Perhaps with words
you will be pierced, broken
to understand. . . .

Aztec Poem
in *Poems of the Aztec People,*
translated by Edward Kissam and Michael Schmidt

Why some people be mad at me sometimes

they ask me to remember
but they want me to remember
their memories
and i keep on remembering
mine.

Lucille Clifton, *Next*

Dangerous Memories

Invasion and Resistance Since 1492

Chicago Religious Task Force on Central America

Authors of *Dangerous Memories*

Renny Golden (Chapter Three), activist and poet, teaches at Northeastern Illinois University. Her newest book, *The Hour of the Poor, The Hour of Women*, recently won the Crossroads/Continuum Women's Studies Award for 1991. *The Hour of the Furnaces* will be published in 1992.

Michael McConnell (Chapter Two), formerly the coordinator of an alternative high school in Chicago and co-author (with Renny Golden) of *Sanctuary: The New Underground Railroad*, was a contributor to *The Moral Nation*, published by Notre Dame University Press, and *Freedom at Risk*, published by Temple University Press.

Cinny Poppen (Chapter One) taught English and writing in public and alternative schools at all age levels for twenty years. Now she is a peace activist, working for the Chicago Religious Task Force on Central America as one of the editors of *¡Basta!*

Authors of "Teaching Strategies"

Peggy Mueller, who has been a teacher, school consultant, and counselor, is currently the director of the Urban Education Program of the Associated Colleges of the Midwest, a teacher training program. She and Marilyn Turkovich have co-authored twelve curriculum books on area studies, multicultural/global education. Turkovich is director of Educational Studies at Columbia College, Chicago. She was the principal writer of three series for Independent Broadcasting Associates, one of which, "Living on the Edge," received the 1990 presidential award for ending world hunger.

Many individuals participated in the production of this book. The authors want to thank them for their help while acknowledging that any errors are our own.

Production Team

Darlene Gramigna
Robin Semer
Claire Stuart

Proofreaders

Melinda Bales
Eileen Gardner
Pat O'Brien

Pre-publication Readers

Carmen Aguilar
Mary Ann Corley
Bill Bigelow
Jan Elliott
Bernard Headley
Faith Smith
Studs Terkel

Task Force Voluteers and Interns

Mary Adderly
Sarah Crean
Mary DiCarlo
Marlise Fratinardo
Chad Goslee
Kristin Pugh

Consultants

John Aubrey, Newberry Library
Maris Cooke, University of Illinois
Meredith Sommers, Central American Resource Center, Minneapolis

The Chicago Religious Task Force on Central America has been involved in Central American issues for over ten years. Originally a local solidarity group primarily concerned with arranging sanctuary for refugees, the Task Force has expanded to become involved nationally and internationally in Central American peace efforts. One of the primary projects of the Task Force is the journal *¡Basta!*

For the past eight years *¡Basta!* has offered regular political and theological commentary on the role of the U. S. government in Central America and the status of solidarity movements in the United States. Each *¡Basta!* focuses on a single issue with insightful political and social analysis. The past three editions were *Challenge to the Central America Movement: Confronting Racism* and *The Dilemma of the '90s: Economic Injustice*, Volume I, *A Critique of Capitalism*, and Volume II, *Hunger and Hope in Latin America*. Individual copies are $5.00 plus $1.50 for postage and handling; a year's subscription (three issues, including postage) is $18.00.

Subjects of the next two issues will be theological reflections on the five hundred years since 1492 and women in Central America.

Special rates are available for multiple copy orders of *¡Basta!* and *Dangerous Memories*.

For information and to place orders contact

The Chicago Religious Task Force on Central America
59 E. Van Buren, Suite 1400
Chicago, IL 60605
312-663-4398

ISBN 0-9631026-0-5
Library of Congress Catalog Card Number 91-076224

Table of Contents

Acknowledgements

The cover of *Dangerous Memories* is taken from the mural in the National Palace in Mexico City by Diego Rivera, courtesy of the Diego Rivera trust.

Many publishers and authors generously gave us permission to quote material: Our appreciation to the following:

Pantheon Books, for excerpts from *Memory of Fire: Genesis* by Eduardo Galeano, translated by Cedric Balfrage. Originally published in 1982 in Spain as *Memoria del fuego, I, Los nacimientos,* Copyright © by Siglo Veintiuno de España Editores, S.A.; copyright © by Eduardo Galeano. Translation copyright © 1985 by Cedric Belfrage. Reprinted by permission of Pantheon Books, a division of Random House, Inc.

Hans Koning, for selections from *Columbus: His Enterprise,* Monthly Review Press, New York City, ©1976, 1991. Reprinted by permission of the author and the Monthly Review Foundation.

Saul Landau, for permission to reprint from *To Serve the Devil,* by Paul Jacobs and Saul Landau, ©1971, Vintage Books, a division of Random House.

Kirkpatrick Sale, for selections from *The Conquest of Paradise.* Copyright © 1990 by Alfred A. Knopf.

Franklin Watts, Inc., New York, for portions of *Columbus and the World Around Him,* copyright © 1990 by Milton Meltzer.

Jose Barreiro, for excerpts from *View from the Shore, Northeast Indian Quarterly,* 7:3 (Fall 1990), published by the American Indian Program, Cornell University, New York.

Zed Books, London, for excerpts from *Indians of the Americas* by Roxanne Dunbar Ortiz.

Thames and Hudson, Inc., New York, for portions of Gordon Brotherston's *Image of the New World.*

Aunt Lute Books, for excerpts from *Borderlands/La Frontera, The New Mestiza.* Copyright © by Glora Anzaldúa.

Selections from the following are reprinted by permission:

Documents of United States Indian Policy, edited by Francis Paul Prucha. Copyright © University of Nebraska Press.

Fulcrums of Change by Jan Carew. Copyright © Africa World Press, 15 Industry Court, Trenton, N.J.

Guatemala in Rebellion by Jonathan Fried, editor. Copyright ©1983, Grove Press.

From Rebellion to Revolution: Afro-American Slave Revolts in the Making of the Modern World by Eugene D. Genovese. Copyright © 1979 by Louisiana State University Press.

Indian Oratory by W.C. Vanderwerth. Copyright ©1971 by the Univeristy of Oklahoma Press.

Cherokee Legends and the Trail of Tears, courtesy of Cherokee Publications, "Native American Collection," P.O. Box 256, Cherokee, NC 28719.

In Pursuit of the Kingdom: Writings 1968-1988, by Bishop Pedro Casadaliga, English translation. Copyright © 1990 by Orbis Books, Maryknoll, NY 10545.

Illustrations and graphics are taken from a number of sources, including archival material, part of the records of Columbus's journey and other explorations to the "new world"; *¡Basta!*; LeRoy H. Appleton, *American Indian Design and Decoration,* a Dover publication; Harvard University's *Black African Art in the Western World,*; Jose Barreiro, ed., *View from the Shore: American Indian Perspectives on the Quincentenary. Northeastern Indian Quarterly,* 7:3 (Fall 1990).

Graphics on the pages marking divisions between sections are taken from a poster produced by Colombian Christian Base Communities. "The Hunted Slaves," engraved by C.G. Lewis (1865), is reprinted courtesy of Moorland-Spingarn Research Center, Howard University; the logo and tree symbol of Peace and Dignity Journeys, is used courtesy of Peace and Dignity Journeys, 1301 W. 16th St., Chicago, IL 60608.

Thanks to Jim Harney for the photographs in Chapter Three and to Mary Johnson, graphic artist at Columbia College, for help with the book cover. Acknowledgement is also given for the invocations honoring Mother Earth, printed throughout,

Foreword

As a native woman active on many fronts of the modern native war, I have searched for the thing that's been so effective in keeping my people down. The one thing I've attributed the largest part of "down" to is the "white historical perspective." I was exposed to that perspective during my entire educational experience, and today I constantly face both the nonnative and native reliance on that perspective. My children are being exposed to the same perspective at this very moment. My partner and I spend a fair amount of time re-educating our children about the truth vs. the white historical perspective, a truth I had to follow an "instinctive" trail to find. This is the most painful experience of discovery I have had to endure, as the trail of truth is a lifelong one.

In my opinion the most powerful institutions of past and modern times are the religious institutions. Second only to them in money and power are the educational institutions of the world, because of their involvement in developing minds. Imagine an educational experience based on the exorcism of one's culture, language, and spiritual beliefs. Imagine that same exorcism based on a white historical perspective.

In contrast to that narrow perspective, I have enjoyed many hours and beautiful moments with our native elders who have received accounts from those who have witnessed the true history of the North American continent. Recently at an occupation camp in the Vallican, British Columbia, the day after a reburial of some ancestors' remains repatriated from educational and government institutions, the elders around the campfire shared memories of school experiences, with much laughter. Although the stories relayed were humorous, the context was very serious, as the impact of schooling on the formation of their minds was immeasurable. The cruelty used against native children of past generations, a double-fisted whammy of church and school, shows that those institutions were willing to travel to great lengths to "take the Indian out of the Indian," since earlier efforts to "take the Indian out of the country" had been abandoned for a more "civilized" way.

I once spoke to my daughter's third grade class. At the time I was excited about having met a native person from Ecuador, whose people are the only ones in the world who know the secrets of head shrinking, the only surgeons in the world who can take the skin off a cranium without committing an incision, who have a medical knowledge much higher than that of the American Medical Association or any other orthodox modern medical association in the world of the 1990s. As I shared my excitement with the third graders, they seemed so hungry, their faces so pure in their thirst for truth and reality. The teacher's face slowly went from interest, to horror, to shut-down. Once I recognized shut-down, I knew it was time for me to wrap it up. She thanked me politely, saying I was "brutally truthful."

It has always been my experience that truth is mostly brutal.

You readers will no doubt find many of the following accounts of white history brutal. White men were brutal. If you bother, you can look around on this day and see these images. Embrace these stories nevertheless . . . they are you. Not until the educational institutions begin to teach and embrace historical truth instead of the white historical perspective will the situation change for my people and all native peoples across the globe. The truth is that the white historical perspective was created as a bit of fiction that white folks could live and feel comfortable with, the same fiction being created on a daily basis now in regard to law, justice, racism, environment, and countless other aspects of our lives. The time of the comfort zone is passed. Changes must be brought home to bear fruit, or I fear for the future—a barren intellectual, cultural, and environmental wasteland.

As I read the transcript of the following text, I thought of one addition I want to make. I suggest a book by Arthur Goodman entitled *American Genesis* for another perspective which will address the theory that natives of the Western Hemisphere came across the Bering Strait, among many other beliefs.

This material is not a pleasant bit of information; in my view, it is an important bit of historical truth.

Marilyn James

Marilyn James describes herself as a native woman who takes the responsibility of being native, being human, and being a mother into action for the quality of life and the sake of the earth. Marilyn is Sinixt (Arrow Lakes Band) and is presently living in Omak, Washington.

How To Use
Dangerous Memories

This book is written in a way different from the usual history text. It is a source book for reading primary documents, comments on history, and historical summaries related to the colonization and conquering of the Americas. The authors have attempted to provide some of the vision and voices of this history which are not usually seen or heard in mainstream educational curricula.

Chapters One and Two

The first two chapters of *Dangerous Memories* present overviews of the European invasion and the subsequent five hundred years of resistance. Each of these two chapters contains two "readings" of this history. One reading (the smaller inside column in bold print) presents an historical context for each subtopic. The other reading (in the wider middle column) presents some of the "missing pages" of history, the voices and commentaries not usually included in texts from which we have learned the history of the Americas. They support, dramatize, explicate, and extend the historical context, leading the reader to possibilities for further research.

Material in italics is directly quoted from the source listed at the end of each passage. The author's name, the title (occasionally in a shortened form), and the page number are given for easy reference. Citations within the historical context follow the standard form: author's last name and page number. Full bibliographic information appears at the end of each chapter.

In several places in the first chapter, we have emphasized particularly important writings by displaying them as one- or two-page spreads, with the hope that they might be useful as easy-to-copy resource material. The pattern of type faces is reversed for easy reading: direct quotations are in plain type; explanations precede the quoted excerpts and are in italics.

The outermost column at the edge of each page contains additional voices on the history, short quotes, poems, and songs which connect dramatically to the other readings.

Chapter Three

The last chapter addresses, in the form of two essays, the war against culture and resistance to that sustained attack. The chapter raises strategic questions about where we go from here. Each of these essays is also accompanied by selected readings, placed in the outermost column at the edges of each page, which present voices and viewpoints of the colonized, again those not usually heard or seen.

Suggestions for Reading

History can be read in many ways. History books typically contain a single line of text telling a story in chronological order, with an occasional interruption of inserts. This book provides several points of entry, and there are numerous ways of reading it. Some readers will choose to go through a short section of the "historical context" column first and then go back to read the related "missing pages" column. Others will read the short excerpts in the middle column first and then read the historical context for background information. Still others may alternate between columns or begin by reading all of the inspirational quotes in the outermost column. The choice can be an individual one or one recommended by a group leader or teacher, depending on the background and skills of the readers. There is no one correct way, although it may be helpful to get an overview of the period by reading the historical context first. It is hoped that reading one column of text will inspire the reader to read the adjacent columns. We also hope readers will be interested enough to consult the sources we've used.

Audience

This book was developed with several audiences in mind. It can be used by an individual or by groups, which might be classes at the high school or college level or adult/community/church study groups in a less formal setting than school. A "strategies" section follows the text and includes ideas for responding to the material in each chapter. Readers are encouraged first to identify their present knowledge about the general topic of the chapter; second, to read and listen to the perspectives and voices presented; and finally, to engage actively in considering the critical meaning of this history for themselves and others. Reflective questions and activities, including role plays, debates, writing assignments, simulations, timelines, and brainstorming, may help readers connect their own lives and experience with new information. The facilitator of these activities might be a teacher or any member of a study group who will help to engage learners in the most critical level of discourse on controversial issues.

The above illustration is from El Primer Nueva Coronica y Buen Gobierno *by Felipe Huamán Poma de Ayala. Ayala wrote his book to inform the King of Spain about the treatment of indigenous people in the colonies.*

maintaining or altering that history and those realities. With Tolstoy, we must ask, "What then must we do?"

This material will undoubtedly raise strong reactions. A deep level of engagement is required to make this history come alive and be a catalyst for change. "Dangerous memories" remain dangerous only if they are not allowed to emerge and be heard.

Memories frame perspectives. This book is meant to frame new perspectives in places where the old ones have fooled us—and failed us.

The Authors

Our Goal

Our primary intent is to engage readers, to challenge them to examine their knowledge and assumptions about the history of a certain time and a certain place. We will be successful if students and readers become seriously critical of their own knowledge base and begin to confront the ways their lives are affected and influenced by their understanding. This book is not meant to be read passively or discussed as mere interesting but irrelevant bits of new information. The material presented here is meant to challenge us to understand and appreciate the last five hundred years in American history from vantage points to which many of us have not been privileged. Furthermore, it is meant to help us realize how present economic, social, and cultural realities of the lives of all Americans, the dominant and the disenfranchised, are intimately connected to the events described. This book is meant to engage us in serious reflection on and questioning of our own knowledge and perspectives, ultimately leading us to a clearer realization of the way we are also actors today in

I·N·V·A·S·I·O·N

A gulf deeper than ocean
yawns between the old world and the new.

Fray Nuñez Cabeza de Vaca quoted in Haniel Long,
The Power within Us

The Europeans who came to the Western Hemisphere in the fifteenth and sixteenth centuries understood the power of memories. The people they conquered, in many cases without much opposition, remembered a different time and a different culture, developed over many centuries, and their memories gave them strength. Some of the existing societies had, in addition to highly refined oral traditions, systems of writing and written documents. In an attempt to counteract the danger of powerful memories among the Mayas, the Spaniards burned their books. Eduardo Galeano suggests what the book burning might have meant to those who witnessed it:

Fray Diego de Landa throws into the flames, one after the other, the books of the Mayas.

The inquisitor curses Satan, and the fire crackles and devours. Around the incinerator, heretics howl with their heads down. Hung by the feet, flayed with whips, Indians are doused with boiling wax as the fire flares up and the books snap, as if complaining.

Tonight, eight centuries of Mayan literature turn to ashes. On these long sheets of bark paper, signs and images spoke: They told of work done and days spent, of the dreams and the wars of a people born before Christ. With hog-bristle brushes, the knowers of things had painted these illuminated, illuminating books so that the grandchildren's grandchildren would not be blind, should know how to see themselves and see the history of their folk, so they should know the movements of the stars, the frequency of eclipses and the prophecies of the gods and so they could call for rains and good corn harvests.

In the center, the inquisitor burns the books. Around the huge bonfire, he chastises the readers. Meanwhile the authors, artist-priests dead years or centuries ago, drink chocolate in the fresh shade of the first tree of the world. They are at peace, because they died knowing that memory cannot be burned. Will not what they painted be sung and danced through the times of the times?

When its little paper houses are burned, memory finds refuge in mouths that sing the glories of men and of gods, songs that stay on from people to people and in bodies that dance to the sound of hollow trunks, tortoise shells, and reed flutes.

Eduardo Galeano, *Memory of Fire: Genesis*, 137

Attempts to burn memory are always futile. The memory of a people is carried in song and story, as inspiration and understanding of a better past, as hope for a better future.

However, what Marilyn James refers to as the "white historical perspective" has had a powerfully negative effect. The history of the last five hundred years in the Americas is for most of us an unknown story. Although we may have studied American history on numerous occasions through elementary, secondary, and post-secondary levels of schooling, we know little of the real story of the first Americans and of the multitudes who have been struggling for five hundred years to preserve their cultures, have their voices heard, and determine their own destinies. The American history we have heard has been told basically from one perspective, that of the invaders and the conquerors. The history we do not know is the story of those who have been colonized and disenfranchised. Without this perspective we cannot understand or analyze with accuracy or objectivity the reality of America today.

Dangerous Memories is meant to challenge our memory of the last five hundred years of history in the Americas, to reassess the origins of the societies that developed in the Western Hemisphere, to question fundamental assumptions about the disenfranchised, to reread history with a more critical eye, to critique our own understanding of that history. It is meant to make us reconsider our fundamental viewpoints and assertions about who we have been and who we are now as nations and peoples.

Writing history is the art of making choices; it requires choosing perspectives and choosing sides. In this book we have tried to present writings that are not well known, to encourage the reader to investigate resources that are certainly available but not widely publicized, with the hope that they will be jolted into an appreciation of the narrowness of commonly held historical perspectives. We have been selective in the voices and events included, choosing to give voice to the marginalized, those who refused to give in or give up in the face of overwhelming firepower. We have chosen to present what was accidentally lost or purposely suppressed.

Some may call this approach one-sided and therefore not objective. Our purpose is not to be objective; our purpose is to try to be honest. The critical question for historians is not "Is your material objective?" but rather "Is it true?" Those who speak from the white European perspective often use the term "objectivity" or the goal of "presenting both sides" as ways to cover their own biases. To present Columbus's voyage to the Western Hemisphere as an "encounter between two cultures" is not objective; it is simply wrong. What most of us have received in terms of history has been one-sided. What

we present here is indeed the other side, the side of the persecuted and the rebels. We do so without apology. As they approach this material, readers should ask the same questions that should be asked of traditional histories: "Is this presentation true to the historical record? Whose interests does this history serve? What is the purpose of its writing?"

Ultimately, the study of the past should enable us to see the present more clearly. The study of the Americas' past should lead to an understanding of present-day realities and injustices. Furthermore, hearing the voices and stories of the courageous, reclaiming dangerous memories, should empower us to take hold courageously of our own responsibility to work together to frame a future which is truly characterized by justice for all of the peoples of the Americas.

Montezuma meets Cortes

13

Europe Before the Conquest

To understand the invasion of the lands known to us as the Americas, it is necessary to know something about Europe at the end of the fifteenth century. In many ways it was a place under siege.

End of the World

Most Europeans were far from rich, and their lives were marked by violence, disease, and famine. The belief that the world would end soon was taken quite serously. In fact,

Life in Fifteenth Century Europe

Not many children lived even to maturity. About half, and not just the poor, died in their first year. If you lived longer, poor diet, disease, and violence threatened to cut life short.

Food supplies were scanty. The usual meal was bread dipped in a thin vegetable soup. To eat fresh meat more than a dozen times a year was very uncommon. Milk, butter, and cheese were too expensive. The family pig was not eaten at home but sold for much-needed cash. The landowners savagely punished poaching for game or fish. If you didn't starve to death, malnutrition was almost sure to keep you so weak you fell prey to disease.

If disease didn't get you, violence might. The frequent wars of this period organized violence on a large scale. On their way to and from battle, armies ravaged the countryside. Bandits attacked travelers and held whole villages for ransom. Violence was a poison running through the bloodstream at all levels of society. People were killed casually in quarrels, for cheating in gambling, over malicious gossip, in drinking bouts, and in urban riots.

Milton Meltzer, Columbus and the World Around Him, 31

Death

The general devastation was so great that a famous demonic preacher and rabble-rouser, Savonarola, could say, in 1496:

There will not be enough men left to bury the dead; nor means to dig enough graves. So many will lie dead in the houses, that men will go through the streets crying, "Send forth your dead!" And the dead will be heaped in carts and on horses; they will be piled up and burnt. Men will pass through the streets crying aloud, "Are there any dead? Are there any dead?"

Quoted in Kirkpatrick Sale, The Conquest of Paradise, 34

. . . And Despair

Always and everywhere in the literature of the age, we find a confessed pessimism. As soon as the soul of these men has passed from childlike mirth and unreasoning enjoyment to reflection, deep dejection about all earthly misery takes their place and they see only the woe of life.

Huizinga, The Waning of the Middle Ages, 138
Quoted in Kirkpatrick Sale, The Conquest of Paradise, 31

Preparation for Overseas Conquest

The Europeans were not the first to undertake sea voyages. In fact they learned valuable techniques from the Arab world and others.

Inuit (Eskimo) plied the entire Arctic circle in their rapid kayaks for centuries and made contacts with many peoples, as

preoccupation with morbid subjects was so great that it was given a name, "the culture of death."

Christopher Columbus concluded, from his extensive study of the Bible and theologians of the time, that Armageddon had a date: it would occur in 1650. There were good reasons for such melancholy.

Violence

Common folk routinely suffered acts of violence from each other in the form of robberies and murders. Revenge was sweet, especially if it came in the form of a public spectacle. Crowds got perverse enjoyment from watching criminals being tortured and then executed on scaffolds in public squares.

The many different units of society contending for domination also constantly fought with each other: earldoms, republics, duchies, noble families, and all kinds of factions engaged in "kidnapping, torture, mutilation, fratricide, patricide, assassination, and fomented rebellion" (Sale, 33).

In addition to these battles among themselves, those who had any power at all didn't hesitate to use it against their disobedient subjects or fellow citizens who had the misfortune of being out of favor. Wars on a large scale were commonplace as newly organized nation-states vied for power.

Disease and Famine

For centuries the Black Death had ravaged the countryside of Europe. By 1450 the population was just beginning to grow back to its preplague levels. Other epidemic diseases also scourged humanity as a direct result of unsanitary and crowded living conditions, general uncleanliness and ignorance, and the constant waging of wars.

Hundreds of thousands also died every year of hunger during recurrent famines when the main crops of wheat and barley failed. The landscape was riddled with pestilence, war, and death. No wonder people whose daily experience was chaotic and dangerous had a preoccupation with death.

Constant Warfare, Holy and Otherwise

Latin Christendom had waged war against Islam for eight hundred years, and portions of Europe, including parts of Spain, were still under Islamic control. The Moors, or Moslems, invaded the Iberian peninsula in 711 from North Africa and conquered it in only seven years. The next seven centuries saw almost constant fighting in what came to be known as the "reconquest." The goal of Christians was to expel from their territory not only the Moors but also others who challenged the prevailing version of Catholicism.

The Crusades, the series of campaigns fought from 1096 to 1291 to recover the Holy Land from the Moslems, were unsuccessful in their main goal but nevertheless had a powerful impact in that they

did Indian and Polynesian fishermen of the Pacific rim. Egyptians and Greeks and Norsemen knew the Atlantic and Indian Oceans.

What was different was the mindset of European merchants and heads of state. Their own society was set up in a hierarchy, in which domination of one class over another was an accepted way of life.

In a sense, the first people colonized under the profit motivation by the use of labour, before overseas exploitation was made possible, were the European and English peasantry. Indeed, whole nations, such as Ireland, Bohemia and Catalonia, were colonized. The Moorish nation, as well as the Judaic Sephardic nation, were physically deported by the Crown of Castile from the Iberian peninsula, an act that was accomplished, significantly, in 1492. All the institutions of colonialism, all the methods for relocation, deportation and expropriation, were already practiced, if not perfected.

Roxanne Dunbar Ortiz, *Indians of the Americas*, 9

The Transformation of Society

The reconquest prepared Spain for its task of conquering a native population. Necessitating almost continuous fighting, the reconquest advanced not by townships but by great regions, emphasizing their importance as the basic unit of Spanish national life and contributing to the rise of nationalism.

Though capable leaders' unity, self-reliance, and resettlement all helped to achieve the Reconquest, the most important factor was probably the willingness of Christian Spaniards to transform their society for this purpose. This transformation was extremely thorough. Late medieval Castile became essentially a society organized for war, a dynamic military machine which would function well so long as it had more lands to conquer. It might be disconcerted by military defeats, but it could survive them. . . .

Only Spain was able to conquer, administer, Christianize and europeanize the populous areas of the New World precisely because during the previous seven centuries her society had been constructed for the purpose of conquering, administering, Christianizing and europeanizing the inhabitants of al-Andalus.

The colonization is a story of military conquest carried out by a people possessing vastly superior arms against sometimes practically unarmed populations, of subduing and sometimes exterminating those populations, of appropriating their land and their labor to the ends of the conquerors.

John Mohawk, "Discovering Columbus: The Way Here," *View from the Shore*, 45

Above illustration: Attending a victim of the Bubonic Plague

Thus if the Reconquest is important in Old World history because it is the primary example of the reversal of an Islamic conquest and because it fostered the transfer of Greek and Asian culture to western Europe, in the general sweep of world history it is vital because it prepared the rapid conquest and europeanization of Latin America.

D.W. Lomax, *The Reconquest of Spain,* 173-178, *passim*
In *1492: Discovery/Invasion/Encounter,* 8

Military Advancements

The constant waging of local conflicts, advancement in existing technologies, and general agreement throughout diverse communities that experimentation was not only acceptable but also inevitable led the nation-states of Europe in the direction of developing new technologies of warfare.

opened the way to a larger world. The many nobles, knights, servants, and churchmen who participated returned from their quest with fantastic tales of great cities and lavish stores of consumer goods.

Trade

As a result of contact with the East, Europe began a brisk trade, centered on the Mediterranean Sea. Venice and Genoa were in the best geographic position to monopolize business arrangements with the powerful Moslem rulers. By the time of the fall of Constantinople in 1453, wealthy Europeans had become enamored of such luxuries as teas, spices, silk, gold, and jewels, and Portugal and Spain wanted to open up their own routes to the riches so they wouldn't have to pay middlemen.

Changes in Spain

Spain itself went through tremendous upheaval during the reconquest. The bulk of the population had converted to Islam, but from tiny remnants of the old regimes grew the mighty kingdoms of Léon, Castile, Aragon, and Portugal, determined to reconquer the whole territory. At the same time, all the various rulers waged wars among themselves, vying for power and internal domination. In retrospect it seems that Spain was preparing itself for the conquest of a new continent, although any notion that such a place existed would have been labeled dreaming in the fifteenth century.

Nationalism

The rise of nation-states and, eventually, nationalism also helped set the stage for conquest.

The disintegration of the Roman Empire in Europe had led to a decentralization of government that in turn led to a fragmentation of power. As the weak sought protection from the strong, the strong forced the weak to do their bidding. The feudal system arose as the method of organizing society after centuries of struggle when Europe was invaded over and over. Peasants suffering from constant encroachment by marauders entered into arrangements with more powerful lords, giving them their land and their service (including military service) in return for protection.

However, the concept of feudalism can't be limited to the single institution of vassalage and lordship. Nor does the term "feudal system" imply that the arrangement was systematic. Patterns varied greatly.

The modern nation-state of Spain was unified by the political marriage between Ferdinand, heir to the throne of Aragon, and Isabella, heiress to the throne of Castile, in 1469 (they met four days before the wedding). From 1479 on, they ruled as "the Catholic monarchs."

The only part of the country not under their control was Granada, the last remnant of the Moorish Empire, established in the ninth century. They used that problem to their advantage, organizing war-hungry barons and nobles to conquer Granada. But when Granada fell in 1492, the war machine ran out

The introduction of new weapons set into motion an arms race which has continued to the present. As new military technologies were introduced the players were forced to buy the new weapons and adopt the new techniques or face annihilation on the battlefield. Each new offensive weapon was countered with a defensive weapon or formation. Huge cannon balls capable of smashing projectiles through thick masonry walls were countered with earthworks which proved impervious to cannonballs. As states grew in size and wealth, the ambitious among them acquired the weapons and armies which helped to spur their growth during periods when offensive weapons overwhelmed defensive ones.

John Mohawk, "Discovering Columbus: The Way Here," *View from the Shore*, 39-40

Patterns of Feudalism

Feudalism in Europe consisted of a wide variety of social organization with two common elements:

1. The individual received protection in return for his personal service to a stronger, richer man.

2. Ownership of land, or some other valuable commodity, passed from the original, weak owner to the lord.

The destruction caused by whole groups of people marching over the countryside and waging war was a prologue to the feudal era. After each conflict new fragments of territory were taken over by someone. Eventually "Europe" became merely a name for a bewildering variety of communities, some autonomous, some interconnected, identified by different terms: the manor, the city, the church, business, the military.

Feudal process was the incessant wrestling within and between these communities to establish relations of dominance and dependency. In such a world the ordering restraints of religion and law often became mere instruments for conquest, petty or grand.

Francis Jennings, *The Invasion of America*, 4

Patterns of Conquest

When the Spaniards entered a village in the "new world," they followed a routine first developed in the Canary Islands called the *requerimiento*. The invaders read outloud, in Spanish or in an appropriate translation if they knew the native language, a formal document that announced their arrival and their intentions and then offered the natives a choice: accept Christianity and Spanish rule or suffer enslavement and/or death.

The experiences of the reconquista had led to the formulation of an elaborate code of rules about the "just war," and the rights of the victors over the vanquished population, including the right to enslave it. These rules were extended as a matter of course to the Canary Islands. The conquerors of the Canaries used, for instance, the strange technique of the requerimiento, which was later employed in America, whereby the bewildered natives were presented before the opening of hostilities with a formal document giving them the option of accepting Christianity and Spanish rule.

It could, however, be argued that there was a difference in kind between the Canary Islanders and the Moors of South Spain, since the islanders were totally ignorant of Christianity until the arrival of the Spaniards, whereas the Moors had heard of Christianity but rejected it. Slavery would surely seem an excessively harsh punishment for mere ignorance.

J.H. Elliott, *Imperial Spain*, 46-7, 58
In *1492: Discovery/Invasion/Encounter*, 9

Much later, in America, the long speech would be read in the middle of the night, without an interpreter, some distance away from the village that would be attacked in the morning, so that the sleeping natives never knew their "options" before the surprise massacre.

Expulsion of Heretics

The Inquisition had a monetary as well as a religious drive. Successful businessmen who also happened to be Jews were envied and distrusted. Many Jews converted to Christianity, to no avail, as the excesses of religious zeal were put to double use. Jews were denounced as heretics, they were arrested and expelled from the country, and their money was confiscated into the coffers of the state.

of land to conquer inside Spain, and the only avenue open was for the barons to go back to fighting each other.

Overseas Expansion

Ferdinand and Isabella came to power because they were able to consolidate the various factions during the long war against the Moors, but they had very little economic power. They looked with longing at the riches the Mediterranean nation-states gained from commerce. In addition to the need to refocus the war machine and the desire for riches, the traditional hostility between Spain and Portugal provided another incentive to acquire possessions overseas. Portugal had already settled the Azores and Madeira, far out in the Atlantic.

Following the lead of Portugal, the Spanish monarchs launched a successful attack against one of the Canary Islands and thereby began their experience with colonization. They then used the Canaries as a sort of laboratory for practicing the techniques later used in the "new world."

In its later stages, much of the reconquest was conducted under control of the crown with financial support from both public and private institutions. This pattern was further developed in the occupation of the Canaries in a contract between the state and a company of merchants from Seville. The combination of money from merchants and legal authority from the royal family provided a useful precedent for the later voyages of discovery. The Canaries would also be critically important as a staging point for the voyages themselves.

All of Columbus's expeditions were launched from the Canary archipelago.

Eventually, Portugal would concentrate its efforts on finding a way to Asia eastward around Africa; Spain, in the person of Christopher Columbus, would sail west.

The Church

During the first three centuries after the birth of Jesus, Christianity had no concern for the punishment of those who disagreed with its precepts. But gradually throughout Europe a notion took hold that the divinity of Jesus Christ was a doctrine that all human beings must believe in. Unlike many other cultures of the world which accept the reality of different belief systems, Christianity developed at its base a compulsive universality, the idea that "Christian truths were absolute and permitted no deviations among believers, nonbelievers, or peoples who had not yet encountered the faith" (Mohawk, 43).

From 1057 on, popes tried to unify all of Europe under their authority. In addition to the reconquest and the Crusades, the major military attempts to expel heretics from European-claimed territory, another device was instituted: the Inquisition, which all the European countries used in various forms to rid their lands of heresy.

The Spanish, after an initial hostility towards its excesses, gradually adopted and greatly refined the methods of the Inquisition. At first the primary targets were Moors and Jews, even those who had converted to Christianity (*conversos*), who were held in general suspicion because of their wealth and power.

The Moors were conquered at Granada, but the victory had emptied the treasuries of the Spanish kingdoms. The power of the Church, never so great as when it stood with cross and sword over the fallen Moslem, had at that moment insisted upon the expulsion from the realms of every person professing the Jewish faith, and thus the country was deprived of a people not only possessing commercial riches but constant producers of national property, a people sober, dexterous, and thrifty.

John Boyd Thacher, Christopher Columbus:
His Life, His Work, His Remains, 172

The country may have been deprived of productive citizens, as Thacher points out, but the treasuries benefited. Indeed, some of the confiscated wealth was used in funding later voyages of exploration.

Church Promotion of Violence

However, the message of the Inquisition was not just for Jews, or for Moors, but for everyone:

The church-sponsored violence known as the Inquisition . . . went, methodically and heartlessly, after any variety of heretic or dissenter, reformer or mystic, attempting to do by the sword—or by the torturer's rack and the auto-da-fé [public burning]—what it could not do by word or prayer, under whose jurisdiction countless millions were imprisoned, by whose decree countless hundreds of thousands were killed.

The Inquisition in Spain was the most brutal of all in the fifteenth century, in part because it was, uniquely, under the control of the crowns of Castile and Aragon. It was in fact the only truly national institution within their territory and as such their single most potent (and indeed most popular) instrument for creating the nation-state that was to be Spain.

The Inquisition, under royal direction from 1483, was the one whose strictures Cristobal Colon would have been careful to heed, and whose ministrations, evidenced in clouds of smoke billowing from town squares throughout the land, he would have witnessed daily.

Kirkpatrick Sale, The Conquest of Paradise, 33

Above illustration:
A public execution

The Economics of Wool

The year 1492 marked a watershed for Spain. The conqest of Granada and the expulsion of the Jews had far-reaching consequences. Centuries of conflict came to an end; so did centuries of religious tolerance. Spain became a nation-state characterized by centralized autocratic government, a homogeneous population, and a theology that allowed for no deviaton. It was also a nation-state badly in need of gold.

When heretics were convicted, by a separate court of the Inquisition, for statements, writings, or actions that didn't follow stringent church laws, they lost their property, their citizenship, and quite often their lives. The accused were presumed guilty; they were not told who had denounced them, and they were strongly persuaded to confess and denounce other "heretics." Torture, although originally unpopular in Spain, gradually became the main method of extracting confessions and was applied widely until the eighteenth century.

The Inquisition spread throughout the Spanish colonial empire hand in hand with the Catholic faith. Later, in Spain, as in the rest of Europe, it was directed against Protestants.

New Philosophies

To the violence and terror of the day, <u>humanism</u> provided answers. Humanists turned to the classics of antiquity, translating and disseminating ideas from Greek and Latin authors to help upper-class citizens find a sense of direction in their lives.

According to humanist philosophy, man is the crown of God's creation, constantly seeking dominion over the world, never satisfied as long as there are lands to conquer. Morality took the form of a secular pragmatism: what's important is what works in the here and now.

Humanism also fit into the prevailing class system. Although the term "man" was used to mean "human," it also had strong connotations of "male human," especially male human of the upper class, the educated, wealthy, urban man of position.

Along with the glorification of the human went a dismissal and fear of nature. Fairy tales and poetry portrayed mountains, forests, jungles, and deserts as terrifying, populated with both real and mythical beasts. Anything wild was feared; man's duty was to tame the wilderness, to bring nature under his control. The early explorers shared with their culture a lack of appreciation of the beauties of the lands they were seeing for the first time; the notion that humans might live in harmony with nature was not a familiar one.

The idea of the Wild Man, a terrifying mythical being who lived in the hills and mountains, frightened both children and adults. In pictures and stories he was portrayed as naked, covered with hair, usually wielding a club, living like a wild beast and ready to do damage to more "civilized" Europeans. The concept of the Savage Beast later had disastrous consequences for the innocent natives who welcomed Columbus.

Another response to the chaos of the Middle Ages was rationalism, the philosophy that forms the basis for present-day scientific methodology. Gradually, over many decades, old worldviews were replaced. Centuries-old beliefs in gods and spirits that inhabited the elements of nature gave way to scientific proof that all combinations of chemical and mechanical properties could be measured and subjected to analysis, prediction, and manipulation.

The only way of getting that universally acceptable means of payment was through the export of wool, a crop produced in a context of extreme economic disparity and hardship.

Ferdinand and Isabella had used the long war against the Moors to strike down the political power of the noblemen, but not their economic power. The nobility, about two percent of the population, owned ninety-five percent of the land. The peasants were not serfs: they had the right to leave their fields. But that freedom has been called "the freedom to die of hunger." There was nowhere for them to go.

The sheep of Spain, some three million of them, belonged to the Mesta, the sheep raisers' corporation, which was really a state within the state. Every spring, these vast flocks of sheep were driven from the high plains of Castile to the mountains of Galicia and León for summer grazing. In the fall they were brought back. They had a guaranteed free passage. The sheep walks could not be enclosed by the peasants, who twice a year saw their land despoiled and their woods cut down by the Mesta shepherds.

The wool went to Flanders for gold, and the Mesta paid no one for the damage done to the land. No one but the King, who got tax monies, and the noble owners, who reaped profits, received anything back.

This, then, is a very brief sketch of the economics of Spain at the end of the fifteenth century: half-starving peasants and noblemen holding enormous estates: townships humbly obedient to an aggressive enormous monarchy and Church. The country was criss-crossed by millions of hungry sheep like a permanent plague of locusts. Wool was the national export but the wool trade brought in diminishing returns, and the damage to the land began causing repeated famines at home.

It was no wonder that envious eyes looked at the riches from commerce, and at the easy prosperity that the trade in spices and gold had brought to Venice, and was bringing to Portugal from its trading stations along the African coast.

The "Catholic Monarchs" felt they had a role to play in the world that could neither be financed by their miserable peasants nor by the Mesta alone. The stage was set for Columbus and the conquistadors who came after him.

Hans Koning, *Columbus: His Enterprise*, 17-18

Nature as the Enemy

The attitude toward nature of Europeans was very unusual.

This separation from the natural world, this estrangement from the realm of the wild, I think, exists in no other complex culture on earth. In its attitude to the wilderness, a heightening of its deep-seated antipathy to nature in general, European culture created a frightening distance between the human and the natural, between the deep silent rhythms of the world and the deep recurrent rhythms of the body, between the elemental eternal workings of the cosmos and the physical and psychological means of perception, by which we can come to understand it and our place within it.

To have regarded the wild as sacred, as do many other cultures around the world, would have been almost inconceivable in medieval Europe—and, if conceived, as some of those called witches found out, certainly heretical and punishable by the Inquisition.

Kirkpatrick Sale, *The Conquest of Paradise*, 78-79

Beginnings of Capitalism

What began as a new way to organize economic interaction, referred to as capitalism or mercantilism, had a profound impact on the next several centuries.

Having brought impoverishment to the domestic peasantry, especially in England, the land-owners and budding manufacturers were stimulated to promote overseas conquest and colonization. With their control of the state they could carry on such commercial activities under the guise of legality, international law and the law of states and conquest.

First the Spanish and Portuguese, and then the British, turned towards America, and the British annihilated whole societies in North America, in both cases rearranging the survivors under their control. The Dutch and French also penetrated North America and the Caribbean with the same motives, goals and results.

The advent of capitalist production brought fundamental changes in the structure of European society, and through colonialism, affected the entire world. Two new classes appeared wherever capitalism intervened: owners of the means of production, and dispossessed persons who were forced to sell their labour cheaply to those owners.

The rise of mercantilism is the story of a struggle to retain and adapt an original Christian morality during the dynamic secularization of a religious outlook as an agrarian society was transformed into a life of commerce and industry.

William Appleman Williams, *The Contours of American History*, 33

Scholars could point to new technological advances such as the printing press to bolster their claims for the validity and significance of rationalism. Printing extended knowledge to a wider audience than ever before. With the development of movable type in the 1440s and the availability of good, cheap paper, came a well-established printing industry by the 1470s. In a fifty-year period, from 1454 to 1504, twenty million books were printed in at least forty thousand separate editions. One of the most successful early books was the log of Columbus's first voyage, translated into four languages and printed in nineteen editions.

A natural adjunct of humanism and rationalism was <u>materialism</u>, the celebration of objects of the "real" world. Possession of material wealth became a primary goal of life and began to replace other values long honored because of ethical and religious considerations. Coveting goods was gradually accepted as tolerable human behavior, not criticized as sinful or immoral, and slowly a new form of economic interaction developed: <u>capitalism</u>. The church accompanied the shift in attitude. The Bible enjoins believers to promote the general welfare and common good of God's "corporate" world. Those words were simply applied to the new definition of God's world as the civil society in which individuals resided.

Under capitalism, morality shifted. The purposes, needs, and limits of human beings no longer had a restraining influence upon industry; rather, the accumulation of money and power became the ultimate end for which human beings worked.

For the first time in human history, the majority of the people depended for their livelihood on a small minority, a phenomenon which became associated with colonialism worldwide.

Roxanne Dunbar Ortiz, *Indians of the Americas*, 10

An artist's interpretation of the mystery of traveling through uncharted waters

Dangerous Voyages

Highly motivated men dared to undertake dangerous voyages to strange lands, willing to risk their lives on the high seas on perilous journeys, traveling farther than anyone had ever ventured before. A combination of circumstances in fifteenth-century Spain provided the incentives and the context: the violence, poverty, and disease common in the lives of the people; the rise of nationalism out of the hierarchical feudal system with its acceptance of the domination of one class over another; an impoverished nobility yearning for wealth; a recognition of the importance of material wealth and an awareness that other nations were getting it through commerce; and an insistence on the universality of the Christian culture, with a tradition of waging battles against heretics and a missionary spirit to "save the world."

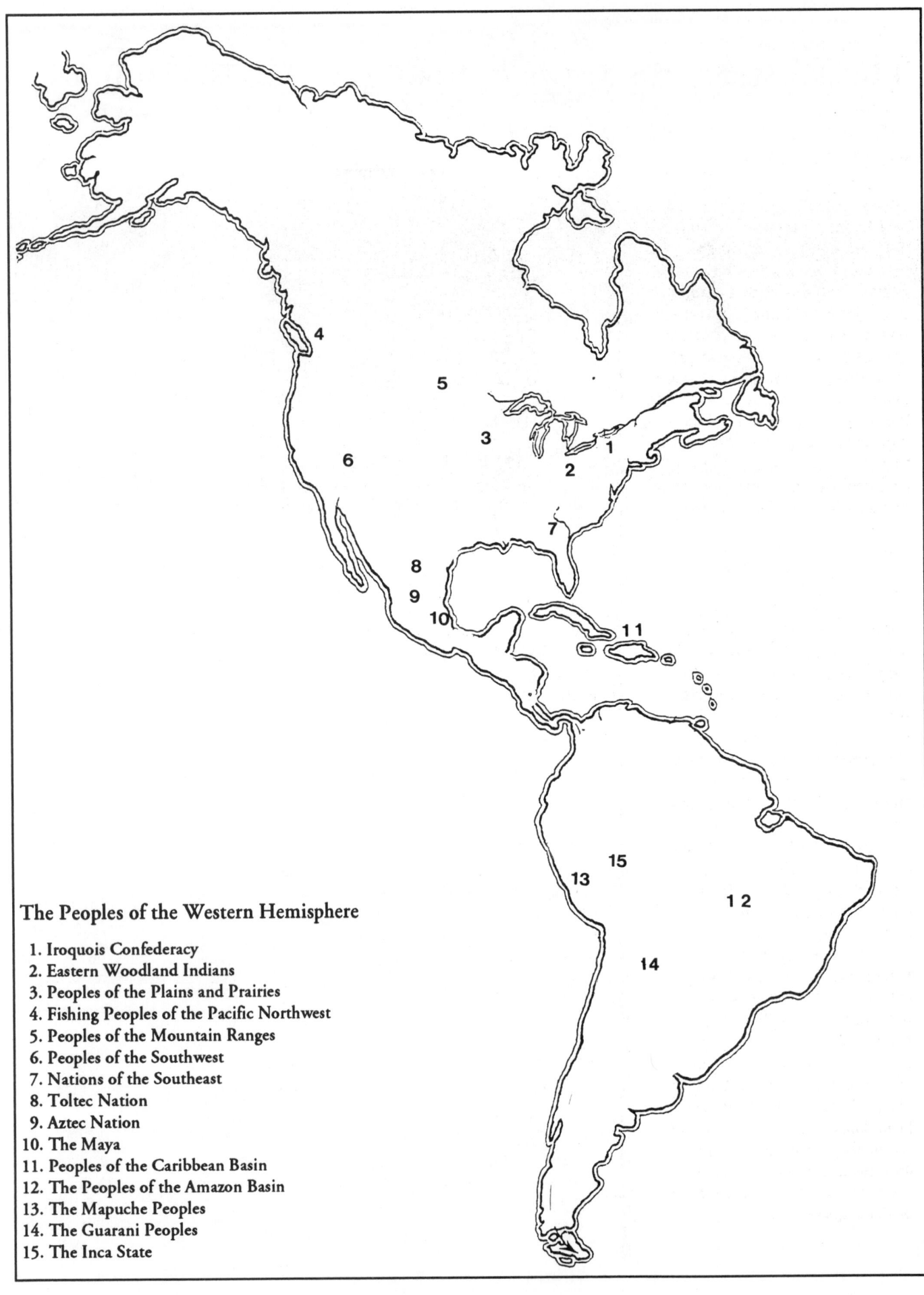

The Peoples of the Western Hemisphere

1. Iroquois Confederacy
2. Eastern Woodland Indians
3. Peoples of the Plains and Prairies
4. Fishing Peoples of the Pacific Northwest
5. Peoples of the Mountain Ranges
6. Peoples of the Southwest
7. Nations of the Southeast
8. Toltec Nation
9. Aztec Nation
10. The Maya
11. Peoples of the Caribbean Basin
12. The Peoples of the Amazon Basin
13. The Mapuche Peoples
14. The Guarani Peoples
15. The Inca State

The Western Hemisphere Before the Conquest

It is difficult to get an accurate picture of the inhabitants of the lands visited by Columbus for two reasons: overall, they were very quickly destroyed, and most of the words we have on the subject were written by the Europeans who were responsible for that destruction. The current state of knowledge about pre-Columbian civilization in the Western Hemisphere reflects scholars' fairly recent attempts to describe the cultures found by Europeans in a fair and nonjudgmental way.

Length of Habitation

For a long time learned writers wanted to justify the conquest by pretending that the hunting and gathering tribes existing in what became the Americas had only recently migrated from Asia over the Bering Strait and therefore had little claim to the vast resources of the "new world." If the explorers and colonizers found only a seemingly endless, relatively unpopulated wilderness, they were clearly entitled, indeed mandated by the presumptions of their own culture, to tame it. And furthermore, if the groups of human beings they encountered were unorganized, unskilled, unchurched, unschooled—in short, "primitive"—then the colonizers had every right to share their superior civilization. According to this line of reasoning, massacres and murders were necessitated by the resistance of the subjects of their generosity.

Iroquois wooden mask

A Multiplicity of People

Civilization in America emerged from certain centers, just as it did in the three other major continental land masses of the world. These centers tended to incorporate groups and territory on their peripheries, sometimes in growth spurts that led to periods of integration, sometimes very gradually through periods of decline and disintegration. The shifting of boundaries and control in the Western Hemisphere resembled that in Europe and Asia, especially in that it occurred over thousands and thousands of years.

Naming every tribe and nation and giving their characteristics would require a huge amount of space. The following list is not intended to be exhaustive, but it gives an idea of the number and variety of groups in the Western Hemisphere at the time of the conquest. Several centers can be identified:

The Iroquois Confederacy

- At first five, eventually six nations formed from thousands of agricultural villages from the Great Lakes to the Atlantic and south to the Carolinas.
- Population around two million.

Indians are traditionally viewed as natural features of the land, rather like mountains or rivers or buffalo or troublesome, if colorful, wild varmints, affecting American history only by at times impeding the civilizing progress of advancing settlers.

William Brandon, *The Last Americans*, 1

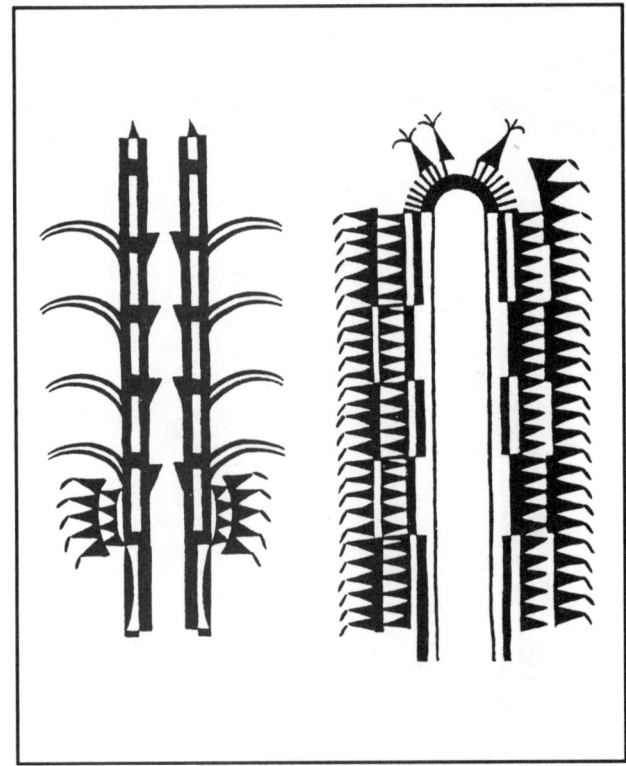

Quillwork of the Blackfoot Indians

[The Iroquois Confederacy] was a highly structured state system which allowed the multi-ethnic state to incorporate many diverse peoples and nations. Undoubtedly, it would have continued to incorporate and annex other peoples in North America. The remarkable aspect of the Iroquois state was its ability to avoid centralization by means of a clan-village system of democracy, based on collective ownership of the land; its products, stored in granaries, were distributed equitably to the people by elected authorities. "Clan mothers" played the key role of supervising all activities, having the final veto on any decision.

All material in italicsis is from
Roxanne Dunbar Ortiz, *Indians of the Americas,* 2-8

Eastern Woodland Indians

- Many diverse groups who lived along the eastern coast, from Nova Scotia to Florida, and west to the Great Lakes.
- Three large language stocks: Algonquian, Iroquoian, and Siouan; included the Delaware, Ojibway/Chippewa, Sauk, Fox, Menominee, Kickapoo, Illinois, Winnebago, Shawnee, Seminole, Creek, as well as thirty or forty more nations.
- Population hard to estimate since thousands were obliterated before awareness of them was developed; certainly in the hundreds of thousands, possibly half a million or more.

Now it is generally agreed that human beings have lived on the American continent for at least twenty thousand years and possibly as much as twice that long. They may indeed be the oldest known people on earth (Brandon, 26).

Scholars disagree about where they originated. It is possible that they crossed to what is now Alaska from what is now Siberia, using a land bridge exposed by the lowering of the ocean during the last Ice Age. Moving southward and populating the whole continent took thousands of generations, until much, much later, by the late fifteenth century, many diverse cultures and civilizations with very long histories occupied the land mass of which Europe knew nothing.

Number and Variety

Population estimates range widely, but a rough academic consensus now maintains that between ninety and one hundred twenty million people lived in the Americas before Columbus's voyage, compared to sixty to seventy million people in Europe at the same time (excluding Russia).

The extraordinarily rich variety of cultures had adapted not only to their wide range of physical environments but also to each other. Some were gentle and peaceful, some were fierce and quarrelsome, some were reserved in their demeanor, some were emotional. Some remained hunters and gatherers, others developed kingdoms and empires.

Languages

Groups in the Western Hemisphere spoke some two thousand distinct languages at the time of the conquest, some as different from one another as Chinese and English. In the entire "old world" about three thousand languages are known to have existed at the end of the fifteenth century. The languages of the "new world" can't be classified as primitive, in vocabulary or in any other respect.

"Whereas Shakespeare used about 24,000 words, and the King James Bible about 7,000, the Nahuatl of Mexico used 27,000 words, while the Yahgans of Tierra del Fuego, considered to be one of the world's most retarded peoples, possessed a vocabulary of at least 30,000 words" (Stravianos, 213-214).

Characteristics

Although generalization is risky because of the variety of lifestyles and systems represented in the many pre-Columbian cultures, it's safe to say that at least some of the cultures of the "new world" exhibited admirable characteristics. People in those ancient societies tried to live according to the moral principles agreed on by their forebears. Among many groups freedom and equality prevailed, with no division between rich and poor, no form of servitude, no money, no meddling governmental bureaucracy, no private property. In many cases governments were established to promote the general good, not to create a state apparatus for repression.

Political organization of these seminomadic town dwellers took the form of large confederacies such as the Three Fires, composed of the Ojibways, Potawatomis, and Ottawas on the eastern end of Lake Superior. Wide trade networks were well established. The people were skilled in hunting; they also cultivated wild rice, squash, corn, and other crops. They developed snowshoes, used birch bark to build canoes and houses, and produced maple syrup. They introduced wampum, seashells strung on strings or braided into belts, used for trading and also as a way of remembering for a non-literate society; for example, belts might embody the terms of treaties in the symbolic placement of the shells. Some tribes were matrilineal; some created clans claiming descent from the spirit of an animal, or special societies formed for a specific purpose such as war or healing. Occasional wars or battles gave the erroneous impression to early settlers that all these people were warlike; the French and English used ancient enmities to turn tribes against each other.

Peoples of the Plains and Prairies

- Several centers of state development, from West Texas to the sub-Arctic.
- Cree in prairies of Canada, Lakota and Dakota (Sioux) in present-day North and South Dakota, Cheyenne and Arapaho to the west and south.
- Human population approximately one million; bison population around eighty million.

Many other bison-hunting peoples occupied various parts of the territories, and territorial disputes occurred. Some peoples, such as the Potowatomie, turned almost entirely to commerce. These groups tended to be peacemakers and negotiators in disputes, speaking many languages, perhaps originating the sign language which became universal in the Western Hemisphere in pre-colonial times.

Fishing Peoples of the Pacific Northwest

- Included the Tlingit, Hoopa, Poma, Karok, and Yurok peoples.
- Total population of four million.

A state system as such is not apparent, although their ceremonial and trade linkages could have supported some sort of state structure. These were wealthy people living in a paradise of natural resources. . . . These people are also the inventors of the potlatch, the ceremonial destruction of accumulated goods, and of the gigantic totems and masks.

Painted paddle of the Tlingit

The great sea has set me in motion.
Set me adrift,
And I move as a weed in the river.

The arch of sky
And mightiness of storms
Encompasses me,
And I am left
Trembling with joy.

Eskimo Song

Villages Between the Two Great Mountain Ranges

- Nez Perce, Blackfeet, Shoshones, Utes, Paiutes and others.
- Inhabited difficult terrain, developed clan-based democratic communities which shifted habitation according to animal migrations and seasons.
- Around two hundred thousand people.

Peoples of the Southwest

- Desert and alpine arid and semi-arid region, fragile land base suffering from drought.
- One to two hundred city-states maintained by Pueblo and Hopi Indians, living according to the "right way": moderation, industry, peaceful interactions.
- Developed vast irrigation systems, including extensive leak-proof canals.
- Also home for the Athabascans (Navajos and Apaches), who hunted and traded, interacted and intermarried with the Pueblo peoples and became involved in the inter-village fights and wars engendered by disputes over water usage and territory.
- Numbered around two hundred thousand.

Major Nations of the Southeast

- One of the most fertile agricultural belts in the world, from the Atlantic Ocean to the Gulf of Mexico along the southeast portion of what is now the United States.
- Muskogee-speaking Choctaw, Creek, and Chickasaw in the south center; Algonquin-speaking Cherokee in the east; Natchez in the west.
- Five major nations, a thriving civilization in 1492.
- Total population of at least two to three million.

These states functioned in a confederacy similar to that of the Iroquois, with decision making based on popular consensus. Among these groups were mound builders who created massive communal graves and temples; it is possible that they had contact with Mayans or other groups in Central America.

The Toltec Nation

- Appeared around two thousand years ago in central Mexico, creating great cities.
- After flourishing for two centuries, wiped out by invaders who waged war among themselves.

The mountains,
I become part of it
. . . the herbs, the
fir tree,
I become part of it.

The morning mists,
the clouds, the
gathering waters,
I become part of it.

The wilderness,
the dew drops,
the pollen. . .
I become part of it.

Navajo chant

Hopi Tray

Attitudes toward Property

One very basic difference between the two worlds, the one known to Europeans and the one unknown, was the attitude toward property.

With some notable exceptions, the European way of life had developed into a focus on individual competition for the acquisition of property. What motivated the early colonizers was desire for gold and other minerals, for land as a means of production, for labor to extract or create wealth and commodities, and for all the other promised riches of the newly discovered territory. From humble settlers looking for small land-holdings to powerful forces of land and mineral speculation, all white frontier expansionists understood the advantages of owning property.

The basic attitude of the inhabitants of the unknown world (also with some notable exceptions) seems to have focused more on cooperation, using property in common rather than competing to acquire private property. In many of the native groups, all members seemed to live as equals, with no hierarchies or class structure. Societies emphasized the nonmaterial satisfaction of being in harmony with nature; individuals didn't appear to work very hard. The profit motive was far from primary.

"It might be said, in sum, that the Indian world was devoted to living while the European world was devoted to getting. This may be the essence of the Indian world and image" (Brandon, 8).

For instance, the people referred to as the Incas, one

of the most highly developed civilizations according to European criteria, valued harmony with the universe as the chief goal of life. Their intricate political organization relied on two principles: reciprocity and redistribution.

Reciprocity, the mutual exchange of gifts, was important to the *allyus*, groups united by kinship ties, that formed the basis of society. Gradually, these small groups organized into much larger units and fed into a central government which had a high respect for local institutions. Farmers paid a tribute from their surpluses to a coordinating center, responsible for storing the collected produce and redistributing it to local chieftains in time of need (Wachtel, 61).

Meaning of the Land

The land that Europeans coveted and eventually took away from the Indians had totally different meanings to the two cultures. To the Indians land was sacred, obviously precious and life-giving and worthy of special reverence, with holy spots that evidenced the oneness of all creation. The souls of the ancestors were mixed with the soil.

"In a way that few Europeans could understand, the land <u>was</u> Indian culture: it provided Native Americans with their sense of a fixed place in the order of the world, with their religious observances, and with their lasting faith in the importance of the struggling but united community as opposed to the ambitious, acquisitive individual" (Segal and Stineback, 28).

Huge buildings, sculptures and markets made up the cities, which housed vast universities and libraries. Their written language was [a forerunner to the later] Mayan form, as was the calendar used in scientific research and study.

The Aztec Nation

- Expanded through wars of conquest to an area from the Gulf of Mexico to the Pacific and northwards.
- Population of some thirty million.

The economy was based on hydraulic agriculture, with corn (maize) as the central crop and many others such as beans, pumpkins, tomatoes, cocoa, tobacco, and cotton, which provided the fiber for all cloth and clothing. The Aztecs created works of art and useful commodities of cloth and metal, built huge stone dams and canals as well as fortress-like castles, had huge markets in each city and a far-flung trade network, using turquoise for exchange. They developed a sophisticated political organization: the land was owned in common and worked by commune members, who lived in clans and elected leaders, including the principal commander of the military who was also the main political and religious leader.

By the late fifteenth century Aztec dominance was in a process of decay. Constant warfare had many negative effects: the equitable distribution of wealth was skewed by rewards of property and land given to distinguished warriors; slavery was becoming an essential institution, with prisoners of war used as slaves; formerly elected offices were being transformed into hereditary ones by the emergence of a clan nobility. The clan structure itself gradually disintegrated, with a corresponding emergence of a class society, similar to the state development taking place in Europe at the same time. Most slaves taken in conquest were used for human sacrifice; eventually the dominant religious cult required the daily human sacrifice of thousands of people to the Sun God.

At the time of the conquest, peasant uprisings were increasing and intensifying all over Mexico; Montezuma II, who came to power in 1503, was making an attempt to reform the regime.

Mayan Civilization

- Prospered for five centuries in the northwest of what is now Central America.
- Population around ten million.

Mayan culture, often compared to that of Greece in the golden age of Athens, amazes everyone who studies it.

Our house on earth we do not inhabit

only borrow it briefly

Aztec poem

Detail from Temple of Quetzalcoatl

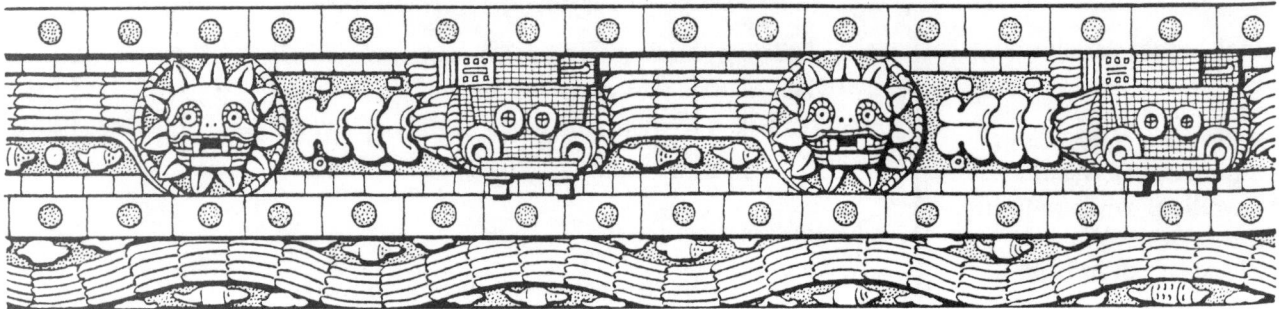

Above illustration: Detail from Temple of Quetzalcoatl

The cultivation of corn was its basis, so essential that a religion was constructed around this vital food. However, methods of agriculture never became more technically sophisticated than slash and burn: hacking down and burning trees and brush, planting a cornfield in the rough clearing, and then repeating the process in another place in a few years.

The Mayans used a variety of materials, including gold and silver, in their highly-developed art, architecture, sculpture, and painting. But it is in the realms of mathematics and astronomy that their achievements are the most impressive. The calendar system developed by the Mayans was one-thousandth of a day per year more accurate than the one we use now, and they were familiar with the concepts of positional numbers and zero, unknown in Europe for another thousand years. They also had a written language with hieroglyphic ideographs, conventionalized symbols standing for certain words, as in Chinese writing, and possibly some symbols representing sounds like modern alphabets.

There was a distinct commercial class, and the cities were authentic urban centres, not simply bureaucratic or religious ones; but ordinary Mayans retained the fundamental features of a clan structure in their communities. They were required to work in the nobles' fields and to pay them rent for use of the land, and also to contribute to the building of roads, temples, noblemen's houses, and other structures. It is not clear whether these relations of production were exploitative or democratically and co-operatively developed. It is clear that certain groups, such as war prisoners, criminals, debtors and orphans were used as slaves, and although easily freed and not hereditary, features of slave-dependence for labour were apparent.

The Caribbean Basin

- Important as the place Columbus first landed.
- Total population of at least several million.

This region, like the resource-rich and temperate Pacific northwest, was a virtual paradise where hunger and want were unknown. Tied by cultural, clan, and trade bonds,

Identification with the land in no way implied ownership. The concept of owning the land was as foreign to the Indians as the idea of owning the air would be to us. The early inhabitants had an intimate and abiding relationship with nature that colored their view of humans as only one of many species participating in an intricate web of life. The rituals, myths, and ceremonies passed down through the ages that helped individuals understand their obligations and responsibilities played a primary role, at the very center of existence.

Living on the land required conscious caretaking, a finely-tuned sense of balance, and respect in such everyday activities as hunting, farming, and foraging.

Importance of Giving Gifts

The generosity of the Indians was extolled by Columbus and other early explorers. It was a natural product of the understanding among natives that life depended on the largesse of nature. Grateful recipients of good harvests and successful hunting expeditions routinely shared their bounty with others in the ritual known as "potlatch" among Northwest Coast Indians.

Detail from a painted Mayan vase

The formal distribution of food and other goods to the community was deeply engrained in the society and went beyond mere customs of hospitality; the colonizers benefited greatly from its practice.

The Natives Who Welcomed Columbus

The natives who rowed out to investigate the strange intruders in their gigantic ships, greatly overdressed for the climate and so eager to display the power of their weapons, were Tainos, related to a larger group known as Arawaks. Evidently they were peaceful and agricultural, living in houses built of perishable materials such as reeds and palm trees.

Some of their household implements have been recovered: small stones chipped and carved in the shape of chisels, gouges, spearheads, hoes, and knives; mortars and pestles, the latter with carved heads, possibly idols; beads of stone and oyster shell and fragments of pottery.

Frederick Ober, commissioned in 1890 as a special representative of the World's Columbian Exposition to follow the path taken by

there may have been state developments or federations that have not been detected; the pre-colonial cultures in the Caribbean have been very little studied, since most were annihilated or merged with African populations during slavery.

Four Major Nation-State Formations in the Southern Continent

- The peoples of the Amazon basin.
- The Mapuche (Araucan) of the Pacific regions.
- The Guarani of Paraguay and Argentina.
- The peoples of the Inca state, present-day Bolivia, Peru, Ecuador, and Colombia.
- Total population fifty million.

The Incas were agriculturalists and stock-breeders, metal-workers and weavers, and notable architects; their science, mathematics, and medicine were much more highly developed than in Europe at that time. The Quechua language had a hieroglyphic script and books were published in it.

Road-building and trade were extraordinarily far-flung and developed in these highlands, where villages are at elevations of several miles. The main social unit in land tenure was the ayllu, or the commune, the members of which worked together to till the land which was distributed equitably to families. The Sapa Inca [leader of the state] was considered the owner of the land, and a portion of the harvest and animal produce went to the state to support its functions, both secular and religious.

The irrigation canals of the sierra and the coast and the agricultural terraces of the Andes, which survive to this day, are evidence of the degree of economic organization reached by the Inca state. As regards religion, the cult of Mama Pacha is considered to be on a par with the worship of the Sun. Like the Sun, Mother Earth represents no one in particular, with a correlation between communal ownership of land and the universal religion of the Sun.

All material in italics is from
Roxanne Dunbar Ortiz, *Indians of the Americas*, 2-8
See also William Brandon, *The Last Americans*

Nazca pottery

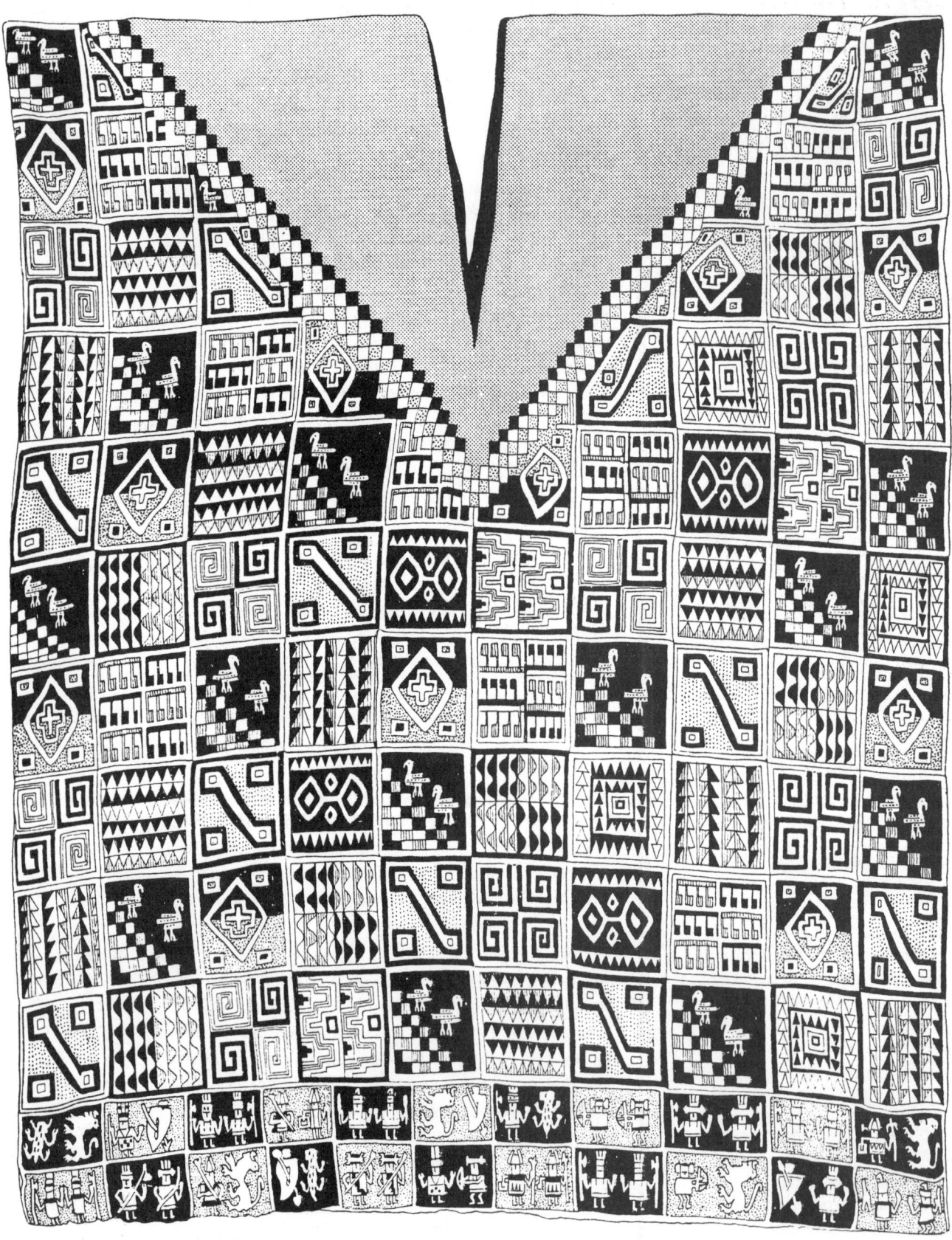

Columbus, reported on his findings, "There yet remain other articles to mention, which show that these barbarians did have among them, or were in communication with, skillful artisans who carved wonderful things in wood and stone, the like of which have not been found elsewhere. . . .

"When the Indies were discovered, all the common people sat on the ground in the presence of strangers, but . . . their chiefs made use of low seats, of stone or wood, carved in the shape of a beast or reptile, with very short legs, its head and tail erect, and with golden eyes" (Ober, 84).

Variety and Harmony

It is safe to say, then, that in the immediate world Columbus and his crew "discovered," human beings lived in harmony with nature and shared nature's bounty, and that the larger world later visited by other Europeans was characterized by a very large population and a wide variety of cultural patterns.

The Lands of the Western Hemisphere

Varied societies, in differing degrees of "civilization," ordering the lives of their members according to deeply held principles and beliefs, lived in the land mass unknown to Europeans, about to be "discovered" and forever changed. Pre-Columbian North America was fairly densely populated, as such cultures go, and certainly was not the empty wasteland and untouched wilderness that Europeans took it to be. . . .

. . . We must imagine a sizable population, such as the European invaders did not achieve until the 1840s, in some areas quite densely settled, that would have been trapping and shooting small game and game birds day after day for centuries, fishing any available stream and clamming any available coast, gathering fruits and nuts and roots of several hundred species over thousands of acres a year, hunting big game over hundreds of square miles with many thousands of pounds of meat every year (more than fifteen thousand for a village of four hundred in southern New England alone, one estimate suggests), ringing and burning trees and planting crops on a scale of perhaps an acre a person, clearing underbrush and driving animals by fires any one of which might be as much as twenty miles around, and, let us assume, occasionally blundering with a fire out of control or a hillside denuded for firewood or a well dried up from overuse—all that, and still occupying an environment that in important ways was ebullient and wild, abundant in both kinds and numbers of flora and fauna, functioning to all intents and purposes in its original primal state.

Kirkpatrick Sale, *The Conquest of Paradise*, 316-317

Pottery bowl of the West Indies

The Natives' View of the Land

The Indians say: The land has an owner? How's that? How is it to be sold? How is it to be bought? If it does not belong to us, well, what? We are of it. We are its children. So it is always, always. The land is alive. As it nurtures the worms, so it nurtures us. It has bones and blood. It has milk and gives us suck. It has hair, grass, straw, trees. It knows how to give birth to potatoes. It brings to birth houses. It brings to birth people. It looks after us and we look after it. It drinks chicha, accepts our invitation. We are its children. How is it to be sold? How bought?

Eduardo Galeano, *Memory of Fire: Genesis,* 225

Illustration on previous page: Incan poncho

Men of the Good

The following excerpts from an article by Jose Barreiros describe in some detail the culture that had enjoyed a long existence in the area where Columbus landed. Although the cultural patterns of the "new world" vary tremendously, this one, as the first to feel the effects of the conquest, is a key example of the values, lifestyles, and community organization practiced by many groups throughout the Western Hemisphere.

The word Taino meant "men of the good," and from most indications the Tainos were good. Coupled to the lush and hospitable islands over a millennium and a half, the indigenous people of "La Taina" developed a culture where the human personality was gentle. Among the Taino at the time of contact, by all accounts, generosity and kindness were dominant values. Among the Taino peoples, as with most indigenous lifeways, the physical culture was geared toward a sustainable interaction with the natural surroundings. The Taino's culture has been designated as "primitive" by Western scholarship, yet it prescribed a lifeway that strove to feed all the people, and a spirituality that respected, in ceremony, most of their main animal and food sources, as well as the natural forces like climate, season, and weather. The Taino lived respectfully in a bountiful place and so their nature was bountiful.

The naked people Columbus first sighted lived in an island world of rainforests and tropical weather, and adventure and fishing legends at sea. Theirs was a land of generous abundance by global terms. They could build a dwelling from a single tree (the Royal Palm) and from several others (gommier, ceiba), a canoe that could carry more than one hundred people.

. . . . The Tainos lived in the shadows of a diverse forest so biologically remarkable as to be almost unimaginable to us, and, indeed, the biological transformation of their world was so complete in the intervening centuries that we may never again know how the land or the life of the land appeared in detail. What we do know is that their world would appear to us, as it did to the Spanish of the fifteenth century, as a tropical paradise. It was not heaven on earth, but it was one of those places that was reasonably close.

The Taino world, for the most part, had some of the appearance that modern imaginations ascribe to the South Pacific islands. The people lived in small, clean villages of neatly appointed thatch dwellings along rivers inland and on the coasts. They were a handsome people who had no need of clothing for warmth. They liked to bathe often, which prompted a Spanish royal law forbidding the practice, "for we are informed it does them much harm," wrote Queen Isabella.

The Taino were a sea-going people, and took pride in their courage on the high ocean as well as their skill in finding their way around their world. They visited one another constantly. Columbus was often astonished at finding lone Indian fishermen sailing in the open ocean as he made his way among the islands. Once, a canoe of Taino men followed him from island to island until one of their relatives, held captive on Columbus's flagship, jumped over the side to be spirited away.

Among Tainos, the women and some of the men harvested corn, nuts, cassava, and other roots. They appear to have practiced a rotation method in their agriculture. As in the practice of many other American indigenous ecosystemic peoples, the first shoots of important crops, such as the yucca, beans and corn, were appreciated in ceremony, and there are stories about their origins. Boys hunted fowl from flocks that "darkened the sun," according to Columbus, and the men forded rivers and braved ocean to hunt and fish for the abundant, tree-going jutia, the succulent manati, giant sea turtles and countless species of other fish, turtles and shellfish. Around every bohio [hut], Columbus wrote, there were flocks of tame ducks (yaguasa), which the people roasted and ate.

. . . . The Taino world of 1492 was a thriving place. The Taino islands supported large populations that had existed in an environment of Carib-Taino conflict for, according to archeological evidence, one and a half millennia, although the earliest human fossil in the region is dated at fifteen thousand years. Tainos and Caribs may have visited violence upon one another, and there is little doubt they did not like each other, but there is little evidence to support any thesis that genocidal warfare existed in this world. A Carib war party arrived and attacked, was successful or repulsed, and the Tainos, from all accounts, returned to what they were doing before the attack. These attacks were not followed up by a sustained campaign of attrition. . . .

Early descriptions of Taino life at contact tell of large concentrations, strings of a hundred or more villages of five hundred to one thousand people. These concentrations of people in coastal areas and river deltas were apparently well-fed by a nature-harvesting and agricultural production system whose primary value was that all of the people had the right to eat. Everyone in the society had a food or other goods producing task, even the highly esteemed *caciques* and *behiques* (medicine people), who were often seen to plant, hunt, and fish along with their people. In the Taino culture, as with most natural world cultures of the Americas, the concept was still fresh in the human memory that the primary bounties of the earth, particularly those that humans eat, are to be produced in cooperation and shared.

. . . . Like all American indigenous peoples, the Taino had an involved economic life. They could trade throughout the Caribbean and had systems of governance and beliefs that maintained harmony between human and natural environments. The Tainos enjoyed a peaceful way of life that modern anthropologists now call "ecosystemic." In the wake of recent scientific revelations about the cost of high impact technologies upon the natural world, a culture such as the Taino, that could feed several million people without permanently wearing down its surroundings, might command higher respect.

. . . There was little or no quarrelling observed among the Tainos by the Spaniards. The old *caciques* and their councils of elders were said to be well-behaved, had a deliberate way of speaking and great authority. . . . The peoples were organized to the gardens *(conucos)* or to the sea and the hunt. They had ball games played in *bateyes*, or courtyards, in front of the *cacique's* house. They held both ceremonial and social dances, called *areitos*, during which their creation stories and other cosmologies were recited. Among the few Taino-Arawak customs that have survived the longest, the predominant ideas are that ancestors should be properly greeted by the living humans at prescribed times and that natural forces and the spirits behind each group of food and medicinal plants and useful animals should be appreciated in ceremony.

As can be seen throughout the Americas, American indigenous peoples and their systems of life have been denigrated and misperceived. Most persistent of European ethnocentrisms toward Indians is the concept of "the primitive," always buttressed with the rule of "least advanced" to "most advanced" imposed by the prism of Western Civilization—the more "primitive" a people, the lower the place they are assigned in the scale of "civilization." The anti-nature attitude . . . [inherent in this idea] came over with the Iberians of the time, some of whom even died rather than perform manual labor, particularly tilling of the soil. The production and harvesting of food from sea, land, and forests were esteemed human activities among Tainos. As with other indigenous cultures, the sophistication and sustainability of agricultural and natural harvesting systems was an important value and possibly the most grievous loss caused by the conquest of the Americas.

Jose Barreiro, "A Note on Tainos: Whither Progress?"
View from the Shore: American Indian Perspectives on the Quincentenary, Northeast Indian Quarterly, 7:3 (Fall, 1990), 66-71

Columbus bearing Christ to the "new world," from a world map by Juan de la Cosa, 1500

The Conquest and Its Consequences

The First Voyage

Cristoforo Colombo, (or Cristobal Colon) son of a weaver from Genoa, went to sea as a young man, probably as a trader or clerk, and turned up in Lisbon, Portugal, the center of European navigation and exploration, around 1476. The long (and growing) list of authors who have written about him disagree about many aspects of his life, but most would say he was driven by an obsession to explore the world.

Strong Determination

The schoolbook story that Columbus knew the earth was round although everyone else thought it was flat is simply not true. Five hundred years earlier, the Greeks knew that the earth is a sphere, and educated Europeans of the fifteenth century shared that knowledge.

What stopped seamen from sailing west across the sea was primarily fear of the unknown. Ships hugged the coastlines, the captains not trusting navigational aids enough to venture forth into uncharted seas. Also, everyone assumed the distance to land was too great to traverse. And, at least in theory, they were right.

Columbus's reckonings of the distance between Europe and Asia, if one traveled across the sea to the west, were dead wrong. He believed, and was finally able to convince others, that Japan was about

Columbus's Reckoning

The more Columbus studied and dreamed, the more certain he became that he was right about the possibility of sailing west to Asia.

Logic had small place in his thinking. Without going into technical details, it may be enough to say that he convinced himself the ocean was narrower than it is, and that Asia was wider than it is. He sifted through the literature, the maps, the charts produced by scholars and seafarers from ancient times to his time, and wherever figures differed from his concept, he "'corrected'" them.

Milton Meltzer, *Columbus and the World Around Him*, 57

Late 1400s: Shipboard Life

It is well to remember, as an antidote to romantic sea tales written in warm libraries, that ships were then floating slums and floating sweatshops. The common fate of crew and officers gave a certain solidarity that would not have been found on land among such disparate men, but they were still masters and servants, and no nonsense. The captain was lord over life and death, and any man who evoked his displeasure could be lashed, locked in irons, keelhauled, or hanged. The food for the crew was vile—though on a normal voyage probably no worse than what they were used to on land. As for their quarters, there weren't any. The men simply had to bunk down for the night wherever they could find a dry spot, which is not easy on a sailing boat; and those who had one change of dry clothes with them were the fortunate ones.

Those were the men who did the work, though. It has been said that the great explorers of Africa were simply the first white men carried around that continent by blacks; likewise, those famous captains were the first men sailed across the oceans by their crews.

Hans Koning, *Columbus: His Enterprise*, 44

[Columbus was] a figure in transition from the dying Middle Ages to the rising world of capitalism and science, blindly credulous and boldly questioning, a medieval mystic incongruously eager for gold and worldly honors.

Benjamin Keen, *The Life of the Admiral Christopher Columbus*, vi

Illustration on preceding page: Columbus bearing Christ to the "new world"

Above illustration: Engraving showing Columbus bidding farewell to Isabella and Ferdinand

October 11, 1492: Somewhere in the Western Part of the Ocean Sea

Clear skies, the moon a few days past full. Three ships from the port of Palos, in Spain, sailed before a brisk wind of about ten knots. The ships, the largest about the size of a tennis court, had been at sea for thirty-two days. In spite of fear and tension built up during the long journey, the crew felt a growing anticipation, for increasingly in the last few days they had seen signs of land.

Around ten o'clock in the evening the captain general of the little fleet thought he saw a light on the western horizon. However, he wrote in his log that he was too uncertain to confirm it as land. He called the royal steward, who said he too saw the light, and the royal inspector, who said he couldn't see anything.

The captain general kept looking, still thinking he could see something out there, "like a little wax candle that was lifting and rising." Since no one on either of the two other

twenty-four hundred sea miles from the Canary Islands, about a quarter of the actual distance. If he had to distort facts and figures to fit in with his notion of the size of the ocean, he didn't hesitate to do so. He was so sure he could do what he dreamed of that finally his dream became more real to him than reality.

In 1484 Columbus began a long period of arguing, cajoling, pressuring, and begging private investors and heads of governments to finance his proposed endeavor to sail west to Asia. Failing to find backers in Portugal, he went to Spain in 1485, where he soon realized he needed the support of the powerful monarchs Ferdinand and Isabella.

Somehow, he managed to get an audience at court in May, 1486. It is known that he spent time in a monastery near the castle; possibly, he had the attention of church leaders who persuaded the king and queen to listen to his plans. "Even in that religious and bigoted age, Columbus stood out as a very fierce Catholic. When he discussed his westward voyage, he always dwelt on its religious aspects: to convert the Asian 'heathens' to Catholicism, and/or to use their gold for the reconquest of the Holy Land from the Moslems" (Koning, 35).

Success

The monarchs took the plan under advisement. While waiting for their answer, Columbus and his brother Bartolomé petitioned the kings of Portugal, France, and England—in vain. After a long time with no response, the report from the royal advisors finally came: it cautioned that the westward-to-Asia plan appeared impossible to any learned person because the ocean was much wider than Columbus supposed. Isabella, however, held out a little hope to the discouraged dreamer. If Spain was victorious in the war with the Moors for Granada, Columbus could apply again.

After the Moors surrendered in January, 1492, Luis de Santangel, the royal treasurer, scraped up enough money from Italian bankers to finance the expedition. Isabella also agreed to Columbus's rather outlandish demands: ten percent of all the wealth that would pour into Spain from his new route to Asia; not only the riches he would personally bring in, but all that everyone else might gather, and for all time, for both himself and his heirs; the title of viceroy and Admiral of the Ocean Sea, together with other honors. With the title of admiral he would become the commander of the Western Atlantic, and would receive a share in all the naval booty to be drawn from that vast region.

The First Voyage

On August 3 the Niña, the Pinta, and the Santa Maria sailed from the small port of Palos, Spain, on their way to their first stop on the Canary Islands. They couldn't use Spain's principal port, Cadiz, because eight thousand people were penned up there in the holds of all kinds of ships awaiting deportation. They were Jews, expelled by the Holy Inquisition in a move toward religious unity.

The crew of ninety men, mostly professional sailors, included an interpreter who

ships called out, the captain general went to bed, after telling his crew to keep a good watch and "to look well for the land." He promised a doublet of silk to the first man to see land. This promise was in addition to the other reward the King and Queen had offered: ten thousand *maravedis* as a yearly stipend, a little less than a seaman's annual wages.

Sometime around two o'clock in the morning the lookout on the Pinta, Juan Rodriguez Bermejo, gave out the cry of *"Tierra!"* A cannon was fired as a signal to the other ships. And there, "at a distance of two leagues," they saw their long-anticipated goal. They lowered sails and lay-to until daylight.

Shortly after dawn the crew of the flagship prepared a display of ceremonial grandeur, including banners, pennants, and the royal standard. Their theatrical efforts were soon appreciated, fortunately, by an audience of naked people on the sands. The captain general boarded the flagship's longboat, taking with him the two royal observors to take notes, the official interpreter, and probably a few armed soldiers, and they were all rowed ashore.

Eduardo Galeano imagines how the scene might have played itself out:

He falls on his knees, weeps, kisses the earth. He steps forward, staggering because for more than a month he has hardly slept, and beheads some shrubs with his sword.

Then he raises the flag. On one knee, eyes lifted to heaven, he pronounces three times the names of Isabella and Ferdinand. Beside him the scribe Rodrigo de Escobedo, a man slow of pen, draws up the document.

From today, everything belongs to those remote monarchs: the coral sea, the beaches, the rocks all green with moss, the woods, the parrots, and these laurel-skinned people who don't yet know about clothes, sin, or money and gaze dazedly at the scene.

Luis de Torres translates Christopher Columbus's questions into Hebrew: "Do you know the kingdom of the Great Khan? Where does the gold you have in your noses and ears come from?"

The naked men stare at him with open mouths, and the interpreter tries out his small stock of Chaldean: "Gold? Temples? Palaces? King of kings? Gold?"

Then he tries his Arabic, the little he knows of it: "Japan? China? Gold?"

The interpreter apologizes to Columbus in the language of Castile. Columbus curses in Genovese and throws to the

... with this act two vastly different cultures, which had evolved on continents that had been drifting apart steadily for millions of years, were suddenly joined. Everything of importance in the succeeding five hundred years stems from that momentous event: the rise of Europe, the triumph of capitalism, the creation of the nation-state, the dominance of science, the establishment of a global monoculture, the genocide of the indigenes, the slavery of people of color, the colonization of the world, the destruction of primal environments, the eradication and abuse of species, and the impending catastrophe of ecocide for the planet Earth.

Kirkpatrick Sale, "What Columbus Discovered," *The Nation*, 446

---

ground his credentials, written in Latin and addressed to the Great Khan. The naked men watch the anger of the intruder with red hair and coarse skin, who wears a velvet cape and very shiny clothes.

Soon the word will run through the islands:

"Come and see the men who arrived from the sky! Bring them food and drink!"

Eduardo Galeano, *Memory of Fire: Genesis*, 45-46

The lookout who first called out the sighting, Juan Rodriguez Bermejo, didn't collect the doublet of silk or the ten thousand *maravedi* annuity. Columbus kept the reward to himself, although it was a small amount compared to the fortune he would later amass. His rationale was that he must have seen the lights of the landfall earlier in the evening. After all, the royal steward said he saw the lights, too.

See Kirkpatrick Sale, "What Columbus Discovered," *The Nation*, 444, 446

First Reports from Columbus

Friday, October 12, 1492

No sooner had we concluded the formalities of taking possession of the island than people began to come to the beach, all as naked as their mothers bore them. . . .

The people here called this island Guanahani in their language, and their speech is very fluent, although I do not understand any of it. They are friendly and well-dispositioned people who bare no arms except for small spears, and they have no iron. I showed one my sword, and through ignorance he grabbed it by the blade and cut himself. Their spears are made of wood, to which they attach a fish tooth at one end, or some other sharp thing.

I want the natives to develop a friendly attitude toward us because I know that they are a people who can be made free and converted to our Holy Faith more by love than by force. I therefore gave red caps to some and glass beads to others. They hung the beads around their necks, along with some other things of slight value that I gave them. And they took great pleasure in this and became so friendly that it was a marvel. They traded and gave everything they had with good

---

knew Hebrew and some Arabic and who, it was hoped, would be able to converse with whatever people they met in Asia; a marshal, or disciplinary officer, on each ship; a secretary to keep the official journal; a comptroller to record the expected riches; a "surgeon," probably with limited qualifications; and various petty officers.

Land!

With amazingly good fortune, given his lack of experience and faulty reckoning, and the increasing tension felt by the crew, farther from land for a longer period of time than anyone had ever been before, Columbus charted a course that led to a landing within thirty days of leaving Gomera, the westernmost part of the Canary Islands, the only Spanish colony, and thus a good staging place for the voyage.

Columbus's Log

During the ninety-six days he spent exploring the lands he encountered, Columbus kept a daily log which he gave to Isabella on his return. In spite of many misadventures the record survived and was translated by Fray Bartolomé de Las Casas, an early admirer of Columbus who later migrated to the "new world" and became the most outraged reporter of the atrocities committed by the Spaniards against the natives.

In his log, Columbus raves about the generosity and simplicity and good-naturedness of the islanders and refers to the beauty of the scenery, but he is quick to possess the land and think what good slaves the people would make.

Given prevailing European attitudes toward nature, it is not surprising that Columbus's descriptions of the landscape lag behind his descriptions of the people. The handsome, naked, trusting islanders understandably grabbed his immediate attention; they were as strange and fascinating to him as the Spaniards were to them. But in the early days he slights what must have been spectacular scenery around them.

"Here he was, in the middle of an old-growth tropical forest the likes of which he could not have imagined before, its trees reaching sixty or seventy feet into the sky, more varieties than he knew how to count much less name, exhibiting a lushness that stood in sharp contrast to the sparse and denuded lands he had known in the Mediterranean, hearing a melodious multiplicity of bird songs and parrot calls—why was it not an occasion of wonder, excitement, and the sheer joy at nature in its full, arrogant abundance?" (Sale, 101).

For the first two weeks of the beginning of his voyage through the Bahamas to Cuba, only a third of the lines of description recorded in the log have anything to do with the natural phenomena around him. And some sights he seems not to have noticed at all. He mentions the nighttime sky in terms of navigation but never describes the sharp, glorious configurations of stars that must have been visible practically every night of his journey.

will, but it seems to me that they have very little and are poor in everything. I warned my men to take nothing from the people without giving something in exchange.

This afternoon the people of San Salvador came swimming to our ships and in boats made from one log. They brought us parrots, balls of cotton thread, spears, and many other things, including a kind of dry leaf [probably tobacco] that they hold in great esteem. For these items we swapped them little glass beads and hawks' bells.

Many of the men I have seen have scars on their bodies, and when I made signs to them to find out how this happened, they indicated that people from other nearby islands come to San Salvador to capture them; they defend themselves the best they can. I believe that people from the mainland come here to take them as slaves. They ought to make good and skilled servants. For they repeat very quickly whatever we say to them. I think they can easily be made Christians, for they seem to have no religion. If it pleases Our Lord, I will take six of them to Your Highnesses when I depart, in order that they may learn our language.

Robert H. Fuson, trans., *The Log of Christopher Columbus*, 75-77

Wednesday, 17 October, 1492, on "Long Island"

The houses look like Moorish tents, very tall, with good chimneys, but I have not seen a village yet with more than 12 or 15 houses. I also learned that the cotton coverings were worn by married women or women over 18 years of age. Young girls go naked. And I saw dogs, mastiffs and pointers. One man was found who had a piece of gold in his nose, about half the size of a castellano, and on which my men say they saw letters.

Log, 86

Tuesday, 6 November, 1492, on Cuba

The Spaniards said that the Indians received them with great solemnity, according to Indian custom, and all the men and women came to see them and lodged them in the best houses. The Indians touched them and kissed their hands and feet in wonderment, believing that we Spaniards came from Heaven, and so my men led them to understand. The Indians gave them to eat what they had.

Log, 103

Monday, 3 December, 1492, on Cuba

I saw and entered a beautiful house, not very large and with two doors, such as they are all built. I saw a wonderful arrangement of chambers, built in a way that I do not know how to describe. The chambers were formed by mats and shells hanging from the ceiling. I thought it was a temple, and I called them and asked by signs if they prayed in it and they said no. One of them went overhead to a loft and gave me all they had there, and I took some of it.

Log, 123-124

December 25, 1492: A Chief's Kindness

On Christmas Day, 1492, an incident occurred that led to the establishment of the first settlement in the "new world." Columbus had been sent a present from a leader, or *cacique,* named Guacanagari, a belt and mask with features of hammered gold, and a promise of "all that he had" if the Admiral would visit him.

On Christmas Eve, the Niña and the Santa Maria made their way along the coast. The entire crew, including the Admiral, went to sleep, and the Santa Maria hit a coral reef a few miles from shore, was quickly stuck firmly, and broke up and sank as the sun arose. Columbus sent a messenger to Guacanagari to ask for help. The *cacique* wept when he heard of the shipwreck.

The Cacique was unwearied in his attentions; his grief at the disaster was so manifest, and his attempts to divert [the sailors] from their trouble so delicately proffered, that finally hope returned to cheer them, and they thought upon their blessings.

The little Niña lay anchored off the village of Guarico, and at sunrise of the day after Christmas, the Cacique paid a visit of state to the Admiral, when Columbus was so pleased with his frank and manly bearing that he repeated his encomiums, declaring him preeminent in virtue.

While the king was on board, his Indian subjects swarmed in canoes around the caravel, holding out pieces of gold, and crying out, "Chug, chug!" intimating that they wished to barter the nuggets for hawks-bells, over which they went wild with joy. Seeing that such trifles brought in exchange great pieces of gold, Columbus was delighted, and at the sight of the pleasure expressed in his countenance, Guacanagari, quick to note the change, assured him that if gold was the object of his desires, he would direct him to a region where the very

Taking Possession

Although he didn't rhapsodize about the physical splendor at first, Columbus had no hesitation about taking possession of all he came across, no question about the possibility that someone else might already have a proprietary relationship with the landscape. Significantly, he assigned names to sixty-two physical features on the islands—capes, ports, mountains—as he possessed them for his king and queen, instead of asking whether or not they had names.

Later he succumbed to the natural beauty around him. In Cuba, toward the end of his journey, he came upon a large harbor which he named Puerto Santo. "As I went along the river," he writes on November 27, "it was marvelous to see the forests and greenery, the very clear water, the birds, and the fine situation, and I almost did not want to leave this place. I told the men with me that, in order to make a report to the Sovereigns of the things they saw, a thousand tongues would not be sufficient to tell it, nor my hand to write it, for it looks like an enchanted land" (Fuson, 119).

First Colony

Columbus didn't find what he was looking for: gold. The natives answered his constant questions the only way they could. They were puzzled by these strangers, but they tried to please them by giving them information about possible stores of the shiny metal they admired so much.

He also didn't find Asia. To make up for those failures he began to consider building a colonial outpost, a military fortress:

"I wanted to see if I could find a place to build a fort. I saw a piece of land that looked like an island, even though it is not, with six houses on it. I believe that it could be cut through and made into an island in two days. I do not think this is necessary, however, for these people are very unskilled in arms. Your Highnesses will see this for yourselves when I bring you the seven that I have taken. After they learn our language I shall return them, unless Your Highnesses order that the entire population be taken to Castile, or held captive here. With fifty men you could subject everyone and make them do what you wished" (Fuson, 79-80). Colonization and slaves began to have as much appeal as gold and a passage to Asia.

The shipwreck of the Santa Maria gave the explorers an excuse to build a colony, named "La Navidad" in honor of the Day of Nativity (Christmas) on which its inadvertent founding occurred. Using salvaged timber, with the help of the willing Tainos, the Spaniards in a few days constructed some buildings, and thirty-eight or forty of the men agreed to stay in the fortress. The rest of the crew, plus Indian captives, set sail in the two remaining ships on the homeward journey.

Engraving of La Navidad

stones were golden, and where it was in such abundance that the people dwelling there held it in light esteem. This region he called Cibao, which Columbus construed to mean Cipango [Japan], so long the goal before him in his voyagings.

Of course, the chief's promise, made out of a desire to please, was never fulfilled.

Frederick Ober, *In the Wake of Columbus*, 224-225

Sunday, January 13, 1493: A Show of Strength

After three months on the islands, the Spaniards for the first time discovered some natives with bows and arrows "as if ready for war." Since the Admiral (Columbus quickly began referring to himself by his new title) had given standing orders that his men should buy or barter away any weapons the Indians might have, the sailors dickered with a few of these men of ferocious aspect and persuaded them to come on board to talk with the Admiral, who sent them ashore to induce the others to bring gold.

Following are two versions of the story, the first written by Columbus's son, the second a commentary on the significance of the episode:

How the First Skirmish Between the Indians and Christians Took Place in Samana Bay on the Island of Española

The Indian who had visited the ship persuaded the others to lay down their bows and arrows and the large cudgels which they use as swords, for they have no iron. The Christians began to buy swords and arrows as the Admiral had instructd them to do, but after the Indians had sold two of their bows they disdainfully refused to sell any more; instead they ran toward the place where they had deposited their weapons, with the design of picking them up and also of getting cords with which to tie our men's hands. But the Christians were prepared for their attack, and though only seven in number, fell upon the Indians with so much spirit that they gave one Indian a slash on the buttocks with a sword and wounded another in the breast with an arrow. Terrified by the valor of our men and the wounds inflicted by our arms, the Indians turned and fled, leaving behind most of their bows and arrows. Many would certainly have been killed had not the pilot of the caravel, who was in charge of the landing party, restrained our men.

The Admiral was not displeased by this incident; for he was convinced these were the Caribs whom the other Indians feared so greatly, or if not Caribs, at least their neighbors. Their appearance, arms, and actions showed them to be a daring and courageous people. The Admiral hoped that when the islanders learned what seven Spaniards had done against 55 ferocious Indians, they would feel more respect for the men left behind in the town of Navidad and would not dare annoy them.

> The Life of the Admiral Christopher Columbus by His Son, 88-90

After just two bows were sold, the Indians turned and ran back to the cover of the trees where they kept their remaining weapons and, so the sailors assumed, "prepared . . . to attack the Christians and capture them." When they came toward the Spaniards again brandishing ropes—almost certainly meaning to trade these rather than give up their precious bows—the sailors panicked and, "being prepared as always the Admiral advised them to be," attacked the Indians with swords and halberds, gave one "a great slash on the buttocks," and shot another in the breast with a crossbow. The Tainos grabbed their fallen comrades and fled in fright, and the sailors would have chased them and "killed many of them" but for the pilot in charge of the party, who somehow "prevented it."

It may fairly be called the first pitched battle between Europeans and Indians in the "new world"—the first display of the armed power, and the will to use it, of the white invaders.

> Kirkpatrick Sale, *The Conquest of Paradise*, 120-121

Captives

Columbus had kidnapped citizens of the island villages he visited, realizing what good servants these gentle, agreeable people could become.

In one harbor, "five young Indian men came aboard for a last visit, and in return for their trust, Columbus held them captive. He wanted to train them as interpreters, he said. Then he sent a boat ashore to kidnap seven women and three boys. Seeing this, the husbands and fathers of some of the victims begged to be taken along with them, rather than suffer the pain of separation. Columbus kindly agreed. A little later two of the young men escaped. The others? All would die before the fleet reached Spain" (Meltzer, 99).

Although he captured a total of thirty-one islanders, the number he actually took with him isn't known. Six survived the difficult voyage, especially difficult for inhabitants of a tropical climate who had never experienced cold weather, and were centerpieces of Columbus's triumphant entry first into Portugal and then into Spain.

After hearing about the first voyage, other writers followed the lead of Columbus in describing the "new world." In the words of Peter Martyr, an early historian, writing after a later journey, "This people are astonished at the sound of our trumpets and drums, stupefied by the thunder of our cannon, speechless at the prancing, running, and trappings of our horses; perplexed at the sight of everything belonging to us. They stand in open-mouthed astonishment. They think our people have come from heaven" (December 29, 1494, letter in Thacher, 70).

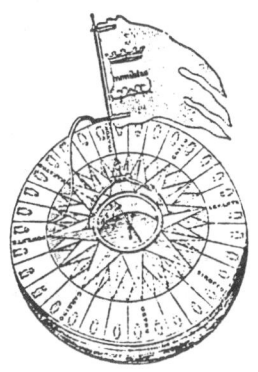

1493: Reaction

Historians hardly knew what to make of the stories Columbus brought back from his first voyage. In an early interpretation, Peter Martyr focused on the riches of the land and the strangeness of the people:

A certain Christopher Columbus . . . followed the western sun from the Gades, with three ships furnished him by my sovereigns, and proceeded to the Antipodes, about five thousand miles.

He ascertained that the land [he visited] produced naturally gold, cotton, spices in form like cinnamon and smooth like pepper, trees of scarlet dyes, the juices of which make a bluish-grey colour, and many other things most precious to us, small samples of which things he brought away.

The island has many kings, but naked, as indeed all are of both sexes. This people, wholly content by nature, naked as they are, feed only on such nourishment as comes from trees, with a kind of bread made of roots. Notwithstanding, they are fond of government, and owing to this desire they wage wars against each other, with bows and with pikes burned into very sharp points. The King who is conquered is considered to be subject to the conqueror.

And the principle of Meum and Tuum [mine and thine] has a part in their lives as it has among us; and so the things belonging to luxury and the accumulation of money are sought by them, a thing you would hardly think necessary for naked people.

Peter Martyr of Anghara in John Boyd Thacher, *Christopher Columbus: His Life, His Work, His Remains*, 58

Later, however, Martyr's views changed somewhat, and he described Cuba as a veritable Utopia:

It is certain, that among them, the land is as common as the sun and water: and that Mine and Thine (the seeds of all mischief) have no place with them. They are content with so little, that in so large a country, they have rather superfluity than scarceness. So that . . . they seem to live in the golden world, without toil, living in open gardens, not entrenched with dikes, divided with hedges, or defended with walls. They deal truly one with another, without laws, without books, and without Judges. They take him for an evil and mischievous man who takes pleasure in doing hurt to others.

Peter Martyr, quoted in Kirkpatrick Sale, *The Conquest of Paradise*, 199

The Later Voyages

The Treaty of Tordesillas

Pope Alexander VI expressed himself (using the royal "we") in no uncertain terms:

We have indeed learned that you, who for a long time had intended to seek out and discover certain islands and mainlands remote and unknown and not hitherto discovered by others, to the end that you might bring to the worship of our Redeemer and the profession of the Catholic faith their residents and inhabitants . . . chose our beloved son, Christopher Columbus, . . . whom you furnished with ships and men equipped for like designs, not without the greatest hardships, dangers, and expenses, to make diligent quest for these remote and unknown mainlands and islands through the sea, where hitherto no one had sailed; . . . and they at length, . . . discovered certain very remote islands and even mainlands that hitherto had not been discovered by others.

Wherefore, as becomes Catholic kings and princes, after earnest consideration of all matters, especially of the rise and spread of the Catholic faith, as was the fashion of your ancestors, kings of reknowned memory, you have purposed with the favor of divine clemency to bring under your sway the said mainlands and islands with their residents and inhabitants and to bring them to the Catholic faith. . . .

And, in order that you may enter upon so great an undertaking with greater readiness and heartiness endowed with the benefit of our apostolic favor, we . . . by the authority of Almighty God conferred upon us in blessed Peter and of the vicarship of Jesus Christ . . . do by tenor of these presents . . . give, grant, and assign to you and your heirs and successors, kings of Castile and Leon, forever, . . . all islands and mainlands found and to be found, discovered and to be discovered towards the west and south, by drawing and establishing a line from the Arctic pole . . . to the Antarctic pole . . . to be distant one hundred leagues towards the west and south from any of the islands . . . commonly known as the Azores and Cape Verde. . . .

You should appoint to the aforesaid mainlands and islands worthy, God-fearing, learned, skilled, and experienced men, in order to instruct the aforesaid inhabitants and residents in the Catholic faith and train them in good morals. Furthermore, under penalty of excommunication . . . we strictly forbid all persons of whatsoever rank . . . to dare, without your special permit . . . to go for the purpose of trade or any other reason to [these] islands or mainlands.

Francis Gardner Davenport, ed., *European Treaties Bearing on the History of the United States and its Dependencies to 1648*, 76-78

Where is it written that the world is already divided up?

—*King of France, 1494*

Quoted in Hans Koning, *Columbus: His Enterprise*, 67

The Church

Columbus stopped first in Portugal, where he heard from John II, the king who had refused to sponsor the expedition, that, based on the terms of a treaty signed between Portugal and Castile in 1479, all the lands visited during the journey would henceforth be Portuguese territory. However, according to the medieval church under the traditions of feudalism, any newly discovered land belonged to the pope and could be given away only by him and only to heads of state who promised to lead the inhabitants to the "true faith."

Although at this time it was unclear what place Columbus had visited, since he and many others assumed he had reached the outskirts of Asia, evidently no one worried about what the Emperor of Japan or the ruler of China might think of Pope Alexander VI dividing up the world between Spain and Portugal. For that's what he did. He granted Ferdinand and Isabella, the "Catholic Sovereigns," all they had already conquered and everything they might discover on the westward journey to the Orient.

King John wasn't happy with this decision, naturally. In 1494 he persuaded the Catholic monarchs to meet with him in the town of Tordesillas where they signed the treaty of that name. An imaginary line now cut vertically through the ocean fourteen hundred miles west of the Cape Verde Islands. Everything west of that line belonged to Spain, everything

east to Portugal. Based on the Treaty of Tordesillas, Portugal later claimed Brazil, and for years any foreign sailors apprehended in Spanish waters were punished by garroting (strangling to death with a rope and stick).

The Second Voyage

The positive reception of the travelers led to a second voyage, this time grandly outfitted with seventeen ships and between twelve and fifteen hundred colonists, including five religious specifically charged with converting the natives, a large band of soldiers, and many adventurers, financed at least partly with funds confiscated from Spanish Jews. Underlying the voyage was the general assumption that surely this time Columbus would reach the Asian islands Marco Polo had described.

On the second voyage, "the pretense was ended, the idyll over. The Indians, who had been praised for their generosity and innocence, were now called savages. The talk was of slavery and gold, rather than brotherhood and conversion. The new relationship between the races was established" (Koning, 69-70).

As the fleet traveled through the islands, the Spanish took captives whenever they could. This time the villages were largely deserted. The Spanish colonizers in La Navidad had set the tone for centuries to come by roaming the islands in gangs, demanding gold and terrorizing the natives, until the gentle, timid Tainos rose against them and killed them in pitched battle, in spite of attempts by the *cacique* Guacanagari to prevent this revenge.

Late April, 1494: Isabella

The tone for the second voyage was set early on. At first Columbus continued his practice of bartering for the largesse his men received from the natives:

As he sail'd close along the Shoar, great Numbers of People came aboard in their Canoes from the Island, thinking the Spaniards to be Men come down from Heaven, bringing them Bread, Water, and Fish, and giving it all freely, without asking for any Return; but the Admiral, to send them away pleas'd, commanded they should be paid, giving them Beads, Bells, and such kind of Baubles.

But soon the voyagers took a more bellicose stand:

The next Day he ran along the Coast to seek out Harbours, and the Boats going to found the Mouths of them, there came out so many Canoes with arm'd Men, to defend the Country,

Above illustration:
A woodcut showing the king sending off travelers to the "new world"

that they were forc'd to return to their Ships, not so much for Fear, as to avoid giving an Occasion of Enmity to those People. But afterwards considering, that if they shew'd the least Signs of Fear, the Indians would grow insolent upon it, they return'd together to the Port, which the Admiral call'd Puerte Bueno, or the Good Harbour. And because the Indians came to drive them off, those in the boats saluted them with such a flight of Arrows from their Cross-bows, that six or seven of them being wounded they were glad to retire.

The American Traveller, 194-195

It has been said of the Spanish conquistadors that first they fell on their knees, and then they fell on the aborigines.

Eric Williams, *From Columbus to Castro,* 30

Murder

As a Spanish longboat returned to the fleet, they observed a Carib canoe paddling around a point on the coastline. It stopped abruptly when those aboard caught sight of the vast Spanish fleet anchored in the harbor.

For a long hour the four men, two women, and a boy aboard the canoe stayed motionless on the water, staring in wonder at the huge ships and the white men gazing at them from the decks. The shore party meanwhile maneuvered their boat so as to cut off the Caribs' escape.

Seeing that flight was impossible, the Indians shot arrows at the Spaniards, wounding one and killing another. But they were soon overpowered and taken to the fleet.

One of the men, whose belly was sliced by a Spaniard's sword, was tossed overboard. He did not sink, but clutching his guts with one hand, swam with the other toward shore. The Spaniards chased after him, pulled him aboard, tied his hands and feet, and threw him back into the sea. The Indian managed to free himself, and again swam off. Then the gallant whites, frustrated in their repeated attempts at murder, shot the Indian through and through with arrows until he died.

Milton Meltzer, *Columbus and the World around Him,* 125-127

Colonization

Another colony, Isabella, was founded in central Hispaniola (today the Dominican Republic and Haiti). The colonists suffered from the tropical heat, the changed diet, the hard work of building a town, and the contrast between the harsh reality they faced and the idyllic descriptions that had lured them. They wanted to return to Spain in spite of Columbus's assurances that gold was plentiful in the interior, where he spent six months searching for it. Columbus himself contracted a devastating illness, quite possibly a mental collapse, with a high fever and crippling arthritis that plagued him the rest of his life.

As more forts were established, governing them became more and more of a problem, since the Spanish soldiers "went their own cruel way, robbing the Indians of their gold ornaments, raping the women, kidnapping boys and girls to serve as slaves, and gobbling up the scarce supplies of food" (Meltzer, 140).

The only way the newcomers could relate to the hospitable tribes Columbus knew from his first voyage was to terrorize them in order to crush the resistance that grew as a result of their own actions—a vicious cycle. The Spanish had horses and dogs, crossbows and arquebuses (portable guns); the Indians carried on a guerrilla war, ambushing soldiers, burning their food supplies, raiding their camps at night.

However, after a year the last remnant of resistance was crushed and the total enslavement of the Indians was inevitable.

The Tribute System

Columbus had another major problem: he still hadn't found a good source of gold. Now governor of Hispaniola, he instituted the tribute system, "a simple and brutal way of fufilling the Spanish lust for gold while acknowledging the Spanish distaste for labor" (Sale, 155).

Every man and woman, boy and girl of fourteen or older was forced to collect gold for the Spaniards. They had to fill a hawks' bell with gold dust and bring it to the fort every three months. (Hawks' bells were the same trinkets the Indians had received from the explorers with such happiness during the first voyage.) The "chiefs" had to produce about ten times as much. In areas with no gold, the requirement was twenty-five pounds of spun cotton.

When the Indians brought their tribute in they were given a copper token to wear around the neck. The punishment for not paying tribute was the cutting off the hands of the offender. A famous engraving from a 1619 book called *Spanish Cruelties* shows Indians stumbling away from the chopping block, looking with surprise at the stumps of their arms pulsing out blood.

Since no gold fields existed, the Indians' only hope was to work all day in the streams, washing gold dust from the pebbles. Meeting the quotas of both gold and cotton was an impossible task. Indians who tried to flee into the mountains were hunted down with dogs and killed as an example. Desperate, the Tainos began killing themselves with cassava poison. In two years, one half the

. . . and Rape

No European women traveled to the "new world" until several years later; obviously the men had implicit permission to use the island women as they wished.

While the great courage of the Indians did not win mercy, it deeply impressed the militaristic Spaniards. They soon found the Carib women were just as brave. Cuñeo [a nobleman and one of the few reporters of the second voyage] tells how he tried to rape one he had made his slave. She fought back so violently he had to whip her with a rope before he could subdue her. That evening, he joined all the other Spaniards in singing a hymn to the Blessed Virgin.

Milton Meltzer, *Columbus and the World around Him*, 127

February, 1495: First Massive Slave Raid

Time was short for sending back a good "dividend" on the supply ships getting ready for the return to Spain. Columbus therefore turned to a massive slave raid as a means for filling up these ships. The brothers rounded up fifteen hundred Arawaks—men, women, and children—and imprisoned them in pens in Isabella, guarded by men and dogs.

The ships had room for no more than five hundred, and thus only the best specimens were loaded aboard. The Admiral then told the Spaniards they could help themselves from the remainder to as many slaves as they wanted. Those whom no one chose were simply kicked out of the pens. Such had been the terror of these prisoners that (in the description by Michele de Cuñeo, one of the colonists) "they rushed in all directions like lunatics, women dropping and abandoning infants in the rush, running for miles without stopping, fleeing across mountains and rivers."

Of the five hundred slaves, three hundred arrived alive in Spain, where they were put up for sale in Seville by Don Juan de Fonseca, the archdeacon of the town. "As naked as the day they were born," the report of this excellent churchman says, "but with no more embarrassment than animals."

The slave trade immediately turned out to be "unprofitable, for the slaves mostly died."

Hans Koning, *Columbus: His Enterprise*, 82

Above illustration: Tainos working for their Spanish masters

Stories of Cannibals

In the tradition of the Wild Man and Savage Beast tales, legends circulated in Europe about man-eating islanders, and Columbus assumed that the inhabitants of the Caribbean islands, the Caribs, were the fierce, warlike, cannibals of whom he had heard. However, he never met or saw any Caribs on his first voyage; on the second voyage his assumptions led him to convey the notion that the islands he visited were populated by Caribs. Yet on Guadeloupe, the only Carib island his fleet stopped at, the natives "as soon as they saw us, instantly ran to the mountains," according to Cuñeo, one of the reporters.

The idea of fierce and hostile Caribs, in short, was never more than a bogey, born of Colon's own paranoia or stubborn ferocity and spread to his comrades, to the chroniclers of Europe, and to history. Certain sixteenth-century sailors did come to grief when landing on those islands—given the fierce reputation of the white man by then, it is not surprising that the Caribs were less than hospitable—but the historical record for that century actually emphasizes the friendliness of the islanders and the passivity of their behavior.

And their rapacious cannibalism? That, similarly, from all the real evidence we have, seems to be a myth. . . . That is all there is. . . . Las Casas, who had considerable experience in the islands over several decades, said flatly that the Caribs were not cannibals, and a nineteenth-century scholar, Wil-

entire population of Hispaniola were killed or killed themselves.

When it became obvious that no gold was left, the Spaniards instituted another system known as the *encomienda*, based on models familiar to the Europeans from their own experience of feudalism. The governor could give ("commend") Indians to the colonists *(encomenderos)* to use as they chose, for tribute or forced labor; the masters would in return provide their servants with instructions on becoming good Christians.

Colonists' Complaints

Columbus's role in the second voyage came to an ignoble end. Reports to Ferdinand and Isabella pictured him as an inept administrator. The colonists complained bitterly that he had led them astray with his tales of instant riches. They were unhappy and sick, unable to become self-sufficient and constantly clamoring for fresh supplies from Spain.

A new disease had appeared, and although historians differ on its origin, many agree that syphillis was first transmitted to Europe by colonists returning from the Indies, who contacted it through sexual intercourse with native women. Evidently among the Indians of the Caribbean it was a widespread, nonfatal condition with almost no symptoms. It flared up in a new and deadly form in Europe, as "the just price the Spaniards paid for their ravaging of Indian women" (Koning, 88).

Because of their history as warriors, the colonists were arrogant and brutal toward the Indians and each other. As Spanish gentlemen, they were unaccustomed to hard work and indeed felt only contempt for those who worked with their hands. "They would rather rot than do anything for them-selves. . . . In a land where it was easy to grow food, easy to catch fish or fowl, they acted as though Hispaniola were some godforsaken desert" (Meltzer, 145).

The Third Voyage

The King and Queen finally had to pay attention to all the complaints against Columbus by the angry men under his command, and they called him back to Spain.

There he lived in the house of a priest and dressd as a friar, evidently to show humility. He continued to petition for another voyage. With financing partly from the sale of enslaved Indians, Columbus made a third trip in May, 1498.

His reports back began to show the effects of his long illness on his mind: he claimed in all seriousness to have found the Garden of Eden and concluded that the earth is not round but pear-shaped, with Paradise at its tip.

He stayed in Hispaniola for two years, governing with his brothers and continuing to bring about the destruction of the island's civilization. The Arawaks were dying out, the colonists waged constant war on each other and all the Indians, and finally the mon-archs sent a commissioner, Francisco de Bobadilla, to investigate. What he found

liam Sheldon, reviewing all the literature, said that he could find no believable evidence of cannibalism. . . .   The anthropologist W. Arens, in his wide-ranging The Man-Eating Myth, *says that he was "unable to uncover adequate documentation of cannibalism as a custom in any form for any society" and adds that "there is little reason to assume that the very aborigines whose name now means man-eaters actually were so."*

Kirkpatrick Sale, *The Conquest of Paradise,* 129-133

. . . and Amazons

Another persistent story was about the Amazons:

He made for the island Guadalupe, where sending his Boats, well-man'd, ashore, before they reach'd Land, abundance of Women came out of the Woods with Bows and Arrows, as if they would defend their Island.

[The wife of a Cacique] told the Admiral that this Island was only inhabited by Women, and that those who endeavour'd to hinder his Men from Landing were all Women, except about four Men, who were there accidentally from another Island; for at a certain Time in the Year, they come to hunt, and accompany with them.

The same Customs, she assur'd him, were also observ'd by the Women of another Island, call'd Matrimonio, of whom she gave much the same Account as we read of the ancient Amazons; all which the Admiral made no Difficulty to credit, because of the surprizing Strength and Courage of these Women, which he himself had been a Witness to.

It is likewise observable, that these Women seemed to be endu'd wih clearer Understandings than those of the other Islands; for in them they only knew to reckon the Day by the Sun, and the Night by the Moon; whereas these Women could reckon by other Stars, it being a common Expression amongst them, when the North Star rises, or such a Star is North, then it is Time to do such or such a Thing.

American Traveler, 118-220

The Tragedy of the Natives

The growing hostility between the colonizers and the natives led to tragic misunderstandings and horrible consequences for the natives. During the third voyage, trouble with the Indians accelerated into open warfare. Columbus captured thirty of them in an ambush and confined them to a lower deck on one of the ships.

But even as he prepared to sail, the Indians chose suicide rather than captivity. During the night they all hanged themselves from beams in the low hold of the ship, bending their knees while they strangled. Much later, writing of it, the admiral's son Ferdinand disposed of the tragedy by saying, "Their deaths were not great harm to the ships. . . ."

Milton Meltzer, *Columbus and the World around Him*, 166

Eduardo Galeano sums up the total lack of communication:

Bartolomé Columbus, Christopher's brother and lieutenant, attends an incineration of human flesh.

Six men play the leads in the grand opening of Haiti's incinerator. The smoke makes everyone cough. The six are burning as a punishment and as a lesson: They have buried the images of Christ and the Virgin that Fray Ramon Pané left with them for protection and consolation. Fray Ramon taught them to pray on their knees, to say the Ave Maria and Paternoster and to invoke the name of Jesus in the face of temptation, injury, and death.

No one has asked them why they buried the images. They were hoping that the new gods would fertilize their fields of corn, cassava, boniato, and beans.

The fire adds warmth to the humid, sticky heat that foreshadows heavy rain.

Eduardo Galeano, *Memory of Fire: Genesis*, 51

led him to arrest Columbus and his two brothers and deport them for trial in Spain. During the arrest, Columbus was manacled. Although later the captain of the ship offered to remove the chains, Columbus insisted on wearing them during the entire trip, until he met with his sovereigns to receive their words of criticism.

Naming of America

By this time other explorers from other countries were filling in more of the details of the newly discovered continent, and recognizing it as such. Amerigo Vespucci sailed with one of Columbus's former lieutenants and wrote brilliant accounts of his voyages. In his honor mapmakers called the new landmass in the Western Hemisphere "America."

The Last Voyage

Ferdinand and Isabella replaced Columbus as governor of the Indies with Nicolás de Ovando. His first action on his arrival in Hispaniola was to massacre the welcoming party of eighty-five chiefs headed by a woman *cacique*, Anacoana, and everyone else they could catch. Hispaniola quickly became a center for the expeditions launched by the Spanish to commit similar atrocities against the people of Cuba.

But Columbus was still determined to find a passage to the Indies. Again he convinced the monarchs to fund him, on condition that he stay away from Hispaniola and search for gold and silver, pearls and spices, but not take slaves. By 1502 he was too old and sick to command the small fleet of four caravels, but he went along, with his brother Bartolomé and his young son Ferdinand, who much later wrote an account of this extremely difficult voyage.

A fourth of the crew, the majority twelve- or thirteen-year-old boys, never returned home. Attempts to colonize again failed. In the end the men mutinied, almost murdering Columbus before they were subdued by Bartolomé.

Columbus returned to Spain a broken old man wracked by illness. Queen Isabella died shortly after his return, and Ferdinand asked the archbishop of Seville to deal with Columbus's appeals for the income and property and titles he had been promised before his first voyage. His demand to be restored as governor of the Indies was refused, in the interests of the state, but he continued to receive the revenues due him. Contrary to the myths that he died penniless, he ended his life a rich but very unhappy man.

The Legend

For many years no one paid much attention to Columbus. The publication in 1571 of Ferdinand's biography of his father caused some stir, but it wasn't until later, in the 1600s, that the legend of Columbus gained a place in European consciousness. The first centennial commemoration was celebrated in Europe and America three hundred years after the first voyage, in 1792.

Later Assessments

The depths of the differences in worldview among the many cultures involved continued to be plumbed in succeeding centuries, as European immigration followed the initial voyages of Columbus. Only very gradually did Columbus become a hero and his voyages something to remember on a special day. On October 23, 1792, on the occasion of one of the first celebrations in America honoring Columbus, Jeremy Belknap delivered an address at the request of the Historical Society in Massachusetts. Three centuries after the event, Belknap raised significant questions about its meaning for humankind. His speech began with a recognition that European travels to the Western Hemisphere had many positive consequences:

The discovery of America has opened an important page in the history of man. We find our brethren of the human race, scattered over all parts of this continent, and the adjacent islands. We see mankind in their several varieties of colour, form and habit, and we learn to consider ourselves as one great family, sent into the world to make various experiments for happiness.

Belknap recognized that the oppressed of Europe have always found safety and relief in North America, and the idea of individual freedom from tyranny has been expanded into a clear vindication of the rights *which are the gift of god to man.*

However, Belknap pointed out, two major flaws undercut the new society that formed in the "new world." The first was slavery:

Our astonishment is excited, by considering that the discovery of America has opened a large mart for the commerce in slaves from the opposite continent of Africa. So much has been written and spoken on the iniquity attending this detestable species of traffic, that I need not attempt again to excite the feelings of indignation and horror, which I doubt not have pervaded the breast of every person now present, when contemplating this flagrant insult on the laws of jusice and humanity.

I shall only observe, that the first introduction of the negro slave into America, was occasioned by the previous destruction of the native inhabitants of the West-India islands, by the cruelty of their Spanish conquerors, in exacting of them more labour than they were able to perform. . . . The commerce of slaves from Africa has proved destructive to human life and happiness, in the same proportion that it has encouraged avarice, luxury, pride and cruelty.

Belknap, clearly a man ahead of his time, was hopeful that slavery would be abolished soon:

But do I not see the dawn of that auspicious day which shall put a stop to this infamous traffic, and shall teach mankind that Africans have a native right to liberty and property as well as Europeans and Americans? May these rights ever be respected, and never more be infringed, especially by those who have successfully contended for the establishment of their own.

Another flaw Belknap recognized resulted from the savagery of Christians who insisted on conversion of all the inhabitants of the lands they conquered. Using Peru as his model, he questioned the need to force obedience from a people whose code of laws *was a work of reason and benevolence, and bore a great resemblance to the divine precepts given by Moses and confirmed by Jesus Christ.*

But when we find that these mild and peaceful people were invaded by avaricious Spaniards, under a pretence of converting them to the catholic faith; when instead of the meek and humble language of a primitive evangelist, we see a bigoted Friar gravely advancing at the head of a Spanish army, and, in a language unknown to the Peruvians, declaring that their country was given to his nation, by the Pope of Rome, God's only vicar on earth, and commanding them to receive their new masters on pain of death; when we consider this parade of arrogant hypocrisy as the signal for slaughter, and see the innocent victims falling by the sword of these ministers of destruction; when we see the whole nation vanquished, disheartened, and either murdered or reduced to slavery, by their savage conquerors; when instead of the worship which they addressed to the luminary of heaven, and which needed but one step more to conduct them to the knowledge of its invisible Creator, we see the pomp of Popish idolatry, with the infernal horrors of the Inquisition introduced into their country; our astonishment is excited to the highest degrees. . . .

If we survey the whole continent, from the first discovery of America, to the present time, the number of converts to christianity, among the Indians, bears but a small proportion to those, who have been destroyed either by war, by slavery or by spirituous liquors.

Belknap suggested that looking inward was in order:

If the truths of our holy religion are to be propagated among the savages, it will become us to consider, whether we had not better first agree among ourselves, what these truths are. . . . It is also worthy of consideration, whether the vicious lives

A Faithful Chronicler

Fray Bartolomé de Las Casas, an early admirer of Columbus who translated his logs into Spanish, spent more than forty years in the American colonies. He came as a colonist and was himself an *encomendero*, but as a cleric and faithful Christian he was outraged at the atrocities he saw being committed in the name of God.

In addition to his many other writings, through the years he produced *The Devastation of the Indies: A Brief Account* in an attempt to persuade the monarchs in Spain to exert some control over their colonizers. King Ferdinand V was sufficiently moved by Las Casas's testimony to initiate an investigation; his heir Charles V eventually ruled that the procedure of the conquistadors had been illlegal and a council should work out a plan by which the colonies could be governed without the force of weapons. However, little changed in actual practice.

Las Casas spent his long life (he died at ninety-two) fighting for the cause of the Indians. One unfortunate conclusion he came to had enormous consequences: he suggested that Africans would make much better slaves than the delicate Indians. Late in life he deeply regretted that suggestion, saying that the right of the blacks is the same as that of the Indians and that the slave trade of the Portuguese in Africa was a crime.

and conduct of our own people, and especially those on the frontiers, with whom the Indians are most acquainted, be not a great obstruction to the spreading of divine knowledge among them. It is very natural to estimate the goodness of any religion, by the influence which it appears to have on those who profess it; and, if they are to regard the conduct of the people by whom they have been cheated, robbed, and murdered, as a specimen of the influence of christianity on the human mind, it would be a greater wonder that they should embrace it than reject it.

Jeremy Belknap, *A Discourse Intended to Commemorate the Discovery of America by Christopher Columbus,* 36, 46-52

Bartolomé de las Casas

These cautionary words would be echoed through the years by many other observers. The saga of conquest continued, in the destruction of the Aztec civilization, in the tremendous increase in the practice of slavery, and in the continued colonization of the Western Hemisphere by the rising nation-states of Europe.

The Devastation of the Indies

One can open any page of the writings of Fray Bartolomé de Las Casas and find descriptions of horrible atrocities. The following is only a sample.

This large island [Hispaniola] was perhaps the most densely populated place in the world. There must be close to two hundred leagues of land on this island, and the seacoast has been explored for more than ten thousand leagues, and each day more of it is being explored. And all the land so far discovered is a beehive of people; it is as though God had crowded into these lands the great majority of mankind.

And of all the infinite universe of humanity, these people are the most guileless, the most devoid of wickedness and duplicity, the most obedient and faithful to their native masters and to the Spanish Christians whom they serve. They are by nature the most humble, patient, and peaceable, holding no grudges, free from embroilments, neither excitable nor quarrelsome. These people are the most devoid of rancors, hatreds, or desire for vengeance of any people in the world. And because they are so weak and complaisant, they are less able to endure heavy labor and soon die of no matter what malady. The sons of nobles among us, brought up in the enjoyments of life's refinements, are no more delicate than are these Indians, even those among them who are of the lowest rank of laborers. They are also poor people, for they not only possess little but have no desire to possess worldly goods. For this reason they are not arrogant, embittered, or greedy. Their repasts are such that the food of the holy fathers in the desert can scarcely be more parsimonious, scanty, and poor. . . .

Yet into this sheepfold, into this land of meek outcasts there came some Spaniards who immediately behaved like ravening wild beasts, wolves, tigers, or lions that had been starved for many days. And Spaniards have behaved in no other way during the past forty years, down to the present time, for they are still acting like ravening beasts, killing, terrorizing, afflicting, torturing, and destroying the native peoples, doing all this with the strangest and most varied new methods of cruelty, never seen or heard of before, and to such a degree that this Island of Hispaniola, once so populous (having a population that I estimated to be more than three millions), has now a population of barely two hundred persons.

. . . .[On the other islands and the mainland] we can estimate very surely and truthfully that in the forty years that have passed, with the infernal actions of the Chris-

tians, there have been unjustly slain more than twelve million men, women, and children. In truth, I believe without trying to deceive myself that the number of the slain is more like fifteen million. . . .

It should be kept in mind that their insatiable greed and ambition, the greatest ever seen in the world, is the cause of their villainies. And also, those lands are so rich and felicitous, the native peoples so meek and patient, so easy to subject, that our Spaniards have no more consideration for them than beasts. And I say this from my own knowledge of the acts I witnessed. But I should not say "than beasts" for, thanks be to God, they have treated beasts with some respect; I should say instead like excrement on the public squares.

Bartolomé de Las Casas, *The Devastation of the Indies: A Brief Account,* translated by Herma Briffault, 37-41

The Spaniards did not content themselves with what the Indians gave them of their own free will, according to their ability, which was always too little to satisfy enormous appetites, for a Christian eats and consumes in one day an amount of food that would suffice to feed three houses inhabited by ten Indians for one month. And they committed other acts of force and violence and oppression which made the Indians realize that these men had not come from Heaven. . . .

They took up arms, but their weapons were very weak and of little service in offense and still less in defense. (Because of this, the wars of the Indians against each other are little more than games played by children.) And the Christians, with their horses and swords and spikes began to carry out massacres and strange cruelties against them. They attacked the towns and spared neither the children nor the aged nor pregnant women nor women in childbed, not only stabbing them and dismembering them but cutting them to pieces as if dealing with sheep in the slaughter house. They laid bets as to who, with one stroke of the sword, could split a man in two or could cut off his head or spill out his entrails with a single stroke of the pike. They took infants from their mothers' breasts, snatching them by the legs and pitching them headfirst against the crags or snatched them by the arms and threw them into the rivers, roaring with laughter and saying as the babies fell into the water, "Boil there, you offspring of the devil!" Other infants they put to the sword along with their mothers and anyone else who happened to be nearby. They made some low wide gallows on which the hanged victim's feet almost touched the ground, stringing up their victims in lots of thirteen, in memory of Our Redeemer and His twelve Apostles, then set burning wood at their feet and thus burned them alive. To others they attached straw or wrapped their whole bodies in straw and set them afire. With still others, all those they wanted to capture alive, they cut off their hands and hung them round the victim's neck, saying "Go now, carry the message," meaning, Take the news to the Indians who have fled to the mountains. . . . And because on few and far between occasions, the Indians justifiably killed some Christians, the Spaniards made a rule among themselves that for every Chrisian slain by the Indians, they would slay a hundred Indians.

Devastation, 43-45

Another thing must be added: from the beginning to the present time the Spaniards have taken no more care to have the Faith of Jesus Christ preached to those nations than they would to have it preached to dogs or other beasts. Instead, they have prohibited the religious from carrying out this intention, and have afflicted them and persecuted them in many ways, because such preaching would, they deemed, have hindered them from acquiring gold and other wealth they coveted. And today in all the Indies there is no more knowledge of God, whether He be of wood or sky, or earth, and this after one hundred years in the New World. . . .

Devastation, 139

The tyranny exercised by the Spaniards against the Indians in the work of pearl fishing is one of the most cruel that can be imagined. There is no life as infernal and desperate in this century that can be compared with it, although the mining of gold is a dangerous

and burdensome way of life. The pearl fishers dive into the sea at a depth of five fathoms, and do this from sunrise to sunset, and remain for many minutes without breathing, tearing the oysters out of their rocky beds where the pearls are formed. They come to the surface with a netted bag of these oysters where a Spanish torturer is waiting in a canoe or skiff, and if the pearl diver shows signs of wanting to rest, he is showered with blows, his hair is pulled, and he is thrown back into the water, obliged to continue the hard work of tearing out the oysters and bringing them again to the surface. . . .

At night the pearl divers are chained so they cannot escape. Often a pearl diver does not return to the surface, for these waters are infested with man-eating sharks of two kinds, both vicious marine animals that can kill, eat, and swallow a whole man. . . .

And it is solely because of the Spaniards' greed for gold that they force the Indians to lead such a life, often a brief life, for it is impossible to continue for long diving into the cold water and holding the breath for minutes at a time, repeating this hour after hour, day after day; the continual cold penetrates them, constricts the chest, and they die spitting blood, or weakened by diarrhea.

Devastation, 109-111

The Conquest of the Aztecs

The Empire of Mexico, Sixteenth Century

Cortes left Cuba with 617 men, eighteen horses, and a small supply of armaments, on his way to subdue the most powerful state on the continent of America.

This was the empire of Mexico; rich, powerful, and inhabited by millions of Indians, passionately fond of war, and then headed by Montezuma, whose fame in arms struck terror in the neighbouring nations.

The empire of Mexico had existed for ages. Its inhabitants were not a rude and barbarous, but a polished and intelligent, people. Mexico, the capital of the empire, situated in the middle of a spacious lake, was the noblest monument of American industry. It communicated to the continent by immense causeways, which were carried through the lake. The city was admired for its buildings, all of stone, its squares, and market-places; the shops which glittered with gold and silver; and the sumptuous palaces of Montezuma, some erected on columns of jasper, and containing whatever was most rare, curious, and useful.

Cortes, in his march along the coast of Mexico, experienced but little opposition. The natives were terrified at the appearance of the warlike animals, on which the Spanish officers were mounted. The artificial thunder which issued from their hands, and the wooden castles which had wafted them over the ocean, struck a panic, from which they did not recover till their ruin was unavoidable. Wherever the Spaniards marched, they spared neither age nor sex, nothing sacred or profane.

John Britten, *Sheridan and Kotzebue*, 6-7

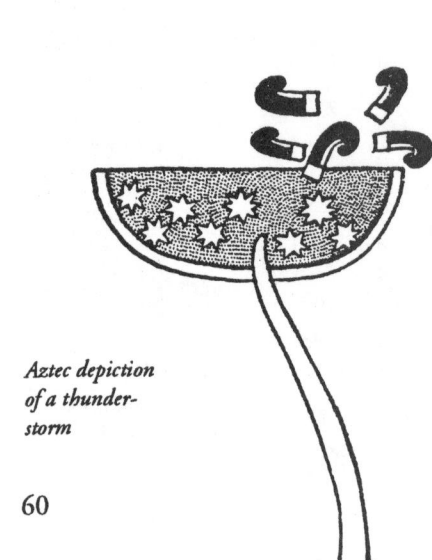

Aztec depiction of a thunderstorm

In 1519 when the Spanish conquistadors, led by Hernando Cortes, reached the capital city of the Aztecs, Tenochtitlan, they gaped in astonishment at its magnificent temples, palaces, and gardens. The Aztec state had reached a climax of development that matched the achievements of Spain, now the greatest power in Europe after the triumphant conclusion of the reconquest.

Aztec prophecies had long foretold the return of Quetzalcoatl and other gods from over the sea, so the Aztecs at first assumed the strangers were their long-lost gods. The Spaniards considered the Aztecs barbarians in spite of their vigorous political, religious, and socioeconomic structures, wanted their gold, and tried to Christianize and subject them.

Survival of Stories

Although the conquistadors burned almost all Aztec writings and destroyed their centers of education, a few missionaries (including Bernadino de Sahagun and Diego de Duran) were able to save some indigenous literature. They transcribed stories and songs memorized and retold by natives into the Latin alphabet so they could record texts in the original words. Because of their efforts, the story of the conquest from the point of view of the victims remains fairly intact.

Destruction

As the Spaniards marched across land to the capital city, they attacked towns and villages mercilessly; other native groups joined them out of fear and also because of longstanding hostility toward the Aztecs, whose own patterns of conquest and enslavement had oppressed their neighbors for decades. The Aztec leader Montezuma heard all the reports of massacres and battles, debated how to receive the conquistadors, and decided a peaceful welcome would be best.

The Lady Malinche

In addition to horses and cannons, Cortes had another significant advantage: the former slave, highly valued as a translator, who became his mistress, the lady Malinche. A brilliant linguist, theoretician, and diplomat, Malinche paved the way for Cortes's troops with her speeches, which combined persuasion and threat and benefited from her understanding of the history and culture of the various nations of the region. She was so clever and valuable that "some historians are almost tempted to think of her as the real conqueror of Mexico" (Brandon, 100).

When the invaders reached Tenochtitlan, Montezuma had them quartered in the palace of his father, an immense house with many rooms and walls of sculptured stone. Several days of polite visits between the Aztec leader and the Spaniards followed, until the guests took the host prisoner. Malinche spent a couple of hours convincing Montezuma it would be to his advantage to come along

Reports of the Messengers

Thanks to the efforts of dedicated priests, we now have direct reports from natives who survived the massacres and told their stories.

For a long time people had noticed omens and signs of the coming of strangers. King Montezuma sent emissaries to the spot where reports indicated something very unusual was happening. When the emissaries returned *they went directly to the king's palace and spoke to him with all due reverence and humility*, describing the light-skinned, bearded strangers who fished from a small boat and then climbed back into their two towers.

The king sent gifts to the person he presumed to be the god Quetzalcoatl, and the messengers dressed Cortes in all the finery: a mask with golden earrings, a vest decorated with feathers from the quetzal bird, a collar with a disk of gold in its center, a blue cloak known as "the ringing bell," a mirror with little bells. *In his hand they placed the shield with its fringe and pendant of quetzal feathers, its ornaments of gold and mother-of-pearl.* Finally they set before him black sandals of fine soft rubber and laid out many other objects of divine finery for him to see.

The Captain asked them: "And is this all? Is this your gift of welcome? Is this how you greet people?" . . .

Then the Captain gave orders, and the messengers were chained by the feet and by the neck. When this had been done, the great cannon was fired off. The messengers lost their senses and fainted away. They fell down side by side and lay where they had fallen.

Later they paddled furiously to get back to their city. *Some of them even paddled with their hands, so fierce was the anxiety burning in their souls.* They told the king about the cannon:

"A thing like a ball of stone comes out of its entrails: it comes out shooting sparks and raining fire. . . . If the cannon is aimed against a mountain, the mountain splits and cracks open. If it is aimed against a tree, it shatters the tree into splinters. . . ."

The messengers also said: "Their trappings and arms are all made of iron. They dress in iron and wear iron casques on their heads. Their swords are iron; their bows are iron; their shields are iron; their spears are iron. Their deer carry them on their backs wherever they wish to go. These deer, our lord, are as tall as the roof of a house.

We only came to sleep
We only came to dream
It is not true, no, it is not true
That we came to live on the earth.

We are changed into the grass of springtime
Our hearts will grow green again
And they will open their petals.

But our body is like a rose tree:
It puts forth flowers and then withers.

Aztec hymn, in William Brandon, *The Last Americans*, 109

Quetzalcoatl from an ancient manuscript

View of Mexico City, 1677

"The strangers' bodies are completely covered, so that only their faces can be seen. Their skin is white, as if it were made of lime. They have yellow hair, though some of them have black. Their beards are long and yellow, and their moustaches are also yellow. Their hair is curly, with very fine strands.

"Their dogs are enormous, with flat ears and long, dangling tongues. The color of their eyes is a burning yellow; their eyes flash fire and shoot off sparks. Their bellies are hollow, their flanks long and narrow. They are tireless and very powerful. They bound here and there, panting, with their tongues hanging out. And they are spotted like an ocelot."

When Montezuma heard this report, he was filled with terror. It was as if his heart had fainted, as if it had shriveled. It was as if he were conquered by despair.

Miguel Leon-Portillo, *The Broken Spears*, 26, 30-31

quietly, and from then on he was in the custody of the Spaniards, still administering the affairs of the kingdom and treated with respect, but giving them enormous quantities of gold and ordering his subjects to follow their bidding. For several months the natives, overawed by the Spaniards' ferocity and their amazing greed for gold, housed and fed their guests.

Massacre

But in the spring, while Cortes was away battling with another conquistador, Panfilo de Narvaez, the Spaniards left behind under the direction of Pedro de Alvarado murdered celebrants at the fiesta of Toxcatl.

Outraged Aztec citizens immediately retaliated with javelins, arrows, and spears. The Spaniards took refuge in the palace, where they shackled Montezuma in chains. The Aztecs, who had been so generous with food and supplies under orders from their king, now refused to feed the Spanish and waited for them to die of hunger.

Cortes returned with extra troops, and the battle raged for four days. When Cortes forced Montezuma to try to calm his furious subjects, the grieving king said, "What more does Malinche want from me?" (Brandon, 107). In the attempt Montezuma was killed, by either the angry Aztecs or the desperate Spaniards. After losing three-fourths of their troops, the Spanish retreated; Cortes and Malinche escaped.

The Final Conquest

A period of relative normalcy followed. But disease, the second line of assault against natives, this time in the form of a smallpox epidemic, decimated the population. A second onslaught from the Spanish was not far behind. Long, devastating battles kept the capital under siege for eighty days. Finally the Spanish were successful in vanquishing the natives. It is estimated that almost half a million people lost their lives in the war: 240,000 Aztecs and 170,000 Spaniards, plus 30,000 members of other tribes who fought with the Spanish.

French watercolor of massacre of Mexican nobles

Massacre at the Fiesta of Taxcatl

At a moment in the fiesta, *when the dance was loveliest and then song was linked to song,* the Spaniards ran forward, armed as if for battle. They closed all the entrances and passageways, posted guards so no one could escape, and began to slaughter all the people.

They ran in among the dancers, forcing their way to the place where the drums were played. They attacked the man who was drumming and cut off his arms. Then they cut off his head, and it rolled across the floor.

They attacked all the celebrants, stabbing them, spearing them, striking them with their swords. They attacked some of them from behind, and these fell instantly to the ground with their entrails hanging out. Others they beheaded: they cut off their heads, or split their heads to pieces.

They struck others in the shoulders, and their arms were torn from their bodies. They wounded some in the thigh and some in the calf. They slashed others in the abdomen, and their entrails all spilled to the ground. Some attempted to run away, but their intestines dragged as they ran; they seemed to tangle their feet in their own entrails. No matter how they tried to save themselves, they could find no escape.

Some attempted to force their way out, but the Spaniards murdered them at the gates. Others climbed the walls, but they could not save themselves. Those who ran into the communal houses were safe there for a while; so were those who lay down among the victims and pretended to be dead. But if they stood up again, the Spaniards saw them and killed them.

The blood of the warriors flowed like water and gathered into pools. The pools widened, and the stench of blood and entrails filled the air.

Miguel Leon-Portillo, *The Broken Spears,* 75-76

Slavery

*Song of the Bornu
Slaves*

*Where are we going?
Where are we going?
Where are we going,
Rubee?**
*Hear us, save us,
make us free.
Send our Arka**
down from thee!
Here the Ghiblee
wind is blowing,
Strange and large
the world is growing!
Tell us, Rubee,
where are we going?
Where are we going,
Rubee?*

*Bornu! Bornu!
Where is Bornu!
Where are we going,
Rubee?
Bornu-land was rich
and good,
Wells of water, fields
of food;
Bornu-land we see
no longer.*

*Here we thirst, and
here we hunger,
Here the Moor man
smites in anger;
Where are we going,
Rubee?*

*gold
**freedom papers

African Civilization

In the sixteenth century, Central Africa was a territory of peace and happy civilization. Traders traveled thousands of miles from one side of the continent to another without molestation. The tribal wars from which the European pirates claimed to deliver the people were mere sham fights; it was a great battle when half a dozen men were killed. It was on a peasantry in many respects superior to the serfs in large areas of Europe that the slave trade fell.

Tribal life was broken up and millions of detribalized Africans were let loose upon each other. . . . Violence and ferocity became the necessities for survival. The stockades of grinning skulls, the human sacrifices, the selling of their own children as slaves, these horrors were the product of an intolerable pressure on the African peoples, which became fiercer through the centuries as the demands of industry increased and the methods of coercion were perfected. . . .

C.L.R. James, *Amistad 1*, 120-121

The Middle Passage

Crew and captives alike were reduced to a brutish state during the crossing, all exposed to disease and death. The total disregard for human life is described in a report to the British House of Commons:

The Negroes were chained to each other hand and foot, and stowed so close that they were not allowed above a foot and a half for each in breadth. Thus rammed . . . like herring in a barrel, they contracted . . . fatal disorders; so that they who came to inspect them in the morning had . . . to pick up dead slaves out of their rows, and to unchain . . . [them] from the bodies of their wretched fellow-sufferers. . . .

Quoted in Louise Daniel Hutchinson, *Out of Africa*, 43

A revival of the ancient institution of slavery occurred in the twelfth century to facilitate the production of sugar. Europeans needed to find a Christian source of sugar so they wouldn't have to depend on Moslem North Africa or the Middle East. Venetians, Catalonians, Genoese, and others established sugar plantations in Cyprus, and a brisk slave trade developed to provide workers.

African Slaves

At first, the slaves were Moslems and Christians taken as prisoners in raids from the Black Sea area. By the early fourteenth century the Mediterranean trade expanded to include captives from sub-Saharan Africa brought to the plantations by professional slave traders.

As plantations spread to Crete, Sicily, and Spanish cities, the international slave trade grew. A gift of ten Africans from the coast of Guinea to Henry the Navigator of Portugal led to more importation of blacks. At first they were used as house servants, but along with the creation of more plantations in Portuguese territories came a greater reliance on African slaves as field workers.

New Possibilities

Voyages to the West opened up many possibilities, among them the transportation of slaves as a source of labor. A small number of black slaves was brought to the newly

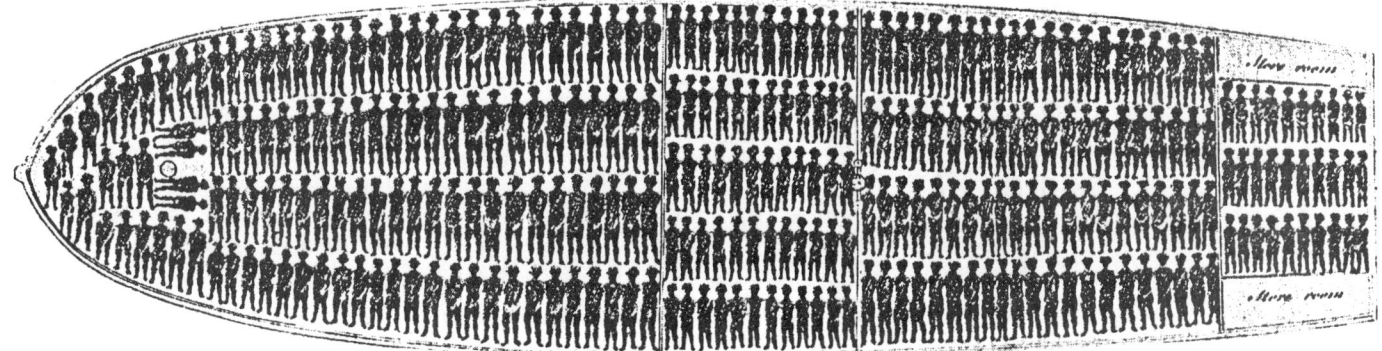

discovered continent for the first time in 1502. Slavery continued to be interconnected with sugar production. Hispaniola first exported sugar in 1522; by the mid-1550s sugar plantations were thriving in Puerto Rico, Jamaica, and Mexico. Brazil became a major producer of sugar in the late 1500s.

England entered the slave trade in the 1560s. The first black slaves in Virginia in 1619 came by accident, brought by a Dutch captain who had captured them from a Spanish ship.

Three different models were evident early on in the "new world": in the highlands of Mexico and Peru, a few Spanish controlled the predominantly Indian population; in North America, a large number of whites held all the power, and the relatively few Indians and blacks had none; in the South Atlantic (Caribbean) area, the white planter elite dominated a primarily black population which included a small number of Indians.

Life on the Republic

A character in Charles Johnson's novel *Middle Passage* recounts a scene on the Republic, a ship out of New Orleans that regularly transported slaves from the West Coast of Africa. Although fictionalized, the story of the slaves' degradation is based on similar tales told by survivors.

The captain of the Republic, Ebenezer Falcon, fancied seeing the slaves dance to music played by the ship's mate, Tommy. Meadows, a crewman, and Ngonyama, one of the slaves, were in charge of bringing the slaves up from the hold of the ship to see the light of day and fill their lungs with sea air.

Twenty blacks were brought from below to dance them a bit to music from Tommy's flute and let them breathe. They climbed topside and stood crushed together, blinded by the sun, for that morning the weather was fair, yet hushed. Meadows and Ngonyama searched the fusty spaces between decks for Africans unable to come up on their own.

There were always a few of these since Ebenezer Falcon rearranged their position after the storm. He was, as they say, a "tight-packer," having learned ten years ago from a one-handed French slaver named Captain Ledoux that if you arranged the Africans in two parallel rows, their backs against the lining of the ship's belly, this left a free space at their rusty feet, and that, given the flexibility of bone and skin, could be squeezed with even more slaves if you made them squat at ninety-degree angles to one another. Flesh could conform to anything.

Where are we going?
Where are we going?
Hear us, save us,
Rubee!
Moons of marches
from our eyes,
Bornu-land behind
us lies;
Hot the desert wind
is blowing,
Wild the waves of
sand are flowing!
Hear us, tell us,
Where are we going?
Where are we going,
Rubee?

Song recorded by abolitionists and published by John Greenleaf Whittier In Louise Daniel Hutchinson, *Out of Africa*, 42

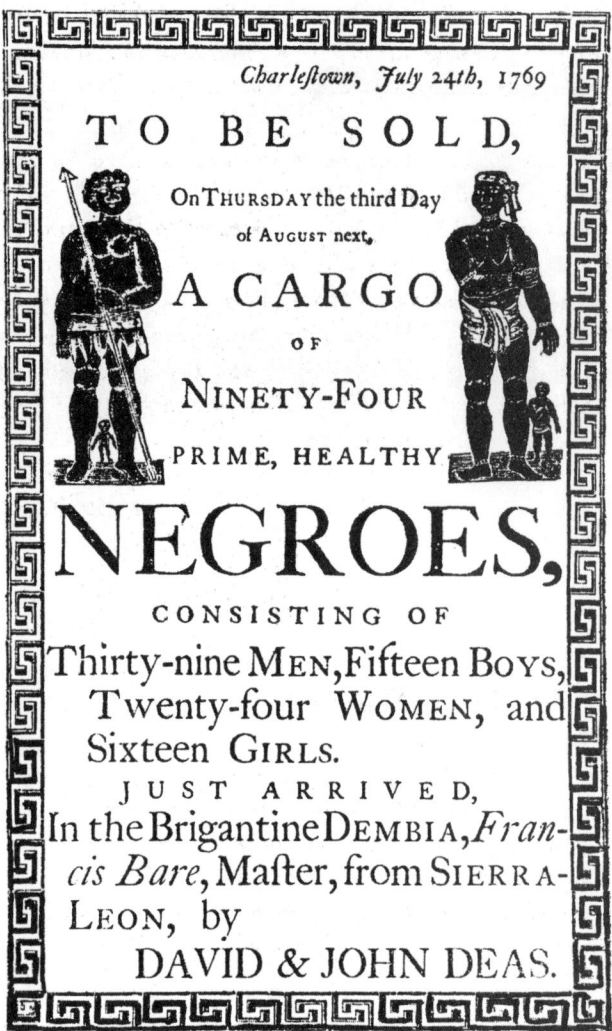

Broadside announcing the sale of slaves, 1769

Charlestown, July 24th, 1769

TO BE SOLD,

On THURSDAY the third Day of AUGUST next,

A CARGO

OF

NINETY-FOUR

PRIME, HEALTHY

NEGROES,

CONSISTING OF

Thirty-nine MEN, Fifteen BOYS, Twenty-four WOMEN, and Sixteen GIRLS.

JUST ARRIVED,

In the Brigantine DEMBIA, *Francis Bare*, Master, from SIERRA-LEON, by

DAVID & JOHN DEAS.

So when they came half-dead from the depths, these eyeless contortionists emerging from a shadowy Platonic cave, they were stiff and sore and stank of their own vomit and feces. . . . Meadows snapped his head away, his nose wrinkled, and he splashed buckets of salt water on them, then told Tommy to play. . . .

Snapping together his three-piece flute and touching it to lips shaped in that strangely mad, distant smile unreadable as a mask, he let his chest fall, forcing wind into wood that transformed his exhalations into a rill of sound-colors all on board found chilling—less music . . . than the boy's air alchemized into emotion, or the song of hundred-year-old trees from which the narrow flute was torn.

One side of Falcon's face tightened. "Methinks that's too damned melancholy. Even niggers can't dance to that. A lighter tune, if you will, Tommy." The cabin boy obeyed,

Black Labor

By 1650, there were more blacks than Europeans in the Americas. Africans were superior to any other national group in their ability to resist disease because they'd been exposed to the greatest variety of human illnesses. All of Europe agreed that without black slave labor America would face absolute ruin. A decree of King Louis XIV of France from 1670 reads, "There is nothing which contributes more to the development of the colonies and the cultivation of their soil than the laborious toil of the Negroes" (Williams, 136).

Catastrophe for Africa

The consequences of the slave trade were catastrophic for Africa. The developing social, economic, and political systems, as well as such by-products as craftsmanship, weaving, metalwork, and agriculture, took second place to a trade which led to the domination of a slave system in most of the states. For nearly two centuries European interests in West Africa were limited to building forts where traders could pick up slaves, captured in the interior through raids or tribal wars by local potentates looking for wealth and power.

Scholars estimate that over four centuries between eleven and fifteen million men, women, and children were deported and survived the horrors of the "middle passage" to reach America. Many more than that figure died during the wars of captivity and the crossing, when three out of every ten perished.

The figures for the West Indies alone are striking: of every one hundred captives who left the African coast, eighty-four reached the West Indies; one-third of these died in three years. Therefore, for every fifty-six slaves on the plantations at the end of three years, forty-four had perished (Williams, 147).

A Boon for Capitalism

In spite of the depreciation from death among the cargo, the slave trade realized enormous profits and was central to the growth of capitalism. It "kept the wheels of metropolitan industry turning; it stimulated navigation and shipbuilding and employed seamen; it raised fishing villages into flourishing cities; it gave sustenance to new industries based on the processing of colonial raw materials; it yielded large profits which were plowed back into metropolitan industry; and, finally, it gave rise to an unprecedented commerce . . ." (Williams, 148).

striking up a tune of lighter tempo. Falcon, pleased, tapped his foot, stopping only to stare as Ngonyama and Meadows carried an African's corpse from below.

As with previous cases like these, Falcon ordered his ears sliced off and preserved below in oil to prove to the ship's investors that he had in fact purchased in Bangalang as many slaves as promised. This amputation proved tough going for Meadows, for the last stages of rigor mortis froze the boy hunched forward in a grotesque hunker, like Lot's wife. Hence, after shearing off his ears, they toted him to the rail as you might a chair or the ship's figurehead, then found him too heavy to heave over.

Charles Johnson, Middle Passage, 120-121

Daily Lives of Slaves

The slave was a slave for life, and any children were destined to slavery. It was the very empire of death, a slow death, even if the life-span of the slave, virtually throughout the Americas, was estimated at seven years. Work under the supervision of a taskmaster was from sunrise to sunset and was enforced by the discipline of the whip. . . .

Tortures reserved for rebellious or lazy slaves were not evidence of the particular cruelty of some masters, but simply part of the structure of the daily practice of slavery. To apply a red-hot iron to the tender parts of the slave, to tie him to a stake so that insects gnawed him to death, to burn him alive, to chain him, to set dogs or snakes at his heels, to rape negresses, served above all to express absolute domination.

Laennec Hurbon, "The Slave Trade and
Black Slavery in America," Concilium, 111

Later Contacts and Devastation

1637: Massachusetts Bay

The phrase "God is an Englishman" sums up the pevailing attitude of the churchmen who left England and formed the early colonies on the eastern coast of the "new world."

John Winthrop, founder of the Massachusetts Bay Colony, was clear about the reason the English could take over the Indians' lands: that which is common to all belongs to none. This "savage" people pretended to rule over many lands without title or property.

The Puritans came to build the new Jerusalem. They fled from the king and his bishops, leaving behind taxes and wars, hunger and diseases, and threats of change in the old order. Winthrop, who was a Cambridge lawyer born into a noble family, operated out of the assumption that God Almighty, in his most holy and wise providence, had determined that some members of mankind must be rich, some poor, some powerful and some powerless.

In commenting on the devastation of Indian communities by smallpox, Winthrop came up with another assumption about God's will: Smallpox was sent by God as a method of clearing the land and obliging English colonists to occupy it.

See Eduardo Galeano, *Memory of Fire: Genesis*, 220-221

In the late fifteenth and sixteenth centuries, contacts between Europeans and North American Indians were of two types. Expeditions of explorers set out from the newly emerging nation-states of England, France, and Portugal in attempts to match Spain's stunning successes in Central and South America, and fishing crews hired for merchants sailed from ports on Europe's Atlantic coast looking for cheap sources of protein.

Later in the sixteenth century, French merchants developed a specialized fur trade with the Algonquin hunters in eastern Canada. As a result, the natives became dependent on a very unpredictable industry, began to compete with each other, and, as in many other places, suffered greatly from exposure to European diseases.

England's Role

England became the primary colonizer in North America for a variety of reasons. Of the European nations, England was the furthest along in capitalist development. Members of the gentry had bought or leased land from feudal lords, raising crops and/or livestock to sell. As the population increased, smaller producers suffered from competition to the point that they were forced to sell their own labor and become indentured servants or travel to North America and settle as colonizers.

Driven out of England by overpopulation, a shortage of tillable land, growing extremes of wealth and poverty, and the breakdown of effective institutions of social control under a rapidly diversifing and changing economy, they migrated to the "new world" where within a century, due to their presence and attitudes, similar conditions prevailed. "Despite the intentions and beliefs of many participants, then, the effect of colonization had not been to halt or reverse the processes forming preindustrial England but to carry them across the Atlantic" (Salisbury, 237).

Puritanism

The adverse circumstances experienced by many during the seventeenth century led to the popularity of religious beliefs which elevated family-oriented economic independence to the status of a divine character trait. Puritans viewed their economic and social crises as evidence of the deep sinfulness of the world, and they tried to separate themselves from it. The need for hard work and self-discipline in a fiercely competitive, rapidly changing economy (quite different from the seasonal agricultural work of their ancestors) plus the need for certainty as the old order declined gave Puritanism a strong appeal.

Its worldview provided economic activities with a spiritual base. A person was "called" to a vocation; fulfilling material goals could at the same time insure a place in heaven. The certainty that they were among the few elect who would be saved by God legitimized Puritans' individual pursuits and gave

Attitudes of Virginians

Conway Whittle Sams wrote an account of the colonization of Virginia from the point of view of the colonists:

The Conquest of Virginia involves the dealings of Englishmen, who became Virginians, with two inferior races. The country they came to acquire was occupied by the one, and, no sooner had they established a foothold here, than there was imported from Africa another.

. . . The real object of the colony was to secure for England, and for Protestantism, a part of the New World then being explored, claimed and occupied by other European Powers, that is, by France and by Spain, both of them Catholic Powers. . . .

The colony was conducted in an as orderly a way as possible by persons of the highest character who were at the head of the movement in England. . . . Religion was a vital feature of the Colony, daily morning and evening prayers being regularly held and attended by the Colonists.

With kindly intentions towards the Indians, and with a high purpose before them, abundantly shown by the solemn public statements that were made on that subject, yet, in carrying out the movement, war with the native inhabitants became inevitable, because they would not accept the situation as the English would have them accept it.

Conway Whittle Sams, *The Conquest of Virginia*, 5, 15, 16

Manifest Destiny

The New England puritans gave the concept of "the American dream" the high visionary meaning it has carried to our own time. To them, and to us, the "discovery of America" became prophecy and promise, "God's country," "manifest destiny."

Other Renaissance explorers and emigrants discovered America as a geographical entity; they put it on the European map of the world. The Puritans discovered America in scripture, precisely as a biblical scholar discovers the meaning of some hitherto obscure text, and they proceeded to put it on the map of sacred history.

America, they explained, was nothing less than the new promised land, held in reserve by God for His latter-day saints.

And what of those who were already acting as the stewards of that promised land?

The misnomer "Indian" is emblematic of the way language could be used, in defiance of historical fact, to denigrate a host of native peoples, each with distinctive traditions and institutions, as "primitives," "savage," "childlike innocents," and so on. This was the way of all the emigrant groups, including the Puritans. But the Puritans went one crucial step further. They "discovered" in the Indians the antagonists to the new chosen people. For other emigrants, the Indians were cultural inferiors, requiring the white gifts of religion and civilization. For the Puritans they were primarily the villains in a sacred drama. . . .

Charles M. Segal and David C. Stineback,
Puritans, Indians, and Maifest Destiny, 16-17

Changes in the Land

In a very real and tangible sense . . . "New England," as we know it in history, was "made" when Indian lands were expropriated for use by English settlers. For it was by that process that the land was removed from a "natural" economy, wherein it was treated as a sacred phenomenon whose powers and gifts were thought to be controlled by supernatural forces, and placed in a nascent capitalist economy where (though hedged in certain respects by the authorities of town, colony, and empire) it became fundamentally a commodity owned by individuals to be bought and sold as they saw fit.

Neal Salisbury, *Manitou and Providence*, 239

them a basis of identity stronger than kinship and geographical ties.

In the 1630s the Archbishop of Canterbury tried to force religious uniformity, in a new phase of the Inquisition. Persecution became an additional motive for migration. Thousands of English Puritans, perceiving themselves as righteous and deprived, hungry for land, desperate for social and cultural order, fled to America.

Indians reacted to their arrival with the goal of maintaining equilibrium and tried to interact as best they could with this new breed of human being. However, the Puritans saw the Indians as not only an obstacle to attaining what they wanted but also as a complete inversion of their ideal world. They turned their quests for land into crusades against the "savages" as they struggled for control over the environment and its inhabitants. Conversion of the natives to Christianity would be an extension of God's will and glory. The antagonism of settlers toward natives set the stage for the later rise of racism in the society that developed in the "new world."

Missionaries

Throughout the hemisphere the conquest followed similar patterns. Initial physical attacks against natives were followed by more subtle—but ultimately just as deadly—attacks on their cultures by missionaries. Churches and missions opened the way for other colonizers. They exploited people, divided families, removed children, robbed natural resources, and forced a shift in traditional values.

Voices of Dissent

Petalesharo

Petalesharo, a principal chief of the Pawnee Indians, gave the following speech at a conference in 1822 which President Monroe also attended. The president had urged the chief and his people to follow "the way of peace" and to be friendly with the people of the United States. In his reply Petalesharo refers especially to the missionaries:

My Great Father: Some of your good chiefs, as they are called (missionaries), have proposed to send some of their good people among us to change our habits, to make us work and live like the white people.

I will not tell a lie—I am going to tell the truth. You love your country—you love your people—you love the manner in which they live, and you think your people brave. I am like you, my Great Father, I love my country—I love my people—I love the manner in which they live, and think myself and my warriors brave.

Spare me then, Father; let me enjoy my country, and pursue the buffalo, and the beaver, and the other wild animals of our country, and I will trade their skins with your people. I have grown up, and lived thus long without work—I am in hopes you will suffer me to die without it.

We have plenty of buffalo, beaver, deer and other wild animals—we have also an abundance of horses—we have everything we want—we have plenty of land, if you will keep your people off of it.

It is too soon, my Great Father, to send those good men among us. We are not starving yet—we wish you to permit us to enjoy the chase until the game of our country is exhausted—until the wild animals become extinct. Let us exhaust our present resources before you make us toil and interrupt our happiness—let me continue to live as I have done.

W.C. Vanderwerth, ed., *Indian Oratory*, 80-82

Red Jacket

In the late eighteenth century a young Moravian missionary asked permission to open a mission on Indian land. In refusing his request, Red Jacket, a famous orator and warrior among Seneca Indians, gave a challenge:

Your forefathers crossed the great water and landed on this island. Their numbers were small. They found friends and no enemies. They told us they had fled from their own country for fear of wicked men and had come here to enjoy their religion. . . . We gave them corn and meat, they gave us poison in return. . . .

You say there is but one way to worship and serve the Great Spirit. If there is but one religion, why do you white people differ so much about it? Why are not all agreed, as you can all read the book?

We are told that your religion was given to your fore-fathers, and has been handed down from father to son. We also have a religion, which was given to our forefathers, and has been handed down to us their children. We worship in that way. It teaches us to be thankful for all the favours we receive, to love each other, and to be united. We never quarrel about religion.

The Great Spirit has made us all, but He has made a great difference between His white and red children. . . . Since He has made so great a difference between us in other things, why may we not conclude that He has given us a different religion according to our understanding? The Great Spirit does right. He knows what is best for His children; we are satisfied.

We do not wish to destroy your religion, or take it from you. We only want to enjoy our own. We are told that you have been preaching to the white people in this place. These people are our neighbors. We are acquainted with them. We will wait a little while and see what effect your preaching has upon them. If we find it does them good, makes them honest and less disposed to cheat Indians, we will then consider again of what you have said.

Roger Moody, ed., *The Indigenous Voice*, 1:247

Legacies of the Conquest

Gifts to the Indians

Hubert Bancroft, an energetic New Englander, was, successively, secretary of the Navy, ambassador to Great Britain, Prussia, and the German Empire, and the president of various scholarly societies during the nineteenth century. Writing in 1883, he asked some critical questions:

What should we do were a foreign power to come in ships to our shore and begin to slaughter our animals, to stake off our land and divide it among themselves? We should drive them away if we were able; but if we found them the stronger, we should employ every art to destroy them, and in so doing regard ourselves as patriots performing a sacred obligation.

This is the Indian's crime; and in so doing we call him cunning, revengeful, hateful, diabolical. But the white man brings him blankets, it may be said, brings him medicine, tells him of contrivances, teaches him civilization. These things are exactly what the savage does not want, and what he is much better off without. The white man's comforts kill him almost as quickly as do his cruelties; and the teachings of Christ's ministers are abhorrent if they are coupled with the examples of lecherous and murderous professors of Christianity. . . .

White men have killed fifty Indians where Indians have killed one white man, and this, notwithstanding that nine-tenths of all injuries inflicted have been perpetrated by white invaders.

A thousand Indian women have been outraged by men whose mothers had taught them the Lord's prayer, where one white woman has been injured by these benighted heathen. At any time in the history of America I would rather take my chances as a white woman among savages, than as an Indian woman among white people.

H. H. Bancroft, *Collected Works*
In *1492: Discovery/Invasion/Encounter*, 72

From the second voyage, the two others later undertaken by Columbus, and the many mounted thereafter by other explorers from not only Spain but also other countries in Europe, comes the legacy of a resounding clash between strikingly different cultures. The overpowering of one by the other led to many of the agonies we suffer from today. Racism and environmental destruction are two that immediately come to mind.

Genocide

Very quickly, the inhabitants of the "new world" discovered that the Spaniards and, later, colonizers from other parts of Europe, notably England, France, and Holland, wanted only their gold, or silver, or pearls, or fur, or land. They themselves were most likely to be killed or enslaved.

Furthermore, the Europeans brought the diseases that ran rampant in the area that had once been so filled with health. "The raging epidemics of Europe's most tragic centuries repeated themselves in America. Not even the most brutally depraved of the conquistadors was able purposely to slaughter Indians on the scale that the gentle priest unwittingly accomplished by going from his sickbed ministrations to lay his hands in blessing on his Indian converts" (Jennings, 22).

Researchers now give the figure of ninety percent decline in population within a century after European contact, much of it due to the viruses and microbes introduced from the "old world." The natives of the West had no immunity to such diseases as influenza, typhus, pneumonia, tuberculosis, measles, pleurisy, diphtheria, or smallpox.

Statistics aren't reliable for many reasons, including the inaccurate estimates of the original size of the population, but the region of Hispaniola can serve as an example. A detailed census taken in 1514 listed twenty-eight thousand people in an area that housed eight millon twenty years earlier. "That is more than decimation, it is a carnage of more than ninety-nine percent, something we must call closer to genocide, and within a single generation. By 1542, according to Las Casas, who was there at the time, only two hundred Tainos remained" (Sale, 161).

It is also known that in central Mexico, the population decreased from thirty million to four million in a few decades. The rapid, massive decline in population, referred to as "the most extreme demographic disaster in human history" (Ortiz, 8), was caused by colonial warfare, massacres, massive deportations of natives as slaves, overwork in the mines, starvation or malnutrition after food production broke down, and suicide, as well as epidemics.

Day of the Indian

In 1977 representatives of nine different tribes issued the following message:

... We want to say that the 22nd of April, 1500, when Pedro Alvares Cabral stepped for the first time on these lands, was the beginning of the expansion of western civilisation and the beginning of the end of the indigenous societies.

With the passage of the years, our destruction was intensified, carried out by western civilisation. The most diverse instruments of degradation were used in the massacre of the indigenous groups. Factors contributing to this process were sicknesses brought by the white man which had until then been unknown to us, the plundering of our lands, and the application of colonialist and ethnocentric educational methods which did not respect our political, economic and religious structure.

So much so that in the sixteenth century the Indians were considered irrational animals, and it was necessary for Pope Paul III to declare to the public of the time that we were human beings, with body and soul. But in spite of this, the destruction of the indigenous people continued.

Roger Moody, ed., *The Indigenous Voice*, 356

Dietary Legacy

A legacy of those colonial days which continues is the custom of eating dirt. Lack of iron produces anemia, and instinct leads Northeastern children to eat dirt to gain the mineral salts which are absent from their diet of manioc starch, beans, and—with luck—dried meat. In former times this "African vice" was punished by putting muzzles on the children or by hanging them in willow baskets far above the ground.

Eduardo Galeano, *Open Veins of Latin America*, 75

Ripple Effects

The ripple effects of the environmental destruction wrought on the land by the colonists were far-reaching.

The destruction of old-growth forests meant the elimination of certain intricate econiches and their microbial and faunal patterns, the emigration of bird and animal populations, and the invasion of pioneer species that prevented the natural succession from ever producing again the great trees or the carpets of native wildflowers. Local and regional climatic changes followed, with new conditions of wind, temperature, humidity, and soil moisture, and even seasons that proved inhospitable to many kinds of plants and animals but to which the vast numbers of new European species—cattle, pigs, horses, rats, dandelions, and so on—adapted rapidly, without predators or pathogens to hinder them.

All in all, the presence of just a few hundred thousands of the European branch of the human species, within just a century after its landing, did more to alter the environment of North America, in some places and for many populations quite irretrievably, than the many millions of the American branch had done in fifteen centuries or more.

Kirkpatrick Sale, *The Conquest of Paradise*, 291-292

Different Worldviews

There was a great difference in the attitude taken by the Indian and the Caucasian toward nature, and this difference made of one a conservationist and of the other a non-conservationist of life. The Indian, as well as all other creatures that were given birth and grew, were sustained by the common mother—earth. He was therefore kin to all living things and he gave to all creatures equal rights with himself. Everything of earth was loved and reverenced. The philosophy of the Caucasian was, "Things of the earth, earth"—to be belittled and despised. . . .

Forests were mowed down, the buffalo exterminated, the beaver driven to extinction and his wonderfully constructed dams dynamited, allowing flood waters to wreak further havoc, and the very birds of the air silenced. Great grass plains that sweetened the air have been upturned; springs, streams, and lakes that lived no longer ago than my boyhood have dried, and a whole people harassed to degradation and death. The white man has come to be the symbol of extinction for all things natural to this continent.

Chief Luther Standing Bear, *Land of the Spotted Eagle*
In *Rethinking Columbus*, 84

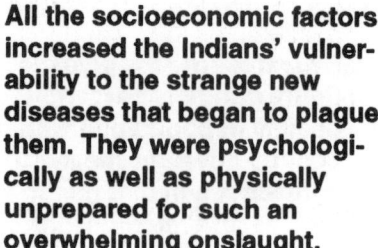

All the socioeconomic factors increased the Indians' vulnerability to the strange new diseases that began to plague them. They were psychologically as well as physically unprepared for such an overwhelming onslaught.

Destruction of the Environment

Besides killing the people with their weapons, demands, and diseases, the Europeans brought about great destruction to the physical environment.

Plant forms were imported with no thought of their effect on the land. Wheat and chickpeas, staples of the Mediterranean diet, withered and died in the heat, and although other plants fared slightly better, at least at first the Spanish seemed to make no effort to adopt the much more productive Taino crops and methods of agriculture.

The animals brought by the Spanish, dogs, cattle, horses, and pigs, dominated and then destroyed native habitats, including carefully-nurtured conuco farms which featured companion planting. They depleted the native grass species and stripped the ground cover, thereby causing erosion.

Invasive plants also had a very negative effect, especially some that were produced for profit such as sugar. Mono-crop open-field planting, in long rows, required cutting and clearing of the forests, as opposed to the Taino method of digging a hole and dropping in a seed, which had nourished both human beings and the eco-system for centuries.

Another long-lasting negative legacy was the new system of

land ownership that created an elite class and denied ownership to indigenous populations, so they couldn't possibly continue their careful cultivation methods.

In a few decades soils were eroded, rivers began to fill up with silt and sometimes went dry, forests were destroyed, and the climate was altered. By 1498 Columbus wrote that in the Cape Verde Islands he couldn't see a single green thing and observed that everything had become dry and sterile.

Two decades after Columbus's tenure as governor, Alonso de Zuaso wrote to a friend at the Spanish court, "If I were to tell you all the damage that has been done, I should never make an end. . . . Although these islands had been, since God made the earth, prosperous and full of people lacking nothing they needed; yet . . . they were laid waste, inhabited only by wild animals and birds, and useless indeed for the service either of God or of Their Highnesses." Some years later de Las Casas wrote of Hispaniola: "It was the first to be destroyed and made into a desert" (Sale, 165-166). But, as we now know all too well, not the last.

Later, in North America, environmental devastation continued. Beavers and other fur-bearing animals; herbivores like deer, moose, antelope, caribou, elk, and wood bison; and game birds like turkeys, ducks, geese, and passenger pigeons were vastly depleted in numbers if not totally exterminated by 1640.

Forests were cleared both to get lumber and to make room for cash crops like tobacco. In Virginia by the end of the

Conquest Myth

European explorers and invaders discovered an inhabited land. Had it been pristine wilderness then, it would possibly be so still today, for neither the technology nor the social organization of Europe in the sixteenth and seventeenth centuries had the capacity to maintain, of its own resources, outpost colonies thousands of miles from home. Incapable of conquering true wilderness, the Europeans were highly competent in the skill of conquering other people, and that is what they did. They did not settle a virgin land. They invaded and displaced a resident population. . . .

The basic conquest myth postulates that America was virgin land, or wilderness, inhabited by nonpeople called savages; that these savages were creatures sometimes defined as demons, sometimes as beasts "in the shape of men"; that their mode of existence and cast of mind were such as to make them incapable of civilization and therefore of full humanity; that civilization was required by divine sanction or the imperative of progress to conquer the wilderness and make it a garden; that the savage creatures of the wilderness, being unable to adapt to any environment other than the wild, stubbornly and viciously resisted God or fate, and thereby incurred their suicidal extermination; that civilization and its bearers were refined and ennobled in their contest with the dark powers of the wilderness; and that it all was inevitable.

Francis Jennings, *The Invasion of America*, 15

Conquest Reality

The story is not a pleasant one. The dramatic meeting of two civilizations had dire consequences that continue to plague the descendants of the main players. One of the greatest tragedies is that the conquerors failed to recognize the true riches they had stumbled upon: the fertile, life-giving land; the wide variety of experiments in human relations practiced by the inhabitants, and especially the patterns of respect for nature and "right living" honored throughout the hemisphere.

Even as the settlers took advantage of the primeval richness of the soil to grow their crops, the pristine quality of the lakes and rivers to provide fish and fur, and the teeming wildlife to give them meat, they saw the land only as a wilderness to be brought under man's control. Even as they used the government of the Iroquois Confederacy as the model for their own and adopted the crops developed by natives as the basis of their agriculture, they thought of Indians as "savage."

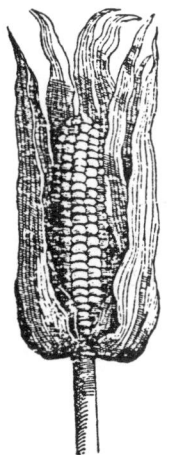

Never once in their arrogance did they stumble upon the single fact that in subsuming the wilderness and the Indian within their synthesis they were irrevocably cutting themselves off from the very substance of the new life they were forging in North America.

Winona LaDuke, "Natural to Synthetic and Back Again,"
Marxism and Native Americans, ii

Challenge by the Natives

From the beginning of the conquest, individuals and groups within the nations encountered by the explorers challenged the worldviews of the invaders. Tundama was the defender of the Sogamoso area in what is now Colombia, which contained an ancient shrine. In 1541, Baltasar Maldonado made Tundama an offer of peace that included a demand of tribute. His reply hints of the hundreds of years of resistance to come:

I am not so barbarous, famous Spaniard, not to believe peace to be the centre on which the bounds of this world depend; but do not think I'm unaware that the bland words with which you offer it to me are much belied by your harsh behaviour.

Who will say that Tundama should give to the vassal the tribute due to the king? I cannot serve someone who serves his king so badly. According to your own accounts of the King of Spain's clemency, it is not credible that he should send you to kill and rob us so.

More barbarian than the Panches and the Muzos [rival tribes], you bathe your horses' mouths in our blood, which they drink out of hunger and thirst and which you spill to display your cruelty. You desecrate the sanctuaries of our gods and sack the houses of men who haven't offended you. Who would choose to undergo these insults, being not insensitive? Who would omit to rid himself of such harassment, even at the cost of his life?

You well know that my people were bred with no fewer natural privileges than yours. We now know that you are not immortal or descended from the sun. Since your people refuse tax and tyranny you cannot be surprised that mine do, with determination.

Note well the survivors who await you, to undeceive you that victory is always yours.

Gordon Brotherston, ed., *Image of the New World*, 48

seventeenth century, half a million acres had been deforested and such species as white oak, white cedar, and black walnut were exterminated.

Our Task

The legacies of the conquest will be with us for years to come. Now it is time to look at the history of the event in a new way, to let the voices of the oppressed speak to us, to tell us their memories and share their wisdom, to teach us from their vast experience of living on the earth.

Unless the conditions that foster oppression are addressed with the urgency and directness they demand, we will continue to suffer from the ignorance, blindness, and greed that have diminished human possibilities during the centuries since 1492.

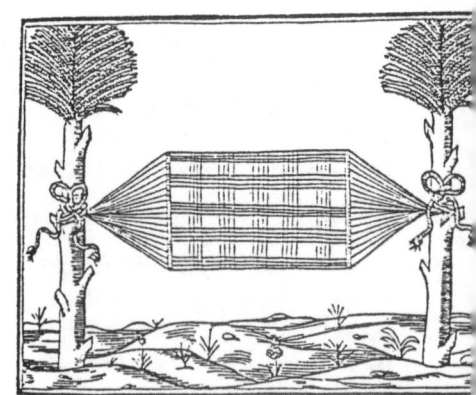

Invasion Bibliography: Works Cited in Chapter One

The American Traveller: Being a New Historical Collection, Carefully Compiled from Original Memoirs in Several Languages and the Most Authentic Voyages and Travels. London: J. Fuller, 1743.

Bancroft, H.H. *Collected Works.* In *1492: Discovery/Invasion/Encounter*, edited by Martin Lunenfeld. Chicago: The Newberry Library, 1989.

Barreiro, Jose. "A Note on Tainos: Whither Progress?" *View from the Shore: American Indian Perspectives on the Quincentenary. Northeast Indian Quarterly* 7:3 (Fall 1990) 66-77.

Belknap, Jeremy. *A Discourse Intended to Commemorate the Discovery of America by Christopher Columbus.* Boston: Apollo Press, 1792.

Brandon, William. *The Last Americans: The Indian in American Culture.* New York: McGraw-Hill Book Company, 1974.

Britten, John. *Sheridan and Kotzebue: The Enterprising Adventures of Pizarro, Preceded by a Brief Sketch of the Voyages and Discoveries of Columbus and Cortez.* London: J. Fairburn, 1799.

Brotherston, Gordon. *Image of the New World: The American Continent Portrayed in Native Texts.* London: Thames and Hudson, Ltd., 1979.

Clifton, Lucille. *Next.* Brockport, N.Y.: Boa Editions, 1987

Davenport, Francis Gardner, ed. *European Treaties Bearing on the History of the United States and Its Dependencies to 1648.* Washington, D.C.: Carnegie Institution, 1917.

de Las Casas, Bartolomé. *The Devastation of the Indies: A Brief Account.* Translated by Herma Briffault. New York: The Seabury Press, 1974.

Elliott, J.H. *Imperial Spain.* In *1492: Discovery/Invasion/Encounter*, edited by Martin Lunenfeld. Chicago: The Newberry Library, 1989.

Fuson, Robert H., trans. *The Log of Christopher Columbus.* Camden, Maine: International Marine Publishing Company, 1987.

Galeano, Eduardo. *Memory of Fire.* Vol. 1, *Genesis.* New York: Pantheon Books, 1985.

____. *Open Veins of Latin America.* New York: Monthly Review Press, 1973.

Hoover, Dwight. *The Red and the Black.* Chicago: Rand McNally College Publishing Company, 1976.

Hurbon, Laennec. "The Slave Trade and Black Slavery in America." *Concilium, 1492-1992, The Voice of the Victims.* Edited by Leonardo Boff and Virgil Elizondo. 91 (December 1990) 109-114.

Hutchinson, Louise Daniel. *Out of Africa: From West African Kingdoms to Colonization.* Washington, D.C.: Smithsonian Institution Press, 1979.

Jennings, Francis. *The Invasion of America: Indians, Colonialism, and the Cant of Conquest.* New York: W.W. Norton and Company, 1975.

Kissam, Edward and Michael Schmidt, trans. *Poems of the Aztec Peoples.* Ypsilanti, Mich.: Bilingual Press, 1983.

Keen, Benjamin, trans. *The Life of the Admiral Christopher Columbus by His Son Ferdinand.* New Brunswick, N.J.: Rutgers University Press, 1959.

Koning, Hans. *Columbus: His Enterprise.* 2d Ed. New York: Monthly Review Press, 1991.

LaDuke, Winona. "Natural to Synthetic and Back Again." In *Marxism and Native Americans,* edited by Ward Churchill. Boston: South End Press, 1983.

Leon-Portillo, Miguel. *The Broken Spears: The Aztec Account of the Conquest of Mexico.* Boston: Beacon Press, 1962.

Lomax, D.W. *The Reconquest of Spain.* In *1492: Discovery/Invasion/Encounter,* edited by Martin Lunenfeld. Chicago: The Newberry Library, 1989.

Long, Haniel. *The Power Within Us: Cabeza de Vaca's Relation of His Journey from Florida to the Pacific, 1528-1536.* New York: Duell, Sloan and Pearce, 1944.

Meltzer, Milton. *Columbus and the World Around Him.* New York: Franklin Watts, 1990.

Mohawk, John. "Discovering Columbus: The Way Here," *View from the Shore: American Indian Perspectives on the Quincentenary. Northeast Indian Quarterly* 7:3 (Fall 1990) 37-46.

Moody, Roger, ed. *The Indigenous Voice.* 2 vols. London: Zed Books Ltd., 1988.

Ober, Frederick. *In the Wake of Columbus.* Boston: D. Lathrop Company, 1893.

Ortiz, Roxanne Dunbar. *Indians of the Americas: Human Rights and Self Determination.* London: Zed Books Ltd., 1984.

Prescott, William. *History of the Conquest of Mexico.* 3 vols. Philadelphia: 1873.

Roberts, Elizabeth, ed. *Earth Prayers: From Around the World.* San Francisco: Harper, 1991.

Sale, Kirkpatrick. *The Conquest of Paradise: Christopher Columbus and the Columbian Legacy.* New York: Alfred A. Knopf, 1990.

___. "What Columbus Discovered." *The Nation,* October 22, 1990, 444-446.

Salisbury, Neal. *Manitou and Providence: Indians, Europeans, and the Making of New England, 1500-1643.* New York: Oxford University Press, 1982.

Sams, Conway Whittle. *The Conquest of Virginia, The Third Attempt, 1610-1624.* New York: G.P. Putnam's Sons, 1939.

Segal, Charles M. and David C. Stineback. *Puritans, Indians, and Manifest Destiny.* New York: G.P. Putnam's Sons, 1977.

Standing Bear, Chief Luther. *Land of the Spotted Eagle.* In *Rethinking Columbus.* Special issue of *Rethinking Schools* (1991) 84.

Stravianos, L.S. *Man's Past and Present: A Global History.* 2d Ed. Englewood Cliffs, N.J.: Prentice-Hall, Inc., 1975.

Thacher, John Boyd. *Christopher Columbus: His Life, His Work, His Remains.* New York: G.P. Putnam's Sons, 1903.

Vanderwerth, W.C., ed. *Indian Oratory.* Norman: University of Oklahoma Press, 1971.

Wachtel, Nathan. *The Vision of the Vanquished: The Spanish Conquest of Peru through Indian Eyes 1530-1570.* Sussex, England: The Harvester Press, Ltd., 1977.

Williams, Eric. *From Columbus to Castro: The History of the Caribbean, 1492-1969.* New York: Vintage Books, 1984.

Williams, William Appleman. *The Contours of American History.* New York: New Viewpoints, 1973.

R·E·S·I·S·T·A·N·C·E

Remember us after we are gone. Don't forget us. Conjure up our faces and our words. Our image will be as a tear in the hearts of those who want to remember us.

Sacred Mayan Prayer
Popul Vuh

The invasion of this hemisphere was not a single event or a series of events of the late fifteenth and early sixteenth centuries. The invasion and destruction have been constant for five hundred years. Christopher Columbus, Hernando Cortes, Francisco Pizarro, Pedro Alvarado, the Puritans, and the other invaders instituted economic and political structures whose legacies still destroy land and people today.

Where once fleets of Spanish galleons transgressed the seas loaded with armored soldiers carrying arquebuses and cannon, now U.S. Marines, rapid deployment forces, and CIA covert activities trespass across borders in order to carry out the will of the powerful. Where once the settlers came with horses and dynamite ripping out trees for plantations and roads for gold miners, now multinationals come to the Amazon rainforest with bulldozers and dynamite to clear away ancient trees for huge livestock plantations and roads for gold miners. Where once French, English, and Spanish traders carried human beings into labor slavery, now multinational traders carry factories to Mexico and Central America, delivering workers into virtual wage slavery. Where once the invaders came with the *requerimiento* signed by Pope and King giving the native people an ultimatum: submit or be destroyed, now world lending institutions like the International Monetary Fund and the World Bank come armed with new requirements: submit your economic system to suit the world's dominant countries or you will receive no new loans and your ravished economies will be destroyed. These new requirements sound much like the old patterns of extracting wealth: institute lower wages, increase exports, import technology and expertise from Europe and the United States, and then pay back the loans at exorbitant rates of interest.

Christopher Columbus planted the first sugar cane, instituting both forced labor to work the huge plantations and an export-based economy that made huge profits for a few white Europeans. Today cane cutters in the Dominican Republic and coffee pickers in Central America receive starvation wages while a few wealthy landowners and huge multinational corporations control the land and reap the profits. All of this is the legacy of invasion.

The first invaders said they were bringing God and civilization. In fact, what they brought was feudalism, deadly microbes, slavery, and lust for wealth. Within five hundred years the invaders annihilated whole tribes, killed millions of Africans, destroyed communal lands, eradicated whole species of plant and animal life, and melted sacred art and religious symbols into bullion. They ripped open the veins of Latin America, extracting blood from its people and gold and silver from its mountains.

Yet if invasion has been constant, the resistance to that invasion has also been ceaseless. From the shores of Africa to the Caribbean islands, from the Andean mountains and Guatemalan highlands to the Western plains, people have refused to submit to injustice and have struggled to preserve their culture and dignity. At times it was individual resistance—a runaway slave, a refusal to name co-conspirators, a revival of an outlawed cultural ritual. At other times it was highly organized resistance involving tens of thousands of people, such as the struggle for the independence of Haiti, Pontiac's Confederacy, the Araucanian resistance, and the Mexican Revolution of 1910. More often than not, however, it was episodic and decentralized. Individuals or small bands of rebels decided to strike for freedom, or peasants organized to reclaim their land. From the first slave ships where Africans mutinied to capture the ship to tin miners striking in Bolivia and university students protesting in Mexico City, every generation since 1492 has resisted the invasion.

It would be impossible to document every act of resistance. For one thing, much of that record has been lost, since history is most often written by the conquerers. White Europeans have, for the most part, written the history of this hemisphere. The words of U.S. history texts used in schools show the perspective. As one textbook summarizes: "Columbus's voyage in search of a western route to Asia ended the isolation of American cultures and brought two worlds together." Those are clearly not the words of an indigenous survivor of the decimation wrought by the European invaders.

The selections in this section follow major periods or patterns of resistance:

African American Resistance

African resistance began in Africa, continued on board the slave ships, and then resumed upon touching the shore of the land the Europeans called America. The African American resistance communities formed in the inaccessible areas of this hemisphere by runaway slaves are a testament to the courage and ingenuity of men and women struggling for freedom at any cost. African American resistance has been constant and multi-leveled. The selections try to show that variety and tenacity, from the anonymous woman rebel on the slave ship "Robert" to the women of Montgomery, Alabama, who were the power behind the successful bus boycott that ignited the civil rights movement; from the Jamaican resistance leader Nanny to Malcolm X and Martin Luther King.

Indigenous Resistance, North and South

The indigenous population, after an inital welcome to the Europeans, began a defense of their lives and land that continues today. We have selected some of the more heroic and successful of those efforts, including the great Araucanian resistance that defeated the Spaniards for three hundred years, keeping their lands in what is now southern Chile from colonization. But even when the Sioux, Cheyenne, and Apache nations succumbed to military firepower, a spirit of resistance could not be extinguished. Eighty years after the supposed final battle of the "Indian Wars," a new native militancy rose up at Wounded Knee, the very site of that last battle, successfully challenging white domination and igniting a new sense of dignity and honor among native peoples.

• In the Andean region that is now Peru and Bolivia, the eighteenth century was a time of upheaval marked by small and great rebellions. We introduce some of the leaders, including Juan Santos Atahualpa, Tupac Amaru II, and Micaela Bastidas.

• In the nineteenth century it was Mexico's turn, as the country erupted in 142 recorded village riots and revolts involving campesinos demanding land and jus-tice. These rebellions that first led to Mexican independence in the early part of the nineteenth century culminated with the Mexican Revolution at the dawn of the twentieth.

Central American Resistance

In this century our attention turns to Central America, where modern-day rebels taking the names of past heroes continue the struggle for land and justice. Even today in the Guatemalan highlands and Salvadoran mountains, communities of resistance continue the struggle begun five hundred years ago.

Resistance Today

One example among many is the struggle to save the rainforest of Brazil. All of the elements of the first invasion are being re-enacted there. Its final fate has become important to the whole world as scientists are realizing the sustaining effect that the world's largest forest has on the ecosphere. Who wins that struggle may well determine the fate of the whole earth.

The selections that follow try to inspire hope; demonstrate that courage was not the sole domain of men or famous leaders; give voice to the anonymous bands of rebels whose names are lost to us, but whose deeds remain; and show that defeat of the rebels has never been final, but has only served to push history to the next stage where resistance emerges once again. Whatever measure of liberty or civil rights that we enjoy today was, in large part, won by these rebels.

We have certainly inherited the winds of destruction, but we are also free to claim the legacy of resistance. Untold people have been killed but multitudes have risen up to take their places.

African American Resistance

Early Resistance

The Shores of Africa, 1500s: The Forerunners

It began at the edge of our homeland where the verdant forests and tropical bush gave way gradually to the sandy beaches of the Guinea coast. It began at the mouths of rivers, from that northern point where the Senegal and the Gambia pour their troubled streams into the waters around Cape Verde, down the thousands of miles of coastline to the place where the mighty river Congo breaks out into the ocean. On these shores near the mouths of these rivers, we first saw the ships.

There was no way to know it then, but their crews of men and boys came from many ports to find the shores of Africa. They sailed from Amsterdam and Lisbon, from Nantes and La Rochelle, from Bristol and London, from Newport and Boston on ships with strange names. They came to us on "Brotherhood" and "John the Baptist," on "Justice" and "Integrity," on "Gift of God" and "Liberty"; they came on the good ship "Jesus." But by the time our weary lines of chained and mourning travelers saw the vessels riding on the coastal

Before the Mayflower

In the sixteenth century, while Spaniards were just beginning the mass trading of human beings, an advanced civilization was developing in Africa. For example, Benin City, in the interior, was a center of art and commerce. The city stretched for twenty-five miles; wide boulevards were lined with sizable houses sporting balustrades and verandas. Travel was not unknown; increasing archeological evidence, including skeletons and carvings, points to the fact that Africans travelled to what is now Central and Latin America several times, centuries before Columbus. Not only slaves but also free Africans arrived in the Western Hemisphere long before the first permanent English colony at Jamestown in 1620.

Position as Slaves

Africans were the only group to come to this hemisphere as slaves, and from the very beginning, African and African American resistance was a constant. Because of the nature of the slave institution, that resistance had to take a variety of forms, many of them disguised. To the whites what seemed like laziness or stupidity was often really a work slowdown or a pretending not to understand in order to deprive the slave owners of labor.

Sabotage, work slowdowns, organized strikes, running away, fires destroying plantations, mutinies on slave ships, ground glass in the master's food, poisonings, feigning sickness or pregnancy, insurrections plotted or carried out—all were acts of resistance perpetrated by slaves for the sake of freedom. Even suicide was an act of rebellion, a way of depriving the white man of his "property." Some slaves also believed that death would take them back to Africa. The resistance of Africans to the dehumanization of chains and the middle passage was so great that some tried to starve themselves. Their captors devised tortures, including hot coals to the lips and a special instrument that wrenched open the jaws of the resisters just to feed them. In many cases, even that did not work.

Historian Herbert Aptheker found 250 instances of revolts and conspiracies in the history of North American slavery; in Brazil, Suriname, and Jamaica, slave rebellion was a way of life.

See Eugene Genovese,
From Rebellion to Revolution

waves, there could be but one meaning: captivity. Thus it was on the edges of our continent—where some of us gulped down handfuls of sand in a last effort to hold the reality of the land—that the long struggle for black freedom began.

Vincent Harding, *There Is a River*, 3

Hispaniola, 1522: First Slave Rebellion

It takes only one generation. Columbus brought the first cane plant to Hispaniola on his second voyage. Two decades later his son Diego is reaping sugar and revolt. This "white gold" savagely devours the fertility of the land and the flesh of the indigenous population. Africans brought to work the land in place of the Arawaks prefer to die in the fire of revolt. Diego sees his plantation and fields burning. When the Spaniards finally stop the revolt, they hang the rebels along the road to stop future uprisings.

It doesn't work.

See Eduardo Galeano, *Memories of Fire: Genesis*, 72-73

Sierra Leone, 1721: Black Women in the Struggle

. . . in spite of constant and costly defeats, the struggles for freedom went on. Often women took a crucial part, making full use of the special status and greater freedom of movement accorded them. Their role was exemplified in the events on board the English ship "Robert" as it stood off the coast of Sierra Leone in 1721. Among the thirty captives on board was a man who called himself Captain Tomba, one of the earliest identifiable leaders of the struggle. He and several other African men and an unnamed woman had developed a plan to attack the crew, overcome them, and make their way back to the shore. The woman, because she had greater freedom of movement, was chosen to inform the men of the best time for the attack.

One night as she roamed the deck, she noted that the number of sailors in the night watch was small enough to make a surprise move more feasible. After she managed to inform Tomba, he prepared to act immediately; but only one of the African men who had promised earlier to assist him was now ready to join Tomba and the woman. Nevertheless, these

We cannot forget that America was built on Africa. . . . America became, through African labor, the center of the sugar empire and the cotton kingdom and an integral part of that world industry which caused the industrial revolution and the reign of capitalism. . . .

W.E.B. Dubois

Quoted in Milton Meltzer, *Slavery II*, 127

83

The cost of rebellion on slave ships was often being thrown overboard. Sharks followed many slave ships, a testament to the constancy of rebellion.

three decided to strike for their freedom. The smallness of their force and an accidental sounding of an alarm worked against them, so that after killing two of the crew they were overwhelmed by others, beaten to the deck and placed in chains. . . .

And what of the black woman who chose the struggle for black freedom over her privileged bondage among white men? We are told that "the woman he hosited up by the Thumbs, whipp'd and slashed her with Knives before the other slaves till she died." And so, not far from the shores of her homeland, the swaying bleeding body of a sister in struggle bore terrifying witness to the cost of the decision for freedom. Yet perhaps she would have considered this lonely vigil above the sea a better use of her body than any that the crew members had had in mind.

Vincent Harding, *There Is a River*, 12-13

Maroon Resistance

Maroons: Communities of Resisters

In 1502, Governor Ovando brought "a few Negroes" to Hispaniola to bolster the faltering colony that Columbus had left behind. Among them was the first African American maroon, who escaped to the Indians soon after coming ashore.

Maroonage or flight was one of the major ways slaves resisted their cruel conditions. It was so common that communities formed by these runaways filled the edges of the Americas from North Carolina to Brazil. Known as *palenques, quilombos, mocambos, cumbes, ladeiras* or *mambises*, these new societies embraced African values and traditions while utilizing skills of the indigenous population. Some survived less than a year, while others lasted for generations or even centuries.

Some became so powerful and so threatening to the plantation system both militarily and economically that the whites had to press for peace agreements with them. The first treaties made by white Europeans in the Western Hemisphere were with the maroons.

Almost constantly at war with the Europeans, the maroon communities had to be nearly inaccessible in order to survive because their former masters usually hunted for them. They had to find land both defensible and hidden, which meant creating a society in the most inhospitable terrain. This required immense creativity and courage to endure daily hardships. For example, in one maroon community the water

San Domingo, 1700s: Ad for Runaways

Zabo, an Ibo, five feet one, quite homely, has scars and lash marks on shoulders having only recently been whipped. Fled the home of the undersigned. Seven newly arrived slaves, part of the cargo of the vessel "L'Aimable," all Congos, not yet branded.

Jean Fouchar, *The Haitian Maroons: Liberty or Death*, 4

Surinam, 1718: Permanent Resistance

The fact that punishments for runaways have to be codified into edicts and laws testifies to the persistence of the maroon resistance.

If a slave runs away into the forest in order to avoid work for a few weeks, upon his being captured his Achilles tendon is removed for the first offence, while for a second offence . . . his right leg is amputated in order to stop his running away; I myself was a witness to slaves being punished in this way.

Richard Price, ed., *Maroon Societies*, 3

Palmares, Brazil, 1695: Maroon Community

For ninety years, maroons have sustained an African society called Palmares led by a small group of chiefs. Economically successful, they have developed trading relations with local plantation owners. Living in a constant state of war, they spread themselves over a large area and engage in general guerrilla war, gradually wearing down the Portuguese. Recognizing the constant threat of the inspiration of their example to other slaves, the Portuguese inflict heavy losses on the Palmarinos, whose supreme chief, *ganga-zumba*, sues for peace in 1678. But the younger leaders, including the *zumbí* (war chief), resume the struggle. Not until 1695 do the Portuguese develop a powerful coalition, including ruffians and mercenaries, to defeat the Palmarinos. The Portuguese describe the *zumbí* as a *Negro of singular courage, great spirit and persistence.*

Eugene Genovese, *From Rebellion to Revolution*, 63

Surinam, 1796: An Adversary Speaks

Captain Stedman, an enemy of the maroons who over-ran some of their villages, is impressed with the life they have created under the harshest conditions. . . . *Their fields are even overstocked with rice, cassava, yams, plaintains, etc. They make salt from palm-tree ashes. . . . We have found concealed near the trunk of an old tree a case-bottle filled with excellent butter, which . . . they made by melting and clarifying the fat of the palm-tree worms; this fully answers all the purposes of European butter, and I found it in fact even more delicious to my taste. The pistachio or pinda nuts [peanuts] they also convert into butter . . . and frequently use them in their broths. The palm-tree wine they always have in plenty. . . . They fabricate pots from clay . . . the gourd or callebasse tree procures them cups; the silk-grass plant . . . supplies materials for their hammocks . . . candles they can make, having plenty of fat and oil; and the wild bees afford them wax, as well as excellent honey.*

Richard Price, ed., *Maroon Societies*, 11

Jamaica, 1730: Nanny, Freedom Fighter

Legend and folklore, they say, embody the spirit of the people who remember and tell the stories. The name and deeds of Nanny still dance on the lips of twentieth-century Jamaicans. Her town is still sacred ground.

Leader of the Windward Maroons, she is so powerful they name a town after her, which becomes known for having the greatest warriors. Completely naked except for a necklace of teeth, she invokes *loa Ogun* (Yoruba god of war) before going into battle. Her followers believe she has magic powers that will make them invulnerable to English weapons. They swear oaths of allegiance to the cause of repelling the intruders from their land. It will take all the magic they can muster to defeat the lust for wealth propelling the white man to this small island.

In battle, Nanny catches British bullets in her buttocks and expels them back. She keeps a large cauldron bubbling without a fire. When the British soldiers come too close they fall in and suffocate.

Nanny is full of magic. The white men's teeth she wears around her neck cannot bite her.

Mavis C. Campbell, *The Maroons of Jamaica 1655-1796*, 4, 11, 50, 51

was filled with worms; the people had to devise elaborate purifying operations just to live there.

Yet amid the brambles or rocks or dense jungles, these maroons created thriving economies that included a wide variety of foods and art and a well-developed political and military organization. Maroon societies raised manioc, yams, beans, bananas and plantains, sugar cane, vegetables, tobacco, and cotton. Through ingenious traps and springs they were able to capture animals and fish.

Maroons throughout the Americas developed incredible skills in guerrilla warfare. The defense of their societies included booby traps, false paths with pointed spikes, and extensive use of the natural environment for defense. The warrior bands became adept at ambush, surprise, crossfires, and extreme mobility. They developed extensive and reliable intelligence networks and often communicated by horns. These tactics were necessary because they were almost always outnumbered, and the Europeans had superior firepower.

The reality of resistance, so integral to the Caribbean, was rooted in the slave's consciousness of his or her human dignity.

See Richard Price, ed., *Maroon Societies* and Mavis C. Campbell, *The Maroons of Jamaica 1655-1796*

The San Domingo Revolution

Slaves Free Themselves

The black-led revolution in San Domingo not only freed the slaves and established a modern state (Haiti), it sent hope to slaves throughout the Western Hemisphere.

It was a brilliant diplomatic and military victory led by Toussaint L'Ouverture and Jean-Jacques Dessalines. What started as thousands of untrained slaves ended up a disciplined army that defeated the greatest military forces of the day, including the Spanish, the English, and the French under Napoleon.

The San Domingo revolution occurred in the context of the French revolution, as the cries for freedom and equality were heard on both sides of the Atlantic.

San Domingo was ripe for revolution because of its decades of successful maroon escapes and warfare. There had been a tradition of freedom. The blacks also significantly outnumbered the whites; as late as 1790, forty thousand new Africans were being imported. Those fresh from Africa were more likely to join the revolt since freedom was still in their hearts. When the slaves heard the French peasants cry for liberty and equality, they made that cry their own.

The following chronology puts the San Domingo revolution in perspective.

San Domingo, 1758: The Precursors

The maroon named Francois Macandal has only one hand, the other sacrificed to a sugar mill and slavery. One day he runs away and becomes the leader of escaped slaves in the mountains, known for poisonings that spread terror throughout the country. He dislikes the pillaging of mansions and the stealing of herds. He wants to make maroonage the center of an organized resistance against the whites in order to free the slaves. He says if the whites catch him and try to burn him, he will become a fly and escape the fire.

He is finally captured and sentenced to death at the stake. Today he is to be burned. A number of slave masters die from poison, thanks to cooks who are his allies. As the flames rise around him, miraculously the iron rings holding him fall from the wood and he is free. Many believe his prophecy is coming true. The whites capture him again and turn him to ash.

See Jean Fouchard, *The Haitian Maroons*, 317-321

San Domingo, 1788: The Colonial Reality

In San Domingo there are big whites and small whites. The big whites are the planters and large merchants. The clerks, artisans, grocers, vagabonds, debtors, thieves are the small whites. No white is a servant, no white does work if he can get a black person to do it for him. Skin color and racial prejudice are the fundamental principles of the society.

A man calls for the barber. The barber arrives dressed in silk with cane and sword followed by four slaves. One slave combs the hair, another curls it, the third dresses it, and the fourth cleans up. One isn't fast enough and the barber smacks him, knocking him down. When they are done they leave, following the white barber, who is walking out like an aristocrat.

The slaves do everything—except receive the money.

See C.L.R. James, *The Black Jacobins*, 33

The Colonial Mentality:

"I want an egg," says the white colonial child.

"There are no eggs."

"Then I want two."

C.L.R. James,
The Black Jacobins, 29

San Domingo, 1790: Arithmetic of Racism

François is the son of a white man and a mulatto. He is a *quarteroon*, 96 parts white and 32 parts black.

Marie is also a *quarteroon* produced by a white and a *marabou* in the proportion of 88 to 40; her half-sister is the product of a white and a *sacatra* in the proportion of 72 to 56.

Christophe is a *sang-melé* with 127 parts white to 1 part black. In the arithmetic of racism, he is still a man of color, not entitled to the privilege of whites.

C.L.R. James, *The Black Jacobins*, 38

San Domingo, 1791: The Beginning

It is becoming a long hot summer. While the rich white planters enjoy cold drinks on the veranda, drums are beating in the hills. They are worshipping their tribal gods, say the whites. How primitive and simple-minded, say the whites.

In the hills, a tall man stands behind a make-shift altar. Speaking in a deep penetrating voice, he tells the assembled slaves that it is time to revolt. It is time to avenge the wrongs, it is time to gain freedom. The man's name is Boukman.

Eight days later, on August 22 at midnight, one hundred thousand slaves begin a movement that will break their chains and found a nation. In a moment, twelve hundred coffee and two hundred sugar plantations are in flames....*the whole horizon a wall of flames.... Such was their voracity that for three weeks we could barely distinguish between day and night....*

Lerone Bennett, Jr., *Before the Mayflower*, 113-115

San Domingo, 1791: Ideas Can Make History

A priest named Abbé Raynal wrote a book, famous in this time, calling for a slave revolution. He wrote:

Natural liberty is the right which nature has given to everyone to dispose of himself according to his will.... These are memorable and eternal truths—the foundation of all morality, the basis of all government; will they be contested?

Chronology

July 14, 1788: • French peasants storm the Bastille; the French Revolution begins under the banner of "Liberty, Equality, Fraternity."

1791: • Boukman begins the slave revolt.

1792: • Toussaint begins training a few hundred troops.

• Six thousand French troops sail for San Domingo to put down the slave revolt.

• Paris masses storm the Tuileries, imprison the royal family, dissolve the legislature, and call for the abolition of slavery. For the first time, the blacks of San Domingo have allies in France.

• Laveaux, the French commander, defeats Toussaint.

1793: • The king of France is executed, the revolutionary armies are winning successes.

• Toussaint issues his call for the blacks to unite.

1794: • Britain sets its sights on San Domingo and other Caribbean islands. The British want to re-establish slavery and make them colonies. One of the leaders of this colonization move says in Parliament that the war in the West Indies was "... not for riches or local aggrandizement but a war for security...." The property owners of San Domingo (even though they are French) rush to welcome the British because they prefer their slaves to the goals of the revolution.

• Toussaint, a Spanish officer now and ally of the British, has been defeating the French. Seeing the wave of British victories in the Caribbean, he weighs the future carefully.

Historian C.L.R. James writes:

"It was a crucial moment in history. If the British could hold San Domingo, the finest colony in the world, they would once more be a power in American waters. Instead of being abolitionists, they would be the most powerful practitioners of the slave trade. . . . If the British completed the conquest of San Domingo, the colonial empire of revolutionary France was gone; its vast resources would be directed into British pockets, and Britain would be able to return to Europe and throw army and navy against the revolution" (James, 136).

• At the French Convention, a member rises to speak: "Since 1789 the aristocracy of birth and the aristocracy of religion have been destroyed; but the aristocracy of the skin still remains. A black man, a yellow man, and a white are about to join this convention in the name of the free citizens of San Domingo." There is an outburst of applause. The National Convention abolishes slavery in the colonies." (James, 139-140)

• Toussaint receives the news of the decree just as the fate of the French sits precariously before the might of the British. Toussaint does not hesitate. He decides to join the French. Laveaux, the French commander, is overjoyed and makes him a Brigadier General. Immediately he undertakes a campaign to retake for the French the cities that he had just a while before captured for the Spanish.

1795: • Toussaint's power grows. To the people, his word is law. He is as much concerned about winning victories over the British as creating a prosperous society. Trying to rein in the chaos of war, he proclaims, "Work is neces-

Yes! . . . A courageous chief only is wanted. Where is he, that great man whom Nature owes to her vexed, oppressed, and tormented children? Where is he? He will appear, doubt it not; he will come forth and raise the sacred standard of liberty.

The man holding the book has read those lines many times. *A courageous chief only is wanted. Who is he?* The man reading those lines is forty-five years old, a carriage driver, steward of livestock, and a slave. Already his hair is turning grey. *It is always the blacks who suffer the most,* is a phrase he often says. His name—Toussaint Bréda, soon to be known to the world as Toussaint L'Ouverture.

C.L.R. James, *The Black Jacobins,* 25

San Domingo, 1793: The Opening

On August 29, Toussaint Bréda makes this call to all slaves:

Brothers and friends. I am Toussaint L'Ouverture. My name is perhaps known to you. I have undertaken vengeance. I want Liberty and Equality to reign in San Domingo. I work to bring them into existence. Unite yourselves to us, brothers, and fight with us for the same cause. . . .

> *Your very humble and very obedient servant,*
> *(signed) Toussaint L'Ouverture*

At the news of another victory by Toussaint, the French say, *This man makes an opening everywhere.* "L'Ouverture" means opening.

C.L.R. James, *The Black Jacobins,* 125

San Domingo, 1797: Declaration of Liberty

Toussaint, not six years out of slavery, dictates a letter to his secretary to be sent to the French Directory. Working from his broken dialect, the secretaries shape Toussaint's eloquent ideas into beautiful prose. Fearing that a movement is underway by some in France to restore slavery, he writes:

Do they think that men who have been able to enjoy the blessing of liberty will calmly see it snatched away? They supported their chains only so long as they did not know any condition of life more happy than that of slavery. But today when they have left it, if they had a thousand lives they would sacrifice them all rather than be forced into slavery again. . . .

But if, to re-establish slavery in San Domingo, this was done, then I declare to you it would be to attempt the impossible: we have known how to face dangers to obtain our liberty, we shall know how to brave death to maintain it. (Toussaint's emphasis)

C.L.R. James, *The Black Jacobins*, 196-197

You think me a fanatic, for you read history with your prejudices. But fifty years hence, when Truth gets a hearing, the Muse of history will put Phocion for the Greek, Brutus for the Roman, Hampden for the English, Lafayette for France: choose Washington as the bright, consummate flower of our earliest civilization; and then, dipping her pen in the sunlight, will write in the clear blue, above them all, the name of the soldier, the statesman, the martyr, Toussaint L'Ouverture.

Wendell Phillips

Quoted in Lerone Bennett, Jr., *Before the Mayflower*, 117

San Domingo, 1800: Toussaint, the Man

In his room there are always flowers. He loves music and children.

One day while he is riding in the countryside, a ten-year-old orphan named Rose stops him crying, *Papa, Papa, take me away with you.* He dismounts, takes her in his arms and carries her home. He hands her to his wife Suzanne and says, *Here is an orphan who has just called me father. I have accepted the title. Accept also the title of her mother.*

sary, it is a virtue, it is for the general good of the state." He orders workers to begin planting twenty-four hours after a territory is liberated by his army. He institutes a conciliatory policy towards whites because he knows their skill, education, and experience are needed by the colony in order to prosper.

1796: • At the end of the year, after three years of war, the British have lost eighty thousand men, half of them dead. It has cost them millions of pounds.

• Toussaint combines military superiority with astute propaganda and wins seven victories in seven days.

• The British ask for a truce.

• Toussaint forbids pillage by his soldiers and so, starving and half naked, they maintain their discipline. No single act of violence happens.

• Toussaint's entry into Port-Républicain is a triumph. Black laborers and ex-slaves come out to hail ex-slaves who have become soldiers and have defeated one of the strongest nations on earth. Even the whites call Toussaint their liberator. An arch of triumph is quickly erected and some of the richest planters, who at one time were his staunchest enemies, invite Toussaint to mount the dais. Toussaint replies, "A dais and incense belong only to God."

• The French send General Hédouville to govern San Domingo. Inept and troublesome, he threatens to have French forces return. Toussaint marches to Le Cap and chases Hédouville from the island. Toussaint addresses the citizens who welcome him:

"Hédouville says that I am against liberty. . . . Who ought to love liberty more, Toussaint L'Ouverture, slave of Bréda, or General Hédouville, former Marquis and Chevalier de Saint-Louis?"

Historian C.L.R. James comments: "At bottom the popular movement had acquired an immense self-confidence. The former slaves had defeated white colonists, Spaniards, and British, and now they were free. . . . Black men who had been slaves were deputies in the French Parliament, black men who had been slaves negotiated with the French and foreign governments. Black men who had been slaves filled the highest positions in the colony. There was Toussaint, the former slave, incredibly grand and powerful and incomparably the greatest man in San Domingo. There was no need of being ashamed of being a black. . . . The revolution had awakened them, had given them the possibility of achievement, confidence, and pride. The psychological weakness, that feeling of inferiority with which the imperials poison colonial people everywhere, these were gone. . . " (James, 244).

1797: • The forces of reaction and counter-revolution are gaining in France. The French leaders suspect Toussaint of wanting complete freedom, Toussaint suspects them of wanting to restore slavery.

1800: • Toussaint marches on Spanish San Domingo and routs the Spanish troops; the Spanish formally hand over the colony.

• Toussaint writes to Napoleon Bonaparte in France telling him that he has relieved the French agent of his duties. Toussaint is laying the ground-

In battle he is one with his men. If a cannon needs to be moved, his shoulder is also at the wheel. Wherever the battle is most intense, there he is in the front. Escaping death many times, he seems to lead a charmed life. Once the plume on his hat is shot off. On another occasion his carriage is riddled. Horses are shot from under him and those next to him are killed. In ten years he is wounded seventeen times.

He governs with the same energy that carried him through years of war. He sleeps only two hours every night. For days he is satisfied with two bananas and a glass of water. He has hundreds of thoroughbred horses scattered throughout the countryside. It is typical for him to ride 125 miles a day.

When he is fighting, it seems to the enemy that he is everywhere, especially where they least expect him. His ability to move troops faster and farther than what seems humanly possible is a main reason for his astounding victories. When governing, he appears out of nowhere to inspect or administer or pass out awards. Then he rides back to his office in order to dictate hundreds of letters.

He dictates to five secretaries at once.

See C.L.R. James, *The Black Jacobins*, 249-250, 255

San Domingo, 1801: Black Consul

He seems to know exactly what to say to people.

When the black laborers come to him, nervous about white domination returning, Toussaint takes a jar filled with black corn and then puts in a few pieces of white corn.

You are the black maize; the whites who would enslave you are the white maize. Then he shakes the jar. The laborers leave satisfied.

Other black laborers come to him because the whites and mulattoes have been spreading insults and treating them unjustly. They no longer want to obey the whites. Toussaint takes a glass of wine and a glass of water and mixes them.

Can you tell which is which? he asks. *We must all live together.* They go away satisfied.

See C.L.R. James, *The Black Jacobins*, 251-252

San Domingo, 1801: Toussaint Prepares for More War

Toussaint proclaims: *I took up arms for the freedom of my color, which France alone proclaimed, but she has no right to nullify. Our liberty is no longer in her hands: it is in our own. We will defend it or perish.*

Toussaint addresses the army:

You are going to fight against men who have neither faith, law, nor religion. They promise you liberty, they intend your servitude. Why have so many ships traversed the ocean, if not to throw you back into chains? . . . Uncover your breasts, you will see them branded by the iron of slavery.

He takes a weapon from a soldier's hand and raises it into the air.

Here is your liberty!

C.L.R. James, *The Black Jacobins*, 226, 281, 307

San Domingo, 1801: The War for Independence

If it was Toussaint L'Ouverture who brought the colony to freedom, it is Jean-Jacques Dessalines who will make it an independent nation. Carrying the scars of slavery, Dessalines is relentless:

Take courage, I tell you, take courage. The French will not be able to remain long in San Domingo. They will do well at first, but soon they will fall ill and die like flies. Listen! If Dessalines surrenders to them a hundred times he will deceive them a hundred times. . . . They will not be able to guard the country and they will have to leave. Then I shall make you independent.

For the first time in the French colony of San Domingo, a black leader speaks that word—independence.

C.L.R. James, *The Black Jacobins*, 314

work for an independent nation. But, according to C.L.R. James, he makes a fatal mistake, his only one in years of battles and maneuvers:

"His error was the neglect of his own people. They did not understand what he was doing or where he was going. He took no trouble to explain. It was dangerous to explain, but still more dangerous not to explain. His temperament, close and self-contained, was one that kept its own counsel. Thus, the masses thought that he had taken Spanish San Domingo to stop the slave traffic, and not as a safeguard against the French . . . ." (James, 240)

• Toussaint sets out to govern the colony under a military dictatorship—albeit a benevolent one. He is still under the French command. He advocates racial equality, hard work, high morality, and public education. Race prejudice, the curse of San Domingo for two hundred years, is vanishing. In a year and a half Toussaint restores cultivation to two-thirds what it was at San Domingo's height. And this is a country devastated by war. He builds schools, roads, theaters. He sends black and mulatto children to school in Europe so that they can return to govern. All he wants is time. Visitors remark that there is a new spirit in the land.

• Toussaint sends many letters to Napoleon asking for teachers and technicians to rebuild the colony. Napoleon never answers. Toussaint knows that he and his people are safe as long as the British and the French are fighting each other. One day the war will end, and San Domingo will once again have to fight for its freedom.

• San Domingo does not have peace. The white colonists cause trouble, while the maritime bourgeoisie in France, the ones who profit so much from trade in human beings, are gaining power. In addition, Napoleon hates blacks.

1801: • England signs the peace treaty with France. Napoleon sends twenty thousand troops to San Domingo under the command of General LeClerc, the largest force ever to leave France. Their purpose—to reinstitute slavery.
.

1802: • Even though he is holding a strong position, Toussaint sues for peace. The terms are that all of the black soldiers and officers maintain their rank. He wants to maintain the army and end the destruction. LeClerc happily agrees.

• Toussaint retires to his plantation.

• Tricked into coming to Le Cap, Toussaint is arrested, bound, and sent to France.

1803: • Toussaint dies in prison.

• Forces led by Jean-Jacques Dessalines defeat the French.

• Declaration of Independence is read. The new state is renamed Haiti.

• Dessalines is crowned.

1805: • Dessalines orders all whites massacred.

C.L.R. James writes: "The massacre of the whites was a tragedy; not for the whites. For these old slave-owners, those who burnt a little powder in the

San Domingo, 1802: Betrayal

French General Brunet writes a flowery letter to Toussaint asking him to come to headquarters for an interview. The general gives his personal assurances of good faith and safety.

It is eight in the evening and Toussaint and General Brunet are talking. Brunet begs to be excused for a moment. Immediately grenadiers with fixed bayonets enter the room. Toussaint rises and draws his sword. Assured that they only want to secure his person, he submits.

They bind him, arrest his son and wife, steal his money and personal papers. They rush him and his family on board a frigate bound for France.

As he steps on the boat, he says to the captain: *In overthrowing me, you have cut down in San Domingo only the trunk of the tree of liberty. It will spring up again by the roots that are too numerous and deep.*

C.L.R. James, *The Black Jacobins*, 333-334

Paris, 1802: Reading Between the Lines

Napoleon carefully reads the letter from General LeClerc. Four-fifths of the army has died from illness. A general insurrection has broken out in the North. The people know of the plan to reinstitute slavery.

. . . Fifty prisoners have been hung; these men die with an incredible fanaticism; they laugh at death; it is the same with the women. . . . It is not enough to have taken away Toussaint, there are two thousand leaders to be taken away.

C.L.R. James, *The Black Jacobins*, 345-346

Fort-de-Joux, France, 1803: One End, One Beginning

He is shivering in this cell in the Jura mountains. The walls drip with moisture, the logs counted so as never to bring real warmth. He collapses every so often into a coma. It is April 7. The guards enter and find Toussaint L'Ouverture sitting in his chair. He is dead.

Napoleon now believes the war is half won.

Across the ocean, in the hills of San Domingo, the former slaves do not know Toussaint has died. They are busy drawing up their declaration of independence.

C.L.R. James, *The Black Jacobins*, 365

San Domingo, 1803: They Advance Singing

It is November 16. The blacks and mulattoes are concentrating for a final assault on the heavily fortified Le Cap and its surrounding posts.

That afternoon, Capois Death, a black officer, leads the charge through a withering crossfire of muskets and artillery.

Forward, forward!

The French drive them back. Capois's horse is killed from under him. He stands up, gestures contempt to the French, and walks ahead crying, *Forward, forward.*

A French soldier, a staunch believer in slavery, would write fifty years later:

But what men these blacks are! How they fight and how they die! One has to make war against them to know their reckless courage in braving danger when they can no longer have recourse to strategem. . . . The more they fell, the greater seemed the courage of the rest. They advanced singing. . . .

C.L.R. James, *The Black Jacobins*, 367-368

Haitians fighting

arse of a Negro, who buried him alive for insects to eat, who were well treated by Toussaint, and who, as soon as they got the chance, began their old cruelties again; for those there is no need to waste one tear or one drop of ink. The tragedy was for the blacks and the mulattoes. It was not policy but revenge, and revenge has no place in politics. The whites were no longer to be feared, and such purposeless massacres degrade and brutalise a population, especially one which was just beginning as a nation and had had so bitter a past. The people did not want it—all they wanted was freedom, and independence seemed to promise that" (James, 373-374).

The United States

Slave Revolts

In addition to the direct evidence for a large number of slave revolts in the United States is the indirect evidence found in the white man's laws that legalized branding, flogging, burning, the amputation of limbs, hamstringing, other gruesome tortures, and death to punish resistance.

Massive successful revolts did not happen in the United States the way they did in Latin America and the Caribbean. Jamaica, Surinam, and Brazil, especially in the area of Bahia, had constant rebellion.

Historian Eugene Genovese has enumerated some of the reasons for the differences. It was not that slavery was somehow more humane in the United States, or that the slaves liked their oppression there. The difference lies rather in the conditions surrounding the plantations —the terrain, the ratio of whites to slaves, etc.

Genovese's analysis suggests that if certain conditions were present there was a higher probability of a slave revolt: (1) absenteeism and depersonalization in the master-slave relationship; (2) economic distress and famine; (3) a large concentration of slaves; (4) splits in the ruling class; (5) blacks heavily outnumbering whites; (6) African-born slaves outnumbering native-born ones (Creoles); (7) a slave-holding structure that allowed the emergence of an autonomous black leadership; and (8) a geographical, social, and political environment providing the terrain and opportu-

South Carolina, 1526: First Slave Revolt

The first settlement within the present borders of the United States sees the first slave revolt. About five hundred Spaniards bring with them one hundred African slaves. The slaves revolt, and the Spaniards are so discouraged and beaten that they return to Haiti, leaving the Africans living with the indigenous population, the first of several black and native acts of solidarity.

Lerone Bennett, Jr., *Before the Mayflower,* 116

Maryland, 1664: Legal Repression

Things are getting bad from the viewpoint of the white planters. The white women are out of control. They refuse to accept white supremacy. They are not only associating with but they are marrying black men! Racism as a system does not yet exist, so the powerful rely on the only other thing besides weapons available to them—the law.

And as much as divers freeborn English women, forgetful of their free condition, and to the disgrace of our nation, do intermarry with Negro slaves. . . . or deterring such free-born women from such shameful matches, be it enacted: That whatsoever free-born woman shall intermarry with any slave, from and after the last day of the present assembly, shall serve the master of that slave during the life of her husband; and that all the issue of such free-born women, so married, shall be slaves as their fathers were.

It does not work. White women defy the law, brave lifetime servitude for themselves and slavery for their children in order to marry the men they love. The mingling of the races continues in Maryland and other colonies where similar laws are established.

Lerone Bennett, Jr., *Before the Mayflower,* 301

Stono, South Carolina, 1739: "Liberty"

In a small town twenty miles from Charleston, a group of enslaved Africans meet together and plot their freedom. With their leader, Jemmy, they break into a

95

weapons storehouse and finally gather about seventy to eighty others. Their aim is to march to the Spanish colony of Florida. They march in the open with two drums beating and shouts of "Liberty" piercing the air. For that moment they are no longer slaves, no longer objects of servitude but men—soldiers of liberty. Their step, their voices, their courage all show it.

Vincent Harding, The Other American Revolution, 13-14

New York City, 1741: A Mob Attacks

Quaco and Cuffee, two slaves, are tied to the stake, the dry kindling reaching up to their knees. The white mob yells and presses close to them. The two confess to being part of a conspiracy to set fire to the white man's fort.

The whites are hysterical. Deep down they know that the oppression of the slave only makes the fever for freedom grow hotter.

The conspirators decided on their strategy a little over a month ago, on a Sunday afternoon, over a bowl of punch. Forty or fifty of them were involved with plans to include other country people and blacks.

The mob presses closer, screaming; the authorities take this last opportunity to get them to name the other conspirators. They dangle life before the slaves like a carrot. Quaco and Cuffee refuse to name the others. They are burned alive.

Thirteen other African Americans are executed on the gallows, one is starved to death in chains, another broken on the wheel. Four whites were also involved. They, too, are executed. Two are women.

The whites carry out the torturous deaths to bring terror to the black and white community. Many slaves are still not cowed.

Years later, a young black boy enters a Louisiana town. On the post by the road are nailed two black hands. They are the hands of a rebel, recently hung on the gibbet. Some pass by in terror. They cower and step back from the line, obedient and silent. For them those black hands mean "stop." Others pass by and remember the rebellion, its cause and courage. For them the hands beckon them forward. They step over the line and join the struggle. The whites intended those hands to intimidate and silence, but in the memory of the defiant and those who want to be, those two black hands become dangerous.

Gary Nash, Red, White, and Black, 124; Herbert Aptheker, ed.,
Documentary History of the Negro People in the United States,
4-5, 31, 36

nity for maroon communities that could last long enough to threaten the plantation culture (Genovese, 11-12).

Blacks and Whites Together

In the historical record of the first Europeans in the Western Hemisphere, they refer to themselves as "Christians," "Puritans," and "English." They do not call themselves "white." The concept of "white" was of no interest in Medieval and Renaissance Europe.

The first settlers in the United States knew nothing of skin color as a distinguishing mark. Racism came later as a system to keep blacks from allying with whites and to keep African Americans first in slavery and later in a state of constant oppression.

Prejudice according to skin color, therefore, is not "natural." It is learned and it has historical roots. Those roots reach into the needs of the aristocratic elite, who wanted to hold on to their power. Divide and conquer tactics, pitting white servants against black slaves, systematically created the institution of racism, which could be called on in times of crises of power.

These crises occurred when the oppressed, no matter what the color, rebelled against injustice. It was then that the whites in power relied on the carefully cultivated system of racism.

See Lerone Bennett, Jr., *Before the Mayflower*, 297-316

Pennsylvania, 1746: Ann Greene

Ann Greene is an English servant woman, indentured to a Maryland man. Besides running away, the main thing wrong with her is that she doesn't know she's white. She has just run away with a mulatto servant named Isaac Cromwell.

Like so many thousands of other black slaves and white servants, the color of their skin is not important. What is important to them is their common oppression and common dreams of freedom. Whites and blacks, like Ann and Isaac, are constantly making common cause against the wealthy in the early days of the colonies. They are also marrying each other.

Lerone Bennett, Jr., *Before the Mayflower*, 304

Philadelphia, 1805: Mixed Marriages

Thomas Branagan is visiting Boston after travelling through the West Indies and the South. Shocked, he writes:

There are many, very many blacks who . . . begin to feel themselves consequential [and] will not be satisfied unless they get white women for wives, and are exceedingly impertinent to white people in low circumstances. . . . I solemnly swear, I have seen more white women married to, and deluded through the arts of seduction by Negroes in one year in Philadelphia, than the eight years I was visiting [West Indies and the Southern states]. . . . There are perhaps hundreds of white women thus fascinated by black men in this city, and there are thousands of black children by them at present.

Quoted in Lerone Bennett, Jr., *Before the Mayflower*, 304

Boston, 1829: Walker's Appeal

On July 2, 1839, on the Spanish slave ship "Amistad," fifty-four African slaves, led by Cinqué, mutinied, killing the captain and three of the crew. For nearly two months the Africans tried to force the remaining crew to sail them back to Africa. When they went on shore at Long Island, New York for provisions they were illlegally captured by the U.S. Navy. Cinqué and the other Africans were imprisoned and tried for murder.

Abolitionists including Lewis Tappan formed a defense committee while the U. S. government argued in court that the Africans were slaves and therefore property and that they had committed murder. The Circuit Court of Hartford ruled that the ship had been taken on the high seas and that the Africans could not be charged with murder.

The Africans were set free. The next year they returned to their homeland, Sierra Leone.

Born free, David Walker is one of those abolitionists who calls for universal emancipation of all balcks in Africa, the West Indies and the United States. His appeal is one of the most militant calls for the end of slavery.

Remember, Americans, that we must and shall be free and as enlightened as you are. Will you wait until we shall under God obtain our liberty by the crushing arm of power? Will it not be dreadful for you? I speak, Americans, for your own good. We must and shall be free, I say, in spite of you. You may do your best to keep us in wretchedness and misery to enrich you and your children, but God will deliver us from under you. And wo, wo will be to you if we have to obtain our freedom by fighting. Throw away your fears and prejudices, then, and enlighten us and treat us like men, and we will like you more than we do now hate you; and tell us now no more about colonization, for America is as much our country as it is yours.

William F. Cheek, *Black Resistance before the Civil War,* 143

Buffalo, New York, 1843: Four Million

A new level of anger is rising in the black community. Impatience coupled with the biblical sense of redemption becomes a volatile mixture, especially in the words of Rev. Henry Highland Garnet. Garnet is a young abolitionist minister from Troy, New York. The grandson of a Mandingo chieftain, he was born on a plantation in Maryland. His father escaped, taking the family to freedom when Henry was ten years old. As this twenty-seven- year-old black man steps to the podium at the

Black Abolitionists

Much of the history of abolitionism has been written about whites struggling to eradicate slavery. Yet black people instigated much of the effort to abolish slavery. They freed themselves in a myriad ways by running away, operating the underground railroad, speaking, and agitating for abolition. Blacks bankrolled and subscribed to William Lloyd Garrison's famous paper *The Liberator.* In the 1830s the pioneer black abolitionists like David Walker paved the way for the giants of the 1840s.

Charles Lenox Remond was the first black preacher to become a professional antislavery lecturer. Samuel Ringgold Ward and Henry Highland Garnet were black pastors and activists. Martin R. Delaney was the first major black nationalist. Delaney wanted people to gain respect and be proud of being black. In the 1850s he advocated for a black state in Central America, the Western United States or Africa. The most famous of the black abolitionists of this period were Sojourner Truth, Harriet

Tubman, and Frederick Douglass. By far the most radical voices calling for an immediate end to slavery were black.

See Lerone Bennett, Jr., *Before the Mayflower*, 140-160

black anti-slavery convention, a rush of anticipation sweeps the crowd.

Think how many tears you have poured out upon the soil which you have cultivated with unrequited toil and enriched with your blood; and then go to your lordly enslavers and tell them plainly that you are determined to be free. Appeal to their sense of justice, and tell them that they have no more right to oppress you than you have to enslave them.

Tell them in language which they cannot misunderstand of the exceeding sinfulness of slavery, and of the future judgement, and of the righteous retributions of an indignant God. Inform them that all you desire is <u>freedom</u>, and that nothing else will suffice. . . . You had better all die immediately—than live slaves and entail your wretchedness upon their posterity.

He then invokes the names of black heroes like Nathaniel Turner and Denmark Vesey who led slave revolts in the South; Joseph Cinqué, the leader of the slave revolt on board the slave ship "Amistad"; Madison Washington, who successfully led the slave revolt on board the slave ship "Creole." The Amistad slaves gained their freedom and sailed back to Sierra Leone. The Creole rebels went to Nassau and freedom.

And then in the style of the great black preachers he ends:

Brethren, arise, arise! Strike for your lives and liberties. Now is the day and the hour. Let every slave throughout the land do this, and the days of slavery are numbered. You cannot be more oppressed than you have been—you cannot suffer greater cruelties than you have already. Remember that you are <u>four millions!</u>

Let your motto be resistance! resistance! <u>resistance!</u> No oppressed people have ever secured their liberty without resistance. What kind of resistance you had better make, you must decide by the circumstances that surround you and according to the suggestion of expediency. Brethren, adieu! Trust in the living God. Labor for the peace of the human race, and remember that you are <u>four millions!</u>

Quoted in William F. Cheek, *Black Resistance before the Civil War*, 143-146, See also Vincent Harding, *The Other American Revoluton*, 49

Georgia to Philadelphia, 1848: Masquerade

"Now William," said Ellen, "listen to me and take my advice, and we shall be free in less than a month." "Let me hear your plans, then," said William. "Take part of your money and purchase me a good suit of gentlemen's apparel, and when the white people give us our holiday, let us go off to the north. I am white enough to go as the master, and you can pass as my servant." "But you are not tall enough for a man," said the husband. "Get me a pair of high-heeled boots, and they will bring me up more than an inch, and get me a very high hat, then I'll do," rejoined the wife. "But then, my dear, you would make a very boyish looking man, with no whiskers or moustache," remarked William. "I could bind up my face in a handkerchief," said Ellen, "as if I was suffering from the toothache, and then no one would discover the want of a beard." "What if you are called upon to write your name in the books at the hotels?" "I would also bind up my right hand and put it in a sling, and that would be an excuse for not writing." "I fear that you could not carry out the deception for so long a time, for it must be several hundred miles to the free States," said William. "Come, William" entreated his wife, don't be a coward! Get me the clothes, and I promise you we shall both be free in a couple of days. You have money enough to fit me out and to pay our passage to the North."

The masquerade succeeds. Abolitionists welcome Ellen and William Craft into Philadelphia on Christmas morning.

Dorothy Sterling, ed., *We Are Your Sisters*, 62-64

The South, 1840s: Day-to-Day Resistance

A daughter remembers what her slave mother taught her:

The one doctrine of my mother's teaching which was branded upon my senses was that I should never let anyone abuse me. "I'll kill you, gal, if you don't stand up for yourself," she would say. Fight, and if you can't fight, kick; if you can't kick, then bite.

Gerda Lerner, ed., *Black Women in White America*, 35

Day to Day Resistance

Slave resistance took a variety of forms, but for every dramatic revolt there were dozens of instances of individual acts of resistance. More common than organized, large-scale rebellion was the daily resistance of running away, slowing down work, refusing to cooperate, striking back at a master, or hiding children in the woods to save them from being sold.

Running away required ingenuity and courage. Some slave women disguised themselves as men or boys. Some lived in caves close to the plantation to keep in touch with their families. One simply walked off the plantation, her children in her arms. Another woman had herself sealed in a crate as cargo, not to be opened until she arrived North.

Running away almost always meant enduring hardships. The Littles were a slave couple who walked hundreds of miles barefoot, with blisters on their feet, braving wolves, bounty hunters, and masses of mosquitos to reach Chicago and freedom.

Those who remained behind also resisted. Milla Granson, a slave woman, ran a midnight school teaching other slaves to read and write from twelve at night until two in the morning. A number of them wrote their own passes and started for Canada. Some mothers worked extra hours doing wash and ironing and after years saved enough money to buy their children from slavery. Some of those purchases cost hundreds of dollars.

As part of resistance, slaves developed a system of reconnaissance among white folks and forms of communication among slaves that were undetected by whites.

All these forms of resistance aimed at reclaiming the power taken away from blacks by the oppressive system of slavery and racism. In a variety of ways slaves were able to take charge of their lives and continue to hold on to their human dignity.

See Dorothy Sterling, ed., *We Are Your Sisters* and Gerda Lerner, ed., *Black Women in White America*

The South, 1840s: "Foolin' Massa"

Without any knowledge of newspapers, or books, or telegraphy, the slaves have their own way of gathering news from the whole country. They have secret signs, an "Underground Telephone". . . . Intuitively they learn all the tricks of dramatic art. Their perceptions are quickened. When seemingly absorbed in work, they see and hear all that is going on around them. They memorize with wonderful ease and correctness. . . .

One former slave woman says, "My father and the other boys used to crawl under the house an' lie on the ground to hear massa read the newspaper to missis when they first began to talk about the [Civil] war ."

"I couldn't read but my uncle could, "says another. "I was a waiting-maid, an' used to help missis to dress in the morning. If massa wanted to tell her something he didn't want me to know, he used to spell it out. I could remember the letters, an' as soon as I got away I ran to uncle an' spelled them over to him, an' he told me what they meant."

I [the interviewer] was attracted by this, and asked if she could do this now.

"Try me missis, try me an' see!" she exclaimed. So I spelled a long sentence as rapidly as possible, without stopping between the words. She immediately repeated . . . without missing a letter.

Gerda Lerner, ed., *Black Women in White America*, 29-30

Massachusetts, 1851: Shadrach

A year before the U.S. Congress passed the Fugitive Slave Law, making it illegal to harbor or help runaway slaves, Rev. Lewis Hayden, a black preacher, and twenty of his friends swept into a Massachusetts courtroom and spirited the slave Shadrach away before he was sent back into slavery.

Several of the abductors are now being tried. Their guilt is undeniable; there were many witnesses. The jury deliberates a long time. All believe them guilty except one. Whatever they do they cannot convince this man to convict them. It is a hung jury. The conspirators go free.

The man who held out for acquittal himself drove Shadrach from Concord to Leominster during his escape.

See Alice Felt Tyler, *Freedom's Ferment*

101

New York, 1857: Liberty Born of Struggle

Frederick Douglass, a freed slave, gives one of his greatest speeches at the West India Emancipation Celebration:

The whole history of the progress of human liberty shows that all concessions yet made to her august claims have been born of struggle. . . . If there is no struggle there is no progress. Those who profess to favor freedom and yet deprecate agitation, are men who want crops without plowing up the ground. They want rain without thunder and lightning. They want the ocean without the awful roar of its many waters. The struggle may be a moral one; or it may be a physical one; or it may be both moral and physical, but it must be a struggle. Power concedes nothing without a demand. It never did and it never will. . . .

Howard Zinn, *A People's History of the United States*, 179

The South, 1873: Reconstruction

The end of the Civil War brings new political power to blacks. Three years before a former slave was elected a U.S. senator from Mississippi, and now seven blacks are in the U.S House of Representatives. There are black postmasters, state legislators, policemen, and mayors. It seems like a new day is dawning. It is an era of firsts: the first black diplomat, the first black woman lawyer, the first black graduate of Harvard University, the first black judges. . . .

Political rights are possible, but economic rights are denied. Frederick Douglass, Thaddeus Stevens, and Charles Sumner lead the fight for *forty acres and a mule.* They want the U.S. government to break up the large plantations and give the newly freed blacks forty acres so they can really start a new life. Congress fails to pass any such legislation, so the southern blacks are forced into sharecropping.

This arrangement soon becomes a new system of oppression, as the black farmers have to rely on whites for loans and for marketing their crops. They fall into debt and the whites hold them in another form of slavery—debt slavery.

See Lerone Bennett, Jr., *Before the Mayflower*

The South, 1890s: Separate and Unequal

In the first generation after the Civil War, blacks and whites mingled in every activity. For two decades whites worked to undermine the gains of Reconstruction. In 1873 the U.S. Supreme Court ruled that there were two kinds of citizenship—state and federal—and that the Fourteenth Amendment that guaranteed civil rights to all people was designed to protect the rights of federal citizenship only.

In a number of civil rights cases in 1883 the high court ruled that states could not discriminate but at the same time created an opening for individuals to do so. By the 1890s many southern states had passed laws segregating railroads and other facilities. There were now two Americas, one white, the other black—separate and unequal.

Chicago, 1901: Ida B. Wells

The century has just turned. Nine out of every ten black people live in the South. The Jim Crow laws are in full effect.

Ida B. Wells was born in Holly Springs, Mississippi. Orphaned at an early age, she worked her way through college and became a journalist. Mobs finally drove her from the South because of her fierce editorials against lynching. Settling in Chicago, she continues to write and speak out against lynching. She reports that from 1878 to 1898, ten thousand black people have been lynched. In the South, the lynchings are justified because the blacks involved have raped a white women. In her careful investigation into the record

... it shows that men, not a few, but hundreds have been lynched for misdemeanors, while others have suffered death for no offense known to the law, the causes assigned being "mistaken identity," "insult," "bad reputation," "unpopularity," "violating contract," "running quarantine," "giving evidence," "frightening children by shooting at rabbits," etc.

And as far as the charge of rape goes, in 1900 less than fifteen per cent were so charged.

Ida B. Wells begins a national campaign to stop lynching.

Herbert Aptheker, ed., *Documentary History of the Negro People in the United States*, 1:804

United States, 1904: Causes of Lynching

Black activist Mary Church Terrell, in her fight to stop lynching, speaks out:

Before 1904 was three months old, 31 negroes had been lynched. Of this number, 15 were murdered within one week in Arkansas, and one was shot to death in Springfield, Ohio, by a mob composed of men who did not take the trouble to wear masks. Hanging, shooting, and burning black men, women, and children in the United States have become so common that such occurrences create but little sensation and evoke but slight comment now.

... It is a great mistake to suppose that rape is the real cause of lynching in the South. Beginning with the Ku Klux Klan the negro has been constantly subjected to some form of organized violence ever since he became free. It is easy to prove that rape is simply the pretext and not the cause of lynching. Statistics show that, out of every 100 negroes who are lynched, from 75-85 are not even accused of this crime,

I have seen very small white children hang their black dolls.

It is not the child's fault, he is simply an apt pupil.

Gerda Lerner, ed., *Black Women in White America*, 147

and many who are accused of it are innocent. . . .

What then is the cause of lynching? At the last analysis, it will be discovered that there are just two causes of lynching. In the first place, it is due to race hatred, the hatred of a stronger people toward a weaker who were once held as slaves. In the second place, it is due to the lawlessness so prevalent in the section where nine-tenths of the lynchings occur. . . .

Lynching is the aftermath of slavery. The white men who shoot negroes to death and flay them while alive, and the white women who apply flaming torches to their oil-soaked bodies today, are the sons and daughters of women who had but little, if any, compassion on the race when it was enslaved. . . .

Gerda Lerner, ed., *Black Women in White America*, 207-209

We return.

We return from fighting.

We return fighting.

W.E.B. Dubois

Washington D.C., 1913: Jubilee

This is the fiftieth anniversary of the Emancipation Proclamation, the year of jubilee. President Woodrow Wilson orders the segregation of restaurants, offices, and facilities in the Post Office, Treasury, Interior Department, and Library of Congress. In four years he will lead the United States into World War I, in order to "make the world safe for democracy."

Today he greets an African American delegation saying: *Segregation is not humiliating, but a benefit and ought to be so regarded by you gentlemen.*

Stereotypes, Distortions, and Omissions, 28

East St. Louis, 1917: Race Riot

Whites are protesting the employment of blacks. The whites call in the militia and police. Lieutenant Arbuckle of the United States Army Reserve Corp is in East St. Louis on business on July 2. He sees whites burning railway cars in yards...members of the militia of Illinois shooting blacks. He sees policeman of East St. Louis shooting blacks. He sees mobs go to the homes of blacks and nail boards over the doors and windows and then set fire and burn them up. He sees the whites take little children out of the arms of their mothers and throw them into the fires and burn them up.

Paul Jacobs and Saul Landau, *To Serve the Devil*, I: 175

Effects of World War I

Many African Americans fought in World War I. Although the army was segregated and they suffered many of the same abuses and name-calling they endured in the United States, there was a change in them when they returned home after being told they were fighting to make the world safe for democracy. The contradictions of their own unjust situation became much clearer. They came home to poverty, discrimination, and the resurgence of white hatred.

Something had to give. And in 1919 it did as the nation exploded into twenty-six different outbreaks of racial violence.

1919: Red Summer

Historian Vincent Harding summarizes the atmosphere of 1919:

"From Charleston, South Carolina, to Longview, Texas, from Washington D.C. to Chicago, Illinois, black and white people went to war on the streets. There were various specific occasions: the taunting attacks of arrogant white servicemen; the movement of white mobs against black people; the violent reaction of whites to the continuing black search for a place to live and breathe.

"Most often the initial intention of the whites was the same: to invade the black community, to attempt another slaughter, another scorched earth. But in 1919, the outcome was different, a new stage in history had been reached.

"Throughout the nation that spring and summer, thousands of black people decided to fight back, to move out into the streets against the white aggressors. Often they pressed on to carry the offensive against their historic oppressors. Especially in Washington and Chicago, the fighting was fierce and extensive.

"Black men set up roadblocks of wood, bricks, and concrete on the streets of their communities. Both blacks and whites used cars of armed men to roar like armed military vehicles through the opposite communities. Black snipers operated from the windows of houses. Bands of attackers swooped down on persons of the opposite race who happened into their territory. Every-

New York, 1917: Silent Parade of Protest

It is July 28 and the National Association for the Advancement of Colored People (NAACP) is waging an effective campaign against lynching. The little children, dressed in white, are leading them. Behind them march the women in white followed by the men in black, the color of mourning. Although silent, they carry their words of protest on banners and streamers.

Just before the American flag is a cloth banner with sewn letters: *Your hands are full of blood.*

The children carry signs: *Mother, do lynchers go to heaven? Mr. President, why not make America safe for democracy?*

On Fifth Avenue, twenty thousand African American feet walk for justice.

Lerone Bennett, Jr., *Before the Mayflower*, 349

Valdosta, Georgia, 1918: Lynching

The white mob hangs Mary Turner from a tree. A couple of them douse her with gasoline and motor oil. Another takes a match. When she has finished burning, a man steps forward with a pocket knife and slits open her abdomen. *Out tumbled the prematurely born child. Two feeble cries it gave—and received for the answer the heel of a stalwart man, as life was ground out of the tiny form.*

During this year, whites lynch sixty people.

Lerone Bennett, Jr., *Before the Mayflower*, 352

France, 1918: Secret Orders

Three of the four all-black regiments fighting in World War I receive the Croix de Guerre for valor. U.S. military police arrest black soldiers for walking down the street with French women.

Secret orders from General Pershing's headquarters to the French Mission:

1. We must prevent the rise of any pronounced degree of intimacy between French officers and black officers. . . . We cannot deal with them [black officers] on the same plane as with the white American officer without deeply wounding the latter. We must not eat with them, must not shake hands or seek to talk or meet with them outside of the requirements of military service.

2. We must not commend too highly the American troops, particularly in the presence of [white] Americans. . . .

3. Make a point of keeping the native cantonment popu-lation from "spoiling" the Negroes. [White] Americans become greatly incensed at any public expression of intimacy between white women and black men.

Lerone Bennett, Jr., *Before the Mayflower*, 348-349

United States, 1919: Red Summer

Black troops come home after fighting what they were told was "the war to make the world safe for democracy." This year there are seventy-six lynchings. Segregation is everywhere. In the South black sharecroppers are en-slaved by a debt system that keeps whites in power. The Ku Klux Klan is resurging. What could not be won with silent protest or rational debate spills into the streets of America.

Poet Claude McKay, part of what is to be called the Harlem Renaissance, writes:

If we must die, let it not be like hogs,
Hunted and penned in an inglorious spot,
While round us bark the mad and hungry dogs,
Making their mock of our accursed lot.
If we must die, O let us nobly die....
Like men we'll face the murderous, cowardly pack,
Pressed to the wall, dying, but fighting back!

Twenty-six race riots explode throughout the country.

Lerone Bennett, Jr., *Before the Mayflower*, 353;
Vincent Harding, *The Other American Revolution*, 105

where, black veterans played a central role in the fighting, often using weapons they had managed to smuggle back into the black commu-nity, weapons as large as machine guns. In Chicago, it lasted for almost a week, spreading over much of that sprawling city" (Harding, 104-105).

A New Form of Resistance

The resistance of blacks in the South took another form as the new century began. They simply left the area. In 1910 the first wave of black migration came north. During that decade 300,000 blacks moved, mostly to the large urban areas of Chicago, Detroit, and New York. From 1920 to 1930 the second wave of 1,300,000 came north. The third wave in the 1930s of 1,500,000 and the fourth wave in the 1940s of 2,500,000 completed the largest migration in U.S. history.

The Black Freedom Movement Continues

The Black Freedom Movement surged forward from 1956 to 1972. The energy of resistance that young African Americans mobilized during that period has rarely been equaled in U.S. history.

In 1954, the U.S. Supreme Court, in its historic Brown vs. the Board of Education case, said that it was illegal to segregate schools according to race.

In 1956 Rosa Parks refused to move to the back of the bus in Montgomery, Alabama, igniting a bus boycott that lasted over a year and began what has been called the civil rights movement.

In 1960 four North Carolina A&T students sat in at a Woolworth's lunch counter in Greensboro. They returned with more students until they were finally served. As a tactic, the sit-ins spread like wildfire across the South. In that year alone fifty thousand protestors carried out sit-ins in seventy-eight communities, resulting in two thousand arrests.

The sit-ins were spontaneous eruptions of pent-up anger over decades of injustices. By themselves they had no direction. Since most were organized by students, Ella Baker of the Southern Christian Leadership Conference brought together some of the leaders, and they founded the Student Nonviolent Coordinating Committee (SNCC). SNCC was to play a role in the future of deepening and advancing the Black Free-

Montgomery, Alabama, 1955: Front of the Bus

A few weeks earlier she was at a leadership training workshop at Highlander Folk School in the Tennessee mountains. Rosa Parks is a seamstress by trade, quiet but determined. When she boards the bus that night after a long day at work, she doesn't feel defiant, just tired. But when the bus driver tells her to move to the back of the bus so that a white can sit in her seat, she refuses. She is arrested and the women of Montgomery swing into action.

Jo Ann Gibson Robinson hears about the arrest and realizes that now is the time for action. For a year, she and other women have been planning a bus boycott, just waiting for the right moment. That moment has now arrived. She mimeographs the first leaflet calling for a boycott. She and other women convince the black Montgomery pastors to lead it. The women organize carpools, raise money, negotiate with the white authorities, pass out leaflets; in short, do all the behind the scenes activities that make the boycott work.

For over a year they walk miles to work, car pool, sing, encourage each other to keep from losing hope. By the end, a black person can sit wherever he or she wants to on the bus.

A young preacher who was thrown into leadership of the boycott becomes known outside of Montgomery. His name—Martin Luther King, Jr.

See Jo Ann Gibson Robinson, *The Montgomery Bus Boycott and the Women Who Started It*

Greensboro, 1960: Sit-in

Late Monday afternoon, February 1, four black freshmen from North Carolina A&T take seats at a downtown Woolworth's lunch counter. They ask for service but receive none. When the counter closes they return to campus.

The following morning thirty students return and occupy half of the lunch counter. They stay for two hours without being served. The next day they return, filling all sixty-six seats at the counter. They are now national news, inspiring sit-ins all across the South. In some places ice cream sundaes are poured over the protestors' heads and they have to endure insults, taunts, and violence. Most protestors keep their poise and their sense of humor.

A waitress tells a pair of sit-inners, *I'm sorry, but we don't serve Negroes here. Oh, we don't eat them either,* comes the reply.

Claybourne Carson, *In Struggle,* 11-12

Jackson, Mississippi, 1961: Freedom Rides

The whites firebomb a bus full of Freedom Riders in Anniston, Georgia. White mobs regularly beat riders as they leave the buses. But Parchman State Penitentiary is reserved for the real criminals—the Freedom Riders themselves. They have all of their belongings taken. Strip searched, they are put under maximum security. When they begin singing the guards threaten to take away their mattresses. They keep singing and the guards take the mattresses.

They write freedom songs: *Woke up this morning with my mind set on freedom. . . .* The guards take their sheets. They keep singing. The guards take their toothbrushes and towels. They keep singing, getting louder all the time.

They sleep for three nights on steel springs without covers and with cold air deliberately blown on them.

And in the morning when they awaken after restless, sleepless nights, *their minds are set on freedom. . . .*

Howard Zinn, *SNCC: The New Abolitionists,* 54-55

McComb, Mississippi, 1962: Defiance

Diane Nash Bevel is charged with contributing to the delinquency of minors because she taught nonviolent tactics to McComb teenagers. She has just found out that she is pregnant and now wants to refuse her option for appeal and take the jail sentence.

I believe if I go to jail now it may help hasten that day when my child and all children will be free—not only on the day of their birth but for all their lives.

The judge, not wanting to risk adverse publicity, suspends her sentence. She still serves ten days for sitting on the white side of the courtroom.

Claybourne Carson, *In Struggle,* 68

dom Movement beyond the immediate goals of civil rights.

Freedom Rides

In 1961 the initiative passed to the Congress on Racial Equality (CORE) as they initiated freedom rides in the South, reviving a tactic used in 1947.

Under federal law, it was illegal to have segregated buses and waiting rooms. But in the South local authorities never enforced the law. Determined to confront this injustice, seven blacks and six whites left Washington D.C. on May 4. They integrated the buses; when the bus stopped the whites went into the black waiting room and the blacks into the white one.

The group was met with violence. One rider had to have fifty stitches in his head, and a white man from Madison, Wisconsin, was so badly beaten by a white mob that he was damaged for life.

SNCC did not want the violence to stop the rides so they took up the call for more riders. When arrested they began to chant, "Jail, No Bail." Their tactic was to fill the jails and bring national attention to the injustice. Their courage and commitment became contagious as thousands of young people joined in the movement.

SNCC tactics were simple. Organizers would go into the most racist communities and look for the indigenous black leadership. One commented, "There was always a mama. She is usually a militant woman in the community, outspoken, understanding, and willing to catch hell, having already caught her share." Women like these were at the heart of the movement.

Respect in the black community as well as in SNCC was measured by how many times an organizer went to jail. As early as 1962 many SNCC organizers had been jailed more than twenty times and some had been beaten.

Voter Registration

In 1962 the spontaneous sit-ins gave way to door-to-door voter registration drives. Whites had systematically denied the right to vote to black people for generations. Using poll taxes, literacy tests, and sheer intimidation, whites kept blacks from registering. SNCC and other civil rights groups were out to change that.

Charles Sherrod and Cordell Reagon talked to people about there being "worse chains than jail and prison." They referred to a system that imprisons the mind and robs people of their creativity. They mocked the system that taught people how to be "good Negroes" instead of good people. As organizers they told people what had been accomplished through resistance and registration.

In 1963 in the South, 930 public protests took place in 115 cities. Over twenty thousand persons were arrested. Ten deaths were directly related to the protests, and at least thirty-five bombings occurred. In Birmingham, the viciousness of racism was brought home to the U.S. public as Eugene "Bull" Connor, director of public

Winona, Mississippi, 1963: Freedom

Fanny Lou Hamer, Annell Ponder, and four other African Americans are returning from a meeting in South Carolina. As a matter of principle, when they get off the bus in Winona, they walk into the white waiting room. The police arrest them all. In jail the police separate them. Annell, in her twenties, begins screaming and praying to God to forgive them. They take Fanny Lou to a cell where the police force two black prisoners to beat her all over her body with a night stick. Fanny Lou Hamer joined the Freedom riders because *the only thing they could do to me was kill me and it seemed like they's been trying to do that a little bit at a time ever since I could remember.*

The next day a group of SNCC people arrive, led by Lawrence Guyot, a twenty-three-year-old graduate of Tugaloo College. Lawrence insists on seeing the prisoners and refuses to answer the State Trooper with "Yes, sir" and "No, sir." After slapping him, the trooper hands Guyot over to the White Citizen's Council, who beat him so badly he cannot lift his arms. His eyes swell shut.

Finally, another SNCC worker arrives and gains entrance to Annell's cell. Her face is also swollen, she can barely talk. She looks at the visitor and whispers one word . . . *freedom.*

Howard Zinn, *SNCC: The New Abolitionists,* 94-95

Mississippi, 1965: Black Power

Black power! shouts Stokely Carmichael, and the crowd enthusiastically responds, *Black power!* The Northern cities are in flames. Four black children are killed in a church bombing while attending Sunday school in a Birmingham Baptist Church. The litany of deaths and violence seems endless. Some blacks are now talking about self-defense.

. . . for once, black people are going to use the words they want to use—not just the words whites want to hear.

Claybourne Carson, *In Struggle,* 219

Harlem, 1964: Malcolm X

When Malcolm rises to speak, he talks in terms that are plain, direct, devoid of flowery trimming. He uses metaphors and figures of speech that are lean and simple, rooted in the ordinary experiences of his audiences. He knows their minds and heart because he identifies with them. They laugh, they learn, they move forward. He is down-to-earth and totally consumed by love for the oppressed.

Malcolm founds the Organization of Afro-American Unity in order to put before the United Nations the petition charging the United States government with genocide against twenty-two million black Americans.

> *The key to our success lies in <u>united action</u>. . . . As long as the freedom struggle of the 22 million Afro Americans is labeled a civil rights issue it remains a domestic problem under the jurisdiction of the United States. . . .But once our struggle is lifted. . .to the level of <u>human rights</u>, our freedom struggle has then become <u>internationalized</u>.*
>
> Malcolm X

. . .We assert that in those areas where the government is either unable or unwilling to protect the lives and property of our people, that our people are within their rights to protect themselves by whatever means necessary. . . .

. . .Basically, there are two kinds of power that count in America: economic and political, with social power deriving from the two. In order for Afro-Americans to control their destiny, they must be able to control and affect the decisions which control their destiny: economic, political and social, This can only be done through organization. . . .

Malcolm X does not equivocate. He goes straight to the point: *We are living in an era of revolution, and the revolt of the American Negro is part of that rebellion against oppression and colonization which has characterized this era . . . We are today seeing a global rebellion of the oppressed against the oppressor, the exploited against the exploiter.*

This man is dangerous. In a few months he will be killed.

Manning Marable, *Race, Reform and Rebellion*, 95
John Henrik Clarke, editor, *Malcolm X: The Man and His Times*,
xvii, 337, 339

New York, 1965: Another Martyr

It is February 21. A few days before, arsonists firebombed the house of Malcolm X where he and his family were sleeping. He is scheduled to speak tonight. Talking to Brother Earl he says, *. . .I always knew it would end like this. . . . Brother, I'm sorry I never had a chance to tell you about my father. He, too, tried to help the people and was hunted and finally killed by the powers of that day. Now, I know how he must have felt, with a family and all.*

. . .Don't look so sad. I'm no stranger to danger. I have lived with danger all of my life. I never expected to die of old age. I know the power structure will not let me. I know that I have done the very best that I could to help our people. . . . I did not want an organization that depended on the life of one man. The organization must be able to survive on its own.

The first shot rings out. Then a pause and a long series of shots. Malcolm X, the *black shining prince*, is dead.

safety, unleashed fire hoses and police dogs against marchers. Martin Luther King was arrested there, writing from prison his famous "Letter from Birmingham Jail." Also that year more than two hundred thousand people converged on Washington demanding "Freedom . . . Now!"

In 1964, SNCC went into Mississippi with a voter education and registration drive that it called Freedom Summer. Organizers set up freedom schools for children to learn about their African American roots of resistance. They went into small towns where the law and the white citizens councils were one and the same. That summer, the bodies of three of those freedom workers were dragged from a ditch on the same day that Lyndon Johnson announced the U.S. bombing of Vietnam.

By 1965, Freedom Summer had put SNCC into the national limelight. More militant than their older counterparts in the movement, they began to see both the depth of racism in the United States and the need to make international connections.

Selma, Alabama, exploded on the scene as state troopers stopped peaceful marchers from crossing Pettis Bridge. When the marchers refused to turn around, the police beat them with billy clubs and threw cannisters of tear gas.

Continued white violence made many blacks wonder about the effectiveness of nonviolence. In a rural Alabama county that year, the Black Panther Party was formed. Stokley Carmichael, a SNCC organizer who had been arrested twenty-seven times, began using the slogan "Black Power." It resonated with the people as their frustration grew in the face of white racism.

In the Watts neighborhood of Los Angeles, the first of several urban riots exploded. SNCC was beginning to make the connections between racism at home and imperialism abroad. Why were young black men dying to save democracy in Vietnam when they were kept from voting at home?

In the summer of 1967, 150 cities were hit by urban rebellions, including Newark and Detroit. The Vietnam War was heating up; four hundred thousand U.S. soldiers were fighting there. Martin Luther King became outspoken in his criticism of the Vietnam War. He too was making the economic and international connections with racism at home and injustice and intervention abroad. Those in power understood how dangerous his statements were for them.

See Vincent Harding, *The Other American Revolution*, and Claybourne Carson, *In Struggle*

Two decades later, evidence will surface of the involvement of the FBI and other federal agencies in his assassination.

John Henrik Clarke, editor, *Malcolm X: The Man and His Times*, 91, 95
Manning Marable, *Race, Reform and Rebellion: The Second Reconstruction in Black America, 1945-1982*, 100

The North, 1967: The Radical King

As the Vietnam War drags on and white violence continues, Martin Luther King becomes radicalized. The FBI is after him because his words sound more and more like those of the young SNCC militants.

He sees now the limits of the U. S. government and how it is imperative for black people to formulate new tactics that no longer depend upon the goodwill of that government. These tactics will have to *compel unwilling authorities to yield to the mandates of justice.*

The dispossessed of this nation—the poor, both white and Negro—live in a cruelly unjust society. They must organize a revolution against that injustice, not against the lives of the persons who are their fellow citizens, but against the structures through which the society is refusing to. . .lift the load of poverty.

The storm is rising against the priveleged minority of the earth, from which there is no shelter in isolation or armament. The storm will not abate until a just distribution of the fruits of the earth enables men everywhere to live in dignity and human decency. The American Negro. . . may be the vanguard of a prolonged struggle that may change the shape of the world, as billions of deprived shake and transform the earth in their quest for life, liberty and justice.

This is not the King who says, *I have a dream. . . .* This is not the King seeking integration and civil rights. This is the King demanding revolution and redistribution of the world's wealth.

He is beginning to see the connections between Latin American problems and United States policies. *Americans must help their nation repent of her modern economic imperialism.* This man is now too dangerous. In a few months he will be killed.

Vincent Harding, *The Other American Revolution,* 198-199

Washington D.C., 1967: COINTELPRO

Black militancy is on the rise. People are in motion. The U. S. government is worried.

J. Edgar Hoover, head of the FBI issues a memo concerning a counterintelligence program (COINTELPRO) against black nationalist groups. . . . *The purpose of this new counterintelligence endeavor is to expose, disrupt, misdirect, discredit, or otherwise neutralize the activities of black nationalist hate-type organizations and groupings, their leadership, spokesmen, membership, and supporters. . . .*

The memo directs field offices to keep these operations totally secret. What emerges is a variety of tactics to carry out this directive.

An internal memo congratulates themselves on a job well done: *shootings, beatings and a high degree of unrest continue to prevail in the ghetto area. . .it is felt that a substantial amount of the unrest is directly attributable to this program.*

In the guise of infiltrating white hate groups, the FBI actually arms, directs, and protects a variety of racist organizations which they use to attack progressive groups.

The FBI targets CORE, SCLC, SNCC—all veteran civil rights organizations. The black leaders who cannot be silenced, embarrassed, discredited, or co-opted are killed.

Brian Glick, *War at Home: Covert Action Against U.S. Activists and What You Can Do About It,* 41-62

Washington D.C., 1969: FBI Internal Memo

For maximum effectiveness of the counterintelligence program, and to prevent wasted effort, long-range goals are being set.

> *. . .Prevent the coalition of militant black nationalist groups. In unity there is strength. . .*
>
> *. . .Prevent the rise of a "messiah" who could unify, and electrify, the militant black nationalist movement. . . .*
>
> *. . .Prevent militant black nationalist groups and leaders from gaining respectability. . . . Prevent the long-range growth of militant black nationalist organizations, especially among youth.*

Brian Glick, *War at Home,* 78-79

Counter Intelligence Program (COINTELPRO)

FBI agents infiltrated progressive groups and became *provocateurs* directed to disrupt, spread rumors, provoke splits, sabotage activities, steal funds, exacerbate rivalries, publicly embarrass leaders and generally undermine trust and instill fear among groups and supporters. From the outside, the FBI waged psychological warfare against progressive groups and leaders by planting false media stories, passing out bogus leaflets and publications, forging correspondence, writing inflammatory letters, tampering with the mail and telephone and generally creating "disinformation." The FBI also used false arrest, conspicuous surveillance, and political trials to harass leaders and activists. And finally, the FBI resorted to violence. The FBI maneuvered the Mafia to move against activist-comedian Dick Gregory and incited violent rivals to attack Malcolm X and the Black Panther Party.

Brian Glick, *War at Home: Covert Action Against U.S. Activists and What You Can Do About It,* 41-62

Oakland, 1969: The Black Panther Party

They run a free breakfast program for young black kids; they monitor police brutality; they open a free health clinic; they educate each other about the history of black struggle in the United States. They also carry guns in self-defense.

Part of their ten-point program says: *We want freedom. We want power to determine the destiny of our Black Community. We want land, bread, housing, education, clothing, justice and peace.*

By July, they are the targets of 233 separate actions under the FBI's COINTELPRO operations. By the end of the year, twenty-seven Black Panthers are dead from police bullets. Over seven hundred are in jail or arrested.

Brian Glick, *War at Home,* 18 and Manning Marable, *Race, Reform and Rebellion,* 122, 125

Chicago, 1969: Fred Hampton and Mark Clark

Fred Hampton is a charismatic black leader pulling together a "rainbow" coalition of progressive groups. Taking on national leadership of the group in the wake of the jailing and exile of other leaders, Hampton becomes a prime target of COINTELPRO. On December 4, after Fred Hampton has been drugged asleep by an FBI infiltrator, a fourteen-man police hit squad with automatic weapons attack. Fred Hampton and Chicago Black Panther leader Mark Clark are killed. A year later, a federal grand jury find that the police fired eighty-three shots into the apartment, while only one shot was fired at the police.

An elaborate cover-up begins. It will take years before the parents and survivors will be paid $1.8 million in damages by federal and local governments for the carnage of that winter night.

Brian Glick, *War at Home,* 63, and Manning Marable, *Race, Reform and Rebellion,* 142

Logo of the Peace and Dignity Journeys, 1992. This non-profit organization plans a cross-country relay from Alaska to Argentina, creating an event that honors and recognizes the indigenous people throughout the continent for their five hundred years of struggle and survival.

Indigenous Resistance: North America

Jamestown, 1622: "Native Infidels"

The joint-stock company from London that financed the Jamestown settlement expected large profits. Edward Waterhouse, an official of the company, writing after the attack by the Powhatans, outlines the theory and tactics that would guide the attitudes of most European settlers for generations in their relations with the native population.

Because our hands which before were tied with gentlenesse and faire usage, are now set at liberty by the treacherous violence of the Savages, not untying the knot, but cutting it: So that we, who hitherto have had possession of no more ground then their waste, and our purchase gained: may now by right of Warre, and Law of Nations, invade the Country, and destroy them who sought to destroy us: whereby we shall enjoy our cultivated places, turning the laborious Mattocke into the

First Settlement

Jamestown, the first permanent European colony in what was to be the United States, was located in the territory of the Great Powhatan Confederacy. The Jamestown settlers came to this hemisphere on business, their chief aim financial profit. They wanted to trade, but first they had to survive.

They survived those first years thanks to the indigenous population. Captain John Smith wrote that they were given "corn and bread ready made." In the winter of 1608-1609, the colonists

114

traded "10 quarters of corn for a copper kettle." Later they got from the indigenous one bushel of corn for every inch of copper. Still later, when the Powhatans were the ones starving instead of the English, the colonists traded four hundred bushels of corn for a "mortgage on their whole countries."

Wahunsonacock (called King Powhatan by the English) tried for peace at all costs. He resolved many incidents without war, including the kidnapping of his own daughter Pocahontas. When Wahunsonacock died, his brother Opechancanough became chief.

The colonists provoked many conflicts. For example, English livestock, especially pigs, would get loose and damage the unfenced gardens of the Powhatans. But if the Powhatans damaged the pig, the English retaliated against the Powhatans until the conflict escalated to the point that the English burned a Powhatan village and killed a dozen people.

Opechancanough had a pessimistic view of what the colonists had in mind for the land and the Powhatans. History has proved him right. When his nation was already suffering terrible losses from European diseases, on March 22, 1622, he led an attack by the confederacy, killing 347 colonists. The response by the colonists was to articulate an ideology that totally dehumanized the native population, equating them with savages and therefore justifying their extermination.

See *Chronicles of American Indian Protest*, 1-6

victorious Sword (wherein there is more ease, benefit, and glory) and assessing the fruits of other labours. Now their cleared grounds in all their villages (which are situated in the fruitfullest places of the land) shall be inhabited by us. . . .

Because the way of conquering them is much more easie then of civilizing them by faire means, for they are a rude, barbarous and naked people. . . . Besides that, a conquest may be of many, and at once; but civility is in particular, and slow, the effect of long time and great industry. Moreover, victorie of them may be gained many waies; by force, by surprise, by famine in burning their corne, by destroying and burning their Boats, Canoes, and Houses, by breaking their fishing Weares, by assailing them in their huntings, whereby they get their greatest sustenance in Winter, by pursuing and chasing them with our horses, and blood-Hounds to draw after them, and Mastives to teare them, which take this naked, tanned, deformed Savages, for no other then wild beasts, and are so fierce and fell upon them, that they fear them worse then their old Devill. . . . By these and sundry other wayes, as by driving them (when they flye) upon their enemies, who are round about them, and by animating and abetting their enemies against them, may their ruine or subjection be soone effected. . . .

Because the Indians who before were used as friends may now most justly be compelled to servitude and drudgery, and supply the roome of men that labour, whereby even the meanest of the Plantation may imploy themselves more entirely in their Arts and Occupations, which are more generous, whilest Savages performe their inferiour workes digging in mynes, and the like. . . .

Following this advice, the English make war on the Powhatans year after year until by 1642 they are almost completely exterminated.

Chronicles of American Indian Protest, 4-5

Connecticut, 1637: "Frying in the Fire"

In May, the English war party surrounds a secondary Pequot village along the Mystic River. Most of the inhabitants are noncombatants, since the main force of warriors is five miles away. The English and their Narraganset allies infiltrate the town and set fire to the wigwams. In the battle as they retreat, the English wound twenty Narragansets because they find it difficult to distinguish their friends from their enemies.

The English regroup and wait for the survivors fleeing from the fire. By sundown, a large majority of the Pequot tribe lies slaughtered.

Could it not be contrived to send the small pox among the disaffected tribes of Indians?
We must on this occasion use every strategem to reduce them.

British Lord Jeffrey Amherst

William Bradford writes, soon after that day, *It was a fearful sight to see them thus frying in the fire and the streams of blood quenching the same, and horrible was the stink and scent thereof; but the victory seemed a sweet sacrifice, and they gave praise thereof to God, who had wrought so wonderfully for them. . . .*

One of the captains who was there writes, *God . . . laughed [at] his Enemies and the Enemies of his People to Scorn, making them as a fiery Oven . . . [and] filling the Place with Dead Bodies.*

The English enslave the survivors and sell some to the West Indies for needed capital. One of New England's first historians writes about the trip on Captain John Gallup's slave ship *which proved [to be] Charon's ferry boat unto them, for it was found the quickest was to feed the fishes with 'em*

An English officer, John Underhill, also keeps a record of the day's battle, reporting that the Narragansets cried out concerning the Englishmen's way of fighting, *Mach it Mach it; that is , It is naught, it is naught [bad or wicked] because it is too furious and slays too many men.*

The savages are appalled at the savagery of the civilized.

Gary Nash, *Red, White, and Black*, 84-85

The Europeans came armed with crossbows, battle axes, armor and firearms. The indigenous had bows and arrows and tomahawks. The unequal forepower resulted in heavy losses for the indigenous population.

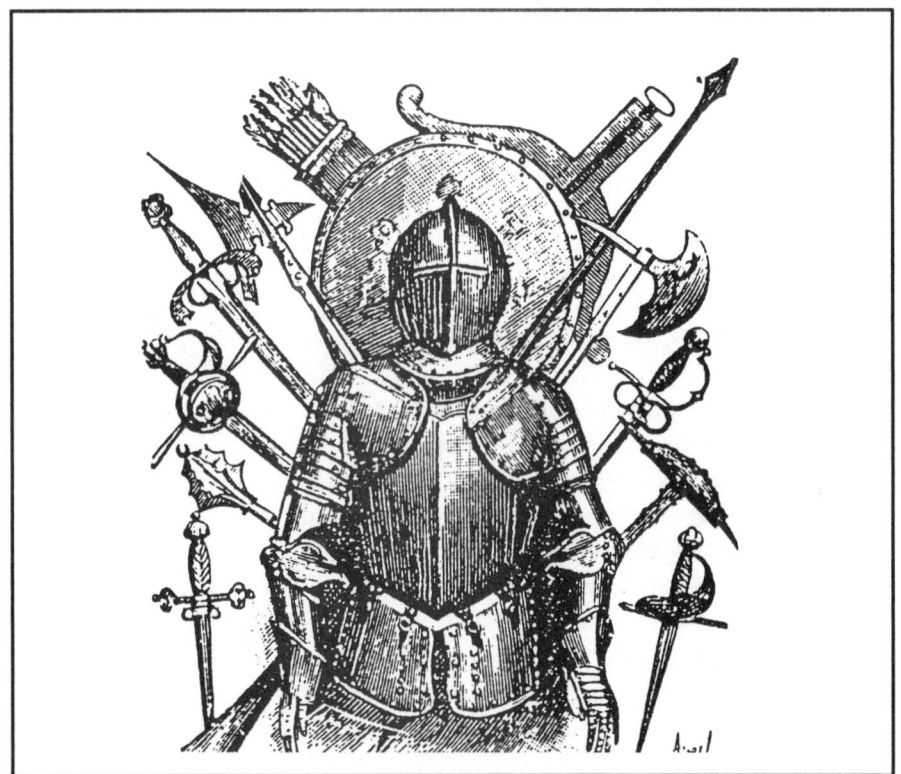

Massachusetts Bay Colony

All the factors that produced conflicts in Jamestown were present in Massachusetts, with the addition of religion. The Puritans believed they were sent to this "hideous and desolate wilderness full of wild beasts and wild men" on a God-directed mission to establish a "city on a hill." This new society would "shine like a beacon" back to England as an example of how pious people should live.

According to historian Gary Nash, the indigenous population became two obstacles to the Puritans. First, they controlled the land that the English wanted. Second, as "savages" they threatened the psychological identity of the Puritans. If they could not control this land and the inhabitants as they thought God had directed them to do, then they would incur God's wrath for their failure.

They did not try to "convert" the "heathen" to Christianity, as the thousands of Catholic missionaries did in the Spanish-dominated parts of the Americas. Rather the Puritans tried to bring the indigenous under civil authority, subjecting them to a white code of behavior. As in the rest of the Americas, here too the indigenous were weakened by Europeans' diseases. But some of the tribes refused to be weakened culturally and politically. Such a tribe was the Pequots.

The Pequots lived in the fertile Conneticut River valley, land that the Puritans wanted. On the pretext of the killing of two English sea captains, one of whom the Puritans themselves hated, they made a punitive expedition into Pequot territory.

The Puritans demanded the murderers and payment in wampum. For good measure they took Pequot children as hostages. The Pequots tried to placate the English, but when that didn't work they resisted. The war was evenly matched until the Puritans massacred a Pequot village. In 1638, the Pequot nation was considered dissolved. For the Puritans, steeped in a theology that good people receive their rewards on earth, their military victory over the Pequots proved their righteousness.

For the Narragansets, allying with the colonists did not help their survival. When the Puritans wanted Narraganset land, they allied with the Mohegans to have a Narraganset chief killed.

Two years later the Massachusetts Bay Colony helped organize the New England Confederation and mobilized for war against the Narragansets. Rather than fight, the tribe submitted to a treaty that cost them large tracts of land.

Neither friend nor foe of the colonists would survive. What could not be pillaged by war was taken by law. The Puritans passed laws that called for the death penalty for "blasphemy," that is, not accepting the Puritan religion. Colonial courts tried, sentenced, and imprisoned indigenous who "trespassed" on lands that the Puritans claimed.

The Wampanoags who once lived on all the land from Narraganset Bay to Cape Cod by 1675 had a few "tongues of land." Metacom, their chief (the English called him King Philip), rallied twenty thousand indigenous from various tribes to rise up in rebellion.

Plymouth, 1676: Metacom's War

In the public square stands a tall pole. On top is impaled the head of the *hellhound, fiend, tawney serpent and dog,* who dared to resist becoming a colonized and culturally submissive person. He dared to drive his forces to within twenty miles of Boston in order to stop the religious and political imperialism of the Puritans. Metacom, chief of the Wampanoags, has mobilized the largest native confederation to resist the onslaught of the whites. His wife and son are now slaves in the West Indies. His head will stay on public display for twenty-five years.

His words will last much longer.

One hundred sixty years later, William Apes will repeat them at the Odeon in Boston.

Brothers,—You see this vast country before us, which the Great Spirit gave to our fathers and us; you see the buffalo and the deer that now are our support. Brothers, you see these little ones, our wives and children, who are looking to us for food and raiment; and you now see the foe before you, that they have grown insolent and bold; that all our ancient customs are disregarded; the treaties made by our fathers and us are broken, and all of us insulted; our council fires disregarded, and all the ancient customs of our fathers; our brothers murdered before our eyes, and their spirits cry to us for revenge. Brothers, these people from the unknown world will cut down our groves, spoil our hunting and planting grounds, and drive us and our children from the graves of our fathers, and our council fires, and enslave our women and children.

This would not be the last time a native from this land the Europeans called America would speak words such as these.

Chronicles of American Indian Protest, 8-11

Northwest Territory, 1763: Pontiac's Speech

It is important for us, my brothers, that we exterminate from our land this nation which only seeks to kill us. You see, as well as I do, that we cannot get our supplies as we had from our brothers, the French. The English sell us merchandise twice dearer than the French . . . and their wares [are worth] nothing. When I go to the English chief to tell him that some of our comrades are dead, instead of weeping for the dead . . . he makes fun of me and you. . . . There is no more time to lose, and when the English shall be defeated . . . we shall cut the passage so that they cannot come back to our country.

Chronicles of American Indian Protest, 40-41

Northwest Territory, 1812: Tecumseh's Plea for Resistance and Unity

Shawnee chief Tecumseh stands in the Great Council before his Choctaw and Chickasaw brothers. He is trying to convince them to join in a unified resistance against the whites.

My heart is a stone: heavy with sadness for my people; cold with the knowledge that no treaty will keep whites out of our lands; hard with the determination to resist as long as I live and breathe. Now we are weak and many of our people are afraid. But hear me: a single twig breaks, but the bundle of twigs is strong. Someday I will embrace our brothers' tribes and draw them into a bundle and together we will win our country back from the whites.

Tecumseh, 1795

The whites are already nearly a match for us all united; and too strong for any one tribe alone to resist; so that unless we support one another with our collective and united forces; unless every tribe unanimously combines to give a check to the ambition and avarice of the whites, they will soon conquer us apart and disunited, and we will be driven away from our native country and scattered as autumnal leaves before the wind. . . .

Every year our white intruders become more greedy, exacting, oppressive, and overbearing. Every year contentions spring up between them and our people and when blood is shed we have to make atonement, whether right or wrong, at the cost of the lives of our greatest chiefs, and the yielding up of large tracts of our lands. Before the pale-faces came among us, we enjoyed the happiness of unbounded freedom, and were acquainted with neither riches, wants, nor oppression. How is it now? Wants and oppression are our lot; for are we not controlled in everything, and dare we move without asking, by your leave? . . . Do they not even now kick and strike us as they do their black-faces? How long will it be before they will tie us to a post and whip us, and make us work for them in their cornfields as they do them? Shall we wait for that moment or shall we die fighting before submitting to such ignominy? . . . The annihilation of our race is at hand unless we unite in one common cause against the common foe. . . .

Will not the bones of our dead be plowed up, and their graves be turned into fields? . . . War or extermination are our only choice. Which do you choose, brave Choctaws and Chickasaws, to assist in the just cause of liberating our race from the grasp of our faithless invaders and heartless oppressors? The white usurpation in our common country must be stopped or we, its rightful owners, be forever destroyed and wiped out as a race of people. Then listen to the voice of duty, of honor, of nature, and of your endangered country. Let us form one body, one heart, and defend to the last warrior our country, our homes, our liberty, and the graves of our fathers.

When U.S. agents approach Tecumseh, he breaks the peace pipe saying, *A chance such as this will never occur again—for us Indians of North America to form ourselves into one great combination and cast our lot with the British*

At the time, however, there were fifty thousand colonists. After initial victories, the sheer numbers of white people proved too powerful.

See Gary Nash, *Red, White, and Black*, 116-121

New Leaders

What has become known as the French and Indian War (1754-1760) ended with the French defeat in Quebec. The English expected the Shawnee, Miami, Kickapoo, Sauk, Potawatomie, Fox, Chippewa, Illinois, Ottawa, and Delaware, who had all allied with the French, to meekly accept the presence of English settlers and traders.

Pontiac

In 1762 an elequent chief and brilliant military strategist rose to power among the indigenous of the Northwest (what is now Ohio, Michigan, and Indiana). He organized a confederacy of eighteen tribes that seized every British post in the Northwest Territory, except Forts Pitt and Detroit. But even at Fort Detroit they managed to hold a siege for eight months—the longest in American military history.

Chief Pontiac and his Confederacy won from the British the famous Crown Proclamation of October, 1763. The Proclamation set an official line of demarcation running the length of the crest of the Appalachian mountains, separating colonial from indigenous land. The Proclamation even demanded those colonists who had gone across the mountains to remove themselves.

Britain had its own reasons for such an agreement. The Crown wanted to stop the native rebellions but also wanted to limit the expansion of the colonies in order to keep them more dependent on the mother country.

Land speculators, including George Washington, Patrick Henry, and Benjamin Franklin, had already purchased millions of acres in what was "Indian Territory."

Chronicles of American Indian Protest,
41-44

Tecumseh and the War of 1812

Both Britain and the United States attempted to gain the indigenous as allies during the War of 1812.

At the beginning the war went well. Tecumseh rallied tribal unity and his military skill helped to force Fort Detroit to surrender with hardly a fight. More tribes began to join the fight on the side of the British. The Potawatomies captured Fort Dearborn, and the Miamis laid seige to Fort Wayne. Tecumseh even convinced the great Creek nation in the South to join.

A change of British command brought in men who were cowards and hated Indians. Tecumseh was finally killed in battle, protecting the fleeing British troops. Those at the battle recalled seeing him being hit several times, with blood pouring from his mouth and covering his body; yet he was still yelling like a "tiger," urging his braves on.

Chronicles of American Indian Protest,
77-81

in this war. Tecumseh believes that if the British win the tribes will keep their land, but if the "long knives" (the colonists) win *it will not be many years before our last place of abode and our last hunting ground will be taken from us, and the remnants of the different tribes . . . will be driven toward the setting sun.*

Paul Jacobs and Saul Landau, *To Serve the Devil,* 53-56

Middle West, 1812: Tecumseh's Way

Tecumseh finds General Procter plying the natives with whiskey and goading them into killing unarmed prisoners. Tecumseh rushes to the scene, sword raised and says, *Are there no men here?* The killing stops. He criticizes General Procter, who only says that Indians cannot be controlled. *You are unfit to command,* Tecumseh counters. *I conquer to save, and you to murder.*

Chronicles of American Indian Protest, 79

Tecumseh, which means "shooting star," was known for his humane treatment of enemies. Even though his father and two brothers were killed by whites, Tecumseh never allowed torture or atrocities.

119

Georgia, 1829: Laws of Conquest

Again, what is too costly to win by armed conflict is taken through laws written by and for the white man without any representation from the people who will suffer. Georgia passes a law that:

1. Confiscates all Cherokee land to be distributed to white owners.

2. Abolishes all authority of the Cherokee government and nullifies all Cherokee laws.

3. Prohibits any gathering of Cherokee people, even for religious purposes.

4. Makes it a crime, punishable by imprisonment, for any Cherokee to advise another not to emigrate.

5. Declares void any contract between Indians and whites unless witnessed by two white men.

6. Refuses the right of any Cherokee to testify in court against any white man.

7. Specifically prohibits any Cherokee to dig gold in the Cherokee gold fields.

Chronicles of American Indian Protest, 113-114

Georgia, 1835: Preamble to Robbery

On December 2, the Georgia legislature passes a law withdrawing the right of occupancy on the land by the Cherokees and requiring their removal to the West. They carefully tell in the preamble the real reasons for their actions so that no one would think it is for greed for the land or hatred of the red skin.

. . . their primary object in the measures intended to be pursued, are founded on real humanity to these Indians, and with a view, in a distant region, to perpetuate them with their old identity of character, under the paternal care of the government of the United States; at the same time disavowing any selfish or sinister motives towards them in their present legislation.

Chronicles of American Indian Protest, 120

Cherokee Trail of Tears

When the Europeans arrived in the Western Hemisphere the Cherokees were a free people and a sovereign nation. Both the English and the French wanted to make alliances with this nation for protection and benefit. The United States recognized its sovereignty in 1785 and 1791, guaranteeing that land not ceded then would remain in Cherokee hands. Whites could not even hunt on Cherokee lands, according to the agreements.

In 1721, South Carolina made a treaty with the Cherokees, the first cession of Cherokee lands. The process was to be repeated so often that by 1835 the Cherokees had concluded more treaties with the United States than any other tribe. Almost without exception every treaty stated that it would be the last one. Treaties contained impressive promises: "The United States solemnly guarantees to the Cherokee Nation, all their lands not hereby ceded"; this treaty will stand "as long as the grass grows and rivers flow." Each treaty stole more from the original land until the Cherokee government finally passed a law making it a capital offense for any tribal member to cede land to the U.S. government.

One of the main ideological arguments used by the Europeans to take the land was that the indigenous were savages and roamed the land as hunters rather than "settling down" and farming the land as "civilized people" do. The Cherokees, however, adapted to many European customs, hoping to maintain their lands not by warfare but through accommodation. By the 1820s, the Cherokees had their own written language and a bilingual newspaper published in English and Cherokee. They had a constitutional government and an eleborate judicial system. Some of them had accumulated considerable wealth and were living on large farms with spacious homes.

The discovery of gold in 1828 in Georgia sent hordes of fortune seekers into Cherokee territory. That same year the Indian fighter Andrew Jackson campaigned on a platform of removal of the Indians to west of the Mississippi. After Jackson became president, Congress granted him power to negotiate treaties that exchanged land in what is now Oklahoma for their original Smoky Mountain land.

Before a treaty was made, Georgia divided up the Cherokee lands and gave it by lottery to whites. Even improved property with houses and barns, cultivated fields, mills, gardens, and orchards was simply given to whites.

On December 29, 1835, a few Cherokees without authority signed the Treaty of New Echota which ceded the remaining territory east of the Mississippi. Chief John Ross, who had recently been released from prison in Georgia, collected over fifteen thousand Cherokee signatures denouncing the treaty as a fraud. In spite of this, and in spite of the fact that it was quite evident that the Cherokees had made it a capital offense to cede territory in order to stop just such a trick, Congress ratified the treaty and gave the Cherokees two years to move.

Smoky Mountains, 1838: Tsali's Sacrifice

Hundreds of Cherokees, under the leadership of Chief Utsala, refuse to be removed and flee to the mountains. An aging Cherokee named Tsali and his family are one of the groups of resistance.

General Scott sends mounted troops to round up the fugitives. They surround Tsali and his family, who surrender. As they are being led to the stockade, one of the soldiers pushes Tsali's wife sharply with his bayonet. Already embittered by the forced removal, Tsali can't bear this last bit of injustice. He tears the weapon away from the soldier and kills him. The rest of the family helps subdue the others, killing a second soldier and wounding a third. Tsali and his family flee to the mountains.

General Scott feels that the "National Honor" is at stake and that the "murderers" have to be punished. Given the rugged terrain, the troops cannot find Tsali or the other hundreds of resisters. So Scott sends word that if Tsali and his sons surrender, thousands of other Cherokees can remain on their land. Knowing the consequences, Tsali and his family surrender.

After a speedy trial, Tsali and his sons are sentenced to death. Facing the firing squad, Tsali's youngest son, Wasidani, is spared at the last minute because of his youth. Before being killed, Tsali tells his son to love the land and never leave it. Because of Tsali's sacrifice, a Cherokee Reservation still exists in the Smoky Mountains.

See *Cherokee Heritage*, 115-16

United States, 1838-39: Trail of Tears

Private John G. Burnett is with the Second Regiment, Second Brigade of the mounted infantry ordered to remove the Cherokees from their land. On his eightieth birthday he records the following for his children, for all children.

The removal of the Cherokee Indians from their lifelong homes in the year of 1838 found me a young man in the prime of life and a Private soldier in the American Army. I was sent as an interpreter . . . in May, 1838, and witnessed the execution of the most brutal order in the History of American Warfare. I saw the helpless Cherokees arrested and dragged from their homes, and driven at bayonet point into the stockades. And in the chill of a drizzling rain on an

October morning I saw them loaded like cattle or sheep into six hundred and forty-five wagons and started toward the West.

One can never forget the sadness and solemnity of that morning. . . . Many of these helpless people did not have blankets and many of them had been driven from home barefooted.

On the morning of November the 17th we encountered a terrific sleet and snow storm with freezing temperatures. From that day until we reached the end of the fateful journey on March the 26th the sufferings of the Cherokees were awful. The trail of exiles was a trail of death. They had to sleep in the wagons and on the ground without fire. And I have known as many as twenty-two of them to die in one night of pneumonia due to ill treatment, cold, and exposure. Among the number was the beautiful Christian wife of Chief John Ross. This noble hearted woman died a martyr to childhood, giving her only blanket for the protection of a sick child. She rode thinly clad through a blinding sleet and snow storm, developed pneumonia, and died in the still hours of a bleak winter night, with her head resting on Lieutenant Gregg's saddle blanket. . . .

The long painful journey to the West ended March 26th, 1839, with four-thousand silent graves reaching from the foothills of the Smoky Mountains to what is known as Indian territory in the West. And covetousness on the part of the white race was the cause of all that the Cherokees had to suffer. . . .

At this time (1890) we are too near the removal of the Cherokees for our young people to fully understand the enormity of the crime that was committed against a helpless race, truth is the facts are being concealed from the young people of today. School children of today do not know that they are living on lands that were taken from a helpless race at the bayonet point to satisfy the white man's greed for gold . . .

Murder is murder and somebody must answer, somebody must explain the streams of blood that flowed in the Indian country in the summer of 1838. Somebody must explain the four-thousand silent graves that mark the trail of the Cherokees to their exile. I wish I could forget it all, but the picture of six hundred and forty-five wagons lumbering over the frozen ground with their Cargo of suffering humanity still lingers in my memory. . . .

Children—Thus ends my promised birthday story. This December the 11th 1890.

Cherokee Legends and the Trail of Tears, 21-27

From 1825 until the moment of their removal, the Cherokees constantly and peacefully petitioned the U.S. government for justice. They sent representatives to the president and to Congress. They testified before committees, passed their own laws, signed petitions, developed their own constitution. Their bilingual newspaper the *Cherokee Phoenix* **, clearly spelled out Cherokee objections to the removal policy. All to no avail.**

In 1838, the newly elected president, Martin Van Buren, stated: "No State can achieve proper culture, civilization, and progress in safety as long as Indians are permitted to remain." So the Cherokees were to be forcibly removed —the bilingual Cherokees whose language was so complex that professional ethnologists at the time could not figure out how it was written. The Cherokee Sequoyah invented an alphabet of eighty-five characters so accurately expressing the roots of the language that any Cherokee could learn to read and write in a few days. The Cherokee rate of literacy was higher than that of the "white rabble" coming to take their lands in the name of "civilization."

In June of 1838, the Trail of Tears began as seven thousand troops marched the Cherokees to concentration camps while the whites looted their houses, burned their crops, and drove off their livestock.

see *Cherokee Heritage*

The Cheyennes Fight Back

In 1851 the Cheyenne, Arapahos, Sioux, Crows, and other tribes met with U.S. representatives at Fort Laramie. The United States wanted access to indigenous lands for roads, forts, and telegraph lines. The tribes granted the access, while not giving up their right to fish, hunt, or roam over the same lands.

Gold had been discovered in California in 1848 and again in Colorado Territory ten years later. Thousands of miners came to Pikes Peak, building the village of Denver City in the process.

In 1860 the United States was on the brink of a civil war. The war slowed down the westward march of the whites, but did not stop it. That same year the first pony express rider reached California. The U.S. Congress also passed the Pre-emption Bill, which provided free land to settlers in western territories. Before the year was out a man named Spencer invented the repeating rifle.

In 1864, Black Kettle, a Cheyenne chief, heard of white soldiers killing Cheyennes without provocation. Black Kettle wanted "to be peaceable and friendly and keep my tribe so." He always camped under the American flag that Colonel Greenwood had given him for protection.

The cavalry raids continued. Officers under the command of Colonel Chivington were ordered to "kill Cheyennes whenever and wherever found." Clashes increased and the younger Cheyenne leaders, members of the Hotamitanio, or Dog Soldier Society, wanted to fight back.

Fort Lyon, 1864: Black Kettle Attempts Peace

One-Eye and Eagle Head, messengers from Black Kettle, approach Fort Lyon. Three soldiers stop them and take firing positions. Quickly the two Cheyenne make hand signals of peace and show a letter from Black Kettle. The soldiers take them prisoner and turn them over to Major Edward W. Wynkoop. In his mid-twenties, with only one battle against the confederates under his belt, he is both afraid and suspicious. The letter says that Black Kettle wants the soldiers to come out to the Smoky Hill camp and guide the two thousand Cheyenne into the reservation. Suspecting a trap, Wynkoop delays a decision. Finally he decides to go.

Releasing the two prisoners, he tells them they are both guides and hostages. *At the first sign of treachery from your people, I will kill you.*

The Cheyennes do not break their word. If they do so I should not care to live longer, replies One-Eye.

On the march Wynkoop has the opportunity to have long conversations with the two Cheyenne. Later he writes:

I felt myself in the presence of superior beings; and these were the representatives of a race that I had heretofore looked upon without exception as being cruel, treacherous, and bloodthirsty, without feeling of affection for friend or kindred.

Black Kettle and the other chiefs hold a council with Wynkoop, telling him of the raids committed against their people. Wynkoop promises to do everything possible to stop the fighting and takes the chiefs to Denver to meet the governor of the Colorado territory and Colonel Chivington.

At Denver, Governor Evans privately tells Wynkoop, *I want no peace till the Indians suffer more. But what shall I do with the Third Colorado Regiment if I make peace? They have been raised to kill Indians and they must kill Indians.* Unknown to Wynkoop was Colonel Chivington's recent order to his soldiers: *Kill all the Indians you come across.*

Because of his friendly attitude toward the indigenous, U.S. military officials replace Major Wynkoop with Major Scott Anthony as the commander of Fort Lyon.

In late November, Colonel Chivington and his troops ride into Fort Lyon. In the officers' quarters, Anthony greets him warmly and Chivington talks of *collecting scalps* and *wading in gore.* Anthony is pleased, since he has been waiting for an opportunity *to pitch into them.*

To tame a savage you must tie him down to the soil. You must make him understand the value of property, and the benefits of its separate ownership.

U.S. Secretary of the Interior, 1851

One does not sell the earth upon which the people walk.

Crazy Horse

123

The next day Lieutenant Cramer and a few others protest going out to Black Kettle's peaceful camp where their safety has been guaranteed. *It would be murder in every sense of the word.*

Chivington becomes violent, angrily slams his fist close to Lieutenant Cramer's head, and says, *Damn any man who sympathizes with Indians! I have come to kill Indians, and believe it is right and honorable to use any means under God's heaven to kill them.*

On the evening of November 28, Colonel Chivington and seven hundred men head out to the Cheyenne encampment in a horseshoe bend of Sand Creek.

Dee Brown, *Bury My Heart at Wounded Knee,* 56-70

Sand Creek, 1864: American Flag, Native Blood

Colonel Chivington orders Robert Bent, twenty-four-year-old guide and interpreter from Fort Lyon, to accompany his soldiers. Bent gives his version of the events at Sand Creek:

The command consisted of from nine hundred to one thousand men. . . . We left Fort Lyon . . . and came on to the Indian camp at daylight the next morning. Colonel Chivington surrounded the village with his troops. When we came in sight of the camp I saw the American flag waving and heard Black Kettle tell the Indians to stand around the flag, and there they were huddled—men, women and children. . . . [I] also saw a white flag raised. These flags were in so conspicuous a position that they must have been seen. When the troops fired, the Indians ran. . . . I think there were six hundred Indians in all . . . thirty-five braves and some old men, about sixty in all. All fought well. . . . I saw five squaws under a bank for shelter. When the troops came up to them they ran out and showed their person to let the soldiers know that they were squaws and begged for mercy, but the soldiers shot them all. There seemed to be indiscriminate slaughter of men, women, and children. There were some thirty or forty squaws collected in a hole for protection; they sent out a little girl about six years old with a white flag on a stick; she had not proceeded but a few steps when she was shot and killed. All the squaws in that hole were afterwards killed. . . .

Every one I saw dead was scalped. I saw one squaw cut open with an unborn child . . . lying by her side. I saw the body of White Antelope with the privates cut off, and I heard a soldier say he was going to make a tobacco pouch out of them. . . . I saw a little girl about five years of age who had been hid in the sand; two soldiers discovered her, drew their

After the Sand Creek Massacre the Cheyenne and the Sioux united to keep the whites out of the Powder River country. They called themselves The People, the last hope to save their ancestral hunting grounds. They were led by Red Cloud, Sitting Bull, Crazy Horse, Dull Knife, and Roman Nose.

In the summer of 1865, a few months after the end of the Civil War, General Patrick Connor invaded the Powder River territory with four columns of troops. Conner built a fort and named it after himself; later it would be called Fort Reno. Connor in 1863 had surrounded a camp of Paiutes and massacred 278 of them. On this mission he was heard to say that the Indians had to "be hunted like wolves." His orders to his men: "Attack and kill every male Indian over twelve years of age." Conner's goal was to open up the Bozeman Trail to give the whites more roads to the West.

Red Cloud and the other chiefs were angry because the whites had not asked permission to build forts and more roads through their country. That summer, the Sioux and Cheyenne killed hundreds of soldiers and cost the U.S. government millions of dollars. It was one of the worst military defeats at the hands of the indigenous up to that time.

The next spring (1866) the whites wanted to talk peace. While Red Cloud and the others were negotiating, an army troop arrived at the fort with orders to build forts up and down the Bozeman Trail with or without treaties. Red Cloud denounced the peace commission and stormed out, taking everyone with him.

A guerrilla war followed. Crazy Horse developed a tactic of luring soldiers out of their defensive positions and into ambushes. It took great riding skill and courage, and earned him high respect from his comrades. The greatest victory was at Fort Phil Kearney, where Crazy Horse drew the soldiers from the fort and the combined forces of the Sioux and Cheyenne annihilated them.

Finally in 1868 the army gave up. Even General Sherman, who had led the Union march to the sea, could not subdue the Sioux and Cheyenne warriors. The United States agreed to abandon the forts. Red Cloud, not trusting the whites, replied that he would not sign a peace treaty until the forts were actually abandoned. As the troops left, the warriors set fire to the forts. Red Cloud still waited to sign, worrying the whites even more. It was one of the few treaties whose terms were dictated by the indigenous.

War for Paha Sapa (Black Hills)

In 1872 rumors abounded that there was gold in the Black Hills. Miners, wagon trains, and cavalry led by General George Armstrong Custer beat a trail known as Thieves' Road to the area. Custer was also known as Squaw Killer because of his massacre of Black Kettle and his people on the Washita River in 1868.

Paha Sapa was sacred to the indigenous people. In the summers they went there to commune with the Great Spirit and seek visions. This was the center of the world, the point from which the hoop of the world bent in four directions.

pistols and shot her, and then pulled her out of the sand by the arm. I saw quite a number of infants in arms killed with their mothers.

Chronicles of American Indian Protest, 206-208

Fort Laramie, 1868: Red Cloud's Victory

It has been two years of resistance and now the whites will have to listen to Red Cloud and Bear Tooth and the others dictate the terms of peace. It is November 6. Red Cloud is surrounded by a small group of triumphant warriors. He has lived up to the message he sent to General Sherman a year before:

The Great Father sent his soldiers out here to spill blood. I did not first commence the spilling of blood. . . . If the Great Father kept white men out of my country, peace would last forever, but if they disturb me, there will be no peace. . . . The Great Spirit raised me in this land, and has raised you in another land. What I have said I mean. I mean to keep this land.

Dee Brown, *Bury My Heart at Wounded Knee,* 116

Washington D.C., 1889: Erasing Dangerous Memory

The Commissioner of Indian Affairs issues a set of instructions to all Indian agents concerning how to train Indians as American citizens and inculcate in them a sense of patriotism.

It is in the highest degree important, therefore, that special attention should be paid, particularly in the higher grades of the school, to the instruction of Indian youth in the elements of American history, acquainting them especially with the leading facts in the lives of the most notable and worthy historical characters. While in such study the wrongs of their ancestors cannot be ignored, the injustice which their race has suffered can be contrasted with the larger future open to them, and their duties and opportunities rather than their wrongs will most profitably engage their attention. . . .

They [teachers] should point out to their pupils the provisions which the Government has made for their education . . . and should endeavor to awaken reverence for the nation's power, gratitude for its beneficence, pride in its history, and a laudable ambition to contribute to its posterity.

Francis Paul Prucha, ed., *Documents of United States Indian Policy,* 180-181

The Wild West, 1885: Sitting Bull

Sitting Bull is the symbol of native resistance. He continually defends his culture from white attack. He is the leader who subjected the U.S. Army to its worst defeat in the "Indian Wars."

He joins the Buffalo Bill Cody Wild West Show. Although he is greeted by boos and catcalls, by the end of the show he has won them over, and they pay him for autographed pictures. But Sitting Bull is poor, he saves nothing of what he earns. He is continually pressing coins into the hands of the ragged and hungry white kids who seem to be at every stop on the circuit.

As a Sioux chief he is responsible for the welfare of his people, which means giving away what he has so that no one will go hungry. He cannot understand how white people can neglect their poor.

He tells Annie Oakley: *The white man knows how to make everything, but he does not know how to distribute it.*

Dee Brown, *Bury My Heart at Wounded Knee*, 338

Pine Ridge Reservation, 1890: Ghost Dance

This generation of Sioux are seeing the end of life as their ancestors knew it. The buffalo and antelope herds are gone. The life of roaming and hunting is as dead as the thousands of warriors buried beneath the white man's railroads and mines and corn fields. In the midst of this ending rises a new beginning—a religious ferment called the ghost dance. A Paiute named Wovoka claims to be the Messiah. He prophesies that by next spring all the whites will be gone and in their place new sweet grass will sprout and all the natives who have ever lived will return to life. The people grasp at this hope and begin to dance the ghost dance in larger and larger numbers. The whites are afraid and they call out the army for protection. The army decides that Sitting Bull is behind this ghost dance phenomenon, even though he is not. They send forty-three Indian policemen to arrest him. In the ensuing melee Sitting Bull is shot.

Bill Zimmerman, *Airlift to Wounded Knee*, 46-47

Just four years, before in the Treaty of 1868, that land had been given to the Sioux forever. Now the government tried to get the Black Hills through treaty, but the Sioux refused. The Peace Commissioners then recommended that Congress decide on a "fair equivalent value" and present it to the Indians as a "finality."

The United States offered the Sioux six million dollars for the Black Hills. The Sioux rejected the offer for good reason: just one Black Hills mine would eventually yield five hundred million dollars. By February 1876, the War Department authorized General Sheridan to begin military actions against the "hostile Sioux," including Sitting Bull and Crazy Horse.

Crazy Horse joined forces with Sitting Bull; they made their camp on the banks of the Little Big Horn. There were ten thousand people with three to four thousand warriors, their camps spreading for three miles. On June 24, 1876, General George Armstrong Custer came looking for the Sioux. He had split his forces into three columns. The Sioux, defending their women and children along the Little Big Horn, wiped out Custer and over 180 of his men. It was the worst military defeat that the U.S government had ever suffered in the wars with the native peoples.

The whites viewed the defeat as a massacre. More soldiers hunted down the Sioux. For over a year Sitting Bull and Crazy Horse kept the soldiers at bay. Finally, Sitting Bull took his people to Canada while Crazy Horse continued to fight. In 1877, after a long winter, the

United States offered Crazy Horse and his people a reservation in the Powder River country, the most precious of territory to the Sioux. Crazy Horse brought his people to the fort and waited for the promised territory. After four months he decided to take the land and marched his people to the Powder River.

Eight companies of soldiers rode out and arrested him. During the arrest procedure, Crazy Horse balked at the prison cell after he saw men in chains. Glad for an excuse to kill him, one of the soldiers ran his bayonet through Crazy Horse's stomach.

The Sioux mourned his death for weeks. His parents finally took his bones and heart and buried them in a desolate spot on their trek to Canada, near a creek called Wounded Knee. The U.S. military had never defeated Crazy Horse in battle.

More and more whites flooded into Sioux and Cheyenne territory, and the U.S. government tried to wrest more land from the tribes. In 1889 they "legally" stole land out of the middle of the Sioux reservation. The stage was set for the end of the frontier and the way of life the native populations had known for millenia.

That end came in 1890 at Wounded Knee. It was the final large-scale military massacre committed by the whites against the indigenous. Many more deaths of native peoples would follow due to poverty, despair, injustice, but not until the 1970s would the big guns again be fired on the Sioux.

Wounded Knee, 1890: The Sacred Hoop Is Broken

Big Foot, hearing about Sitting Bull's death, begins to move his tribe to the Pine Ridge Reservation for safety. The tribe has grown because many homeless widows have joined it recently. It is December, cold and snowing. They meet the Seventh Calvary, Custer's old outfit, who order them to camp at the place called Wounded Knee. Sleeping on both sides that night are survivors from the Battle of the Little Bighorn. Over the Minneconjou Sioux camp flies the white flag. When they awake the next morning the Seventh Calvary has them surrounded and there are four Hotchkiss guns peering down from a nearby hill. The Minneconjou surrender their weapons and place them in the center of the camp. Not satisfied, the troops search for more and find two rifles. In the ensuing confiscation, a gun goes off. Suddenly an explosion cracks through the shallow valley. The troops open fire. Within seconds dozens of unarmed Sioux are dead. Defenseless, many of the Sioux try to flee. The big Hotchkiss guns open fire. Shells tear through the camp at the rate of almost one a second, shredding tepees and human flesh. Flying shrapnel does not discriminate between men, women, and children. *We tried to run but they shot us like we were buffalo.* Some say the Seventh Cavalry killed three hundred. One hundred fifty-three bodies are found soon afterwards on the site. Many more crawl off to die in the snow. Twenty-five soldiers are killed, mostly by their own bullets or shrapnel.

A few hours later Black Elk, a leading Oglala Sioux medicine man, arrives to find many bodies, including that of Big Foot, frozen into grotesque shapes. Decades later Black Elk describes what he saw:

I did not know then how much was ended. When I look back now from this high hill of my old age, I can still see the butchered women and children lying heaped and scattered all along the crooked gulch as plain as when I saw them with eyes still young. And I can see that something else died there in the bloody mud, and was buried in the blizzard. A people's dream died there. It was a beautiful dream. . . .

The nation's hoop is broken and scattered. There is no center any longer, and the sacred tree is dead.

Wagonloads of wounded Sioux, mostly women and children, reach Pine Ridge reservation after dark. The army leaves them in the open cold for hours because the army is living in the barracks. Finally an Episcopal Church offers to take them in. It is December 29; Christmas decorations still adorn the church. Just above the pulpit is a crudely lettered banner:

Between 1870 and 1890, the number of buffalo on the great plains dropped from fifty million to eight hundred.

Dee Brown, *Bury My Heart at Wounded Knee*

127

Reservations and Renewed Resistance

Eighteen U.S. calvalrymen receive the Congressional Medal of Honor for their actions at Wounded Knee. The United States is two years shy of the four hundredth anniversary of Columbus' invasion: four hundred years of a massive assault by mostly white Europeans against the forests, animals, and people that have lived there for millenia; four hundred years of constant resistance as the native peoples defend their lives, culture, and land. It takes four hundred years to break the sacred hoop.

Dee Brown, *Bury My Heart at Wounded Knee,* 351;
Bill Zimmerman, *Airlift to Wounded Knee,* 48

Pine Ridge Reservation, 1925: Why They Rebel, Part I

At seven, Gladys Spotted Bear enrolls in the Holy Rosary Mission School. The teachers beat her if she and her classmates speak their native Lakota language. Converted to Catholicism, she speaks English and prays in Latin. The school makes a conscious effort to destroy the Sioux culture, including their clothing, hair length, skin color, and, of course, religion.

The children perform badly when asked to raise their hands and give the correct answer. None of the children want to be first because they do not want any of their classmates to look less intelligent. The school teaches them that this sort of cooperation is bad and that they should compete with one another.

As Gladys gets older, the Bureau of Indian Affairs (BIA) launches a campaign to wipe out her native religion. The BIA forbids the Sioux to perform cermonies like the Potlatch (where all or most of one's possessions are given away to other people in the tribe) and the Sun Dance.

When Gladys is sixteen, the U.S government decides that the way tribes are organized is wrong. Indian leaders should be elected by ballot, the way the whites do it. For centuries the Sioux and other tribes have been organized in kinship groupings. The chief has as much power as the people allow him to have, given his wisdom, courage, and persuasive power. The Indian Reorganization Act changes all that. The United States government presents each reservation with a model pre–packaged constitution and removes the tribal chiefs from power.

Bill Zimmerman, *Airlift to Wounded Knee,* 58-59

The reservation system, set up by the U. S. government, destroyed the native people. The Bureau of Indian Affairs institutionalized the theft and manipulation of native land and systematically stripped the native peoples of their culture, religion, language and way of governance. Mission schools specifically saw their purpose as "civilizing" and "Christianizing" the children and making them patriotic U.S. citizens.

Decades of this system led in the 1970s to an eruption of protests and demonstrations on the part of native people and their allies to reclaim the civil and human rights and economic development that the United States took from them. Takeovers at Alcatraz and Wounded Knee galvanized native peoples into a new resistance struggle. The ecological awakening during that period, continuing until today, sparked a renewed interest in the indigenous way of life, including their culture, religion, and view of the earth.

On November 9, 1969, seventy-eight native people made a predawn landing on Alcatraz Island in San Francisco Bay. The takeover was extraordinarily dramatic and focused world attention on Indian protest. By November 30, nearly six hundred Indians, representing more than fifty tribes, were living on the island. Their numbers decreased drastically in later months, as the U.S. government cut off telephones, electricity, and water in the hope that they would leave altogether. But the Indians

were unyielding. They incorporated themselves as Indians of All Tribes and remained until they were forcefully removed a year and a half later.

See *Chronicles of American Indian Protest,* 310; Dee Brown, *Bury My Heart at Wounded Knee,* 226-233; Bill Zimmerman, *Airlift to Wounded Knee* , 42-48.

San Francisco, 1969: Alcatraz Reclaimed

Proclamation: To the Great White Father and All His People

We, the Native Americans, reclaim the land known as Alcatraz Island in the name of the American Indians by right of discovery. We wish to be fair and honorable in our dealings with the Caucasian inhabitants of this land, and hereby offer the following treaty:

• We will purchase said Alcatraz Island for twenty-four dollars ($24) in glass beads and red cloth, a precedent set by the white man's purchase of a similar island about 300 years ago. We know that $24 in trade goods for these 16 acres is more than was paid when Manhattan Island was sold, but we know that land values have risen over the years. Our offer of $1.24 per acre is greater than the 47 cents per acre the white men are now paying the California Indians for their land.

• We will give to the inhabitants of this island a portion of the land for their own to be held in trust by the American Indian Affairs and by the bureau of Caucasian Affairs to hold in perpetuity—for as long as the sun shall rise and the rivers go down to the sea. We will further guide the inhabitants in the proper way of living. We will offer them our religion, our education, our life-ways, in order to help them achieve our level of civilization and thus raise them and all their white brothers up from their savage and unhappy state. We offer this treaty in good faith and wish to be fair and honorable in our dealings with all white men.

We feel this so-called Alcatraz Island is more than suitable for an Indian reservation, as determined by the white man's own standards. By this we mean that this place resembles most Indian reservations in that:

1. It is isolated from modern facilities, and without adequate means of tranportation. 2. It has no fresh running water. 3. It has inadequate sanitation facilities. 4. There are no oil or mineral rights. 5. There is no industry and so unemployment is very great. 6. There are no health care facilities. 7. The soil is rocky and nonproductive; and the land does not support game. 8. There are no educational facilities. 9. The population has always exceeded the land base. 10. The population has always been held as prisoners and kept dependent on others.

Further, it would be fitting and symbolic that ships from all over the world, entering the Golden Gate, would first see Indian land, and thus be reminded of the true history of this nation. This tiny island would be a symbol of the great lands once ruled by free and noble Indians.

Chronicles of American Indian Protest, 310-311

Pine Ridge Reservation, 1973: Why They Rebel, Part II

Twelve thousand Sioux live on the reservation. Sixty percent are unemployed and only nine percent of the homes have electricity. A few people are living in chicken coops and in the shells of abandoned cars. The rest live in one- and two-room tar-papered shacks. Occasionally someone freezes to death. The Federal Trade Commission's latest study shows that prices at the trading post are twenty-seven percent higher than the national average.

The infant mortality rate is four times the national average and life expectancy is only forty-four and a half years. The suicide rate is five times the national average and Sioux teenagers are killing themselves at fifteen times the rate of their counterparts in the rest of the country.

While the land is parcelled out to individual Sioux, they do not actually own it. The Bureau of Indian Affairs (BIA) holds it in trust for them. The BIA, instead of serving the Sioux, helps local white ranchers buy and lease land for their own profit.

The reservation is like a ghetto on the plains.

Bill Zimmerman, *Airlift to Wounded Knee*, 60-63

Poster from Akwesasne Notes of the Mohawk Nation *commemorating the history of native oppression and struggle*

130

Pine Ridge Reservation, 1973: Occupation of Wounded Knee

In the last election for tribal chairman, Richard Wilson was elected. Less than fifty percent of the people voted. They now want to impeach him, but Wilson postpones his own hearing. In the meantime, an exchange of ugly remarks in a white bar leads to a fight between a Sioux and the whites. The Sioux is struck from behind with a beer bottle. When the police arrive they arrest the Sioux; when other Sioux hear about this they tear apart four other white bars that have a reputation for being abusive to natives. The police arbitrarily arrest forty Sioux, and the people protest.

In this highly charged atmosphere, Sioux leaders ask members of a new organization called the American Indian Movement (AIM) to come onto the reservation and help publicize the situation. AIM is dedicated to reclaiming the civil rights of the native population and see that the government upholds its past treaty obligations.

The police openly ride around with shotguns in their cars, and vigilante groups form. Dennis Banks and Russell Means, two AIM leaders, promise that they will give the people the protection they need and will help to bring the situation to the attention of the U.S. government.

One of their first actions is to form a caravan of sixty to seventy cars. They stop first at Wounded Knee where a mass grave of the massacre victims lies. As they reflect on the past, they begin to see a way toward the future. The only way to expose their living conditions and sue once more for their rights is to retake Wounded Knee.

They begin their action on February 27. The first building they occupy is Sacred Heart Church, beside which is the long trench containing the bodies of the 153 victims of the original massacre. They block the roads and occupy the remaining buildings. They have three demands. They want 1) Richard Wilson removed from office and preferably a return to the traditional way of tribal chiefs, 2) dismissal of two BIA officials and a Senate investigation of corruption in the BIA, and 3) the Senate Foreign Relations Committee to hold hearings on 371 treaties negotiated between the United States and various indigenous nations, few of which have been honored by the United States.

The U.S. government refuses to negotiate and calls in the FBI with automatic weapons, helicopters, gas grenade launchers, tracer bullets, and armored personnel carriers.

The standoff begins. There are intermittent fire fights. Wounded Knee is difficult to defend militarily because it is in a shallow valley surrounded by hills. The FBI places their guns on the same hills where the old Hotchkiss guns were mounted in 1890.

From all over the country, native peoples respond to the occupation by sending supplies or coming themselves. At one point representatives from sixty-five different tribes are present. The FBI tries to block all reinforcements and supplies. Hikers go through the back trails in the dead of night to carry in food. The FBI charges those caught with a felony violation punishable up to five years in prison and a ten thousand dollar fine. As the siege heads into its second month, the food supplies run low and it looks as though the occupiers may have to give up. Then a clandestine airlift drops parachute after parachute of food in a predawn flight.

As the siege goes on, the fire fights increase in duration and intensity. More than ten thousand bullets stream into Wounded Knee from the surrounding hills in just one night of fighting. One of the vigilante goon squads turns off the water supply, leaving the occupiers without sanitation facilities or safe drinking water.

The Peace and Dignity Journeys, 1992, is a continuation of the indigenous struggle. This tree symbol represents one aspect of the transcontinental relay run commemorating 500 years of resistance. The run will go from Alaska to Argentina. Those who cannot run but want to support the project can adopt a tree. Trees will be planted throughout the journey.

Peace and Dignity Journeys, 1301 W. 16th St., Chicago, IL 60608

132

Inside, the occupiers develop a cooperative community. Work is shared. They hold a spiritual gathering, build a sweat lodge, and learn more about their own culture. On March 11 Wounded Knee declares its sovereignty from the United States of America. It is now land controlled by the Independent Oglala Sioux Nation.

A Harris Poll finds that fifty-one percent of the U.S. population supports the Sioux occupation of Wounded Knee. Finally an agreement is reached to allow the AIM leaders to meet at the White House. The meeting never takes place. Once the leaders are out of Wounded Knee, the U.S. government demands that they lay down all of their weapons before there are further negotiations. Remembering what happened when Big Foot gave up his weapons in 1890, the occupiers refuse.

The occupation lasts for seventy-one days. Two occupiers are dead and fifteen others wounded. In the end a group of Sioux elders, the traditional tribal leadership, negotiates with the U.S. government, demanding and receiving assurances on virtually the same set of demands that the occupiers orignally made.

Wounded Knee is no longer just the site of a massacre —it is also the site of a victory. Wounded Knee and AIM become a rallying point for a new spirit of resistance among the native peoples.

See Bill Zimmerman, *Airlift to Wounded Knee*

One of the many violent encounters between the indigenous and the Spaniards, a battle in 1660.

Indigenous Resistance: South

Hispaniola, 1494: First Resistance

It takes only a few months for the Tainos to realize the real intentions of the Spaniards. The Spaniards demand more and more women, some taking as many as five apiece. They keep asking for gold. When the Santa Maria runs aground, they build a fort, La Navidad . Spanish cruelty and terror continue until a local *cacique* named Caonabo can take it no longer. He and his followers kill all the Spaniards and destroy the fort. Continuing to fight, he organizes the first guerrilla war against the invaders.

Other resistance leaders follow him: Guaynabo and Otoao in Puerto Rico, Hatuey and Guamax in Cuba. The resistance continues for fifty years even though the Tainos are decimated by disease.

See José Barreiro, "A Note on Tainos," *View From the Shore*, 7:3, 73, 76

The Invasion of Latin America

After celebrating mass and communion, Francisco Pizarro set off from Panama in 1530 to steal the wealth of the Andes for himself and his king. At the end of 1532 he and his men arrived in the land of the Incan king Atahualpa, whom they lured into a trap. The night before the ambush, the Spaniards spent praying and polishing their swords. The next day they slaughtered thousands of Incans and took Atahualpa prisoner.

Knowing that the Spaniards wanted gold, Atahualpa offered a large room full of gold treasures in return for his release. Pizarro agreed and watched for two months as Incans brought their finest pieces of artwork as ransom. Pizarro commanded the people to melt down their art into bars.

After receiving reinforcements, Pizarro charged Atahualpa with treason. He was tried, baptized, and strangled. Pizarro and his men moved on to invade Cuzco, the dazzling capital of the empire. Entering the sacred Temple of the Sun in order to sack it, a contemporary observed:

"Struggling and fighting among each other, each trying to get his hands on the lion's share, the soldiers in their coats of mail trampled on jewels and images and pounded the gold utensils with hammers to reduce them to a more portable size. . . . They tossed all of the temple's gold into a melting pot to turn it into gold bars: the laminae that covered the walls, the marvelous representations of trees, birds, and other objects in the garden" (Pendle, 44).

The invasion of Chile followed. Diego de Almagro led an expedition in 1535. Finding no great wealth, he returned to Spain, only to be followed by Pedro de Valdivia, who founded the city of Santiago in 1541. Six months later local indigenous natives almost destroyed it.

Before Pizarro died he ordered one of his captains, Francisco de Orellana, to sail down a wide river which they later named the Amazon after the marvelous women they saw there. Orellana sailed two thousand miles to the Atlantic Ocean.

The history of Chile, Peru, and Bolivia was shaped by the forced labor of the indigenous population and imported African slaves. Even though in

Caribbean Islands, 1511: Hatuey

Cacique Hatuey sees it is useless to fight directly against the Spaniards with their criminal ways. And so he, like thousands of others who will follow him in the centuries to come, flees into the brambles. He knows if they capture him he will be killed. The Spaniards always kill the leaders because once they are dead, it is easy to subdue the rest. With a small band, Hatuey flees by canoe to Cuba (one reason why he is claimed today as a Cuban national hero).

The Spaniards search for him for days. Every native captured alive they torture for information about Hatuey. No one speaks. Finally after three months they find him.

When they are ready to burn him at the stake, a Franciscan friar urges him to die a Christian and be baptized.

Hatuey asks, *Why should I be like a Christian? They are bad people who only worship the God of gold.*

The priest responds, *Because those who die Christians go to heaven where they eternally see God and rest.*

Do Christians go to heaven? asks Hatuey.

Certainly.

Then I do not wish to go there, Hatuey says defiantly.

The torch touchs the wood. He burns alive.

Eric Williams, ed., *Documents of West Indian History*, I:92-93
Also see Eduardo Galeano, *Memories of Fire: Genesis*, 57

San Dominque, 1519: Enriquillo

It has been sixteen years since they brought Enriquillo, son of beautiful Queen Anacaona, to a convent of the Franciscan monks to be raised. On that day most of his family were massacred by the Spaniards. He is now a young man of nineteen, speaks Spanish well, and is tall and aloof, speaking little and sleeping even less. His royal lineage does not keep him from being enslaved—after all, he's an "Indian." One night, the arrogant man who bought him tries to rape his wife Mencia. Outraged, Enriquillo tries to gain justice for this crime through the courts, but to no avail. Having exhausted all legal means, he leaves for the mountains with his people and several trained and armed slaves.

After fourteen years of resistance, the Spanish Emperor Charles V is humiliated and so anxious to gain peace that he directs the governor to deliver a royal letter to Enriquillo. Enriquillo accepts the terms of peace while maintaining the secrecy of his camp. In his bones he knows the deceit of these Europeans. When the treaty is signed the people rejoice, for they are declared free. Enriquillo dies in 1535, leaving behind the memory of his heroic struggle that will take nearly three centuries to complete.

See Jean Fouchard, *The Haitian Maroons*, 304-306

Caribbean, Sixteenth Century: Ciguayo and Tamayo

Inspired by Enriquillo, Ciguayo recruits ten or twelve others and rises in rebellion. They attack the Spaniards on their estates and in the mines. Fear and panic spread. The Spaniards pursue him to a gorge where he is hiding. Later, Spanish priest Bartolomé de las Casas writes: *He fought like a mad dog, as if he wore armor from head to toe . . . a Spaniard passed a lance half through his body and even then he fought like a Hector. Finally, when he was bleeding and losing strength, all the Spaniards rushed up and put an end to him.*

The Spaniards find it easier to kill Indians than to kill the spirit of rebellion. No sooner is Ciguayo dead than Tamayo organizes another band to carry on the rebellion. The Spaniards don't even feel safe in their towns now. How is it that four thousand Spaniards are afraid of only two hundred fifty natives? The first priest ordained in the Americas writes: *This can only be attributed to the Divine Judgement, which wished to prove to us three things: first that the Indians did not lack courage . . . even though they were naked and very peace loving; secondly, that if only they had weapons like ours, and horses and arquebuses, they would not have been exterminated from the face of the earth as we exterminated them; thirdly, that that was an indication of the condemnation of such deeds, and of the punishments we shall suffer in the life to come for the heinous sins committed against God and against our fellow men, if we do not repent in this life.*

Quoted in Eric Williams, *Documents of West Indian History*, I:93-94

The Amazon, 1542: "Raining Arrows"

Francisco Pizarro, not content with the riches of Peru, sends his brother Gonzalo and Francisco de Orellana to look for El Dorado and the Land of Cinnamon. Orellana is a gifted linguist who seems to understand the native tongue. The group encounters a village where members of the tribe are subjects of a group of women who the Spaniards refer to as Amazons. Drifting further down

1528 the king of Spain ordered that the Indians should not be used in forced labor, the Spaniards ignored his edict. The *encomienda* became a system of rewarding Spaniards for military service. The crown then "commended" the care of groups of the indigenous to that *encomendero* for two or three generations. The *encomendero* was supposed to provide for their Christianization and care.

In reality, the Spaniards exploited their labor to make quick profits. In 1620 indigenous and *mestizo* laborers living on the haciendas were required to work 160 days a year. The situation didn't change much over time: in 1953, Chilean rural tenants and laborers typically worked well over 200 days including the labor of the whole family.

The quest for indigenous and workers' justice has been a constant throughout Latin America. In Chile, the Araucanians resisted the Spanish invasion longer and more successfully than any other indigenous group. It took over three centuries before they were finally defeated and their lands taken. During that period the region south of the Bió Bió River most of the time remained liberated territory.

See Brian Loverman, *Chile*, and George Pendle, *A History of Latin America*, 44-47

Amazon women demonstrating their legendary rigor against invaders in their territory.

river they are met by fierce resistance by the indigenous wielding bows and arrows. The Spaniards respond with crossbows and arquebuses. Even in the face of superior firepower the natives fight on.

A Dominican friar accompanying the group, Gaspar de Carvajal, writes in his journal:

. . . It seemed to rain arrows. . . . I want it to be known what the reason was why these Indians defended themselves in this manner. It must be explained that they are subjects of and tributaries to, the Amazons. . . . There came as many as twelve of them, for we ourselves saw these women, who were fighting in front of all the Indian men as women captains. . . . the Indian men did not dare to turn their backs, and anyone who did turn his back [the women] killed with clubs right before us. The women are white and tall, and have hair very long and braided and wound about the head, and they are very robust and go naked, [but] with their privy parts covered, with bows and arrows in their hands, doing as much fighting as ten Indian men.

The women are unmarried and when they desire men, they capture them. If they became pregnant they either kill the male children or send them to their fathers. The females they solemnly raise and instruct them in the art of war. Their leader is called Coñori and they worship in elaborate temples lined with the colored feathers of parrots and macaws.

The Spaniards, fearless conquerors of the Incan empire and wild jungles, see the women and feel a new excitement . . . and dread.

Abby Wettan Kleinbaum, *The War Against the Amazons,* 119-123

Chile, 1553: Araucanian Victory

The Requerimiento

Pedro Alvarado: "In the name of the King of Spain I require you to acknowledge the supremacy of the Pope and the Crown over these lands or else we have the right to attack and you will suffer war and enslavement."

The indigenous send back the reply: "We do not know either of them."

Jonathan Fried, et al., eds., *Guatemala in Rebellion*, 9-10

It's Christmas Day and Pedro de Valdivia wants presents of concubines and slaves to replace the *encomienda* Indians decimated by forced labor, mistreatment, and smallpox. Lautaro, chief of the Araucanians, used to be Valdivia's page. While attending to Valdivia's needs, he has also served the needs of his people by learning Spanish military tactics and their weaknesses. Ingeniously, the Araucanians have tipped their lances with Spanish swords; they wear helmets and vests made of sealskin and whalebone. They try to fight in the rain to make it difficult for the Spaniards to light the fuses of their arquebuses.

Lautaro lures Valdivia and his fifty men into a trap. No Spaniard survives. Some say Valdivia died in battle, his severed head on the tip of an Araucanian lance made of metal forged in Seville. Others say the Araucanians poured molten gold down his throat because that's what he thirsted for so badly. Still others say it was Araucanian soil that filled his stomach until he burst. No matter. Whichever is true, he received in death exactly what he lusted for in life, some say what he deserved.

See Brian Loveman, *Chile*, 53;
Eduardo Galeano, *Memories of Fire: Genesis*, 119-120

Chile, 1560: Why They Rebel, Part I

Hernando de Santillán, advisor to the governor, has tried for three years to prohibit the indigenous people from being used as pack animals. He has failed. Upon leaving Chile he writes about his own countrymen:

[They] killed, maimed and set dogs upon the Indians, cut off feet, hands, noses and teats, stole their lands, raped their women and daughters, chained them up and used them as beasts of burden, burned their houses and settlements and layed waste their fields.

Fray Gil de San Nicolás, in the tradition of Bartolomé de las Casas, also writes about the real conditions of the indigenous:

They take the Indian men and women prisoners in chains and use them for "dog bait," watching the dogs tear them apart for sport. They destroy the crops, burn the houses and villages full of Indians, shutting the doorways [of the houses] so none can escape.

Brian Loveman, *Chile*, 60

Spanish Atrocities

Spanish abuses against the indigenous population became so numerous and ghastly that even the Spanish king became shocked. The priests profited from enforced labor, and the conquistadors killed and maimed far beyond what was needed for military reasons.

Peru, 1613: Why They Rebel, Part II

Felipe Huamán Poma de Ayala, descendant of an Incan chief, is an artist with a conscience. He sits down to write a letter to King Philip III telling him of the abuses against his people by the clergy. At this time there is one priest, friar, or nun for every ten Peruvians.

. . . The various religious orders established in Peru . . . show an unholy greed for wordly wealth and the sins of the flesh and a good example would be set to everyone if they were punished by the Holy Inquisition.

These priests are irascible and arrogant. They wield considerable power and usually act with great severity towards their parishioners. . . . They readily engage in business, either on their own or other people's account, and employ a great deal of labor without adequate payment.

A favorite source of income for the priesthood consists in organizing the porterage of wine, chillies, cocoa, and maize. These wares are carried on the backs of Indians and llamas and in some cases need to be brought down from high altitudes. The descent often results in death for the Indians, who catch a fever when they arrive in a warm climate.

Three years later, Felipe finishes the letter that now includes four hundred line drawings and a catalogue of abuses, atrocities and resistance. It is twelve hundred pages.

H. McKennie Goodpasture, ed., *Cross and Sword*, 44

Peru, 1749: Why They Rebel, Part III

Two brothers, Jorge Juan and Antonio de Ulloa, ship captains of the Royal Armada, visit Peru. They too write back to the king:

The tyranny suffered by the Indians stems from the insatiable desire for riches on the part of those who come from Spain to rule over them. The latter have no other means of satisfying this lust than by exploiting the Indians. Using every oppressive measure at their disposal, officials exact more through cruelty than they obtain from their own slaves. . . .

In those kingdoms Indians are veritable slaves. . . . The Indians do not retain even the tiniest part of the sum which their toil, sweat, and hard work have earned. . . .

They use fines or court costs to gain ownership of an Indian's cow, mule or other cattle. . . . These continuous extortions have reduced the Indians to such a miserable state that they cannot even be compared to the poorest, most abject people imaginable. . . .

The repartimiento system, so cruelly wicked that it appears as if it were imposed on the people as a punishment . . . a more tyrannical abuse could not be imagined. . . .

Jorge Juan and Antonio de Ulloa, eds., *Kingdoms of Peru*, 70, 76, 77

The Age of Andean Resistance

Peru, 1742: Juan Santos Atahualpa

Juan Santos is tall, a Jesuit-educated *mestizo* with light skin and short hair worn in the style of the indigenous. He speaks Spanish, Quechua, and Latin. He dresses like those who live in the jungle and around his neck is a crucifix which he always wears.

It is May. The messengers he had sent out days ago are returning to his jungle encampment. The message they carried to the pueblos and colonial missions was that an Incan Lord had appeared, a direct descendant of the murdered Atahualpa. He was sent by God to set the world right and usher in a new order that would free the tribes from oppression and bring in prosperity. The message ends asking for their help to reclaim history.

The messengers return with word from the outlying regions. The word is *Yes*.

See Steve Stern, ed., *Resistance, Rebellion, and Consciousness in the Andean Peasant World*, 43; Daniel Valcárcel, *Rebeliones Indigenas*, 50-51

Peru, 1746: Guerrilla Victory

General José de Llamas exudes arrogance when he walks. The most prestigious officer in Peru, he is fresh from the war with England where he commanded twelve thousand men. Rejecting suggestions to plan carefully, Llamas has nothing but disdain for these jungle "savages" whom he will put down in quick order.

At the beginning of March, he heads into rebel territory with 850 soldiers. The humidity rots their supplies and the mules go lame. The men fall sick and some die. When they reach Mount Salt they are fatigued and demoralized. They were supposed to meet other soldiers under the command of Troncoso. But at that moment Troncoso is being beaten so badly by the indigenous forces of Juan Santos that he has to retreat to avoid total annihilation.

With the indigenous is a woman named Doña Ana who was born from the union of an indigenous and a black slave. She commands a company of fifty women.

Neither Llamas nor those who follow him can either find or defeat Juan Santos.

See Steve Stern, ed., *Resistance, Rebellion, and Consciousness in the Andean Peasant World*, 43, 44; Daniel Valcárcel, *Rebeliones Indigenas*, 61, 62

In what is now Peru and Bolivia, the years 1742-1783 marked a period of intense and constant rebellion by the indigenous people.

History of Defiance

Well over one hundred times between the years 1720 and 1790 the native Andean people rose up in defiance of colonial authorities. The causes of the rebellion were rooted both in the repressions that the indigenous population had to endure under colonialism and the vision of the return of the great Incan creator. The *Inkarri* myth envisioned the return of an Andean god who would bring in an age of justice. This belief both unified and legitimized the great rebellion of Juan Santos Atahualpa.

Also during this time, resurrection stories circulated telling of the reappearance of the messiah who would come and recover the Incan greatness. When the invaders decapitated Tupac Amaru I in 1572 the great Incan dynasty came to an end. But they believed that his body had been regenerating underground for possible return.

A New Leader

In 1742 in the Andean jungle, a man calling himself Juan Santos Atahualpa Apo Inca arose as a leader. He was a direct descendant of the Inca king Atahualpa who had been betrayed and strangled by Pizarro. He called upon the indigenous population to join in an insurrection that would bring in a new order by outlawing slavery and expelling the whites.

The colonial authorities, deeply threatened by a possible insurrection, organized military campaigns against Juan Santos in 1742, 1743, 1746, and 1750. Never defeated, Juan Santos controlled the jungle regions, keeping this area from further colonization for over a century. The Spaniards finally had to rely on a defensive strategy that kept the rebellion from spreading to the sierra.

Frequent Upheavals

From 1751 to 1765 evidence reveals fourteen upheavals against *corregidores* (local governors) and priests. Economic repression was behind most of the revolts of this whole period. The indigenous were under a multiple system of taxes, forced labor, indebtedness, and payments that left them destitute.

The three main types of economic activity were mines, *obrajes* (weaving mills), and haciendas, or plantations. The *mita* system required the indigenous to work unpaid in mines, *obrajes,* or haciendas from six to twelve months during the year. This requirement would be repeated every second or third year.

In addition, the *reparto* system forced the indigenous population to purchase European and native goods at inflated prices from the local *corregidor.* They quickly became indebted to the *corregidor* and therefore had to work for him in the mines, *obrajes,* or *haciendas.* The *reparto* proved more effective at guaranteeing forced labor than the *mita.*

Peru, 1780: El Grito de Tinta

November 4: José Gabriel Condorcanqui is having dinner in the home of his former tutor. The other dinner guest is the local *corregidor* Antonio de Arriaga, an intransigent man who has used his power to cruelly oppress the people. José Gabriel excuses himself on the pretext of having an unexpected visitor. With a small band of loyal followers he waits and captures the *corregidor.*

November 10: José Gabriel proclaims that he is the legitimate heir of the last Incan ruler Tupac Amaru I. He takes the name of Tupac Amaru II and declares a royal order giving him the power to seize, try, and punish *corregidores* and their aides. He promises the people that he will abolish the *mita* and the *reparto* and other forms of labor abuses. He calls upon the people to follow him.

He then takes his first act as their new ruler, and the body of Antonio de Arriaga swings from the scaffold, surrounded by indigenous men with muskets, pikes, and slings. The people pledge their lives to him.

November 18: After hearing of Arriaga's execution, Spanish authorities in Cuzco send a force of six hundred soldiers and seven hundred loyal Indians. Tupac Amaru II marches out to meet them at Sangarará where he wins a great victory. The Inca's ranks swell to sixty thousand.

November 26: Tupac Amaru II issues a proclamation of emancipation freeing everyone, including the slaves.

December 6: Micaela Bastidas, the wife of Tupac Amaru, is back at the command post, governing the country and sending letters to her husband. She is the movement's chief strategist. She understands better than he that their power lies in moving quickly before the Spaniards can call up reinforcements.

Dear Chepe:

You are causing me grief and sorrow. While you saunter through the villages . . . our soldiers rightly grow tired and are leaving for their homes. . . . I have warned you sufficient times against dallying. . . . I gave you plenty of warnings to march on Cuzco immediately. . . .

Your wife

After I finished this letter, a messenger arrived with the news that the enemy from Paruro are in Archos. I shall march out to meet them though it cost me my life.

June E. Hahner, ed., *Women in Latin American History,* 36-37

I am the liberator of the kingdom, the common father of those who groaned under the yoke of the repartimiento.

Tupac Amaru

Added to this burden were local priests who began demanding free personal services from the indigenous while charging for religious services. For example, a high mass with a procession cost twelve pesos. The longer the *reparto* remained in effect, the more pressure it created, because the debt of the indigenous only increased.

Most of the uprisings of this period can be traced to these economic injustices.

See Steve Stern, ed., *Resistance, Rebellion, and Consciousness in the Andean Peasant World,* and Scarlett O'Phelan Godoy, *Rebellions and Revolts in Eighteenth Century Peru and Upper Peru*

A great many people gathered that day, but nobody uttered a cry or spoke a word. . . . Although the weather had been fine and dry, that day dawned overcast, without a sign of the sun, and threatening rain; and at twelve o'clock, when the horses were tugging at the Indian, a strong wind arose, followed by a sudden downpour, so that everybody, even the guards, had to run for shelter. As a result of this the Indians are saying that the heavens and the elements were lamenting the death of the Inca whom the cruel, impious Spaniards were putting to death so inhumanely.

A contemporary witness

In Emir Rodríquez Monegal, ed., *Borzoi Anthology of Latin American Literature,* I:170

Micaela is very beautiful. Her thin neck belies her indomitable spirit. She was the one who had advocated the death of Arriaga. She carried bullets in her mantilla, to shoot him in case he escaped the hanging. While her husband is away she is the government—issuing passports, sending supplies, preventing crime, issuing edicts, appointing officials, and taking charge of prisoners. Generals report to her and priests ask her for assurances and help. She is the chief propagandist for the cause, recruiting new followers. She even goes out personally on expeditions saying, *I will die where my husband dies.*

See Lillian Fisher, *The Last Inca Revolt*

Peru, 1781: Death of the Leaders

May 18: Nine prisoners are led forth, their hands and feet shackled. Seven hang from the gallows. The Inca's son and uncle have no tongues. The executioner takes Micaela up the scaffold, where, in the sight of her husband, her tongue is cut out and a metal collar with screws is tightened around her neck. Her slender neck defies the screws so the executioners tie ropes around her neck, and each pulls in a different direction, and with kicks in the stomach and breast they finally kill her. The general in charge accuses José Gabriel of being an accomplice to insurrection and treason. José Gabriel looks at the general and says, *There are only two accomplices here, you and I. You in the repression and mistreatment of the people and I in their liberation.*

They bring José Gabriel into the middle of the square and the executioner cuts out his tongue. They tie four ropes to his hands and feet and fasten the ropes to the girths of four horses, a sight the city has never seen before. The horses cannot tear him apart, even though they tug at him for a long time so that he springs in the air like a spider. Finally the commander sends word to the executioner to cut off his head, and this is done.

Emir Rodríquez Monegal, ed., *Borzoi Anthology of Latin American Literature,* I:169-170

Peru, 1781: Speaking the Language of the Conquerors

José Antonio de Areche, representative of the king of Spain, commander of the army and judge of the high court, knows the danger of memory. He decrees:

Illustration from The Letter to the King *written by Felipe Huamán Poma de Ayala, depicting the death of Tupac Amaru.*

Indians are forbidden to wear the dress of the gentry, and especially of the nobility, which serves only to remind them of what the ancient Incas wore, bringing back memories that merely cause them to feel more and more hatred for the ruling nation. . . . They should adopt our Spanish customs and the Castilian [Spanish] language. . . .

But it didn't work. In Uruguay in the 1960s and 1970s, there arose a group of urban guerrillas struggling to free the country from an oppressive dictatorship. They called themselves the Tupamaros, after Tupac Amaru. Today in Peru, women attempting to work for social justice have formed a reflection and action group called the Micaela Bastidas Committee.

See Eduardo Galeano, *Memories of Fire: Faces and Masks*, 57, 59

Men and women fought side by side in the Mexican Revolution from 1910-1920. Their rallying cry was "Tierra y Libertad—Land and Freedom."

Rebellion and Revolution: Mexico

Yucatan, 1761: Canek

Legend and history mingle like a braided tapestry. Both could well be true. The revolt lasts a few days; the stories last generations. The stories, the memories, are the fuel that feed the fires of resistance. Two centuries later, one of the spiritual descendants of Canek writes down the stories (see reference below).

The whites have heaped murder on top of abuse. The indigenous are hungry, miserable. The whites say that there will be no reduction in tribute because the Treasury has great needs. The whites brand indigenous with the same iron that they use for the cattle. Canek breaks the iron. In the church, the offerings from the indigenous go to buy incense and candles. *Why not use some of that money to cure the sick?* asks Canek as he smashes the statue of San Antonio.

Mexican Revolts 1700-1910

In Mexico from 1700 to 1900, the rural peoples showed an unparalleled defiance. Historians have recorded around 142 village revolts and rebellions between the years 1700 and 1820. And scarcely a year passed from 1810 to 1920 without some kind of rural uprising. The Mexican countryside probably had more rebellion during those two centuries than any other part of the hemisphere.

144

Why did people revolt? Much of the resistance centered on local grievances. Small farmers, sharecroppers, and the indigenous protested unfair taxes and issues surrounding concentration of ownership of the land in a few hands. Land became the central issue of the Mexican revolution in 1910 as haciendas kept taking over the land of small farmers and villagers.

Sometimes these local revolts became regional rebellions through the development of alliances with other sectors of the population. There were also caste wars in which the indigenous population fought to expel white authorities. The Yaquis in Sonora and the Maya in the Yucatán were never decisively defeated during the nineteenth century. The indigenous population, nearly wiped out by disease, recovered by the eighteenth century. As their numbers grew, so did their ability to carry out successful resistance campaigns.

The revolt in the Yucatán of the Mayans led by Jacinto Canek was quickly put down but long remembered. The Mayan people have a strong sense of continuity with their past. They pass on their oral history from generation to generation. Their history became alive ninety years later as a new, more successful revolt called the War of the Castes raged for fifty years. Their rallying cry was "Jacinto Canek."

The Yaquis

The Yaquis formed the dominant thread of rebellion from 1740 to 1976. This rebellion at times took the form of armed struggle, and at other times was a cultural resistance that found nonviolent ways to defend the culture, identity and way of life

The Indians are in revolt! yell the whites.

The whites go from house to house seeking the rebels. If they find a machete hanging on the wall, they kill the inhabitants as suspected rebels. If they don't have a machete, they kill them anyway. *They are bound to have a machete someplace,* the Captain explains.

The whites burn the ranch of an indigenous family. *Leave the Indians inside. A burned Indian makes good fertilizer.*

The call to war goes out to the surrounding villages. It is not in writing. The messengers simply dip their hands in the blood of the martyrs assassinated by whites.

Canek calls the people together. Without a word he points to the table filled with bread and weapons. Some take the bread. To those he gives guns and tells them to defend their homes. Some take the weapons. To those he gives bread and tells them to mount the barricades. Others take both guns and bread. Because they are so clever, he makes them the captains.

The white soldiers slaughter the indigenous in the plaza. Row upon row fall. They capture Canek. They tie his hands. *It's useless, Captain, you don't have enough rope to tie the hands of all the people.*

When Canek mounts the gallows he is smiling, but the people don't see it because they are looking at the ground. Some say that they saw him, up ahead, on the road to Cisteil. His steps make no noise and the birds do not flee when he passes. His body is clear, like a bright light burning in the sun. He keeps on walking and when he reaches the horizon he begins to ascend.

Ermilo Abreu Gómez, *Canek: History and Legend of a Maya Hero,* 51-66

Mexico City, 1909: The Eve of Revolution

Porfirio Díaz, strongman of the Americas rules Mexico like an aristocrat. In dress uniform covered with medallions, he looks like a Prussian kaiser. Near him is the archbishop, baptizer of the aristocracy, presiding over a very wealthy church that has accumulated centuries of profits from the backs of the indigenous and campesinos.

While peasants cultivate the huge haciendas with oxen and wooden plows, the wealthy attend the Italian marble opera house with its fabulous glass curtain made by

Tiffany. The mines are owned by a few capitalists, one of them a citizen of the United States, Meyer Guggenheim. William Randolph Hearst, the San Francisco newspaper tycoon, owns thousands of acres of Mexican land. Some haciendas, like the one owned by the Terrazas family, extend for one million acres. And the haciendas are grabbing more and more land, taking the *ejidos* (traditional communal lands) of the villages. Ninety percent of the population is living in poverty, ten percent in splendor.

The sugar plantations that have dominated the land in the South since the sixteenth century are expanding. Well-paid lawyers use tricks to grab land and water from their rightful but weaker users. Where the refinement of law fails, plantation foremen beat and cheat field hands. Racism undergirds the theft: *The Indian . . . has many defects as a laborer, being as he is, lazy, sottish and thieving.* Villages begin to disappear. One plantation owner uses his irrigation system to flood a whole village. The plantation owners meet resistance with brutality.

See Anita Brenner and George Leighton, *The Wind that Swept Mexico*

Anenecuilco, 1909: Emiliano Zapata

He just turned thirty. Over the last three years he has been active in village defense, signing protests and generally keeping up village morale. He is elected president of the village council. He is not a poor man, for his family owns livestock, but he is one of the people. Short in stature and weighing only 130 pounds, he usually wears an oversize sombrero that hides his dark intense eyes.

John Womack, Jr., *Zapata and the Mexican Revolution*, 5,6

Tlaltizapán, 1911: Zapata and the Liberating Army of the South

His men follow him out of *cariña*. They admire and respect him, feel tender toward him because he trusts them and does not seek power or glory for himself. He is so loyal to his own troops that his enemies defect to join him. The people of the South believe he is the champion who will right all wrongs. To some he is a father, to others a son or brother, to still others—*a savior*.

He is obsessed with staying true to the people. Never able to betray a promise, he detests the politicos in Mexico City and continually refuses to go there for talks. His headquarters are out in the countryside he loves so dearly. He says, *The land free, the land free for all without overseers and without masters, is the war-cry of the revolution.*

of the people. The Yaquis were able to remain separate while also partially integrating their economy into the larger Mexican society. This feat was central to their lengthy survival.

In 1740, the Yaquis revolted against the paternalism and exploitative labor practices of the Jesuit mission. The Yaquis' grievances were put forward by El Muni, their new leader. In 1736, the priests had El Muni arrested, provoking an outcry and spontaneous demonstration by two thousand Yaquis.

By 1740, many Yaquis were going hungry because the Jesuits had sent out of the territory surplus grains which the Yaquis had grown. The Yaquis raided granaries which they thought were theirs anyway. The rebels never killed any priests and generally left the mission property unharmed.

During the nineteenth century, the Yaquis were in almost continual revolt. They opposed white colonization and the dividing of their communal lands into individual plots. They first appealed through legal channels. When that failed, they relied on armed struggle.

By 1873, a new leader, Cajeme, had arisen, who emphasized Yaqui self-sufficiency and autonomy and who initiated a cultural awakening through the recreation of traditional festivals and ceremonies, and the reactivation of councils as a democratic form of government. The Yaquis were, at this point, a state within a state, which the Mexican government could not tolerate. A new cycle of attacks against them began.

By the end of the nineteenth century, their resistance took the form of guerrilla bands under their new leader Tetabiate. The Yaquis were more dispersed geographically, but they formed communities in exile that financially supported the guerrilla war.

Mexican president Díaz reacted by deporting Yaquis to distant parts of Mexico. When the revolution of 1910 broke out, the Yaquis joined the revolutionary forces of Pancho Villa and Alvaro Obregón.

In the 1930s the government of Lázaro Cárdenas created a *zona indigena* (reserve) which included most of the traditional Yaqui land which they were able to hold in common. New treaties in the 1950s integrated the Yaquis into the large Mexican state through the building of large dams that forced them into export and large-scale agriculture.

Importance of Rural Revolts

Rural revolts played a central role in the significant changes in Mexican society during the two centuries. Mexico is the only country in the Western Hemisphere where every major social change has been linked to rural revolts. Rural unrest against the Aztecs aided the Spanish invasion. Likewise, rural unrest was the force behind the Mexican independence movement. And finally, in 1910, rural villages, particularly in the South, behind the leadership of Emiliano Zapata, fueled the revolution.

See Evelyn Hu-Dehart, "Peasant Rebellion in the Northwest: The Yaqui Indians of Sonora, 1740-1976," *Riot, Rebellion and Revolution*, 141-175

The liberating army of the South is a people's army. The men and women are primarily villagers and secondarily soldiers. Zapata insists on the primacy of village democracy and control. The national duty is to uphold the dignity of village life.

He sets up his headquarters in Tlaltizapán; his offices are in an old rice mill on the edge of town. It is a little town with a shady square where people relax in the evening with a beer and talk of the weather and prices. Zapata joins them when he can, savoring a good cigar and savoring his people.

John Womack, Jr., *Zapata and the Mexican Revolution*, 241-243

Mexico City, 1911: Zapata meets Madero

The two revolutionary leaders meet in Mexico City conferring on the future of the revolution. Zapata is clear: *What interests us is that, right away, lands be returned to the pueblos, and the promises which the revolution made be carried out.*

In the late nineteenth century haciendas extended their power by using new technology, irrigation systems, and foreign capital to produce cash crops for export. These crops included cotton, sugar cane, tobacco, cacao, and vanilla. These practices drove the peasants off the land.

Madero says that the land issue is complicated. The most important thing is for Zapata to disband his troops. *I'll disband my boys as soon as the land is divided.*

Zapata, his rural and indigenous roots out of place in this ornate city room, rises, walks to Madero and points his rifle at Madero's gold watch.

Look, Señor Madero, if I take advantage of the fact that I am armed and take away your watch, and after a while we meet, both of us armed the same, would you have a right to demand that I give it back? Madero says that he would have that right and he would ask for interest as well. *Well, that's exactly what has happened to us in Morelos, where a few planters have taken over by force the villagers' lands. My soldiers— the armed farmers and all the people in the villages— demand that I tell you, with full respect, that they want the restitution of their lands . . . right now.*

John Womack, Jr., *Zapata and the Mexican Revolution,* 96

Mexico City, 1913: Defense of the Revolution

Madero has trusted the military and the *hacendados* and has distrusted Zapata and the men of the South. Those, he realizes as he sits waiting for execution, are his two crucial mistakes. In a few days he will be dead. The man who rose up against him in a military coup was Victoriano Huerta. And, ironically, it is Zapata who tried to save him.

Huerta needs Zapata so he tries to negotiate with him. When that fails he tries to buy him off. Not today or ever will Emiliano Zapata betray the cause of his people. He tells Huerta:

We do not want the peace of slaves, nor the peace of the grave. . . . We want peace based on liberty, on the political and agrarian reform promised by our political creed; we are incapable of trafficking with the blood of our brothers and we do not want the bones of our victims to serve as a staircase to public offices. . . .

Robert P. Millon, *Zapata: The Ideology of a Peasant Revolutionary,* 19-20

The Mexican Revolution

In 1910, Mexico was a nation dominated by haciendas, large plantations worked by peasants and sharecroppers. These laborers were usually in debt to the hacienda owner who lived a comfortable life from the profits produced by cheap labor. In Morelos, for example, the ownership of the land was so concentrated in the hands of a few people that thirty haciendas controlled almost all of the cultivated land there.

Sugar production was strong, based on export and maximizing profits. The sugar plantations and other haciendas were hungry for more land and so ate up the small plots worked by peasant farmers. The political life of the nation was controlled by the elite sectors of the military, wealthy merchants, and the hacienda owners.

Porfirio Díaz, aligned with these wealthy elites, had been president of Mexico since 1884. In 1910, Francisco Madero, son of a wealthy *hacendado*, began the revolution that in a few months toppled Díaz from power. Joining Madero were Pancho Villa and Pascual Orozco in the North and Emiliano Zapata in the South.

The *Zapatistas*, as the people who followed Zapata were called, at first were very sympathetic to Madero because he talked of a land reform plan that would return some land to the peasants. Even though Zapata won a crucial victory in the South, once Madero came to power in 1911 he wanted Zapata to disband his troops. Madero also refused to implement any of the land reform that he had promised. The agrarian reform was such a central part of the *Zapatistas'* struggle that they broke with Madero and fought against him in the name of the true revolution.

The Plan of Ayala

That same year, the *Zapatistas* drew up their own land reform proposal called the Plan of Ayala. The plan called for the restoration of land taken from the peasants; one-third of the lands of the haciendas would become *ejidos*, the traditional communal lands of the indigenous; and all those owners and politicians who opposed this redistribution would have their land taken without compensation. The plan also authorized the people to take the land immediately when possible. That plan would be their banner for the remainder of the revolution.

Government Atrocities

General Victoriano Huerta carried out a military coup against Madero and had him assassinated. Huerta and his men, under the direction of Juvencio Robles, wrought horrible destruction to the South. The government armies tortured, mutilated, and killed unarmed villagers and raped the women. They burned whole villages and used the tactic of creating concentration camps where they took the villagers.

The *Zapatistas* in the South and Villa and Venustiano Carranza in the North kept up the revolutionary struggle. In 1914, they defeated Huerta. Carranza and his wing of the revolution, called the Constitutionalists, came to power. Carranza refused to implement the kind of sweeping land reform that Zapata wanted. After a short peace,

Mexican Countryside, 1917: Women in the Revolution, *Adelitas*

They do everything. They cook and they command troops. They accompany their husbands and they lead them. Some disguise themselves as men, others enter the army as wives and mothers, taking care of their families under hazardous and difficult conditions. They ride the tops of trains heading into battle. Some come because their husbands make them; others come dragging their husbands. Margarita Neri and Carmen Alanís command troops, while Jauna Belén and Dolores Jimenez de Muro rise to the rank of colonel.

They would call us Adelitas because we were revolutionaries. But the real Adelita was from Ciudad Juarez. This Adelita would say, "Let's go. The one who is afraid stays to cook beans!" And amid gunshots and gunshots, the one who disobeyed— she herself would kill them. She was very brave.

Like women always, they do what is necessary. When commanders need secret information, they are spies and couriers. When the battle is fierce, they carry and shoot carbines and pistols. When uniforms need mending, they are seamstresses. When the outside world needs information, they are journalists and propagandists and secretaries. When the injured come back from the battle, they are nurses and doctors. They formulate plans, write declarations, make tortillas and love.

Julia Tuñón Pablos, *Mujeres en Mexico: Una Historia Olvidada,*
133-140

The women who fought in the revolution were called Adelitas. The feminine presence in the revolution was widespread. This image of the woman soldier has formed part of the legends of the revolution.

Morelos, 1919: Betrayal, Death and Resurrection

Zapata returns to Morelos with new energy for the struggle. He is negotiating with Colonel Jesús Guajardo to defect to the rebels. If that happens there will be the troops and the army to retake all of Morelos for the true revolution. His spies pick up rumors of a trick, but Zapata restrains his suspicions. Zapata meets Guajardo in his home territory, thirty-five miles from the village of Ayala, the town whose name bears the plan at the heart of the revolution.

At 2:10 p.m. on April 10, Guajardo orders a bugle honor call for Zapata. As the last note dies away, Zapata reaches the doorway where the soldiers presenting arms shoot him at point blank range. Emiliano Zapata, the "Savior," is dead, killed by the orders of a Jesús who gets a fifty thousand peso reward. Many months before, Emiliano Zapata had said, *I want to die a slave to principles, not to men.* He does.

The government sends the corpse back to the people of Morelos, so that they will verify his death. The government believes that killing Zapata will kill the revolution. *Los humildes*, the humble common people, file past the body and tremble from head to toe. *It hurt me as much as if my own father had died.* Some say it is not Zapata because the face is missing a mole or the hand is not missing a finger. Some say they saw him riding in the hills. But there is no such resurrection.

The resurrection of Emiliano Zapata comes in the people he loved. The resistance continues with Gilgardo Magaña as Zapata's successor. A message circulates: *Rebels of the South, it is better to die on your feet than to live on your knees.*

John Womack, Jr. *Zapata and the Mexican Revolution,* 326-330

Morelos, 1920: Triumph

The year ends with agrarian reform as a national policy. The *Zapatistas* are integrated into the national army. The area of Morelos, on whose behalf Zapata had taken up the revolution, has survived systematic arson, concentration camps, and mass executions. The people of Anenecuilco, hometown of Zapata, filter back and gain plantation lands as their own under the new law. Most large sugar plantations are gone. *What was called prosperity for the state was misery for us. We are [now] growing what we want to grow and for our own use.*

John Womack, Jr., *Zapata and the Mexican Revolution,* 369-374

Zapata and Villa once again began fighting for what they believed was the real revolution. Carranza became more conservative, siding with the *politicos* in Mexico City and losing sight of the campesinos in the countryside. His troops carried out some of the same atrocities as Huerta, and in 1919 Carranza had one of his men betray and assassinate Emiliano Zapata. The *Zapatistas* continued fighting under the leadership of Gildardo Magaña.

A Triumph

Alvaro Obregón, a radical Constitutionalist, came out of retirement because of Carranza's move to the right, and overthrew him in 1920. With Obregón in power, much of what the *Zapatistas* had fought for became part of the revolutionary government. Zapata's desire to promote popular education resulted in the building of thousands of schools in the countryside. The villagers of Morelos held onto their lands and the new government of 1920 instituted guarantees to them that they could keep it. Twice during the Mexican Revolution the U.S. government directly intervened with troops—once at Vera Cruz in 1914 and again in the North in 1916-1917. These and other U.S. interferences kept the revolution from achieving all that it had hoped for. Some of the best achievements had to wait for the regime of Lazaro Cardenas (1934-1940).

See John Womack, Jr., *Zapata and the Mexican Revolution,* and Robert P. Millon, *Zapata: Ideology of a Peasant Revolutionary*

The image of Augusto Cesar Sandino became a rallying point for the new generation of Sandinistas in Nicaragua during the 1970s and 1980s.

Central American Resistance

Nicaragua

San Albino Mines, 1926: Beginnings

Augusto Ceasar Sandino has just returned from Mexico where he worked at the Huasteca Petroleum Company. He brings his life savings of five thousand dollars, which he is ready to give over to the revolutionary struggle that is in its beginning stages.

Meeting with miners from San Albino, he hears and sees the wretchedness of their lives. The United States owns the mines. The workers tell him how they are barely paid in coupons, which are of no value except at the company store. They work fifteen hours a day and then return to their huts where they have to sleep on the floor because they have no beds. The mines are under constant guard so there cannot be resistance.

These miners will become the first soldiers in Sandino's struggle for liberation.

see Gregorio Selser, *Sandino*

Nicaragua: Early Resistance

In the seventeenth and eighteenth centuries the Subtiava tribe fought the Spaniards. In 1811-1812 indigenous insurrections arose in Leon, Masaya, Granada, and Rivas, the people armed with only sticks and machetes. The 1820s and 1840s were periods of renewed rebellion.

In 1856 a U.S. citizen named William Walker came to Nicaragua, proclaimed himself president, made English the official language, and reinstituted slavery. He confiscated Nicaraguans' land to give to U.S. citizens and received backing from the slave states and immediate diplomatic recognition by the U.S. government. Uprisings ousted Walker and chased him from Nicaragua.

Zelaya

When the Panama Canal was built in 1903, Nicaraguan president Jose Santos Zelaya investigated the possibility of a second canal through Nicaragua. That suggestion, along with his willingness to trade with Britain and Japan, infuriated the United States, whose government believed it should have sole control over Central America.

In 1908 Zelaya contracted for a loan from a British firm to build a railway in Nicaragua. The United States accused him of breaking the Monroe Doctrine by having such close relations with outside countries. When two U.S. citizens were caught sabotaging Nicaraguan ships and were tried and executed, the U.S. government had the pretext it needed to intervene. Four hundred Marines arrived to "protect U.S. lives and property." The assault was financed by a contribution of one million dollars by U.S. businessmen. After the overthrow of Zelaya's presidency, the United States finally installed its man, Adolfo Diaz, as president. Diaz eventually modified the Nicaraguan constitution to allow for U.S. intervention, and U.S. bankers rapidly assumed control of the country's finances.

More Resistance

In 1912, in response to the rise to power of the U.S.-backed Conservative Party, General Benjamin "El Indio" Zeledon began a popularly based resistance movement. After the rebels won several important victories, the U.S. troops were called in. They stormed Zeledon's position, killing him and more than six hundred of his followers.

Moncada's Camp, 1927: First Manifesto

Moncada has made his deals with the U.S. government and is ready to surrender. He calls his generals together to tell them how to give up their arms. Everybody is there—except Sandino. Moncada rushed the meeting so that when Sandino arrived he'd be too late.

Moncada: *As my subordinate, you must accept the decision to disarm.*

Sandino: *I protest that this meeting was called so that I could not be present.*

Moncada: *And who made you a general?*

Sandino: *My comrades in arms, señor. I owe my rank neither to traitors nor invaders.*

Sandino consults his troops. Twenty-seven refuse to surrender. Sandino issues a manifesto:

Seeing that the United States of North America, lacking any right except that with which brute force endows it, would deprive us of our country and our liberty, I have accepted its unjust challenge, leaving to History the responsibility for my actions. To remain inactive or indifferent, like most of my fellow citizens, would be to subject myself to this vulgar multitude of parricide merchants.

Gregorio Selser, *Sandino,* 76-77

Yalí, 1927: Father and Son

Don Gregorio, Sandino's father and a friend of Moncada, comes to persuade his son to surrender. They move out to a little open area, but still in earshot of Sandino's small band of followers. Don Gregorio tells him that in this world saviors end up on the cross and the people are not grateful and forget. Sandino remains adamant that this is the proper course. His gestures and his words tell his men that he will not turn back or surrender. *Viva Sandino,* they shout.

Don Gregorio leaves. He writes a letter to his other son Socrates saying, *Come, join your brother's cause.*

Gregorio Selser, *Sandino,* 78

Ocotal, 1927: Ultimatum

G.D. Hatfield, commanding officer of the U.S. Marines in Nicaragua, is growing impatient. He writes a final letter to Sandino:

It does not seem possible that you remain deaf to reasonable proposals, and despite your insolent replies to my suggestions in the past, I hereby offer you one more opportunity to surrender with honor. . . . Otherwise you will be proscribed and placed outside the law, hunted wherever you go and repudiated everywhere, awaiting an infamous death: not that of the soldier who falls in battle but that of a criminal who deserves to be shot in the back by his own followers. . . .

In conclusion, I wish to inform you that Nicaragua has had its last revolution. . . .

Gregorio Selser, Sandino, 79

Camp El Chipote, 1927: The Ant Confronts the Elephant

Sandino responds:

Captain G.D. Hatfield, Ocotal

I received your communication yesterday and fully understand it. I will not surrender and await you here. I want a free country or death. I am not afraid of you; I rely on the patriotic ardor of those who accompany me.

A.C. Sandino

Gregorio Selser, Sandino, 79-80

Ocotal, 1927: Massacre

President Coolidge calls it *an heroic action.* Diaz, the U.S.-picked man in Nicaragua, calls for medals for the airmen. The Marines call in air support in Ocotal, planes that rain bombs down upon the town. Following orders to *gun the bandits down mercilessly where they are encountered,* they empty their bomb racks and then swoop low and empty their machine guns on the fleeing people. One U.S. soldier is killed. Three hundred Nicaraguans—men, women, and children are killed and one hundred are wounded.

Illinois Governor Edward Dunne writes:

In all of U.S. history there has been no action of such indecency as we now see in Nicaragua. . . . The slaughter of 300 Nicaraguans by the Americans is a blot on the United States. . . .

H.H. Knowles, former minister to Nicaragua, says in a speech:

I know of no inhuman actions and crimes greater than those committed by the United States against the defenseless

The twenty-seven hundred U.S. Marines, their job finished, left, but very soon they were called in again. In 1927 the United States feared intervention from Mexico. Asserting that only the United States could intervene in other countries, the government sent four thousand Marines and soldiers to Nicaragua.

At the time two Nicaraguan factions were fighting each other. The United States imposed a ceasefire and required all arms to be handed over to the Marines. Jose Maria Moncada, leader of one of the factions, surrendered. In his army was a man named Agusto Ceasar Sandino.

Sandino, with only a few men at first, refused to surrender. He said that the real problem in Nicaragua was U.S. intervention and called for a Nicaragua free from outside domination. His fight against U.S. imperialism inspired a new wave of Nicaraguan insurrection that would last decades.

see George Black, *Triumph of the People*

The First Sandinistas

Augusto Caesar Sandino and the twenty-nine men who refused to surrender took to the hills of Segovia, mountainous jungle, perfect for guerrilla warfare. Sandino's army grew, as did the popularity of his cause. Under the slogan "Free Country or Death," his main goal became driving the "gringos" from Nicaraguan soil.

At first the untrained and ill-equipped army suffered defeats. Then they began to change their tactics and develop real guerrilla war manuevers. The local population acted as spies and assisted with developing a communications network, allowing Sandino to learn quickly about U.S. troop movements. As Sandino's forces began scoring victories over the "Yanqui invaders," the United States turned to using air power against Sandino. However, even with their vastly superior air power, the United States could not defeat the Sandinistas.

Sandino became a folk hero throughout most of Central and Latin America, but in the U.S. press he was portrayed as a "bandit." Cecil B. DeMille wanted to do a movie about him but the State Department did not allow it.

By 1930, the United States planned to leave Nicaragua, but not before training and equipping a Nicaraguan National Guard which would act as an agent of U.S. interests. The clear advantage of this arrangement was protecting U.S. interests without risking the lives of U.S. citizens. In 1932, U.S. troops left Nicaragua, leaving Anastasio Somoza as head of the National Guard. Somoza would soon became dictator, and his family ruled Nicaragua until 1979, the longest dictatorship in Central America. In 1933, Somoza lured Sandino to Managua under the pretext of signing a peace agreement. With approval and direction from the United States, Somoza arranged the assassination of the great leader and folk hero.

See Gregorio Selser, *Sandino* and George Black, *Triumph of the People*

peoples of Latin America through its legally authorized agents and representatives. . . .

We have imposed our force upon weak, defenseless, and completely powerless countries, murdering thousands of their subjects, and we have attacked them when they expected us to defend them. We have used the Monroe Doctrine to prevent European countries sympathetic to those republics from coming to their aid. Instead of sending them teachers, instructors, and elements of civilization, we send them hunters of usurious banking concessions, avaricious capitalists, corrupters, soldiers to shoot them down, and degenerates to infest them with every disease.

Gregorio Selser, *Sandino*, 80-81

Nicaragua, 1929: The People

While Sandino's guerrilla band is fighting in the mountains, the people are waging their own struggle in the cities. Children are refusing to learn English in the schools. The United States forces them to attend a U.S. military parade. The people refuse to sing the national anthem and instead shout out Sandino's war cry, *Death to the traitors!* The elderly refuse gifts made in the United States.

A reporter writes, *Sandino has the whole continent behind him.*

Gregorio Selser, *Sandino*, 228

Managua, February 21, 1933: Betrayal

5 p.m.: Sandino arrives at President Sacasa's home.

Early evening: The National Guard holds a Council of War. At dusk Somoza arrives. *I come from the American Embassy, where I have been conferring with Ambassador Arthur Bliss Lane. He has assured me that the Washington government supports and recommends the elimination of Augusto Caesar Sandino, considering him as it does a disturber of the country's peace.* They draw up a document implicating all of them in the assassination plot—an insurance policy against anyone betraying the others.

At the same time Sandino is having supper in the home of President Sacasa, who himself will be overthrown by Somoza in 1936. They talk of peace and gold mining and Nicaragua's future.

10 p.m.: Sacasa accompanies Sandino; Gregorio, Sandino's father; and Sandino's generals, Umanzor and

Estrada to the door. The guests get into the car and head toward the National Guard's Campo de Marte where they encounter a stalled vehicle. Generals Estrada and Umanzor, sensing an ambush, pull out their revolvers. Sandino urges them not to shoot, since Salvatierra and his father are not fighting men. Major Delgadillo, disguised as a Guard corporal, approaches the car and tells them to drop their pistols because they are under arrest. Sandino, Estrada, and Umanzor are ordered into a truck marked GN No. 1 *(Guardia Nacional)* while Salvatierra and Gregorio stay behind. The National Guard takes them to a place called La Calavera (the Skull). Sandino is calm. He asks for a drink of water. The request is denied. Estrada says, *Don't ask these fellows for anything, general, let them kill us.* Standing with his hands in his pockets, Sandino refuses to allow them to search him. His last words: *My political leaders have played jokes with me.*

11 p.m.: Sandino sits on a rock on the right, Umanzor in the middle and Estrada to the left. A shot crackles in the air, the signal to begin. The machine guns open fire. A bullet enters Sandino's brain and chest. Umanzor dies with five in the head, Estrada two in the chest. From the distance, Gregorio hears the shots and says, *Now they're killing them. It always happens; try to be a redeemer, and you get crucified.*

Somoza, knowing the danger of memory, erases the struggle of Sandino's forces from Nicaraguan history books and makes it a crime to speak the name of Sandino.

Gregorio Selser, *Sandino*, 174-177

United States, 1935:
A Henchman Speaks the Truth

Moments occur when the powerful, or those who serve them, speak the truth about what they have done. In his memoirs Major General Smedley Butler, a Marine who led many invasions into Central America, sets the record straight.

I spent 33 years and four months in active service as a member of the . . . Marine Corps. . . . And during that period I spent most of my time being a high-class muscle man for Big Business. . . . Thus I helped make Mexico and especially Tampico safe for American oil interests in 1914. I helped make Haiti and Cuba a decent place for the National City Bank to collect revenues in. . . . I helped purify Nicaragua for the international banking house of Brown Brothers in 1909 and 1912. I brought light to the Dominican Republic for American sugar interests in 1916. I helped make Honduras "right" for American fruit companies in 1903.

Joyce Hollyday, ed., *Crucible of Hope*, 10

The Second Sandinistas

For forty years the Somoza family ruled as a dictatorship becoming the nation's largest landholders. The U.S. government calculated their worth at close to a billion dollars by the 1970s. That wealth was in stark contrast to the poverty suffered by the majority of Nicaraguans.

Frente Sandinista de Liberacion Nacional (FSLN)

In 1961 the Sandinista Front was born, taking its name and aspirations from Sandino. By 1963, sixty combatants grouped in Honduras, among them Santos Lopez, a soldier who fought with Sandino. The early years brought depravation, sacrifice, and only a few victories. The guerrilla force established itself on the Rio Coco on the Honduran/Nicaraguan border.

As one combatant related: "There was nothing to eat, not even animals. There was no salt. It wasn't just hunger that was terrible, but constant cold twenty-four hours a day, because we spent all our time in the river. We were always wet through with the clinging rain of that part of the country, the cold a kind of unrelieved torture, mosquitoes, wild jungle animals, and insects. No shelter, no change of clothes, no food." (Black, 78)

All recruits to the guerrilla force had to commit themselves to live as campesinos. In the late 1960s the guerrilla force remained on the move and hidden while at the same time building the credibility of the movement in the cities and rural areas. In 1974 the

Tegucigalpa, Honduras, 1961: Resurrection

Three former university students, Tomas Borge, Carlos Fonseca Amador, and Silvio Mayorga meet in the Honduran capital to discuss creating a national liberation front in Nicaragua. They have devoured the writings and autobiography of Augusto Caesar Sandino and see that many of Sandino's goals are the same for them: stopping U.S. intervention, creating real independence, and forming a guerrilla army in the mountains that will build local support among the campesinos.

They emerge from the meeting committed to national liberation. Their name: *Frente Sandinista de Liberacion Nacional* (FSLN), the Sandinista National Liberation Front.

In Nicaragua some now dare to speak the name of Sandino.

George Black, *Triumph of the People,* 75-76

El Naranjo, 1974: Fire from the Mountain

It was only a few years ago that he was a university student and organizer for the FSLN. In 1970, he had made the momentous decision to leave the city and join the guerrillas in the mountains. Omar Cabezas will some day be a Sandinista leader. Now he is still battling the mud and exhaustion of the mountains. He and his *compañeros* are always wet. Some days they only eat three spoonfuls of corn meal while marching up and down the mountains. They contract a skin disease called mountain leprosy that rots the skin from their legs and arms. He sleeps on the ground with a piece of plastic for a bed. Mud is everywhere and in the mountains it is cold, and like the cold nights, the loneliness penetrates to the bone. But a transformation is taking place:

As if the mountain and the mud, the mud, and also the rain and the loneliness, as if all these things were cleansing us. . . .

That is why we said that the genesis of the new person was in the FSLN. The new person began to be born with the fungus infections and . . . feet oozing worms; the new person began to be born with loneliness and eaten alive by mosquitos. . . . That's the outer part, because inside, by dint of violent shocks day after day, the new person was being born with the freshness of the mountains. A person—it might seem incredible—but an open, unegotistical person,

Forward we march, compañeros, we advance toward the revolution. Our people are the owners of their history, architects of their liberation.

Combatants of the Sandinista Front, forward, the future is ours, red and black flags cover us, free country, to win or to die.

The children of Sandino do not sell out or surrender, never! We struggle against the Yankee, the enemy of humanity.

Today the dawn is no longer a temptation, tomorrow, some day, will rise a new sun that will illuminate all the land that the heroes and martyrs bequeathed us, in abundant rivers of milk and honey.

Forward, we march. . . .

Hymn of the Sandinistas

no longer petty—a tender person who sacrifices. . . . for others, who suffers when others suffer and who also laughs when others laugh. . . . You always cultivated that tenderness in the mountains. I took care not to lose my capacity for that beauty. The new person was born in the mountains. . . .

Omar Cabezas, Fire From the Mountain, 87

Monimbo, 1978: The People Take the Lead

In the town of Masaya is the Indian barrio (neighborhood) called Monimbo. Speak the name Monimbo these days and you speak the name resistance. Benjamin "El Indio" Zeledon died there in 1912 at the hands of the U.S. troops. A few miles away is Niquinohomo, the birthplace of Sandino.

The people begin organizing masses and demonstrations protesting the death of *La Prensa* newspaper editor Pedro Joaquin Chamorro, assassinated by Somoza. On February 21, thousands take to the streets to mark the anniversary of the death of Sandino. The National Guard launches an aerial attack on the crowd marching to the cemetery.

A series of sporadic attacks occurs in the next few days. The people erect barricades in the streets and Monimbo becomes a sea of red and black Sandinista flags. They make and throw *bombas de contacto,* weapons that will pass into the folklore of the revolution as symbols of the ingenuity and determination of a people.

As the days pass, a single barrio takes on the accumulated power of the whole National Guard. Tanks, armoured cars, helicopters, and heavy machine guns attack the people. They fight back with machetes, sticks, contact bombs, and stones. The National Guard attack some young boys carrying Sandinista flags and cut off their hands with bayonets. Other children and adults cry out *Vive el frente Sandinista!* The Guard cuts their tongues out. The Guard attacks with brand-new rifles, M-16's, given to them by the United States. Some of the Guard, ashamed at the killing, go to the side of the people. At the end of the battle, two hundred people, including children, lie dead.

Within days another insurrection in another barrio peopled by the Subtiava Indians erupts in insurrection.

The indigenous are leading the people.

See George Black, Triumph of the People, 113-114

Sandinistas boldly broke their silence by kidnapping wealthy landowners and government officials close to Somoza. The raid harmed no one; in exchange for release of the hostages, the Sandinistas received from Somoza two million dollars, release of Sandinista prisoners of war, and access to the press to proclaim their political program. The daring action gave new visibility to the FSLN among the people.

Somoza's Reign of Terror

In 1967 Somoza ordered the killing of six hundred people at a demonstration. Throughout the late 1960s and 1970s the United States trained the Nicaraguan National Guard and sent arms. When Nicaragua suffered an earthquake in 1972, Somoza stole most of the money sent by international aid organizations and governments to repair the damage and help the people. Somoza's power rested on the ruthlessness of the National Guard and the support of the United States, who considered him a trusted friend because he always voted with the United States at the United Nations. When the Central Intelligence Agency invaded Guatemala in 1954, they used Nicaragua as a base of operations.

In the late 1970s even the middle class became disgusted with Somoza and worked for his removal. Somoza's assassination of popular newspaper editor Pedro Chamorro, galvanized the whole nation for the battle to oust the dictator.

In 1978 the Sandinistas took the lead as the people looked to them for direction. A number of popular insurrections spread thoughout Nicaragua in 1977 and 1978. Somoza sent in the National Guard to brutally suppress the revolts. They killed thousands of people, including children playing in the streets, but they realized that even with their superior weaponry they were no match for the poorly armed people. The people refused to give up even in the face of massive losses.

Insurrection followed insurrection. The Sandinistas made another daring raid, this time on the National Palace, and held hostage many of Somoza's family and close associates. Again Somoza was forced to give in to their demands. This action prepared the way for the final insurrections and battles leading to the triumph of the revolution on July 19, 1979.

See George Black, *Triumph of the People*

Chinandega, 1978: Seizing the Land

The mobilization of the people is becoming a way of life. Rebellion spreads throughout Nicaragua. In Tonala in the far north, the people seize the land. A peasant says,

This land is ours and we've taken it . . . so that we can work, so that we can live. The poison dust from the fumigation of the cotton fields is killing our pigs and chickens. At night, the place is alive with mosquitoes from the Standard Fruit Company's banana plantations. . . . They poison us . . . women, children and old people. Either God will save Tonala or we'll save it ourselves. Tonala will be Nicaragua's second Monimbo.

It is.

George Black, *Triumph of the People*, 123

Managua, 1978: Strike at the Heart

Insurrection and the possibility of insurrection are everywhere. But the Sandinistas feel they need some bold action to galvanize the resistance. Keeping the tightest secrecy, three people plot "Operation Pigsty," the taking of the National Palace in broad daylight and holding members of the House of Deputies hostage. With a total force of only twenty-six people, they choose the best combatants, who happen to average eighteen or nineteen years of age. They disguise themselves as National Guard troops, enter the National Palace, and pretend that Somoza himself is coming. The people inside hide in fear of the dictator, and before they realize that they have been tricked, the Sandinistas capture the whole House of Deputies. Somoza rings the building with Guard troops and orders a helicopter to fire on the building. When he learns some of his friends are inside he stops. The Sandinistas demand the release of their *compañeras* in Somoza's prisons, many of whom are

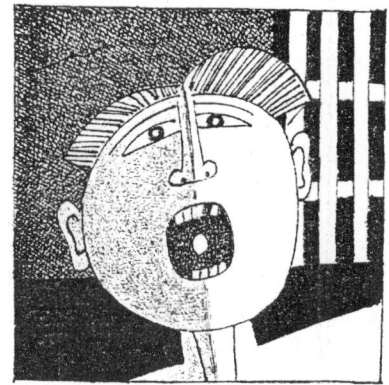

The jails of Somoza were notorious for torture. They were a "test by fire" for those combatants who were captured. These illustrations portray both the pain and the hope that Sandinista prisoners experienced as they waited for the revolution to triumph.

Nicaráuac

being tortured. The siege lasts for forty-five hours. Somoza meets the demands. As the Sandinistas leave the National Palace, thousands of Nicaraguans line the streets, while others form a motorcade of cars, trucks, and motorcycles. The red and black Sandinista *banderas* are everywhere.

In Matagalpa, the daring action has already had an effect. The city erupts in a spontaneous insurrection.

George Black, *Triumph of the People*, 124-126

Managua, 1979: Triumph of the Revolution

May 29: A three-hundred-person column of the famous *Frente Sur* (Southern Front) crosses the border from Costa Rica.

May 31: The FSLN calls for a national insurrection and general strike: *Heroic people of Nicaragua, the hour of the overthrow of the infamous dictator has come. . . .*

June 4: The Sandinistas take Leon.

June 7: Somoza declares martial law and a state of siege.

June 9: The Managua insurrection begins.

June 16: The provisional government junta of National Reconstruction is named, starting a parallel government in Nicaragua and preparing for the fall of Somoza.

July 2-6: Strategic cities fall to the Sandinistas.

July 16: Esteli barracks of the National Guard, the last military installation outside of Managua, falls.

July 17: Somoza resigns and leaves for Miami.

July 19: Radio Sandino awakens the country with sounds of victory—the Sandinista national anthem, slogans, folk songs. The new junta requests discipline, vigilance, and generosity to the defeated enemy. The people of Manuagua take over the city even before the troops arrive. They line the streets to greet the troops who are their sons and daughters, classmates whom they have not seen for years. It is like a family reunion with red and black flags covering the streets, the plaza which will soon be named after Carlos Fonseca. Pandemonium reigns.

The people have regained their memory and their voices. There is one name repeated over and over again, without fear of reprisal. *Viva Sandino!*

The people are reclaiming their history, their land, and a memory that is dangerous.

See George Black, *Triumph of the People*, 155-157

Guatemala

First Invaders

Pedro Alvarado, the first Spanish invader in Guatemala, arrived in the early 1520s. Accompanying him were smallpox, influenza, and the bubonic plague. Up to one-third of the population of the highlands area died during this first epidemic alone. Other epidemics followed in 1545-1548 and 1576-1581. The disruption of the economic and social life due to disease alone was horrific.

Guatemalan historian Severo Martínez Paláez sums up the colonial period as a "regimen of terror for the Indians." He writes, "What we must recognize [is that] the cruel treatment of the Indians was not a sporadic phenomenon, but . . . inherent in the social structures of the colony, absolutely necessary to maintain subjected to incredible forms of exploitation a mass of serfs with enormous numerical superiority." (Handy, 14-15)

The Killers: Disease, War, and Economics

Disease and war took their toll on the indigenous population during the first years of contact with the Spaniards. The economic systems that the Europeans established were equally devastating. The *encomienda* and *repartimiento* systems that prevailed in Peru, Bolivia, and Chile were also fundamental to Guatemala. Spanish wealth depended upon the exploited labor of the indigenous population.

Pangán, 1530: Beginning of the Tribute from the Annals of the Cakchiquel

During this year heavy tribute was imposed. Gold was contributed to Tunatiuh [Pedro Alvarado]; 400 men and 400 women were delivered to him to be sent to wash gold. All the people extracted the gold. Four hundred men and 400 women were contributed to work in Pangán on the construction of the city, by order of Tunatiuh. All this we ourselves saw, oh, my sons! . . .

Jonathan Fried, et al., ed., *Guatemala in Rebellion: Unfinished History*, 15

Guatemala, 1560: The Plague

An anonymous Cakchiquel historian is shivering while writing. Fever overtakes the body, the enormity of destruction overtakes the mind. Both cause the body to quake. Writing it down . . . to remember. . . .

Little by little it arrived here. In truth a fearful death fell on our heads. . . . Many families [succumbed] to the plague. Now the people were overcome by intense cold and fever, blood came out of the noses, then came the cough growing worse and worse, the neck was twisted, and small and large sores broke out on them. The disease attacked everyone here. On the day of Circumcision [January 1, 1560], a Monday, while I was writing, I was attacked by the epidemic.

Jonathan Fried, et al., ed., *Guatemala in Rebellion: Unfinished History*, 15-16

Kingdom of Guatemala, 1648: The System of *Repartimiento*

In the 1540s and 1550s the Dominicans removed the indigenous from their traditional homes and nearer to the Spanish settlements. In this way it was easier to use them for *repartimiento* labor. Thomas Gage, a Dominican friar, writes a century later what this "cheap and lazy way" of colonial living has done to the native population:

It would grieve a Christian's heart to see how by some cruel Spaniards in that week's service those poor wretches are wronged and abused [Indians were partitioned or "shared" by the week]; some visiting their wives at home, whilst their poor husbands are digging and delving; others whipping them for their slow working; others wounding them with

161

their swords, or breaking their heads for some reasonable and well grounded reason in their own behalf; others stealing from them their tools; others cheating them of half; others of all their wages. . . .

Jonathan Fried, et al., ed., *Guatemala in Rebellion: Unfinished History,* 21

Guatemala, 1769: Eighteenth Century Colonialism

Archbishop Pedro Cortes y Larraz has been sent by the Spanish king to investigate the conditions of the indigenous people. In his report back to the king he writes:

This partitioning of Indians for labor service is done with great violence, without respect for the Indian's own need to work his land, or for his own health, or life. . . .

. . . they have experienced two years of calamitous starvation because of which many have died and many have fled the villages. Many have also died spinning cotton which the Spanish administrator makes the Indian women do all year long so they cannot do anything for their families. . . .

The truth is, that at whoever's command, these wretched Indians are tied to the whipping post; men, women, young and old, they are whipped with excessive cruelty, sometimes without any reason at all, and almost always for things which they would not be whipped for if they were not Indians. . . . Of this cruelty I cannot produce greater evidence except to say that frequently enough I hear screams and cries from my room or inn even though the beatings are taking place at a great distance. . . .

Jonathan Fried, et al., ed., *Guatemala in Rebellion: Unfinished History,* 23

Guatemala City, 1838: Revolt from the Mountains

On February 1, the rebel forces of Raphael Carrera march into Guatemala City, and the Spanish and *ladinos* cower behind their doors. They have been taught that the "Indians" are "savages," so they expect the worst. The four thousand rebels are wearing green bushes in their hats so they look like *a moving forest*. The rebels treat the population well, only wanting their basic rights.

Carrera and the rebels are protesting the "liberal reforms" that, from the perspective of the local village, only mean more taxes and less land. At first, Carrera leaves the politicians in power, but by 1839 he sees the interests of the indigenous are not being met. He triumphantly re-enters Guatemala City in that year and assumes the presidency until his death in 1865.

The native-born Spaniards would not allow *Criollos*, Spaniards born in Guatemala, to have any jobs other than that of *corregidor*, or managers of the estates. The tyranny and oppressive behavior of the *corregadores* was notorious throughout Guatemala. They robbed and exploited the indigenous population and became the objects of numerous revolts.

By 1750, attempts by the indigenous population to reclaim their communal practices and Mayan religion led to a number of revolts in outlying villages. The Catholic Church responded by trying to banish these "pagan" practices. Near the town of San Cristóbal, the Tzotzil tribe received inspiration from a young woman who said that the Virgin told her to eliminate the Spaniards. Two thousand people rose up in revolt.

After the death of Raphael Carrera, who led a successful revolt against the wealthy landowners, "liberal" reforms took most of the communal lands of the indigenous population. During the last part of the nineteenth century, Guatemalan economy became export-oriented, with control of the land in the hands of large plantation owners, ensuring vast fortunes for a few people. Tens of thousands of indigenous people lost their land. Dictatorship became the norm.

Coffee was king until the beginning of the twentieth century when large U.S. corporations either bought or were given huge tracts of land for bananas. These corporations benefited from lax regulations. The United Fruit Company, for example, did not have to pay taxes for twenty-five years.

Jorge Ubico became dictator in 1931. He regularly used repression to maintain power, registered all printing presses to cut down on the amount of opposition literature, militarized the public schools, and suggested to United Fruit that the daily wage of the peasants be reduced from seventy to thirty cents. United Fruit was only too happy to oblige. Ubico believed he was the reincarnation of Napoleon, and was so paranoid that he said he had no friends, just "domesticated enemies."

Years of Spring

Led by students, the people overthrew Ubico in 1944. What followed has been called ten years of spring in Guatemala, the only significant time in this century when there was truly civilian rule. Juan Jóse Arévalo was elected president with eighty-five percent of the vote. He was a professor, rather than a politician.

Calling his plan "spiritual socialism," Arevalo instituted a number of political reforms that affected Guatemala City more than the countryside. A social security law and a labor code protecting the rights of workers were two of his accomplishments. He did not attempt to change the distribution of the land for fear of being overthrown by the military and wealthy landowners.

However, his successor, Jacobo Arbenz, did finally institute a mild land reform that bought the vacant lands from their owners at a fair market value and distributed them to landless peasants. The 1950 census showed that two percent of the population controlled seventy-four

This is the only time in the history of Guatemala that peasants, *ladinos,* and the indigenous are able to effect legislation in their own interests.

See Jim Handy, *Gift of the Devil,* 35-54

Guatemala City, 1944: Ubico Flees

A new generation of students has had enough of Ubico's dictatorship. Under Ubico, Guatemala has been sold to U.S. corporations like United Fruit and the Great White Fleet. At the University of San Carlos an association of students protests the tyranny and organizes a series of strikes. Ubico strikes back, saying, *While I am president, I will not grant liberty of press nor of association, because the people of Guatemala are not prepared for democracy. . . .* The students up the pressure and Ubico resigns, but a military group takes over and refuses to allow elections.

Students and professionals organize the Civic Union and plan a general strike. The junta arrests their leaders. Finally the Honor Guard of the Military School joins the students in a bloody battle that chases the junta from power.

See Jim Handy, *Gift of the Devil,* 104-5

Guatemala City, 1954: Bitter Fruit

The United States Information Agency (USIA) is ready to lie itself into history. They launch a sophisticated propaganda campaign designed to destabilize the government of Jacobo Arbenz. They distribute thousands of pamphlets and cartoons to newspapers and others ridiculing the Guatemalan government. They produce three movies on communism in Guatemala. A clandestine radio undertakes a classic disinformation campaign. *Our job is to intimidate listeners. . . .* Panic and fear spread inside Guatemala.

The Central Intelligence Agency (CIA) prepares and arms Castillo Armas with 170 mercenaries. The CIA calls them the *Liberation Army.* When they finally cross the border into Guatemala, the people do not support them and they quickly lose ground. The people do not want them. The United States does not let the will of the people or reality get in their way. The CIA and the USIA fabricate their own reality.

First they tell Castillo Armas not to move or engage in any battles. CIA pilots then leaflet Guatemala City, telling the people how the *Liberation Army* is winning great victories. One CIA propaganda chief says, *Now is the time for the big lie.* CIA radio broadcasts tell of the advance of two non-existent columns of troops, complete with fake conversations between the two imaginary commanders. Frightened Guatemalans flee the city until it is almost a ghost town. The CIA, with the help of the U.S. embassy, spreads rumors that a non-existent cruiser and an imaginary aircraft carrier are off the coast of Guatemala. Jacobo Arbenz and the people of Guatemala are the victims of two months of psychological warfare. Believing that thousands of people will be killed, Arbenz steps down as president to save lives. As he leaves the national palace he addresses the nation:

The United Fruit Company, in collaboration with the governing circles of the United States, is responsible for what is happening to us. . . .

In whose name have they carried out these barbarous acts? What is their banner? We know very well. They have used the pretext of anti-communism. The truth is very different. The truth is to be found in the financial interests of the fruit company and the other U.S. monopolies which have invested great amounts of money in Latin America and fear that the example of Guatemala would be followed by other Latin American countries. . . .

Stephen Schlesinger and Stephen Kinzer, *Bitter Fruit*, 192-199

The sight of children taking care of children in Guatemala is common. Due to the violence of the military against the people, there are tens of thousands of orphans and children who have lost one parent.

percent of the arable land. Seventy-six percent of the population owned only nine percent of the land. The Agragian Reform Law of Arbenz's government, by shifting land away from the largest owners to one hundred thousand peasants, changed the economic structure of Guatemala more than any other event in the previous century.

Part of the expropriation of land hit the United Fruit Company. The Guatemalan government bought unused land of United Fruit for the value they had put down on their tax returns for the last ten years. Company owners were outraged, saying the land was more valuable and they needed it in case something happened to their other land.

End of Spring

They cried to their connections in the highest reaches of the U.S. government that communism was taking over in this hemisphere in Guatemala. John Foster Dulles, Secretary of State, and Allen Dulles, his brother, head of the Central Intelligence Agency, hatched a plot for a CIA-directed invasion of Guatemala.

The CIA armed a man called Castillo Armas and trained a small band of fighters in Nicaragua. The CIA then manipulated the media in Guatemala to such an extent that the people, including Arbenz himself, thought that a huge conquering army was entering Guatemala. The CIA-backed coup overthrew Arbenz; thirty years of military dictatorships followed.

Continued Repression

The late 1970s and early 1980s were periods of unimagineable repression in Guatemala. Under generals like Lucas Garcia and Rios Montt, the Guatemalan army committed at least 225 Indian village massacres in the highlands areas. Not coincidently, those are also areas of Guatemala's greatest mineral wealth, including oil reserves.

Since 1954 the Guatemalan military has killed one hundred thousand people. Presently, there are forty thousand disappeared, people presumed dead but whose bodies have never been found. Familes of the disappeared don't know whether their relative is dead or alive.

In 1962 the first guerrilla group was founded to struggle against the oppressive conditions that the military and wealthy landowners created. In 1982 several guerrilla groups united under the URNG, the Guatemalan National Revolutionary Unity.

Guatemalan Highlands, 1979: Torture

Rigoberta Menchú, one of the leaders of the Guatemalan resistance, tells of the most painful experience of her life.

One of my brothers was a catechist. The other was secretary for a cooperative in the village; that was his only crime. They kidnapped him, and he spent days in the hands of the army, who tortured him. He was only 14 years old. They ripped off his fingernails, cut out his tongue, they destroyed the soles of his feet and burned his skin. I saw him with my own eyes and will never forget it!

. . . At 8:00 a.m. a military truck arrived. They made about 20 men get off the truck; men who no longer looked human, and among them was my little brother. It was hard to identify him. . . . He was so disfigured. . . .

They lined up the prisoners, dressed up like soldiers. . . . They hit them with their rifle butts to make them stand, but they would just fall down again. When [the captain] gave the order to undress them, they had to cut the uniforms because the blood from the wounds made the uniforms stick to their bodies. . . . They tied them and piled them up together, then the captain ordered his soldiers to pour gasoline over them and set them on fire. I was looking at my brother. He didn't die right away, nor did the others. Some screamed; others could no longer breathe so they didn't scream, but their bodies were writhing. Unfortunately, there is no water in our villages, so we couldn't put out the fire that was burning them. When water arrived, it was too late.

I am no longer the owner of my small existence; the world I live in is so cruel, so blood-thirsty, that it is going to annihilate me at any moment. Therefore, the only thing I can do is struggle . . . if I fight, it is to be treated like a human being. . . .

This is what I can give as testimony. . . . If I have narrated my life, if I have taken this opportunity, it's because I know that my people cannot tell their story; but it's no different than mine. I am not the only orphan. . . .

Rigoberta Menchú, *I . . . Rigoberta Menchú*, 198-201

Spanish Embassy, Guatemala City, 1980: Massacre

The occupation and village massacres by the army in El Quiché province have provoked the people to action. They send 130 campesinos to Guatemala City to raise the issue publicly. No one will listen to them. Out of desperation they take over two radio stations. The government warns that they are guerrillas and not to be trusted. Again cut off from raising public awareness, they occupy the Spanish Embassy. Their plan is to occupy the embassy peacefully in order to demand the removal of the army from El Quiché. The dictator, Lucas Garcia, tells his henchmen to take them out.

Guatemalan police surround the embassy, throwing grenades. Inside, the twenty-nine peasants and other visitors take refuge in the ambassador's office. Lucas Garcia says, *Set them on fire.* The police lock the door and throw fire bombs.

From the streets below, the people see thirty-nine human beings writhing and dying, burning.

Vicente Menchú, the father of Rigoberta, is burned alive. She says, *The only thing left were their ashes. . . . What hurt me very, very much was the lives of so many compañeras, fine compañeras who weren't ambitious for power in the least. All they wanted was enough to live on, enough to meet their people's needs. This reinforced my decision to fight.*

Thousands risk death and flood the streets of Guatemala City in the funeral procession honoring the people who died in the Spanish Embassy. Within days a new opposition group is organized called the Vicente Menchú Brigade. Rigoberta joins it. Her father had said: *Some have to give their blood and some have to give their strength; so while we can, we'll give our strength.*

Jonathan Fried, et al, editors, *Guatemala in Rebellion*, 204-206, and Rigoberta Menchú, *I...Rigoberta Menchú*, 185

"Who in your family has disappeared?"

"My father, Rigoberto,

My brother, Máynor,

My brother Otto,

My brother, Armando,

My uncle Moisés,

My uncle Salomón,

My aunt, Lilián,

My aunt, Elizabeth,

My aunt, Sipirana,

My cousin, Damaris,

My cousin, María,

My cousin Hector,

My cousin, Noé,

My cousin, Abygail,

My cousin Claudia."

Jean-Marie Simon,
Guatemala, 195

Guatemala City, 1984: GAM Begins

They gather in the house of the Archbishop. Twenty-five of them in a circle, each one stands and tells the story of their disappeared relatives. The air is thick with sadness. Two of them had met at the morgue. Nineth de Garcia is one of the founders of the Mutual Support

Group *(Grupo Apoyo Mutuo,* or GAM) for relatives of the disappeared. Her husband Fernando was abducted three months before. But this group is not being formed simply to hold hands. They are supporting each other to protest the injustice of the disappearances.

They hold a press conference. They make the crimes public and lay blame on the government and military. They seek international support and protection.

In spite of threatening phone calls and the assassination of several of their leaders, GAM members remain public in their denunciations.

See Americas Watch, *Guatemala: The Group for Mutual Support*

The Sierra, 1991: Communities of the Population in Resistance

They are not from one village or ethnic group. They are *ixiles, chiquimultecos, quichés, aquacatecos.* They have fled from the Guatemalan army and its massacres, tortures, pillage, disappearances. They have seen their crops and houses burned, cadavers eaten by dogs, villages bombed by planes and helicopters. As one says, *nine years of persecution, nine years of destruction, nine years of resistance.* They live in the mountains, they carry no weapons, and they call themselves the Communities of the Population in Resistance (CPR).

They create their own democracy. There are area committees, *responsables* (responsible ones), and an assembly open to all the people. Everybody comes, including the children. One boy stands with a festering sore covering the left side of his head. The army denies medicine to the community. *All of our children were born here in the mountains, on top of the mud, under violent storms, without covering; therefore, there is much illness because we are unaccustomed to this.*

So many of the murdered and disappeared are husbands and fathers. *We widows have learned to work. We work our land with a machete. We widows have double work. We work the land with our children on our backs. We cut our wood; we bring our water; we cook our food.* Many of the women wear the traditional Mayan dress of their town. They themselves weave the bright reds and deep purples and blacks into *trajes* and headbands. It is an art centuries old passed on from generation to generation. The symbols woven in the clothing recount the history of their people. These women become the artists and the bearers of dangerous memory.

See Informe de la Comision Multipartita, *CPR*

El Salvador

San Salvador, 1931: Farabundo Marti

Two years ago Farabundo Martí returned to El Salvador. On the streets of the capital he found ox carts of the people mingling with Pierce Arrows and Packards of the oligarchs. The price has dropped out of the coffee market, and unrest among the workers is spreading. Military repression increases and Martí leads a protest march. He is arrested and sent to the Central Penitentiary where he begins a month-long hunger strike. Massive demonstrations in his support force the government to release him. He emerges as a national hero and symbol of the opposition to the repressive conditions. Protest demonstrations increase and the police and military kill dozens of protestors. The government is chasing Martí all over the countryside because they hold him responsible for all their trouble. In a military coup General Maximiliano Hernández Martínez comes to power. He believes it is worse to kill an ant than a human being. He will soon act on that belief.

Robert Armstrong and Janet Shenk, *El Salvador: The Face of Revolution*, 21-25

Salvadoran Countryside, 1932: *La Matanza*

The insurrection is planned for January 22. The authorities find out and arrest Farabundo Martí on the 18th. Mass arrests begin. In the countryside the peasants do not know and so the revolt moves forward. Years, generations, and even centuries of abuse create the long fuse that is finally lit. The rebellion is strongest in the coffee growing areas, the indigenous leading the way. Mostly armed with machetes and stones, they are up against rifles and machine guns. "Red Julia" leads a force of five thousand near Sonsonate. Martínez mobilizes his forces to crush the rebellion. The rebels' arms are no match for the weapons of the army, but they fight on for days. Wave after wave brave a hail of bullets. Finally, they are defeated.

The ruling class is outraged and cries for vengeance, and the *matanza* begins. In Izalco, groups of fifty, thumbs tied together, meet their death against the wall of a church before a firing squad. Victims dig mass graves, and when they are finished a machine gun fills their bodies with lead and the graves with bodies. Miguel Mármol, one of the leaders in the Salvadoran Communist Party, later writes:

Coffee and Unrest

El Salvador is the smallest country in Central America, about the size of Massachusetts, yet it has the densest population. As in Guatemala, coffee is king. Fourteen families have controlled the wealth and power in this country for several generations.

In the period from 1930 to 1932 there was general unrest among the peasants. The lack of land coupled with an economic depression left most people without food or a livelihood. The Communist Party began organizing actively. Farabundo Martí, a Salvadoran who had served as Sandino's personal secretary and lieutenant, returned to El Salvador to help organize an insurrection.

Economic Disaster

The same issues facing the people in 1930 face the vast majority today. Lack of basic human needs, like running water, electricity, clean water, access to the land, have remained constant for fifty years.

In the early years of the century, coffee was like gold in terms of the disruption it caused in the lives of the indigenous. In the late nineteenth century communal lands were abolished by decree and large coffee *fincas* (plantations) were created. The peasants who were shoved off the land had to work on the *fincas* for intolerable wages. Coffee as an export crop meant that the profits from its sale enriched the owners of the *fincas* but did not raise the standard of living of the workers. Since so much land was used to cultivate coffee for export, there was little left for subsistence crops for domestic consumption.

Protests in the coffee fields grew in 1930. On May Day of that year, eighty thousand workers and peasants marched into San Salvador, demanding a minimum wage for farmworkers and relief centers for the unemployed. In the rural areas, regular armed skirmishes between the army and peasants occurred.

By 1932 the opposition forces were ready for a general insurrection set for January 22. Betrayal led to the arrest of Martí and other leaders. They tried to call off the insurrection, but those in the rural areas did not know how to stop the momentum. Thousands of farmworkers and peasants, primarily indigenous, stoned government offices, occupied city halls, and set fire to the houses of the rich.

General Maximiliano Hernández Martínez, who had overthrown the elected government the year before, crushed the rebellion. Within weeks the army, the wealthy landowners, and paramiltary forces carried out a massacre that killed thirty thousand. Peasant leaders were hanged in the town square to deter future rebellions.

Church Reform

Throughout Latin America, the 1960s brought tremendous changes within the church. For centuries the Catholic Church had sided with the wealthy against the poor. The church blessed the theft of lands and perpetuated the miserable

General Ochoa . . . made everyone who had been captured crawl on their knees to where he was seated in a chair in the courtyard of the fort and he said to them: "Come here and smell my gun," The prisoners pleaded with him in the name of God and their children, having heard the intermittent shots before entering the courtyard. But the General insisted. "If you don't smell my pistol then you are a communist and afraid. He who is without sin knows no fear."

The campesino smelled the barrel of the gun, and in that instant, the general would put a bullet in his face. "Bring the next one in," he said.

The Salvadoran ruling class and military kill thirty thousand people—two percent of the population.

Robert Armstrong and Janet Shenk,
El Salvador: The Face of Revolution, 28-30

San Salvador, 1975: Salvadoran Kent State

On July 30, students from the San Salvador National University stage a protest march against the army's invasion of a branch campus. In Latin America the neutrality and safety of a university is nearly sacred. The student marchers go up 25th Street heading for the highway bridge just south of the U.S. Embassy. As they enter the bridge, soldiers take up offensive positions on the other side, blocking their advance. Not wanting to risk a confrontation, they turn around, only to see more soldiers blocking their exit. The soldiers open fire on the unarmed students. Some jump off the bridge, others lie flat. In a few moments, the army kills twenty students.

With complete orchestration, military ambulances pick up the bodies, some still alive. Immediately following are the street sweepers washing the blood away. None of the twenty are ever heard from again. The military says, "What massacre?"

See Robert Armstrong and Janet Shenk,
El Salvador: The Face of Revolution, 73-74

San Salvador, 1975: Remembering

Blood can be washed from a bridge. Washing away the memory of those students proves impossible.

As word spreads of the massacre, hundreds converge on the cathedral in the capitol. Gathering both spontaneously and as the fruit of years of organizing, the diverse groups proclaim that *unity is our strength.* They shout *El pueblo unido, jamas sera vencido! (The people united will never be defeated!* Today they take a new name that reflects their unity. They call themselves the People's Revolutionary Bloc (BPR) which becomes known as *El Bloque.* Composed of a variety of popular organizations, they offer the people an alternative to corrupt political parties. Emphasizing democracy, equality, and civil disobedience, they fight for higher wages, land for the landless, electricity for poor neighborhoods. They hate the oligarchy and the army. They simply pledge to end their rule.

See Robert Armstrong and Janet Shenk,
El Salvador: The Face of Revolution, 73-74

Aguilares, 1977: Option for the Poor

God is not somewhere up in the clouds, lying on a hammock. God is here with us, building a kingdom here on Earth.

Father Rotilio Grande has brought the new theology of liberation to the poor communities of Aguilares, a town of ten thousand. Now a pastor near his birthplace of El Paisnal, he awakens the campesinos to their dignity. They are worth more than the $1.75 a day they get from the rich plantation owners. They are worth more than the rocky land they are forced to rent.

Government informers spy on his sermons. On March 12, he takes the parish jeep to drive to his birthplace to say mass. With him are two friends and three children. On a lonely stretch of the road he notices that he is being followed. The car overtakes them and fires. Father Rotilio is shot twelve times by 9mm. armor-plated dumdum bullets from Mantzer automatic rifles, the kind issued to police. One campesino is killed in the barrage of bullets. The other is found with a bullet in his forehead fired at point-blank range. The three children escape to tell the story.

William J. O'Malley, *The Voice of Blood,* 43-46

Escalón, 1977: Being Patriots

In the plush neighborhood of Escalón, a flyer circulates throughout the summer: *Be a Patriot, Kill a Priest.*

In July, the White Warriors Union, a right-wing death squad, sends this note:

conditions of the indigenous, saying that God meant them to be poor but they would get their reward in heaven.

There were, of course, some notable exceptions to this trend, including Bartolomé de Las Casas and Bishop Antonio Valdivieso, both of whom defended the indigenous, and Father Miguel Hidalgo, who was a leader in the Mexican independence movement. But for the most part, the institutional church was one of the main forms of cultural invasion in Latin America that stripped the native population of their gods, their dignity, and their very lives.

In 1963, after the second Vatican Council met, Pope John XXIII wrote an encyclical entitled *Pacem in Terris* (Peace on Earth) that led the way for priests, nuns, and lay leaders to see organizing for justice as a fundamental tenet of the Christian faith. The 1968 conference of Latin American bishops in Medellin, Colombia, further confirmed this direction, and the movement known as liberation theology began.

One of the great decisions of the conference was that the church would "make a preferential option for the poor": the church would actively take the side of the poor and begin to view the world from their perspective.

In Latin America, priests and nuns left the safe confines of rectories and convents to actually live with the poor. They realized the daily injustices and indignities suffered by the poor at the hands of the rich. They read the Bible as a group and discovered together that God did not intend people to live in humiliating poverty.

All God's children deserved basic human rights of food, clothing, shelter, and access to the land. The church began organizing cooperatives so that small farmers could get higher prices for their goods, helped organize land take-overs because the children of the campesinos were dying while the rich were growing weeds on their vacant land, and supported unions demanding better wages and working conditions.

All these actions were so threatening to those in power that the church itself became the target of repression. Catechists, priests, and nuns were kidnapped, tortured, and killed. The powerful considered the Bible a "subversive document."

Increase in Repression

The repression was particularly acute in El Salvador. During the 1970s Father Rotilio Grande organized peasants in Aquilares and trained campesinos as Delegates of the Word, leaders of liturgical services.

The emphasis among these leaders was one of service and collective leadership. At the same time, popular organizations were organizing throughout El Salvador. In 1977 the conflict came to a head. Security forces murdered Father Rotilio Grande and arrested, tortured, and expelled priests. A right-wing terrorist organization threatened to kill every Jesuit in the country. That was also the year that Oscar Romero was named archbishop of El Salvador.

All Jesuits without exception must leave the country forever within thirty days. . . . If our order is not obeyed within the indicated time, the immediate and systematic execution of those Jesuits who remain in the country will proceed until we have finished with all of them.

Robert Armstrong and Janet Shenk,
El Salvador: The Face of Revolution, 94

San Salvador, 1980: Romero's Last Homily

Decapitated bodies lie in the streets every morning. Heads are found on poles along country roads. A business will one day develop selling heads at exorbitant prices to grieving families who want to unite the bodies of their loved ones for burial. Ten bodies a day appear as mothers gather with their small pictures of their sons or daughters outside the morgue.

Oscar Romero had been the oligarchy's choice for archbishop three years ago. But he has had a conversion. The murder of his friend Rotilio Grande started it, but the people completed it. He sees into the humble lives of his flock and has gained courage to speak out. He writes a letter to President Carter: *If you truly want to defend human rights . . . [then] guarantee that your government will not intervene directly or indirectly, with military, economic, diplomatic, or other pressure determining the Salvadoran people's destiny.*

And now as he stands in the Cathedral he addresses the army directly:

Brothers: you are part of our own people. . . . God's law must prevail that says: Thou shalt not kill! No soldier is obliged to obey an order against the law of God. . . . It is time to take back your consciences. . . . In the name of God, and in the name of the suffering people, whose laments rise to heaven each day more tumultuous, I beg you, I beseech you, I order you in the name of God: Stop the repression!

Five times the applause of the people who love him so dearly interrupt him. He has to shout the last sentence as the cheering of the people lifts his words to heaven.

James Brockman, *Romero: A Life,* 241-42

Pictures of Archbishop Oscar Romero cropped up everywhere in El Salvador, even though having one could mean being charged with subversion by the army.

San Salvador, 1980: The Shepherd Murdered

It is March 24 and Romero is tired. So many are depending upon him for strength. Some try to dissuade him from saying the Mass at the hospital because it was publicized in the newspapers and there have been threats against his life. He has refused bodyguards because he says the people can't have them. He wants to share the fate of the campesinos.

He begins Mass and reads from the Gospel: *Unless the grain of wheat falls to the earth and dies, it remains only a grain. But if it dies it bears much fruit. . . .* He takes the body and blood of Christ and begins to pray. A bullet from a gun with a silencer pierces his chest. Blood pours from his mouth and nose. Some of the people rush up. They carry him to a hospital where he dies without regaining consciousness.

On a much earlier occasion he said, *If I die, I will rise again in the Salvadoran people.*

James Brockman, *Romero: A Life,* 244-245

San Jose, Costa Rica, 1980: Last Resort

It is May and on the stage of the theater stands the whole spectrum of Salvadoran society. On one end is Enrique Alvarez, a member of one of the fourteen familes, now president of the Democratic Revolutionary Front (FDR). Rejecting his wealth and family breeding, he has joined the people's struggle. On the other end is Juan Chacon, leader of *El Bloque.* A field hand and factory worker, Juan remembers his father, killed and dismembered by the National Guard for being a Delegate of the Word in the church. Alvarez announces to the crowd:

The stealing of elections was common in El Salvador, so the vast majority of people had no hope in an electoral system filled with fraud. The popular organizations and then the guerrilla groups were the only hope most of the people had for fundamental change in El Salvador. The popular organizations were composed of peasants, workers, teachers, and students who were engaging in nonviolent actions to bring about change. These actions included demonstrations, land occupations, and strikes. The government responded with greater and greater violence and repression.

In 1980 the repression reached another height when Archbishop Oscar Romero was assassinated while saying mass and four North American church women were raped and murdered on their way from the airport. In all, ten thousand civilians were murdered that year, the vast majority by right-wing death squads and government security forces.

Since then, seventy thousand civilians have been killed in El Salvador, most at the hands of their own government—a government which has received over four billion dollars in U.S. military and economic aid during those years. The year 1980 also saw the escalation of the guerrilla movement, fueled by the government's killing of opposition leaders and students demonstrating in the streets.

The 1990s

As the 1990s began, the FMLN gained control of much of the countryside and showed their ability to carry out an effective armed struggle in the capitol itself. In 1991, the United Nations began mediating negotiations between the Salvadoran government and the guerrilla forces. Guerrilla demands included a purging of the armed forces of those guilty of human rights violations and the integration of FMLN militants into either the armed forces or the police.

The Salvadoran people have had to take up arms to end the conditions we have been subjected to for the last fifty years — by military governments, by the oligarchy and U.S. imperialism. The people have risen in arms to say "Enough" and to take power the only way they leave us, the way of armed struggle.

The name of this new guerrilla army, a coalition of various forces, is the Farabundo Martí Front for National Liberation (FMLN). Another name of a fallen hero takes its place in the continuing resistance of the people.

Robert Armstrong and Janet Shenk,
El Salvador: The Face of Revolution, 168

San Salvador, 1980: *Adelante*

Members of the FDR and opposition groups decide to return to El Salvador. They are meeting at the Jesuit High School to plan a press conference. Two hundred police surround the building. Men in plain clothes and guns kidnap the five FDR leaders. It is the work of the Maximiliano Hernández Martínez Brigade, named after the general of the *matanza*. Recently, they decapitated four young men, leaving their bodies on the Avenida España with a note: *Long live El Salvador! Long live the massacre of 1932!*

Five bodies are found on the shores of Lake Ilopango. Enrique Alvarez's left arm is missing. Juan Chacon's face is mutilated, his left fist clenched in defiance above his head as if to encode in his body in death, the very essence of his life: *Adelante! Forward!*

See Robert Armstrong and Janet Shenk,
El Salvador: The Face of Revolution,

San Salvador, 1991: The Struggle Continues

The united people have not been defeated. The guerrilla army has fought the Salvadoran military to a standstill. Even though the Salvadoran military has received over four billion dollars in U.S. military and economic aid in the past decade, the FMLN and the popular organizations have something more important—the people.

More than seventy thousand civilians have been killed, the vast majority by government forces and right-wing death squads. The cost has been incredible, but the determination to continue the struggle is even more incredible. Liberated zones are everywhere.

Resistance Today

Rainforest

Pará, Amazon Valley, 1976: King Fires

A fire as big as the state of Rhode Island rages out of control. The A.G. Ranch, a subsidiary of the King Ranch of Texas, is clearing more land. The fire is so intense that it creates its own thunder, lightning, and mini-tornadoes. A land rush of poor migrants looking for survival outside the poverty-stricken cities clears more and more land until much of the area is like a wasteland.

Without the forest the tappers cannot make a living and the indigenous cannot live. Without land the small farmers cannot survive. The large plantation owners live off the misery of all of those groups. The only hope for the tappers and indigenous is to organize.

See Alex Shoumatoff, *The World Is Burning*, 55

In the Amazon today, the invasion of 1492 is being re-enacted. The Brazilian rainforest, or Amazon jungle, is the last remaining territory in the Western Hemisphere that has not been totally invaded by white Europeans.

Treasure, Imagined and Real

It's not that Europeans haven't tried to take over the Amazon. Inspired by the legends of El Dorado, the magnificent City of Gold, conquistadors from Portugal, Spain, the Netherlands, France, and Britain all lusted for the lush riches.

No one ever found the City of Gold, but the Amazon itself is a world treasure. It contains billions of dollars of mahogany and cedar, eight to sixteen billion tons of iron ore deposits, gold, bauxite (essential in making aluminum), limestone, nickel, copper, manganese and seventy-eight percent of the world's supply of niobium. By 1988 approximately eight to ten percent of the rainforests of the Amazon had been cleared. The fate of the rest of the forest is the modern-day counterpart of the invasion of 1492 and the resistance to it.

There were many attempts to invade the forest, enslave the indigenous, and extract its bounty for profit. The familiar pattern of white disease, greed, and inhumanity occurred in the Amazon as well as everywhere else in the hemisphere. Only two hundred thousand Amazonian indigenous have survived from an estimated total of six to twelve million present in 1492.

The Carajas and Others

For example, the Caraja tribe, living close to the Amazon River, experienced smallpox epidemics in 1812 and 1817 after contact with white men. The French explorers described the Caraja as excellent crafts-people, fine weavers of cotton, and artisans with feathers. They had a beautiful and expressive ritual life and they had made agricultural areas out of the jungle, a feat which defies modern techniques. In the early nineteenth century there were fifty-seven thousand Caraja. By 1991 they were reduced to one thousand who now serve as tourist guides and sell their crafts at airports.

The Brazilian anthropologist Darcy Ribeiro found that eighty

Seringal Santa Fé, 1976: *Empate*

Wilson Pinheiro, head of the rubber tappers' union, creates a new tactic in the struggle to save the forest from being cleared and burned. The tappers learn about a clearing taking place on the plantation of Jorge Horácio. Forty tappers, all unarmed, stand in the way of the bull—dozers. The workers doing the clearing, many of them as poor as the tappers, stop. It is an *empate*, a standoff.

In the next five years they organize forty-five *empates*. Chico Mendes adds another element, bringing women and children too to stand in front of the bulldozers and chain saws. When they hear of a part of the forest that is being cleared, they round up everyone and form a wall on the edge of the land. Even the *pistoleiros*, the hired guns, do not dare shoot. In all of the *empates* four hundred are arrested, a few are killed, some are tortured, but they succeed in saving three million hectares of the forest from being destroyed. Chico says, *Thirty of our blockades failed and fifteen worked, but it was worth it.*

Alex Shoumatoff, *The World Is Burning*, 67.

The Amazon, 1980: The Historical Actors

Four distinct groups living in the rainforest at the present time are the main actors in this historical drama:

Indigenous: two hundred thousand are defending their land, culture, and lives.

Garimpeiros: three to five hundred thousand miners, often portrayed as the villains, murdering the indigenous, polluting the rivers and lands. They are in turn victimized by the Brazilian economy and practices of the development "miracle" that made it impossible for them to make a living as farmers or in the crowded cities.

Extractors: two million—while keeping the forests intact they harvest nuts, rubber, resins, palm products, and medicines. The forests that they depend upon and they themselves are under attack. As gatherers, they have been the base of the Amazon economy for five centuries.

Settlers: two to three million drawn by government promises of land and loans. Some are adventurers, other simply trying to survive. They are refugees from the general economic devastation of Brazil.

See Susanna Hecht and Alexander Cockburn, *The Fate of the Forest: Developers, Destroyers and Defenders of the Amazon.164-178*

Acre, Brazil, 1988: Chico, the Man

Chico Mendes has cut rubber full-time for twenty-eight years. Since 1980 he has been full-time head of the union of rubber tappers. He still spends hours playing with his two children, Sandino, named after the Nicaraguan hero, and Elenira, named after a Brazilian guerrilla leader.

I became an ecologist long before I ever heard the word. The tappers take from the forest what can be replenished. They know that the forest is their partner, their sustenance. Devour it and the source of life is gone. Take what is given and there will be more tomorrow.

The tappers love him. The middlemen and plantation owners hate him. Chico hates violence. He pleads against it, *I don't believe in bodies.* The tappers say, *he never [gets] mad at anybody . . . he never [gets] a thing for himself. He has a magnetic presence and a real way with words.*

Alex Shoumatoff, *The World Is Burning,* 8, 23, 28, 29

New York, 1988: Fire

The headlines of the *New York Times* scream out a warning:

Vast Amazon Fires, Man-made, Linked to Global Warming

Satellite studies of Amazon fires in 1987 finally make the international news a year later. The mathematics of de–struction are almost inconceivable:

> • eight thousand fires per day in the Amazon;

> • two hundred thousand square kilometers of forest burned;

> • the fires may account for one-tenth of all man-made carbon dioxide (five hundred million tons), the cause of the greenhouse effect and global warming;

> • smoke clouds rising to twelve thousand feet.

Marlise Simons, the *Times* reporter, writes: *From the flames, tons of fumes and particles are hurled into the sky . . . and at night the forest looks to be at war.*

Alex Shoumatoff, *The World Is Burning,* 127-128

indigenous tribes had been destroyed between 1900 and 1957. Many of the surviving tribes were on the verge of extinction. In 1967, a government investigation found that tribes were being massacred through dynamite, machine guns, and poisoned sugar, and deliberately infested with smallpox, tuberculosis, and measles germs.

And yet the forest and the people have survived to a greater degree than any other region or people in the hemisphere, due to a tradition of indigenous and worker resistance, as well as the massive burgeoning jungle, so full of life and growth, which has defied human destruction.

The Capitalist Miracle

But resistance and defiance, on the one hand, and final victory, on the other, are two different things. Unfortunately, the destruction is escalating. The increase can be traced to 1964 when a military coup installed a dictatorship that promised to provide a "capitalist miracle" for Brazil. With advice from the staunchest capitalists in the United States and internationally, the military generals embarked on a campaign to make the rainforest profitable.

First, the generals destroyed the peasant leagues and outlawed all strikes. To please foreigners, they passed laws that required minimum wages for workers and health benefits, but these laws were never enforced. In order to keep meat and food prices down while continuing major exports of beef, the generals opened the Amazon to "development." Called Operation Amazon, the program gave tax breaks and investment credits to investors. The onslaught of fortune seekers drove the indigenous off the land they had held for centuries, bulldozed forests, and burned the valuable Brazil nut trees. Guns, threats, and the ever-present legal document led the charge.

Twenty thousand Brazilian soldiers trained in counter-insurgency warfare wiped out the communist guerrillas, who mobilized to stop the destruction. The generals developed a new slogan: "A land without men for men without land." The themes and ideologies of the first invasion were being repeated. The idea that the land was vacant and that the indigenous were not human gave the invasion its moral right to proceed without concern for the fate of the people or of nature.

Settlers flooded in, some buying the land, others grabbing it through fraud or intimidation. The small settlers eventually failed because the larger economic forces of capitalism favored the large landowners who snapped up the land of the failed small farmers. In a third of the cases, the large landowners used threats and violence to run the small farmers off.

And More Capitalism

As the Brazilian "miracle" began to lose ground in the early 1970s, the generals looked to large-scale capitalist development projects in the Amazon as their salvation. These massive projects created the greatest or potentially greatest ecological damage. Several huge dams flooded millions of acres of forest.

Chicago, 1988: Indigenous Fight Back

Paulinho Paiakan is a Kayapó militant who speaks before the World Bank and international audiences to stop the destruction of the forest, to stop the building of dams, and to gain recognition for the rights of the indigenous. At the University of Chicago he says:

The forest is one big thing; it has people, animals and plants. There is no point in saving the animals if the forest is burned down; there is no point in saving the forest if the people and the animals who live in it are killed or driven away. The groups trying to save the races of animals cannot win if the people trying to save the forest lose; the people trying to save the Indians cannot win without the help of the Indians, who know the forest and the animals and can tell what is happening to them. No one of us is strong enough to win alone; together we can be strong enough to win.

Alex Shoumatoff, *The World Is Burning,* 220

Xapuri, 1988: Chronicle of a Death Foretold

On the night of May 24, Chico receives an anonymous call telling him that he will not live out the year. He is now *anunciado*. The *anuncio* is a peculiar form of Brazilian torture in which a killer derives a certain pleasure in telling the victim that he or she will die, and then watching the psychological pain as the victim wonders when and where.

Chico has already survived five assassination attempts. The first was just after the head of the tappers' union, Wilson Pinheiro, was gunned down on the porch of the union hall. Knowing he is next, Chico hides for ninety days, sleeping in a different place every night.

With this latest phone call, everyone knows who is out to kill him. Darli Alves is the owner of land that he planned to clear. An *empate* organized by Chico just a month before stopped the clearing and made the land an extractive reserve. From then on Darli has gone around publicly telling people he is going to kill Chico.

Chico's friends go to the police. The police do nothing. All efforts to arrest Darli or protect Chico are blocked by the authorities.

We all knew it would happen around Christmastime, says one of his friends later. His friends and co-workers try to convince him to go to Sao Paulo for the holidays. Chico

Two Central Commandments of the Oppressed:

One. Do not conform with the situation.

Two. Do not conform with purely individual promotion and success.

Or, in positive terms: struggle, and struggle together.

Clodovis Boff

In Alex Shoumatoff, *The World Is Burning,* 73

wants to stay with his family in Xapuri for Christmas. Like all great leaders he resists giving in to fear. Give in to it once and soon it dominates and defines your life. Alter your plans this week and soon the whole direction of your life is changed forever—led more by fear than hope and justice. The great ones keep their eyes on the prize. But he is no martyr: *Public gestures and a well-attended funeral will not save Amazonia. I want to live.*

On December 18, Chico tells his brother, *The situation is ugly. The circle is closing.* On December 22, Chico returns from an organizing trip. Late in the afternoon he visits a mother whose son was almost killed by a bus. He sits with her at the kitchen table consoling her. He returns home and by 6:00 p.m. it is dark. He throws a towel over his shoulder to go out in back to the outhouse. He opens the back door; it's so dark he sees nothing. As he steps out the door an explosion rocks the house. Chico staggers back into the kitchen, his chest and right shoulder filled with buckshot. Careening from the table to the wall to his bedroom, he finally collapses face up on the floor. His wife Ilza runs in. He clings to life a few more seconds, his eyes peaceful. *Damn, they got me.* And then he is gone. His blood, his red fingerprints cover the table, the plates, the wall.

His life, and now his death, spread like an *empate* throughout the world, creating an international stand-off that slows and at times stops the destruction of the forest he loved so much.

Alex Shoumatoff, The World Is Burning, 109-113

Amazon, 1990: Chico's Legacy

The government of Brazil founds four large extractive reserves. Taken together they are the size of the state of Massachusetts. One of them is called the Chico Mendes Reserve.

Mining polluted the waters, and deforestation destroyed the ecological balance of the forest, creating fires that added carbon to the atmosphere and increasing the greenhouse effect. These projects emphasized the maximum extraction of profit from the forest without any concern for the people or the ecological damage. For example, one of the proposed projects was to create the world's largest rice plantation; another involved the manufacture of wood pulp on a massive scale. A charcoal project would have required 1,680,000 acres of eucalyptus plantations. Public colonization for the small farmer gave way to corporate colonization for the rich.

The Continuing Drama

The forest people are struggling today to stop many of these projects. In 1980, the military dictatorship of Ernesto Geisel was under attack. The "miracle" was not happening. The standard of living of the average person had fallen, while inflation was rampant and the value of the Brazilian currency had declined rapidly. Brazil's debt soared, and the "miracle" still needed billions in foreign capital to fuel its huge projects. The dictatorship was followed by a return to democracy, but the struggle for the Amazon rainforest is still being waged.

See Susanna Hecht and Alexander
Cockburn, The Fate of the Forest:
Developers, Destroyers and Defenders
of the Amazon.

Resistance Bibliography: Works Cited in Chapter Two

Aptheker, Herbert, ed. *Documentary History of the Negro People in the United States.* Vol.1. New York: Citadel Press, 1951.

Armstrong, Robert and Janet Shenk. *El Salvador: The Face of Revolution.* Boston: South End Press, 1982.

Bennett, Lerone, Jr. *Before the Mayflower.* New York: Penguin Books, 1984.

Black, George. *Triumph of the People.* London: Zed Books, 1981.

Brenner, Anita and George Leighton. *The Wind that Swept Mexico.* Austin: University of Texas Press, 1971.

Brockman, James R. *Romero: A Life.* Maryknoll, New York: Orbis Books, 1989.

Brown, Dee. *Bury My Heart at Wounded Knee.* London: Picador, Pan Books, 1970.

Cabezas, Omar. *Fire from the Mountain.* New York: New American Library, 1985.

Campbell, Mavis C. *The Maroons of Jamaica 1655-1796.* Trenton, N.J.: African World Press, Inc., 1990.

Carson, Claybourne. *In Struggle: SNCC and the Black Awakening of the 1960s.* Cambridge, Mass.: Harvard University Press, 1981.

Cheek, William F. *Black Resistance before the Civil War.* Beverly Hills, Cal.: Glencoe Press, 1970.

Cherokee Heritage. Compiled by Duane H. King. Cherokee, N.C.: Cherokee Communications, 1988.

Cherokee Legends and the Trail of Tears. Adapted by Thomas Bryan Underwood, courtesy of the Museum of the Cherokee Indian. Cherokee, N.C.: Cherokee Publications, 1989.

Clarke, John Henrik. *Malcolm X: The Man and His Times.* Trenton, N.J.: Africa World Press, Inc., 1990.

The Council on Interracial Books for Children. *Chronicles of American Indian Protest.* New York, 1979.

___. *Stereotypes, Distortions and Omissions.* New York, 1977.

de Ulloa, Don Jorge Juan and Don Antonio de Ulloa. *Kingdoms of Peru.* Edited with an introduction by John J. TePaske. Norman: University of Oklahoma Press, 1978.

Fouchard, Jean. *The Haitian Maroons: Liberty or Death.* New York: Edward W. Blyden Press, 1981.

Fried, Jonathan L., Marvin E. Gettleman, Deborah T. Levenson and Nancy Peckenham, eds. *Guatemala in Rebellion: Unfinished History.* New York: Grove Press, 1983.

Galeano, Eduardo. *Memory of Fire: Genesis, Faces and Masks.* New York: Pantheon Books, 1985.

Genovese, Eugene. *From Rebellion to Revolution.* New York: Vintage Books, 1981.

Glick, Brian. *War at Home: Covert Action Against U.S. Activists and What We Can Do About It.* Boston: South End Press, 1985.

Godoy, Scarlett O'Phelan. *Rebellions and Revolts in Eighteenth Century Peru and Upper Peru.* Koln, Germany: Bohlau Verlag, 1985.

Gomez, Ermilio Abreu. *Canek.* Berkeley: University of California Press, 1979.

Goodpasture, H. McKennie. *The Cross and the Sword.* Maryknoll, New York: Orbis Books, 1989.

Grupo de Investigaciones Agrarias. *Historia del Movimiento Campesino.* Chile: Academia de Humanismoristiano, 1983.

Hahner, June E., ed. *Women in Latin American History.* Los Angeles: University of California, 1980.

Handy, Jim. *Gift of the Devil.* Boston: South End Press, 1984.

Harding, Vincent. *The Other Amercan Revolution.* Los Angeles: Center for Afro-American Studies and Institute of the Black World, 1980.

___. *There Is a River.* New York: Harcourt, Brace, Jovanovich, 1981.

Hecht, Susanna and Alexander Cockburn. *The Fate of the Forest: Developers, Destroyers and Defenders of the Amazon.* New York: Harper & Row, 1990.

Hollyday, Joyce, ed. *Crucible of Hope.* Washington, D.C.: Sojourners, 1984.

Jacobs, Paul and Saul Landau. *To Serve the Devil.* Vol. 1. New York: Vintage Books, 1971.

James, C.L.R. *The Black Jacobins.* New York: Vintage Books, 1989.

Katz, Friedrich, editor. *Riot, Rebellion, and Revolution: Rural Social Conflict in Mexico.* Princeton, N.J.: Princeton University Press, 1988.

Kleinbaum, Abby Wettan. *The War Against the Amazons.* New York: New Press, McGraw-Hill, 1983.

Lerner, Gerda. *Black Women in White America: A Documentary History.* New York: Vintage Books, 1972.

Loveman, Brian. *Chile.* New York: Oxford University Press, 1988.

Marable, Manning. *Race, Reform and Rebellion: The Second Reconstruction in Black America, 1945-1982.* Jackson: University Press of Mississippi, 1984.

Meltzer, Milton. *Slavery II.* Chicago: Cowles Book Co., 1972.

Menchu, Rigoberta. *I . . . Rigoberta Menchu.* Edited and introduced by Elisabeth Burgos-Debray. London: Verso, 1989.

Millon, Robert. *Zapata: The Ideology of a Peasant Revolutionary.* New York: International Publishers, 1972.

Nash, Gary. *Red, White and Black.* New York: Prentice Hall, 1982.

O'Malley, William J. *The Voice of Blood.* Maryknoll, N.Y.: Orbis Books, 1980.

Pablos, Julia Tuñon. *Mujeres en Mexico: Una Historia Olvidada.* Mexico: Grupo Editorial Planeta, 1987.

Pendle, George. *A History of Latin America.* Middlesex, England: Pengin Books, 1963

Price, Richard, ed. *Maroon Societies: Rebel Slave Communities in the Americas.* New York: Anchor Books, 1973.

Prucha, Francis Paul, ed. *Documents of United States Indian Policy.* Lincoln: University of Nebraska Press, 1990.

Robinson, Jo Ann Gibson. *The Montgomery Bus Boycott and the Women Who Started It.* Knoxville: University of Tennessee Press, 1987.

Selser, Gregorio. *Sandino.* New York: Monthly Review Press, 1981.

Shoumatoff, Alex. *The World Is Burning: Murder in the Rain Forest.* New York: Avon Books, 1991.

Simon, Jean-Marie. *Guatemala: Eternal Spring, Eternal Tyranny.* New York. W.W. Norton, 1987.

Sterling, Dorothy. *We Are Your Sisters.* New York: W.W. Norton & Company, 1984.

Stern, Steve, ed. *Resistance, Rebellion and Consciousness in the Andean Peasant World, 18th to 20th Centuries.* Madison: University of Wisconsin Press, 1987.

Tyler, Alice Felt. *Freedom's Ferment.* New York: Harper & Row, 1962.

Valcárcel, Daniel. *Rebeliones Indigenas.* Lima, Peru: Editorial Lima, 1946.

Williams, Eric, ed. *Documents of West Indian History.* Vol. 1, 1492-1655. Trinidad, West Indies: PNM Publishing Company, 1963.

Womack, John, Jr. *Zapata and the Mexican Revolution.* New York: Vintage Books, 1968.

Zinn, Howard. *A People's History of the United States.* New York: Harper & Row, 1980.

___. *SNCC: The New Abolitionists.* Boston: Beacon Press, 1965.

C·U·L·T·U·R·E

They plucked our fruit
They cut our branches
They burned our trunk
But they could not kill our roots

Committee of United Campesinos,
Guatemala

Culture is as physical as texture of hair, hue of skin, and inflection in speaking one's language; it is as historical as your mother's people, their relationship to land and community; it is as traditional as holiday customs or a grandfather's precise use of tools or language; it is as mythic as symbol and folk tales; it is as spiritual as hope or despair. Culture is the teacher which instructs us through the voice and eyes of parents or guardians in what it means to be human. Through folktale, fairytale, or lullabye we learn the ways and values of our people.

In school, official history conveys national culture, which is the story of the dominant culture, the culture of the military, political, and economic dominators—white European culture. When European culture encountered the culture of the "new world," a profound clash of worldviews occurred. Indian and African cultures were subjugated by European culture. Five hundred years later the suppressed cultures of the Americas have kept alive cultural vision and values that hold strategic keys to the survival of the earth and the spiritual redemption of the West. The conquest and its continual legacy exact a cultural price not only for the subjugated but also for the dominant culture.

> When the colonizers exterminated the indigenous inhabitants in many regions of the Americas, they severed connections with a vast network of secret tributaries that led into the mainstream of the memory of mankind [sic]. The total reservoir of memory was seriously impoverished by this loss. The colonizer, reaching into the cultural reserves he believed he had brought with him, discovered that these were soon exhausted, leaving him with psychic voids that could not be filled.
>
> Jan Carew, *Fulcrums of Chage*, 103

Psychic void and loss of cultural memory confront the West. How can we recover our identity and cultural meaning without confronting five hundred years of cultural invasion and cultural resistance? The way to new myths is through the path of truth which uncovers the suppressed history and myths of the defeated.

> We live in an age which portends danger and even disaster . . . the expanding hole in the ozone layer, the "greenhouse effect," the accelerating extinction of plant and animal species, and a dozen more. . . . The roots of these problems are cultural in nature. Humans have been known to inhabit environments for thousands of years with little life-threatening impact. It is modern Western culture which has created the most alarming of these problems.
>
> The West has achieved world domination. Western worldviews and political agendas dominate every political capital in the world. . . . Western ideologies, views toward nature, versions of economics, art, literature, popular culture, products, and prejudices are practically universal. . . . The West assumes that, to the extent that other peoples are legitimate, they have the same wants and desires, the same propensity for deviousness and competition, the same or nearly the same ambitions as Westerners. . . .
>
> The West has long erred in the direction of dangerous speculation and absence of respect for the obvious dependency of our species on the world which has in fact created us. Science and technology could conceivably exist in a cultural environment of respect and reverence with the forces of life designated as nature. Human knowledge about how natural phenomena function does not necessarily lead to irresponsible behaviors, animal and plant extinction, and the destruction of the biosphere. . . .
>
> The element of our culture which makes a dangerous distance from the natural world is its anthropocentrism—the belief that we are not only different from others, but inherently superior. . . . To recover a relationship to nature we must adopt an art which not only tolerates but celebrates difference and complexity in all things, including life forms and cultures. The reason whole species of plants and animals are being destroyed is that the West is so anthropocentric that there is simply not enough value placed on other species of life. Our culture suffers from an inadequate tradition of delight found in things different from ourselves, an inadequate body of stories, images, sounds, and experiences which reinforce that celebration of difference.
>
> John Mohawk, "Toward a Reverence for Nature," unpublished paper

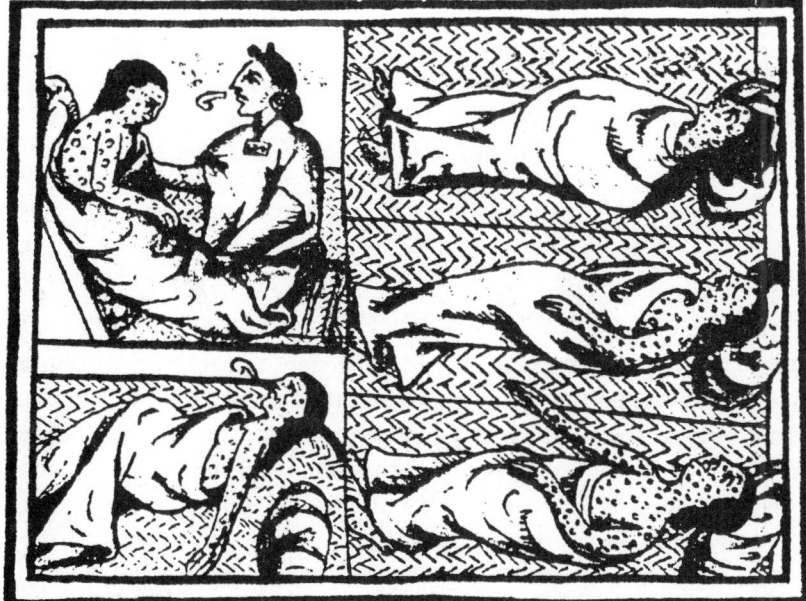

Smallpox: an unknown disease in the Americas

The White Way, the Native Way

The invasion of the Americas by Europeans was a war in which steel, crossbows, mastiff attack dogs, swift horses, and cannons were pitted against native people with lances and arrows. Where weapons failed, an even deadlier contribution of the Europeans was the introduction of bubonic plague, malaria, yellow fever, and smallpox to cultures who had never known such virulent diseases. Another aspect of the invasion, less visible, less an assault on the body of a people than on the spirit, was the cultural war. This war was waged against both the Indian and black visions of the world, visions radically dissimilar from the white way. In the process the red and black visions were discredited. The cultural war, however, remains a battle that has never ended.

Conquest seeks not only to subordinate an "inferior" culture but to crush native culture. European nations differed in the form and intensity of their conquests, but for Africans and Indians the results were the same: death and destruction. The cultural resistance of Africans, Indians, and the later evolving Latino peoples took dissimilar cultural forms. One experience was common, however—pain, and a singular unending refusal to be obliterated as peoples, as cultures.

Culture is the expression of a people's creativity—everything they make which is distinctively theirs: language, music, art, religion, healing, agriculture, cooking, style, customs, and institutions governing social life. To suppress culture is to aim a cannonball at the people's heart and spirit. Such a conquest is more accomplished than a massacre. "We have seen that colonization materially kills the colonized. It must be added that it kills him spiritually. Colonization distorts relationship, destroys and petrifies institutions, and corrupts . . . both colonizers and the colonized" (Memi, 151).

Culture provides a background to the world in which we live. Our eyes are the eyes of the culture to which we were born and which has formed our group and individual identity, including our sense of place in the world.

John C. Mohawk, "Toward a Reverence for Nature," unpublished paper

183

European culture suppressed indigenous and slave culture, but it did not prevail. Where the memory of the ancestors is long and keen, the truth about "discoveries" contends with the official version of the dominators. The "song" of America, for instance, belongs to the vanquished. The blues and gospel of slaves, every boogie, jive, rock n' rollin', jazzy, reggae, mariachi, tango, rumba note the white world has sung or danced has been an imitation, if not a theft.

Cultural war is difficult to see. The militarily and economically powerful nation (the colonialist power) imposes its culture, while at the same time it takes on desired aspects of the culture of the natives. The erasure of the Indian contribution to North American culture has been so accomplished that many descendants of indigenous people never knew their ancestors' contribution to the world. Generations after the conquest of the Americas, the descendants of the colonizers also don't recognize the contributions of the victims. For instance, who "owns" rock n' roll, jazz, salsa, the names of cities—Chicago, Sheboygan, Cheyenne, Minocqua? Where have textbooks revealed that Native Americans discovered the cure for malaria, amoebic dysentery, scurvy, tetanus/lockjaw; that Aztec doctors developed obsidian scalpels for brain surgery; that Mayan and Incan Indians revolutionized world agriculture; that the League of the Iroquois was the model of democracy which shaped the construction of the U. S. political system; that runaway African slaves—maroons—created in the uninhabitable swamps, jungles, and mountain-forests new cultures where ingenuity necessitated the invention of herbal and bark healing systems, agricultural patterns of intercropping, and a whole technology of defense and survival?

Dangerous Memory as Cultural Resistance

Can a people's spirit be killed off? Eduardo Galeano says not as long as someone remembers. Remembers who they are by knowing who they came from. Remembers their people's struggle. This is the danger of cultural memory. It contains spiritual visions and historical lessons which contest the vision of the dominator. Dangerous memory is a weapon of the colonized.

The reason African and Indian culture was dangerous to waves of conquistadors who came to the Americas is because it was the only

Cultural invasion has been devastating:

weapon conquered people could conceal and wield into the future. "They carried in them mankind's [sic] original memories. To have survived the savageries of slavery in the New World, to have retained essential elements of his African culture while at the same time quickly adjusting to and assimilating new ones— Amerindian, European, and in some instances Asian—remains a unique and miraculous achievement" (Carew, 76).

The memories endured. Slave and indigenous poets have scribbled lost words on reservation long-house doors, on the hulls of slaver ships, on prison and garrison walls, in books that were incinerated. The Ghost Dances were forbidden; Mayan art was thrown into bonfires; the bones of Indian ancestors dug from holy soil now lie naked and humiliated in museum display cases which instruct visitors: "These remains are sacred to Indians." Still, memory endured. Each generation that remembered the people's stories remembered who they were. Not slaves, but a people. Cultural memory, says Galeano, is a memory of fire. It is dangerous. Remembering is an act of resistance.

Here is such a story told after five hundred years of resistance— a long enough time to forget. Pedro Hernandez Cobas is one of a few thousand Indians who are direct descendants of the Taino Arawaks who greeted Columbus on his first voyage to Cuba. Cobas remembers the ancestors' stories of those times:

> *I would say Columbus (Colon) and his people treated us in a bad manner. We suffered fright* (susto). *The treatment they gave us was pure whip. The conquistador lied about the Indian. They said we were stupid, imbeciles. But I think the old Indians knew a lot. I think that our ancestors were good, quiet people. They didn't like to hurt anyone. But they ended up whole families jumping off cliffs to avoid slavery. Here our Indian people have been like a fish in a cooler, eyes open but not seeing. For many years nobody spoke about anything Indian, for a long, long time.*
>
> Quoted in Jose Barreiro, "Toward an Indian Voice in 1992,"
> *View From the Shore*, 5

In order to resist cultural death, slaves and Native Americans remembered the people's communal life before the pale strangers who invaded their world arrived. What was the link to the life of tribes in Africa, in the Mayan or Andean highlands, the plains and plantations of North America? It was story—the people's own version of their lives and culture.

It is a story that begins on the golden sands of the Carribbean, the foothills of the Sierra Madres and the peaks of Macchu Picchu, in the great temples of Teuctepec, on the shores of the Yucatan, above the thunderous falls of Iguazu, along the great rivers and plains of Africa, in the bush of Surinam, within the stinking holds

To correct so many generations of bad faith and cruelty . . . you will meet the most fantastic, the most brutal, and the most determined resistance.

James Baldwin
In Rick Simonson and Scott Walker, eds.,
Multicultural Literacy, 3

of slave ships. This story has been dragged through fields, swamps, jungles, along a trail of tears, told in backwoods, backroads, back alleys, and back rooms. It is a story of refusal to die—a story painted on canvas, bark, and leather in colors of sky, earth, and sun; a story woven into the wedding and death dress, festooned with feather, palm, pearl, and jade; a story sometimes moaned on the honey saxophone, chimed on a marimba, slammed on a bongo drum, wept on a *fluta*, laughed on a *guittara*, danced before the sun; a story whispered, roared, chanted, testified, harmonized, and rapped. In different languages, in different voices, the same chorus: No to the white way; Yes to our beauty, art, and sacred ways.

Accumulation vs. Sharing

How has the European worldview which Columbus brought to his encounter with the natives of the Americas shaped five hundred years of history? According to Columbus's log, the Taino Indians were so generous that "if it be asked of them they never say no; on the contrary they invite you to share it and show you as much love as if their hearts went with it." How then explain the fact that all Taino men, women, and children were ordered to mine a gold tribute of three-quarters of an ounce every three months? Indians who refused had their hands cut off. How can one account for the brutality of a slave system causing such despair that, as Pedro Hernandez Cobas relates, whole families of Tainos flung themselves off cliffs to end their misery? How so from a navigator on a mission of God?

The European race to acquire gold locates a fundamental clash of values—for the European, accumulation (of treasure, currency, land) wins cultural and individual honor. The practice of accumulation, historically the basis of a capitalist economy, was as foreign to the Indian and African world as were the tall bearded strangers bearing long knives and muskets. Accumulating abundance for purposes other than to distribute it to the community found no favor with the tribe. The Indian practices of collectivity, sharing, and sexual freedom so captivated the Europeans that they wrote back to the "old world" of encounters with "paradise" and utopia.

While these freedoms attracted the imagination of some Europeans, most found them threatening. The powerful of Europe (Church and State) were undivided in their desire to control the newly "found" lands and peoples. The European worldview is best revealed in the Papal Bull of Alexander VI, which granted by right the lands of the "new world" to Spain and Portugal for the "spread of the Catholic faith." (See page 48) This document reveals both Church and State's belief in the legal and ecclesial right of the powerful to take the lands of the less powerful. The one transgression that was punishable by excommunication was not ownership of people and not, obviously, the ownership of land, or for that

. . . The sailor relates that in Utopia neither money nor private property exist. There, scorn for gold and superfluous consumption is encouraged, and no one dresses ostentatiously. Everybody gives the fruits of his works to the public stores and freely collects what he needs. The economy is planned. There is no hoarding, which is the son of fear, nor is hunger known. The people choose their prince and the people can dispose of him; they also elect the priests. The inhabitants of Utopia loathe war and its honors, although they fiercely defend their frontiers. They have religion that does not offend reason and rejects useless mortifications and forcible conversions. The laws permit divorce but severely punish conjugal betrayals and oblige everyone to work six hours a day. Work and rest are shared; the table is shared. The community takes charge of children while their parents are busy. Sick people get privileged treatment; euthanasia avoids long painful agonies. Gardens and orchards occupy most of the space and music is heard wherever one goes.

Eduardo Galeano, *Memory of Fire: Genesis*, 61

Siphoning for gold

matter the appropriation of others' land, because the Papal Bull legitimated the European state's right to the lands of the Americas. The great sin that merited virtual damnation was for either nation to cross the Pope's demarcation line and attempt to take the land or inhabitants of the other. The key here is the right (moral and legal) to property (human and nature).

The native worldview had no such concept as private property. Although there were over two thousand indigenous languages and thousands of diverse cultures amongst the Indians, few, if any, of the indigenous language forms had a word to express possession. The Indians of "paradise" could not comprehend what was in store for them when they brought offerings of corn, berries, wild turkeys, and beads as tribute to the strangers. In a few years their sharing would be seen as childlike naivete. When they resisted the enforced tribute of gold, their leaders would be hanged or burned; the less radical punishment would order the resister's hand or foot to be severed.

The story of Guaironex, a leader of Indians from the La Vega Valley of Santo Domingo, epitomizes the divergent views of relationship (to land, people and things, i.e., treasure) held by Indians and Europeans:

> *In 1494-95, after Columbus imposed a tribute of gold to be paid by every Taino man, woman, and child, Guaironex went to the first colonizer with a counter offer. Guaironex's main chiefs gathered over one thousand men with coas [planting sticks] in hand. They offered, if Columbus would drop the gold*

tribute, to plant all the food the Spanish would ever want to eat. They said to Columbus, "We will feed you here on the island and also all of your people back in Castille. You don't even need to work." But of course, the colonizers wanted gold or, in lieu of it, slaves and precious woods.

Lyman Tyler, *Two Worlds,* quoted in Jose Barreiro, "A Note on Tainos: Whither Progress?" *View From the Shore,* 7:3, 69

Western moral code demanded an upholding of law which mandated the rights of the emerging nation-states of Europe to acquire property. Accumulation of treasure was the Crown's objective, and church codes gave the enterprise moral justification. Pillage, execution, destruction of entire communities of native peoples, and enslavement were seen as necessary tactics to civilize and "save the souls" of heathens. European society recognized the rights of the powerful (the aristocracy who owned lands) but gave little or no protection to landless serfs and peasants. Nevertheless, poor Europeans were considered Christians and civilized. Indians and Africans were neither. They were "savages" whose refusal to convert to Christianity (and to give up their land and culture) brought upon them whatever "force" was necessary to change their minds. The *requerimiento* is an example.

The *requerimiento* was legally required to be read aloud to the Indians notifying them that God, through his Vicar on earth who was the Pope, had given the Spanish King the power to grant them salvation. This document, read to the Indians in Latin, was legally required before all invasions. (See also pages 20 and 138)

Requerimiento/ The Requirement

In 1514 the lawyer Martin Fernandez de Enciso read the *requerimiento* in the name of King Ferdinand and Queen Juana to the Indians of Sinu. Enciso read the warning that if the Indians wished to stay on the land they must pay the gold tribute to their highnesses. If not they must leave.

. . . The two [Sinu] Chiefs listen, sitting down and without blinking, to the odd character who announces to them that in case of refusal or delay he will make war on them, turn them into slaves along with their women and children, and sell and dispose of them as such and that the deaths and damages of that just war will not be the Spaniards' responsibility. The chiefs reply, without a glance at Enciso, that the Holy Father has indeed been generous with other people's property but must have been drunk to dispose of what was not his and that the King of Castille is impertinent to come threatening folk he doesn't know.

Then the blood flows.

Subsequently the long speech will be read at dead of night without an interpreter and half a league away from the village

---

*The old history is finished,
it can never return.
Now it's another history . . .
Now history is what the people make.
History will now change its name.
Perhaps it shall simply be called people.
Perhaps it shall simply be called life.*

Jose Coronel Utrecho
In Alejandro Murguia and Barbara Paschke,
Volcán, 155

that will be taken by surprise. The natives that sleep won't hear the words that declare them guilty of the crime committed against them.

Eduardo Galeano, Memory of Fire: Genesis, 60

Hernan Cortes faithfully read the *requerimiento* throughout Mexico and the Yucatan. The document he read warned that failure to accept the King's summons would force him to

powerfully invade and make war upon you in all parts and modes, so that I can subdue you to the yoke and obedience of the Church and of His majesty's command, and I will take your effects and will do all the harm and injury within my power, as vassals who will not obey or receive their sovereign and resist and oppose him. And I protest that the death and disasters which may come about because of this action will be the fault of yourselves and not of his majesty, nor of me. . . .

From Cortes's Letter to King Charles
In Irwin Black and Henry Rosen, The Conquest, xvi

The "deaths and disasters" which soon followed the conquest of Mexico and the Yucatan measured eighteen million. By 1650, only one and a half million full-blooded Indians were alive. Cortes faithfully upheld the law of *requerimiento* each time his soldiers pitched battle.

Moral Superiority: The White Man's Burden

The slave trade was also a system governed by the laws of the nation-states. In this case the law dictated the form of punishment to be meted out to runaway slaves of the Caribbean. Maroons were punished by castration. Such cruelty was meant to suppress rebellion, but the punishment fell short of execution in order to continue to reap the benefits of slave labor. Within one hundred years a "reform" law, "Le Code Noir," was signed by Louis XIV of France, in 1685. The edict declared that

A Negro who is absent for a month shall have his ears cut off and shall have a fleur de lys branded on his left shoulder. If he again runs away, his knees shall be lacerated and his other shoulder branded. Finally if he runs away for a third time he shall be sentenced to death.

Jose L. Franco, in Richard Price, ed., Maroon Societies, 38

In effect, native people were children if they submitted and savages if they resisted. In either case, Europeans saw themselves as the superior culture bringing civilization to an inferior culture. The colonial worldview split reality into polar parts: good and evil, body and spirit, man and nature, head and heart, European and

Symbols of Freedom

Every memorial or symbol of the white nation's triumph becomes the occasion that sparks the fire of dangerous memory. Statesman Frederick Douglass, a former slave, gave a speech commemorating America's day of freedom and independence on the Fourth of July, 1852.

What to the American slave is your Fourth of July? I answer, a day that reveals to him more than all other days of the year, the gross injustice and cruelty to which he is the constant victim. To him your celebration is a sham; your boasted liberty an unholy license; your national greatness, swelling vanity; your sounds of rejoicing are empty and heartless; your denunciation of tyrants, brass fronted impudence; your shouts of liberty and equality, hollow mockery; your prayers and hymns, your sermons and thanksgivings, with all your religious parade and solemnity, are to him mere bombast, fraud, deception, impiety, and hypocrisy—a thin veil to cover up crimes which would disgrace a nation of savages. There is not a nation of the earth guilty of practices more shocking and bloody than are the people of these United States at this very hour.

Howard Zinn, A People's History
of the United States, 178

Tainos translates to "men of the good"

Repentance

Fray Toribio de Motolinia placed ten crosses in the Mexican earth to atone for sins of European Christians.

"This cross, my God, is for the diseases that were not known here and that rage so terribly among the natives.

"This one is for war, and this for hunger, which have killed as many Indians as there are drops in the sea or grains of the sand.

"This is for the tribute collectors, drones who eat the honey of the Indians; and this one for tribute which the Indians must sell their children and their lands to pay.

"This is for the gold mines, which stink so of death that one can't go within a league of them.

"This is for the slaves who have been dragged here from all directions like herds of beasts, branded on the face; and this one for those who fall by the wayside carrying the enormous loads to maintain the mines.

"And this one, Lord, for the perpetual conflicts and skirmishes of us Spaniards, which always end with the torture and murder of Indians."

Eduardo Galeano, *Memory of Fire: Genesis,* 95

primitive. Indian spirituality lacks these dualisms: language expresses the oneness of all things. God is not the transcendant Father but Mother Earth, the Corn Mother, the Great Spirit who nourishes all.

For the European such beliefs were pagan. Thus, the conquest was rationalized as a necessary evil that would bestow upon the heathen Indians a moral consciousness that would redeem their amorality. The impetus which drove the conquistador's invading wars was not exploration, but the desire to expand empire, not discovery of new land, but the drive to accumulate treasure (gold), land, and cheap labor (slaves). The worldview which converted bare economic self interest into noble, even moral, motives was a notion of Chrisitanity as the one redemptive religion which demands fealty from all cultures.

There were some Christians who were converted to the Indians and slaves. Bishop Bartolomé de Las Casas refused the land grant afforded him by the Crown, then preached and cried out against the enslavement of Indians by writing to the Council of the Indies and to the Pope documenting "cruelties more atrocious and unnatural than any recorded of untutored and savage barbarians ... [because of] the greed and thirst for gold of our countrymen." Although de Las Casas lost the argument in which he challenged the European worldview, his prophetic voice earned him the friendship of the voiceless Indians. (See also pages 56-59)

The Bishop's intense written debate with the prestigious jurist Sepulveda, chaplain for Charles V, reveals the supremacist worldview of European colonizers. The Bishop argued for the abolition of the *encomienda* system of gold tribute which he called tyrannical, inhuman, and an offense to God. Sepulveda said it was a system suited to the nature of Indians who, unlike the Spaniards, were somewhere between humans and monkeys, and thus it was "natural" and an expression of God's will that barbarians and the unjust should experience punishment.

190

Spiritual vision informs values. A fundamental difference between the European value system and Indian and African values is centered on relationship to the community of ancestors which includes the living and dead. For Indian people, right relationship includes relationship with all beings, including the natural world which surrounds the human world. The destruction of the environment was, from the Indian perspective, a destruction of spiritual equals.

> *It is more than a coincidence that the modern age of extinction begins in 1680. It is often cited as the foundation of the Enlightenment. . . . During the Enlightenment, there arose notions of a mechanistic universe and that humankind can use science and technology to shape his own ends subject only to the physical laws. . . . The idea of the sacredness of nature is, however, a strong central theme in many non-Western cultures. . . . Those cultures tend to see a supportive kind of magic in the process of birth, death, and transformation which recognizes that human beings are part of a wonderful process that can be celebrated and revered. . . .*
>
> *Respect is not something that can be readily generated through dissection. Scientists can wonder at the complexity of the biology of a leaf, can achieve something approaching awe, and even spiritual reverence, through study of the vast system of the stars, and can even grow to achieve profound respect for the complexity of life, but they have been only marginally successful at creating stories and images which transmit those feelings to young and old alike. They have not been successful, in short, in challenging the element of Western culture which views Nature through primarily materialistic lenses because they are viewing reality through such lenses themselves. . . .*

> John Mohawk, "Toward a Reverence For Nature," unpublished paper

In this short description John Mohawk delineates the radical opposition with which Western and Native American worldviews regard nature, spirituality, and science. But it is the Western European worldview that dominates and thus appears natural.

> *Because [the Eurocentric worldview] is the one we have grown up with, it is sometimes hard to see it as just that—one of several different ways of relating to reality. Eurocentrism is distinguished by a kind of one-dimensional seeing—that of a privileged white Western male. It is a perspective that assumes the thinking "I" as the center of the universe. Descartes: "I think, therefore I am." How different this is from the African worldview in which the individual is affirmed as being only in relation to the "we" of his/her community—family/clan—including those not born and those who have departed.*

> Sheila Collins, "Are the Multiculturalists Politically Correct?" 7

In 1524, facing waves of massacres, an Aztec holy man addressed this prayer poem to the Giver of Life:

Nothing but flowers and songs of sorrow are left in Mexico and Tlatelolco, where once we saw warriors and wise men.

We know it is true that we must perish, for we are mortal men. You, the giver of Life, have ordained it.

We wandered here and there in our desolate poverty. We are mortal men. We have seen bloodshed and pain where once we saw beauty and valor.

We are crushed to the ground; we lie in ruins. There is nothing but grief and suffering in Mexico and Tlatelolco, where once we saw beauty and valor.

Have you grown weary of your servants? Are you angry with your servants, O Giver of Life?

In Robert Venables, "The Cost of Colombus: Was There a Holocaust?" *View from the Shore*, 72

African Creation Myth

The Africans . . . do not on the whole share the almost universal preoccupation of Amerindians with the creation of the world. [However] . . . African myths are impregnated with realism and in them gods and humans are never far apart, and the former are eternally responsible to the people they both rule and serve. The genesis myth of the Amerindians around Lake Titicaca portrayed the world as beginning when the Great Serpent stirred under the sea and pushed the earth upwards from murky depths. This makes the whole conceptual framework of creators and creation far more abstract than that of the West African myths which tell of the creation of people and not the world. The maroons of Jamaica, for example, tell of how Damballa, one of the senior West African members of their pantheon of gods, created humans by baking cakes. The burnt cakes were the ancestors of black people, those that were neither well baked nor underdone were the ancestors of brown people, while white people were sired by cakes Damballa neglected to bake at all.

Jan Carew, *Fulcrums of Change*, 75

A Tradition of Individualism vs. Communalism

A fundamental value that shapes Western European emphasis on the right to accumulate, and to ownership of property and people, is the right of the individual. Western law, for example, legalizes the individual rights of property owners. The U.S. Constitution gave states the power to determine who was allowed to vote. The states in turn enfranchised property owners and denied the vote to the nonpropertied, nonwhite, and nonmale—Indians, blacks, women, and propertyless indentured servants. "The Supreme Court of the United States to this day says that the U.S. government is free to take away Indian land, to confiscate it, to extinguish aboriginal Indian title without due process of law, without any compensation and without any regard whatever for the Fifth Amendment" (Coulter, 62). Communal, not individual rights, formed the moral and public codes and laws which governed tribal life in the Americas and Africa. It is one's obligation to community, not oneself, which is binding. Indians, blacks, and Latinos discover their identity in and through community.

The hero of Western literature, on the other hand, discovers himself by separating from others, striking out for independence, and becoming his own man. In Western culture, independence, and thus maturity, is achieved in separation . Native writer Paula Gunn Allen says Native American literature focuses on themes of modern enslavement and colonization to reveal these ruptures of communal identity and meaning. "A theme that shows up frequently in Native writers' stories [is] about jail, boarding school, war and abduction. In all these stories the underlying theme is about forced separation, signifying the loss of self and the loss of personal meaning" (Gunn Allen, 8).

Slaves and maroons of the Caribbean and Latin and North America preserved the African tradition of *mati*, which emphasizes a ritual of kinship that implies a friendship based on deep bonds of solidarity. This practice, referring to the experience of having shared passage on the same slave ship, extended the sense of community care and responsibility for the people that slave culture embraced. As in Indians' culture, black identity is discovered through solidarity with one's people, not through the Western hero's quest.

For Caribbean writer Jan Carew, identity was achieved by recovering his memories of Guyana village life which culturally located his connection to generations of ancestors.

Leaving Agricola, I soon began to realize that my village in the sun was an important spectrum through which, for the rest of my life, I would view the world. The more widely I travelled, the more forcibly it struck me that Agricola with all its mysteries—its deceptive facade of poverty, squalor, and appar-

ent hopelessness—was, in fact, a microcosm of the Third World. Growing up there, I made the acquaintance of secret sorrows and beheld the vision of hidden, stubborn hopes from my soul landscapes within. I needed to have true images of myself and a sense of identity clearer than the one I carried in my mind's eye and ear. All the scattered pieces of my life in Agricola and the complex configurations of my ancestral links had to be shaped into a whole if I was going to live with myself . . . it slowly dawned on me that I was the product of a bewildering array of races, colors, creeds, and cultures; that I carried in me the blood of masters and slaves, bondsmen and overseers, renegades, rebels, castaways, and convicts.

Jan Carew, *Fulcrums of Change*, 119

Reclaiming culture requires recovery of the people's lost voice and history. To remember is to discover the culture of ancestors and in the process to discover oneself. Jamaican writer Michelle Cliff describes this process.

Jamaica is a place halfway between Africa and England, to put it simply, although one culture (guess which one) has been esteemed and the other denigrated. . . . As a writer, as a human being, I have had to accept that reality and deal with its effect on me, as well as finding what has been lost to me from the darker side, and what may be hidden, to be dredged from memory and dream. And it is there to be dredged.

To write as a complete Caribbean woman, or man for that matter, demands of us a retracing of the African part of ourselves, reclaiming as our own, and as our subject, a history sunk under the sea, or scattered as potash in the canefields, or gone to bush, or trapped in a class system notable for its rigidity and absolute dependence on color stratification. On a past bleached from our minds. It means finding the art forms of these of our ancestors and speaking in the patois forbidden us.

Michelle Cliff, "A Journey Into Speech"
In Rick Simonson and Scott Walker, eds., *Multicultural Literacy*, 58-59

The Legacy of Colonialism Today

The memory of the colonized is dangerous because it is an account of theft and bravery that would make the colonizer look, at least, ignoble. None of us wants to look bad in front of our children, or before the eyes of history. So the colonizer repeats his version of the "facts" about the superiority of Western medical, scientific, military technology, or art and literature—in a word—culture.

The first task of the colonizer, or generation of colonizers after the conquest, is to erase the very notion of colonization. This can be done by possessing control of the culture's institutions and communication systems. At its simplest, this process begins with the story itself—who tells it, who sings it, who writes it, and whose language is used.

A Caribbean Notion of Time

An Acewayo droger [Guyana porter] . . . who had remained outside the awful grinding inevitability of linear time that the Columbian era had imposed upon his people . . . told me of the journeys he took in and out of the regions of the mind. The band across his forehead, and the harness strapped under his armpits distributed the hundred and twenty-five pounds he carried in his wareshi *[back-pack with a harness around the forehead and shoulders] so that by thrusting his head forward he could walk at a steady, rhythmic shuffle from dayclean [dawn] to sunset. We were averaging twenty-five miles a day in the mountainous Potaro district.*

"How do you manage?" I asked, thinking of the thirty pounds I was carrying and the way it seemed to double itself after every ten miles. After a long pause he replied, "It's like this, skipper. Most of the time you see me walking here, carrying this big load, I'm not here at all . . . is only shadow here, the substance is back home in Aquero, hunting agouti or deer or labba, playing with my children, catching a gaff, listening to the Old Ones speak, talking to the Ancestors or to God. You can ask me how can I be in two places at one time, I will tell you the secret: the pressure of this wareshi *on my brain makes it easy for me to send my mind away. . . . At the start I feel like a drunken man, there's a singing inside my head, my body feels heavy and the* wareshi *feels like a mountain on my back. Then all of a sudden everything gets lighter and lighter until I feel like a silkcotton blossom floating on wind. Once I reach this stage, I can walk from here to the Forest of the Long Night without feeling any weariness."*

Jan Carew, *Fulcrums of Change*, 108-109

193

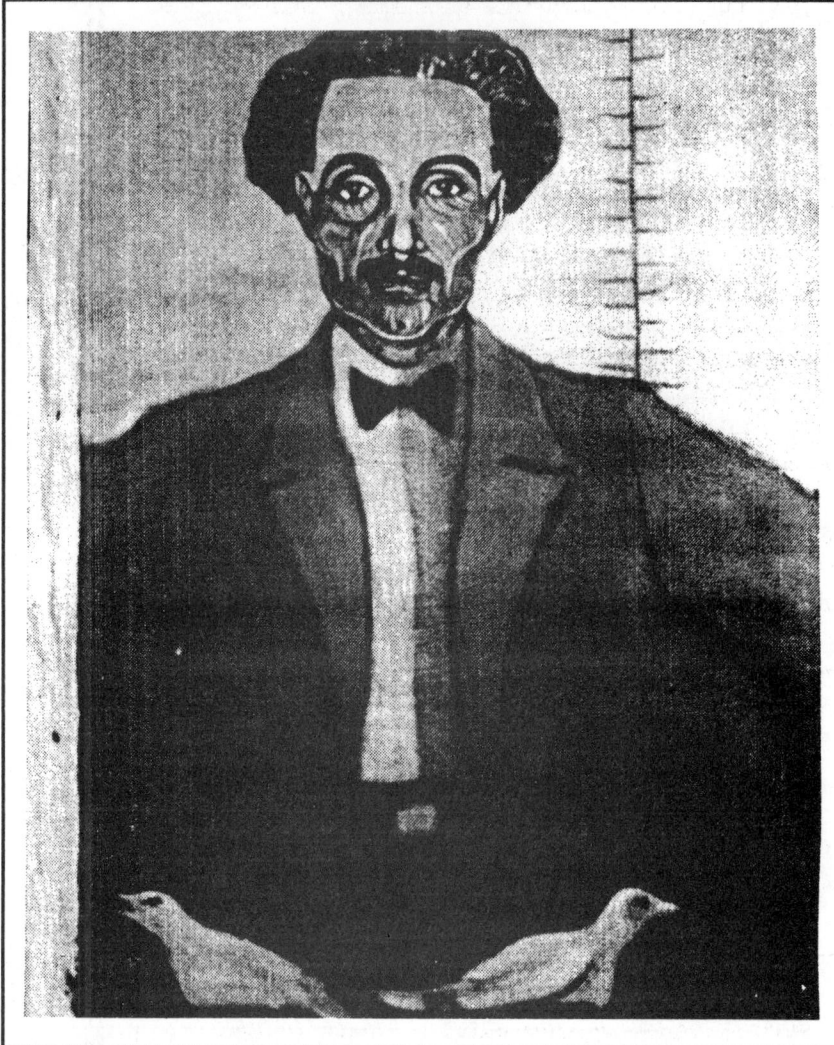

"Albizu Kósmico"

Pedro Albizu Campos, "El Maestro," (the teacher), was a Harvard graduate, lawyer, and leader of the Nationalist Party who reignited the struggle for Puerto Rican independence in the 1930s. A leader of two uprisings and the attack on the U.S. Congress in 1954, for which he was imprisoned for twenty-five years, Pedro Albizu Campos remains dangerous memory.

Painting by Elizam Escobar, a Puerto Rican independista currently serving sixty-eight years in a U.S. prison.

Puerto Rico has the right to independence because when the Treaty of Paris was signed, by which the United States took possession of the island, Puerto Rico already had its sovereignty and, besides, Spain did not have the right to cede it to the United States.

Pedro Albizu Campos, *Claridad*, San Juan, Puerto Rico, Sept. 12, 1991

But, it can be argued, haven't things changed in five hundred years? The quincentennial celebration—in which President Bush honored the brilliant discoverer Christopher Columbus, while at the same time American Indian Movement (AIM) activist Russell Means poured blood on the statue of Columbus in a public protest—makes clear that just as dangerous memory continues amongst the colonized, so too the European worldview has carried its own memory into the future.

The relationship of the United States to Puerto Rico is a case study which reveals the continuation of colonialism from Columbus's encounter with the Taino Indians to relations with their descendants today. Following Columbus's journey to the "new world," Spain soon colonized Puerto Rico, Cuba, Jaimaca, and Hispaniola. The people of Puerto Rico (then called Borinquen) were Taino Indians. Those Taino who were not killed off by the diseases or slavery brought by the Europeans fled to the mountains. The Tainos intermarried with African slaves imported by the Spanish. Five centuries later, currents of Indian, African, and European blood run in the veins of Puerto Ricans.

In 1868, Puerto Rican nationalist Ramon Emeterio Betances led an uprising in the town of Lares (Grito de Lares) against the Spanish colonizers, declaring Puerto Rico an independent republic. That insurrection, along with the rebellion of Yanco in 1897, failed. But Spain was losing its grip. In an effort to hold down rebellion, the Spanish conceded some freedoms. They awarded Puerto Rico the power to ratify treaties and set tariffs and to grant citizenship to the Puerto Rican population.

In 1898, the United States usurped Spain's control of Puerto Rico, landing Marines on the island and signing the Treaty of Paris with Spain which gave the United States control of Puerto Rico. The rights Spain had granted were then revoked; the Puerto Rican provisional assembly and cabinet were abolished; Puerto Ricans were denied a vote in the U.S. Congress; English was made the official language of the island. Between 1900 and 1947 the dollar became the national currency, U.S. laws replaced Puerto Rican law, the House of Delegates' decisions were subject to U.S. veto, and U.S. citizenship was imposed by an act of Congress, in spite of protest by the House of Delegates. In 1952, Puerto Rico became a Commonwealth of the United States, adopting its "own" constitution which has an amendment that states: "Any revision of this constitution shall be consistent with the resolution enacted by the Congress of the United States approving this constitution. . . ."

In addition to virtual political control of the island, the United States also possesses economic control.

Puerto Rico is the largest per capita purchaser of U.S. goods in the world. . . . Eighty-five percent of industries in Puerto Rico are owned by U.S. interests. They do not have to pay island taxes for ten to twenty-five years. This, along with the lower wages than those they pay in the United States has allowed U.S. industries to average twenty percent profit per year, far higher than comparative profits in the United States. . . . The ultimate effect of Operation Bootstrap (which opened two thousand factories in the 1940s, converting the economy from an agricultural economy to an industrial economy) has been to assure complete U.S. control of Puerto Rican economy, as well as to increase social dislocation and economic inequality. . . . It is the distortion of the economy of Puerto Rico for the profit of U.S. capital which has forced one-third of the Puerto Rican nation to move to the United States and accept low-paid menial and service occupations. . . . The incidence of both poverty and unemployment among Puerto Ricans is more severe than that of virtually any other ethnic group in the United States, and the incidence of poverty has been rising since 1970.

The Council on Interracial Books for Children, *Stereotypes, Distortions and Omissions in U.S. History Textbooks,* 96, 98-99

She walks with the stride of her borinquen ancestry as a "Taina Casica." . . .
She knows where she is headed,
for her commitment is to her people.
She is captured by the enemy
But she does not despair. . . .

Dylcia Pagan, Puerto Rican prisoner of war

In *Que Ondee Sola*, student newspaper, Northeastern Illinois University, March 1981, 9

Graphic from Que Ondee Sola

*Glory to these aboriginal hands
  because they've worked.
Glory to these black hands because
  they've worked.
Glory to these white hands because
  they've worked.
Through these hands, Indian, black,
  white,
Through these hands the country
  remains in us.*

Juan Antonio Corretjer,
national poet of Puerto Rico and former
U.S. political prisoner

Currently Puerto Rican *independistas* (Puerto Ricans seeking independence from U.S. colonial control) sit in U.S. prisons with twenty-five and thirty year sentences for seditious conspiracy against the United States. The activists refused to recognize the U.S. court's right to jurisdiction over Puerto Rican patriots, claiming the rights of the colonized under international law to defend themselves against their colonizers. Such arguments were, of course, useless when argued before a U.S. judiciary which denies Puerto Rico's status as a colony of the United States.

Few North Americans know this history; rather, they assume, as they do about African Americans, that Puerto Ricans' poverty and unemployment are due to some lack of ambition, not the result of centuries of colonization. Memories of independence, of Puerto Ricans not having to depend on the United States, are a danger to the powerful.

Not all white Americans fear the memories of the subjugated. There are many white people who, although they are the cultural beneficiaries of colonialism, want to know the truth about history, even the painful truth. To the powerful, however, the memory and voice of the colonized are always a threat because such memory challenges the myth of European white supremacy. People's history reveals that the "new world" empires were built by the killing labor of Indian and African slaves. That theft of human life and labor becomes almost unrecognizable as the economic process becomes systematized. Years and years of an economy which rewards accumulation of wealth and punishes poverty has made the system appear natural. Yet systems based on human sharing rather than accumulation, and politics based on true democracy, may not be so threatening to most Americans. In fact, those systems are what they've been led to believe the

196

American Revolution achieved. The economically and politically powerful work hard at fooling most of the people most of the time. Their best tactic is instilling fear of those who pose a threat— people of color, women, gay people, the "undeserving poor." What is lost in this suppression is, of course, the truth—not just about the cultures of the colonized, but also the "new world" culture.

The Gifts of the Colonized

What were the cultural contributions of the colonized that shaped the "new world"? Historian and anthropologist Jack Weatherford provides the following research which documents the contributions of Indians of the Americas to the world.

Political Contributions: The Gift of Democracy

The democratic system which the United States fought two world wars to defend, and one war of independence to invent, owes much of its formation to the Iroquois Confederation. Founding Father Benjamin Franklin, who studied Indian culture and later became the Indian Commissioner of Pennsylvania, implored the Albany Congress of 1754 to construct a model of governance like that of the Iroquois League. The Iroquois League, initially encompassing five nations—the Seneca, Oneida, Mohawk, Onondag, and Cayuga—was composed of five councils of delegates elected as representatives of each tribe. These councils represented their specific nations but were also formed into one Council of the League which represented the entire League of the Iroquois. The League governed the territory from New England to the Mississippi River. "This model of several sovereign units united into one government presented precisely the solution to the problem confronting the writers of the United States Constitution. Today we call this a 'federal' system in which each state retains power over internal affairs and the national government regulates affairs common to all" (Weatherford, 137).

Not all aspects of the Iroquois democratic political process were adopted by the Founding Fathers. The council delegates elected from each tribe, called sachems, could be recalled or impeached for misconduct or incompetence through the decision of the women of the tribes, who then elected the replacement sachem. Imagine the development of democracy if women could recall and appoint congressional leaders!

The notion of impeachment was foreign to the Europeans whose monarchs ruled for life. Moreover, the very notion of elections was foreign to colonists whose conception of government was based on the British Parliament and imitation of the Greek city-states which, according to Weatherford, were considerably less egalitarian than the Indians' models of democracy.

Yaqui Early Democracy

The documented example of the Yaqui Tribes (who still reside in the Sonora desert of Arizona) demonstrates the Indians' early practice of democracy.

In July 1739 the Yaquis sent two emissaries named Muni and Bernabe to Mexico City for a rare audience with the Spanish Viceroy to plead for free elections of their own government administrators. . . . Thus in the wilds of Mexico a full generation before the Revolution in the English colonies of North America, we see evidence of the Indians demanding the franchise and free elections in order to maintain their traditional political values. In almost every North American tribe, clan, or nation for which we have detailed political information, the supreme authority rested in the group rather than in an individual.

Jack Weatherford, *Indian Givers*, 139

Under the old laws, the Iroquois were a mother-centered, mother-right people whose political organization was based on the central authority of matrons, the Mothers of the Longhouses (clans). . . . The sachems were chosen from certain families by the matrons and set forth in the Great Law of Peace of the Iroquois Confederacy.

Paula Gunn Allen, *The Sacred Hoop*, 33

So fundamental a political process as the caucus was a contribution of the tribes of North America. The word "caucus," which comes from the Algonquin language, describes a process of discussion which explores ideas without making a formal decision or voting. This process was integral to the Indian decision-making process of making a pow-wow and talking through issues affecting the community or councils.

Economic Contribution: The Gift of Silver

The communal traditions of the Indians shaped the political structure which the Founding Fathers constructed, but Indians were not responsible for the economic system based on accumulation that the Europeans imported from the "old world." The Incan Indians of the Andean nations provided the forced labor that impelled a world economic transformation that shaped generations and gave rise to a capitalist world economy.

The silver mined from the Cerro Rico of Bolivia initiated a new currency, which, unlike gold, could be used by the emerging merchant class of bakers, fisherman, candlemakers, and cloth weavers. Never before had this common sector of society been major actors in the economy:

> Never before in the history of the world had so much silver money been in the hands of so many people. Kings, emperors, czars, and pharaohs had always accumulated great wealth in their jewels, their hordes of gold, and their coinage, but the total amount of gold and silver was quite limited by the scarcity of precious metals. . . . This changed with the opening of the Americas. . . . Precious metals from America superseded land as the basis for wealth, power, and prestige. For the first time there was enough of some commodity other than land to provide a greater and more consistent standard by which wealth might be measured. This easily transported and easily used means of wealth prepared the way for the new merchant and capitalist class that would soon dominate the whole world.

> Even though the Indians made possible the greatest economic boom in the history of the world . . . they still languish in poverty. . . . Potosi, the city which supplied the silver for the rise of capitalism, is now out of silver. . . . The great mint of Potosi that swallowed eight million Indian miners and turned out billions of coins from the sixteenth century into the twentieth century operates now as a museum for visiting children.

Jack Weatherford, *Indian Givers*, 13, 18-19

*nothing from our impossible past
has died*

Mirna Martinez
In Zoe Anglesey, ed., *Ixoc Amar•go*, 249

Agricultural Contribution: The Gift of Food

More precious than the silver the Incans were forced to take from the earth is a food root the Incans seeded into the earth. The potato, given to the world by the Incans, saved more lives than silver ever has. Moreover, the lowly potato eventually shifted the power centers of Europe.

Before the conquest, Europeans depended on grain crops which needed warm climates and predictable weather conditions to be harvested. The colder Northern European countries had to import grains and thus remained dependent on the more stable Southern European grain-growing nations. With the arrival of the Incans' potato, which could be grown in cold climates, the Northern European countries were able to feed their masses with a cheap, nutritious crop that needed only four months to harvest.

Five hundred years after the conquest, environmentalists are desperately trying to reconstruct a world where appropriate technology will lead to an atmosphere that is not life-threatening. Our food, water, and atmosphere are so poisoned that scientists predict a possible future of human species extinction unless rapid and radical changes in the use of technology, chemicals, and energy sources are adapted to a simpler and less consumptively driven lifestyle. Clues to such a life are buried in the history of suppressed cultures. The remarkable agricultural system of Caribbean farmers was efficient and abundant.

Mayan and Aztec agriculturalists had developed brilliant methods of irrigation, continuous harvesting, and recycling of waste. In the Aztec city of Tenochtitlan the *chinampa* system of organic farming fed over one hundred thousand inhabitants by adapting the city to its location on a lake. The Aztec farming experts created floating plots of land where food crops or gardens of flowers flourished.

This intricate terraced cultivation had been in use for over fifteen hundred years before Cortes destroyed Tenochtitlan, the ancient city whose wealth, in the eyes of the Europeans, lay in gold and slaves, not an urban geography of beauty, abundance, and unparalleled environmental architecture.

Medical Contributions: The Gift of Healing

Incan, Mayan, and North American medicine healers have saved the world from major illnesses, too. At the time of the conquest, European medicine was more a practice of witchcraft than science. Native healers discovered the cure for malaria, amoebic dysentery, scurvy, and lockjaw. The Incans used a bark called *quinaquina* to cure malaria, a disease introduced by Europeans to the "new world." The word "quinine" is derived from the Quechua word *quinaquina*.

The Power of a Potato

With the new calorie source and the new source of nutrition, the potato-fed armies of Frederick of Prussia and Catherine of Russia began pushing against their southern neighbors. During the Age of the Enlightenment these northern cultures wrestled free from the economic, cultural, and political domination of the South. Power shifted toward Germany and Britain and away from Spain and France, and finally all were eclipsed by Russia. . . . [Russia's] adoption of the potato as their staple food preceded their rise as a world power.

American foods (including corn and varieties of beans) brought about the miracle that centuries of prayer, work, and medicine had been unable to do: they cured Europe of the episodic famines that had been one of the major restraints on the population for millennia.

Jack Weatherford, *Indian Givers*, 69-71

Appropriate Technology

By using imaginative and well-designed systems of irrigation that were both simple and eminently appropriate, they [the Aztecs] could ensure an adequate supply of water during the seasons when it was most needed. Their cultivation of crops was labor-intensive and highly productive; they used biological control of pests, organic fertilizers, plants that trapped nitrogen in the air and encircled the soil, crop rotation and effective methods of storage. They also supplemented their diet with fruit that was both wild and cultivated, roots, fish, grubs, and game.

Jan Carew, *Fulcrums of Change*, 148

Aztec Environmental Engineering

The chinampa . . . is anchored by roots of the ahuehuete tree and by posts and vine walls. Mud from the canals is piled up on a bed of wattles and vines, and layers of water weeds which serve as compost form the upper section of the plot. This is covered with a layer of fresh mud, which provides a fertile medium for planting. The chinampa plots are usually surrounded by an intricate network of canals. These canals are stocked with carp and other fish, and a giant salamander called axolotl, which is considered a delicacy. The canals also provide organic fertilizer and mulch in the form of abundant green algae which is skimmed off the water and applied to the plots. . . . Human wastes were collected, treated, and recycled as fertilizer without polluting its indispensable canals. Urine was collected separately, broken down, and two of its by-products were paint and sulphate of ammonia. This was all part of a ryhthm of recycling that had become as natural as breathing.

Jan Carew, *Fulcrums of Change*, 151-153

Aztec Surgeons

Indian surgeons sewed facial lacerations by using bone needles threaded with human hair. They set bones in plasters made of down feathers, gum, resin, and rubber. They gave enemas with rubber hoses, and they invented the bulbed syringe for use in a variety of medical treatments. . . . European doctors quickly adopted both the rubber hose and syringe and continue to use them today.

Indian healers lanced boils and removed tumors by surgery. Surgeons amputated limbs, prescribed artificial legs, removed teeth and castrated men and animals . . . they mastered the application and use of tourniquets and cauterization.

Jack Weatherford, *Indian Givers*, 188

The new medicine made extensive European settlement of America possible. For example, the 167 records of Governor Berkeley of Virginia show that before the introduction of quinine into Virginia one colonist of every five died within the first year from malaria. "After the incorporation of quinine no one died. . . . But until the research of [Sir Ronald Ross], no one knew that the mosquito transmitted it into the human bloodstream. This discovery led to the Nobel Prize in medicine for Ross in 1902, three hundred years after the unknown Quechua Indians had given the cure for the disease to the world, a gift for which they received no recognition" (Weatherford, 178).

The Huron Indians of North America were able to cure French sailors who were dying of scurvy. French Commander Jacques Cartier wrote in his log that the *annedda* bark administered by the Indians accomplished in one week what "no amount of drugs from Africa or Europe could have done" (Weatherford, 183). A variety of North American tribes contributed witch hazel, wintergreen, blue cohosh, petroleum jelly, and numerous herbs to the stack of medicinal aids used by the early colonists. Aztec surgeons using obsidian scalpels performed brain surgery almost five hundred years ago.

What the Indian healers received for their healing gifts was an influx of European diseases so virulent that the Indians who lacked immunities for killer diseases such as smallpox, bubonic plague, tuberculosis, yellow fever, influenza, and malaria perished by the millions. Their helpless doctors, who'd been used to the practice of preventive medicine with an essentially healthy population, had to watch their people die off.

The Gifts of Africans

Culture

The African gift to the world was culture itself. Archaeologists indicate that civilization began in the great river valleys of Africa and Asia.

> *For some 600,000 years Africans and Asians led the world. . . . Blacks or people who would be considered black today were among the first people to use tools, paint pictures, plant seeds, and worship gods.*
>
> *In the beginning, then, and for a long time afterwards, black people marched in the front ranks of the emerging human procession. They founded empires and states. They made some of the critical discoveries and contributions that led to the modern world.*

Lerone Bennett, Jr., *Before the Mayflower*, 5

The founders and creators of civilization were bound into servitude with little compunction on the part of European "civilization" because they were an uncivilized and inferior race by European standards. Even if this mythology was invented to justify the colonizers' economic needs for a strong laboring class that would facilitate the expansion of empires, the myth would endure and form the racist basis of white superiority.

W.E.B. DuBois confronts the myth of white cultural superiority by listing the cultural gifts Africans brought to America two hundred years before the Mayflower even landed.

> *Your country? How came it yours? Before the Pilgrim landed we were here. Here we have brought our three gifts and mingled them with yours: a gift of story and song—soft, stirring melody in an ill-harmonized and unmelodious land; the gift of sweat and brawn to beat back the wilderness, conquer the soil, and lay the foundations of this vast economic empire two hundred years earlier than your weak hands could have done it; the third, a gift of the spirit.*
>
> Quoted in Lerone Bennett, Jr., *Before the Mayflower*, 29

These three gifts then, story and song, labor, and the gift of the spirit, came from a people who were branded, 'buked, flogged, raped; whose children were torn from their mothers; who were castrated and hanged if they resisted; and who, in the twentieth century, were attacked by police dogs, clubbed, hosed, imprisoned, and beaten to death.

Story and Song

Slaves sang in the hissing fields to lighten the burden of toil from sunup to sundown, sang spirituals that told the burden of their suffering, sang in chain gangs breaking rocks under the guns of Southern prison guards, sang in swamps and backwoods. No sorrow was sufficient to stop their singing.

> *Music was everywhere and it was grounded in two techniques which survived in the "new world": polyrhythmic percussive technique and the call-and-response pattern (leader and chorus alternating). The poetry of tom-toms, the symphonies of synchronized bodies: these ebbed and flowed with the rhythm of life. Men and women danced because dancing had a social and religious meaning and because dancing was meaning, was life itself. This attitude came to America, too.*
>
> Lerone Bennett, Jr., *Before the Mayflower*, 25

Story is the basis of African American aesthetic expression. Oral tradition remembers the beloved culture, the people's suffering, and their resistance to their colonizers. Such an aesthetic is grounded in the community and is accountable, not to the art/

Brer Rabbit and Freedom

Tar-baby is an archetypal symbol of the oppressed—black and indestructible, endowed with the strength and powers of resistance of both male and female. Its tormentors were themselves worn out raining blows upon its head and in the end the aggressor becomes the victim. Tar is black, plastic, capable of being poured into any mold; the harder it becomes, the more vulnerable it is, the more easily it can be pounded into dust; its strength lies in appearing to be soft and yielding. For the slave the rabbit was a communal creature, swift, fragile, cunning, its habit of procreation legendary. It had survived down the ages when stronger and more ferocious enemies had in their pride rushed into extinction. The rabbit, too, was gentle, loyal, loving. Although each warren was a fortress unto itself, it lived and survived in groups.

For slaves anxious to conceal their persistent longing for freedom, the animal story was a perfect vehicle. To those unschooled in the subtleties of an oral tradition in which speech inflections, facial expression, gestures and the infinite variety of feelings that weave themselves in and out of the storyteller's narrative, animal stories could easily be dismissed as infantile, but because of this, political, historical and cultural messages could be more safely woven into a seemingly amusing or innocuous story. The storyteller could also implant in every tale the idea of the moral right of the weak to struggle against the mighty by any means necessary.

Jan Carew, *Fulcrums of Change*, 84-85

literary world, but one's people. For the African American, story addresses the concerns of a people; the literary character's journey is immersed in the people's struggle. Western aesthetic does not require this accountability, rather the opposite. The hero or anti-hero is distinctive because he or she achieves independence from the family, the community. The character's personhood (usually manhood) is achieved through separation from the crowd or from constraints.

The song and story the Africans gave America was communal and integral to the life of the people. "Art and aesthetic expression were collective experiences in which all the people participated. Art, in short, was not for art's sake, but for life's sake" (Bennett, 25).

Story is a crucible which reinvents culture for each generation. Each village in the Carribbean had its storyteller carrying on the African tradition of story and myth-making. In Guyana, children gathered beneath the silkcotton tree where the storyteller "would chant poem hymns to the accompaniment of drums, repeating stanzas over and over until his head felt light as air and his body became a house of dreams; then the tales would unravel themselves" (Carew, 121).

It was the storyteller who conveyed the folk archetype myths from East and Central Africa that became part of the slave mythology of the Americas. The stories of Brer Rabbit, and B'ra Anancy in the Carribbean islands, were tales of resistance and strategic cunning in impossible situations.

Labor

The black gift of labor was the gift of wealth to other nations—a gift all but invisible. While the Incan Indians of Potosi transmuted the world economy, African labor and agricultural skills built Caribbean and North American Empires. There could have been no agricultural economies without slaves to work the lands of the "new world." And land was the basis of power. When that human labor source was withdrawn, as happened with the slave revolts in the Caribbean, the European world economic order was threatened and altered. Moreover, the slave revolts contributed to the "movement for freedom, equality, and democracy, while they foreshadowed the movement against capitalism itself . . . the revolts . . . formed part of the political opposition to European capitalism" (Genovese, 84).

Spirit

As for the gift of the spirit, never before in the history of the United States did a movement of such spiritual force confront the moral contradictions of the white world than did the Civil Rights

To Love the Land

Marko, a Grenadian farmer, describes the human labor from "breast to death" that sustained the land and people as they toiled for colonizers from generation to generation, and how his "heart jumped" when the young Grenadian, Maurice Bishop, came to power. The old farmer's hopes were pinned on the new government, which successfully initiated land reform and an educational and health care sysytem geared to the needs of the Grenadian peasants. Sadly, Marko's reflections preceded the United States' invasion of Grenada, resulting in the death of Bishop and his entire government cabinet.

Ah can't tell you how long we wrestled with these hills and valleys from breast to death . . . this land makes you old before your time, greyhairs your life while you're still young . . . and if it's not one thing it's the other—hurricane, landlords, drought, flood—farmers are going to have to make a better living or this country will die. This is a country of youths, and yet the age of the average farmer is fifty-five . . . part of it is that before you can buy enough land to make a living you're too old to work it well . . . but all that is changing. The morning after Gairy fell, I heard Brother Bishop say, "This is a revolution for land , for jobs, for liberty," and I felt my old heart jump. . . . This time, me, and all the farmers around, those with land and those without, are part of the settlement . . . we will take over the land from those who owned it since long time past days, and who used it so badly. . . . Anyway, only He who created the land got a right to own it, land is for all of we. . . .

Jan Carew, *Fulcrums of Change,* 158

movement. Singing through that struggle with its beatings and bombings, clapping and dancing to a God who would deliver the people from the "Pharaohs" of this land, the spirit of black people revealed, and some would say redeemed, the diseased soul of a nation. That eruption of spirit was not the genius of a charismatic minister named Martin Luther King, Jr. He was only one voice that remembered with his people the moral resistance they'd continued from Africa to plantation cabins, from farm shacks to storefront churches.

It would be hard to name popular music forms that remain separate from or unaffected by this spirit. Negro spirituals inspired blues, jazz, rock n' roll, much of folk music, and, currently, rap.

The Gift of Resistance

Maroons contributed not only a fighting spirit, but also a demonstration of the power of resistance. Historian Eugene Genovese argues that the maroon establishments, such as Palmares in Brazil, sought to reconstruct the communal traditions of Africa but failed to overthrow the colonial powers that continued to hold other blacks in slavery. The desire of runaway slave communities to restore traditional ways limited their political and/or economic impact. Even so, "however traditional or backward-looking the world of the Palmarinos, every blow they struck at the Dutch and the Portuguese forced some slight alteration in the course of European capitalism" (Genovese, 84). The San Domingo revolution, led by Touissant l'Overture, however, provided the world with a revolution which led to a modern black nation capable of export trade and entrance into the world market. (See page 87)

> *The great revolution marked the turning point in the history of slave revolts in the "new world." The people of San Domingo successively humiliated the Spanish, British, and French and inflicted some of the heaviest losses those supreme imperialists ever suffered. . . . W.E.B. DuBois argued that the revolution in San Domingo enormously strengthened the anti-slave movement in England and prepared the way for its flowering in America; that it ended Napoleon's dream of an American empire and led him to the sale of Louisiana, which doubled the size of the United States; and that it influenced, perhaps decisively, the decision of the Southern states to close the African slave trade. . . . Haiti stirred the slaves and free Negroes to rebellion under a modern ideology that posed a new and more dangerous threat to the old regimes than anything else previously encountered. . . . The revolution in San Domingo propelled a revolution in black consciousness throughout the "new world."*

> Eugene Genovese, *From Rebellion to Revolution*, 87, 93, 96

And my special geography too;
the world map made for my own use,
not tinted with the arbitrary colors of
* scholars,*
but with the geometry of my spilled blood.

Aimé Césaire, *Collected Poetry*, 77

. . . l'ouverture / dessalines on horsback /
you will ride back thru here / invoke those
same spirits you called on at the citadel /
there are half-naked women sleeping at
your feet / children begging under yr
bridled stallions / what 3 horses would
balk at / one black man carries on his
back / his sweat falls into the streams of
blood. . . .
where are you now
Haiti's in need. . . .

Ntozake Shange, *A Daughter's Geography*, 34

That revolution in black consciousness which has sparked slave revolts and uprisings in South Africa, Algeria, the Frontline nations of Africa, and the Civil Rights movement in the United States remains an ever-present dangerous memory that could ignite and burn away the economic and political cages that enslave the black world.

Killing the Spirit, Keeping the Spirit

A people's spirit can be wounded, dishonored, and diminished. Their land can be stolen, their leaders killed, their people enslaved, their children starved. Remembering the spirit of their people's resistance they will, nevertheless, endure. The most dangerous and insidious tactic of the colonizer is the attempt to destroy the people's spirit. Such a strategy aims a weapon at the people's culture, attempting to "adapt" that culture to the "civilized" culture by negating the culture of the colonized. This leads to self-hatred on the part of children who grow up in the shadows of the hated (or feared) subjugating culture. This strategy also reinforces in the colonizer's descendants a legacy of moral superiority, which, because it is a lie, is morally corrosive.

Consider, for example, the damage to the Indian spirit, as well as the moral character of Americans, to have U.S. government policies state an objective of cultural destruction of Indian nations. After the buffalo were killed off the great plains, after wild horses no longer ran the open range, and after red people of this land were penned into reservations, the white fathers in Washington made policies to win the final war against the Indians. This was the cultural war; the weapon used was law and policy. The objective of U.S. Indian policy was to deny Native American cultural identity. Psychologists insist that the failure to know who you are leads to madness, suicide, or violent rage. It is psychic death. Yet this was Indian policy. Here is an extract from the *Annual Report of the Commissioner of Indian Affairs* in 1889. "The logic of events demands the absorption of citizens. . . . The Indians must conform to 'the white man's ways,' peaceably if they will, forcibly if they must. . . . They cannot escape it and must conform to it or be crushed by it" (Prucha, ed., 177).

Indian Commissioner Morgan then goes on to identify the essence of U.S. "civilization" and the Indian cultural practices which presented obstacles to their inculturation. "The tribal relations should be broken up, socialism destroyed, and the family and autonomy of the individual substituted. The allotment of lands in severalty, the establishment of local courts and police, the development of a personal sense of independence, and the universal adoption of the English language are the means to this end" (Prucha, ed., 177).

They took away everything
except the spirit,
which they were incapable of seeing.
Julia Esquivel, *You Can't Drown the Fire*, 197

205

Our ideas will overcome your ideas. We are going to cut the country's whole value system to shreds. It isn't important that there are only 500,000 of us Indians. . . . What is important is that we have a superior way of life. We Indians have a more human philosophy of life. We Indians will show this country how to act human. Someday this country will revise its constitution, its laws, in terms of human beings, instead of property. If Red Power is to be a power in this country it is because it is ideological. . . . What is the ultimate value of a man's life? That is the question.

Vine Deloria, Jr.
In *Touch the Earth*, 159

The following excerpt from the *Annual Report of the Secretary of the Interior* also identifies the Indian cultural values of community and nonownership of sacred land as obstacles to their civilization. "The value of property as an agent of civilization ought not to be overlooked. When an Indian acquires property . . . he has made a step forward in the road to civilization" (Prucha, ed., 161).

The clash of cultures centers on the property right and individualism of the white way and the communal and nonacquisitive values of the Indian. Identifying individualism and private property as civilization not only destroys Indian culture but exposes the spiritual bankruptcy of white mainstream culture. The most morally damaging aspect of U.S. Indian policy for the "civilized" citizens of the United States was and is presented as a moral effort much the way modern wars against "communist" or "terrorist" nations are fought in the name of God to save civilization from the new "savages." The forms of "morality" used to justify destruction of Indian culture can be overtly racist or sympathetic, as the next two government documents illustrate. Whether the conservatives or the liberals decided Indian policy, the result was still the same: reservations, broken treaties, the banning of Indian language and rituals in the reservation schools: in short, cultural destruction. Indian Commissioner Price recommended a policy that would solve the "Indian Problem" in 1881:

> *To domesticate and civilize wild Indians is a noble work, the accomplishment of which should be a crown of glory to any nation. But to allow them to drag along year after year, and generation after generation, in their old superstitions, laziness, and filth, when we have the power to elevate them in the scale of humanity, would be a lasting disgrace of our government . . . savage and civilized life cannot prosper on the same ground. One of the two must die. If the Indians are to be civilized . . . they must learn our language and adopt our modes of life. We are fifty millions of people, and they are only one fourth of a million. The few must yield to the many.*

From the *Annual Report of the Commissioner of Indian Affairs*, Oct. 24, 1881, in Francis Paul Prucha, ed., *Documents of United States Indian Policy*, 156

Is the more sympathetic "liberal" approach of Indian Commissioner Walker, which follows, much different in practice from Commissioner Price's harsh tone?

> *Had the settlements of the United States not been extended beyond the frontier of 1867, all the Indians of the continent would to the end of time have found upon the plains an inexhaustible supply of food and clothing. Were the westward course of population to be stayed at the barriers of today . . . the Indians would still have hope of life.*

The freedom of expansion which is working these results is to us of incalculable value. To the Indian it is of incalculable cost. Every year's advantage of our frontier takes in a territory as large as some of the kingdoms of Europe. We are richer by hundreds of millions; the Indian is poorer by a large part of the little he has. This growth is bringing imperial greatness to the nation; to the Indian it brings wretchedness, destitution, beggary. . . .

Can any principle of national morality be clearer than that, when the expansion of development of a civilized race involves the rapid destruction of the only means of subsistence possessed by the members of a less fortunate race, the higher is bound as of simple right to provide for the lower some substitute for the means of subsistence which it has destroyed? That substitute is, of course, best realized, not by systematic gratuities of food and clothing continued beyond a present emergency, but by directing these people to new pursuits which shall be consistent with the progress of civilization upon the continent; helping them over the first rough places on the "white man's road."

Commissioner Walker, *Annual Report of the Commissioner of Indian Affairs,* in Francis Paul Prucha, ed., *Documents of United States Indian Policy,* 137

Indian Policy and the Black Hills

It's no wonder that the Indian cannot understand the white way or that native people have come to assume that whites are only capable of cultural theft of art, medicine, and ideas, of human labor and of land. Sitting Bull articulated the cultural clash of worldviews and the resulting tragedy for the Sioux nation which defended the Indian way:

What treaty that the whites have kept has the red man broken? Not one. What treaty that the white man ever made with us has the white man ever kept? Not one. When I was a boy the Sioux owned the world; the sun rose and set on their land; they sent ten thousand men to battle. Where are the warriors today? Who slew them? Where are our lands? Who owns them? What white man can say I ever stole his land or a penny of his money? Yet they say I am a thief. What white woman, however lonely, was ever captive or insulted by me? Yet they say I am a bad Indian. What white man has ever seen me drunk? Who has ever come to me hungry and unfed? Who has ever seen me beat my wives or abuse my children? What law have I broken? Is it wrong for me to love my own? Is it wicked for me because my skin is red? Because I am Lakota, because I was born where my father died, because I would die for my people and country?

Quoted in Peter Matheissen, *In the Spirit of Crazy Horse,* 33

Address delivered by Chief Seattle to Governor Stevens of the state of Washington in 1853 after his Suquamish and Duwamish tribes were removed to reservation lands.

There was a time when our people covered the land as the waves of a wind-ruffled sea cover its shell-paved floor, but that time long since passed away with the greatness of tribes that are now but a mournful memory. . . .

Your God is not our God! Your God loves your people and hates mine. He folds his strong protective arms lovingly about the pale face and leads him by the hand as a Father leads his infant son—but He has forsaken His red children. . . . Our people are ebbing away like a rapidly receding tide that will never return. The white man's God cannot love our people or He would protect them. . . . We are two distinct races with separate origins and separate destinies. . . . To us our ancestors are sacred and their resting place is hallowed ground. You wander far from the graves of your ancestors seemingly without regret. Your religion was written on tables of stone. . . . Our religion is the traditions of our ancestors . . . and the visions of our sachems, and it is written in the hearts of our people.

Your dead cease to love you . . . as they pass the portals of the tomb. . . . Our dead never forget the beautiful world. . . . Even the rocks, which seem to be dumb and dead as they swelter in   the sun along the silent shore, thrill with memories . . . and the very dust upon which you stand responds more lovingly to [our people's] footsteps than to yours. . . . When the last Red Man shall have perished, and the memory of my tribe shall have become a myth among the White Men, these shores will swarm with the invisible dead of my tribe, and when your children's children think themselves alone in the field . . . or in the silence of the pathless woods, they will not be alone.

In W.C. Vanderwerth, ed., *Indian Oratory,* 118-119

And now, five hundred years later, the colonizers still seek treasure. Today treasure is not gold, but uranium; Indians within the United States are not reduced to slaves, but leaders are criminalized and imprisoned. Law is able to accomplish what the whip and sword accomplished in the time of Columbus. Just as Chief Guaironex and Sitting Bull cherished the land, Lakota leader Russell Means fights for the Black Hills today:

> *Right now, today, we who live on the Pine Ridge Reservation are living in what white society has designated a National Sacrifice Area. What this means is that we have a lot of uranium deposits here, and white culture (not us) needs this uranium as energy production material. The cheapest and most efficient way for industry to extract and deal with the processing of this uranium is to dump the waste by-products right here at the digging sites. Right here where we live. This waste is radioactive and will make the entire region uninhabitable forever. This is considered by industry, and the white society that created this industry, to be an "acceptable" price to pay for energy resource development. Along the way they also plan to drain the water table under this part of South Dakota as part of the industrial process, so the region becomes doubly uninhabitable. This same sort of thing is happening down in the land of the Navajo and the Hopi, up in the northern Cheyenne and Crow, and elsewhere. . . .*
>
> *We are resisting being turned into a National Sacrifice Area. We are resisting being turned into a national sacrifice people. The costs of this industrial process are not acceptable to us. It is genocide to dig the uranium here and drain the water table, no more, no less.*

Quoted in Peter Mattheissen, *In the Spirit of Crazy Horse,* 525

It's sadly ironic that the clash between the red and white vision is symbolized today in the Black Hills, the sacred land of the Great Sioux nation. A legal fight rages over the 1868 Sioux claim to South Dakota lands, including seven and a half million acres of the Black Hills that were "lost" when Congress nullified the 1868 treaty following Custer's defeat. In the 1980s when the Sioux appealed to the Supreme Court, the government's "right" to the land was upheld. But the Sioux nation, faithful to tribal ethics and believing the earth is sacred and not for sale, refused the money.

The Black Hills is the land where the U. S. government chose to symbolize its democratic achievement. Chiseled into the stone hills of South Dakota are the faces of Presidents Washington, Lincoln, Jefferson, and Theodore Roosevelt. The government of the United States seeks to renovate the Mt. Rushmore National Memorial in South Dakota— "a shrine of democracy," according to President Bush. The Sioux nation protests. "Not only did they desecrate our sacred land," said Tim Giago, an Oglala Sioux who is an editor of the *Lakota Times*, "they also memorialized four Presidents who committed acts of atrocity against our people. . . . They want to spend $40 million to repair Mt. Rushmore and it's 70 miles from the poorest county in America, where our people are destitute" (Chu and Shaw, 69-70).

Destitute indeed. The annual income in the area is twenty-four hundred dollars, with an unemployment rate of eighty-five percent (Chu and Shaw, 70). Impoverished and defiant, the Sioux will not accept money for the sacred. Who is spiritually destitute, spiritually alive? If the lands of the Americas are to be saved from destruction, it is the Indians of America, who by their faithful reverence for the living world, will save it. This sacred love of all beings is the profound spirituality that has enabled Indian people to continue to resist five hundred years of assault and degradation. Indian spirituality is the hidden cultural weapon that sustains resistance in the face of hardship and death. Penned in reservations, marginalized, made invisible, the red nations refuse to die.

Five hundred years after the conquest of the Americas, an environmental crisis confronts the world. Scientists predict that the destruction of the rainforest, industrial pollution, acid rain, nuclear radiation, and destruction of animal species has so altered the environment that the earth itself is in mortal danger. Some of the Indian medicine people echo the Indian prophecy which foretells apocalyptic destruction as a result of the whites' failure to respect the mother, Earth. Lakota Wallace Black Elk articulates that vision.

> *The white people have to surrender their arms to the great Spirit.*
>
> *This purification is coming real soon, and all the guns and gold will melt. The holy spirit, the atom, the power of god, will melt those guns and tanks and poison gasses they create. . . . They will be standing by themselves. . . . When the time comes there won't be no amnesty.*
>
> *We're going back to the beginning of time. . . . I have no fear, I have no slightest fear whatsoever. Even if I have to face death like Chief Big Foot, it's very beautiful.*
>
> *We hold the key to eternity, where it is beautiful and it is everlasting for everyone. That's where we're going. We're going home. And finally we will be back in the Great Spirit's hands again. Grandmother's arms again. She'll cradle us in her arms again.*
>
> Quoted in Peter Matthiessen, *In The Spirit of Crazy Horse,* 547

[Indians] believe that the roots of oppression are to be found in the loss of tradition and memory because that loss is always accompanied by a loss of a positive sense of self. In short, Indians think it is important to remember, while Americans think it is important to forget.

Paula Gunn Allen
In Rick Simonson and Scott Walker, eds.,
Multicultural Literacy, 15

This is remembering, waki-ksuya. *It means to recall, to travel back into the past, to hold communion with the spirits, to receive a message from them, to bring to one's mind the dead friends, to hear their voice once again, even to the point of having a vision.*

John Lame Deer
In Alan R. Velie, ed., *American Indian Literature,* 239

Before she died, Anna Mae Pictou Aquash expressed both the spiritual vision and cultural resistance which sustain Native American hope and courage.

I am part of this creation as you are, no more and no less than each and every one of you within the sound of my voice. I am the generation of generations before me and the generations to come. . . . If I have gone against this creation—no man on this Universe holds the power to punish me other than the Creator himself. . . .

You are continuuing to control my life with your violent, materialistic needs. I do realize your need to survive and be part of this Creation—but you do not understand mine.

Quoted in Peter Matthiessen, *In the Spirit of Crazy Horse*, 252

Let us all return.
It is the people who give birth to us,
to all culture, who by their labors
create all material and spiritual values. . . .
only they have the future in their hands.
Only they.

Meridel Le Seur, *Ripening*, 239

Anna Mae Pictou Aquash, a Micmac Indian, faced her own death with the same openness that Black Elk reveals. A mother and activist involved at Wounded Knee, she was mysteriously murdered and found frozen in the snow in a remote area of Pine Ridge reservation. Her hands were cut off and sent in a jar to the FBI in Washington for a fingerprint check. Her sister Mary Lafford believes someone connected with the FBI killed her. AIM leader Dennis Banks said that her killer was not just the triggerman but the cultural triggermen of centuries. "She wasn't killed by just one person. It was what she represented and what kind of person she was. What happens to a people in four hundred years? Maybe that is the answer. Maybe four hundred years killed Anna Mae" (Matthiessen, 268).

How Cultural Invasion has Affected North American Culture

Native American philosopher John Mohawk links the birth of racism to the conquest of the fifteenth century and a white European worldview that continues its mission of conquest through today's mission of bringing "progress" to less developed nations.

It is said that the Conquistadors spilled more blood than any group of people ever spilled up to that time. . . . [Their] mentality also said that they had to dehumanize the victims of the conquest. . . . Even modern scholars identify the period of the conquest as the birth of racism in the modern world. It was the first time that arguments were seriously put forward in courts of Spain, especially at Vallaloid, arguing that the Indians were biologically inferior beings, that they were not even human beings at all, that they were really beasts of burden, that they were sub-humans as you would treat a burro or as you would treat a monkey. Some of the same things are still being argued in the Western Hemisphere, whether peoples of different physical characteristics are fully human and have full human rights and have full civil rights. All those arguments still go on right to the 1980s, certainly in places like Guatemala, and Peru, and Mexico where the conquest, I say, is not ended.

John Mohawk, "The Indian Way Is a Thinking Tradition," *Northeast Indian Quarterly*, 15

Photo by Jim Harney

Crossing the Borders

Who is America? Where is the America that Langston Hughes says has yet to be? Official history remembers one America. Red, black, brown, and yellow peoples remember another America, the America whose memory is a danger. That rainbow America continues to create history and to be a sign of blood and hope.

The America of the conquerors identifies with whiteness, manliness, and keeping a correct order. The other America has mixed things up and is full of color; its song and art break the rules. The other America is the real frontier, the place where something new can happen, the place where history is made. It is a place of possibility, but it is also a dangerous place. It is the border.

Borders are made by the powerful, but they can be subverted. Sometimes the border is a nineteen hundred mile wire fence with armed border patrol guards, checkpoints, and helicopter surveillance, like the Mexican/United States border; sometimes the border is a line drawn around the Black Hills. Sometimes border lines divide rich suburbs from slum neighborhoods where police

Cursed be
all your fences
which encircle you
from within,
fat, isolated,
like man-eating pigs. . . .
Cursed be all fences!
Ours is another land. . . .
The human earth made free, sisters and
brothers!

  Pedro Casaldaliga, *In Pursuit of the Kingddom,* 48

211

In school I learned of heroic discoveries
Made by liars and crooks. The courage
Of millions of sweet and true people
Was not commemorated.

Let us then declare a holiday
For ourselves, and make a parade that
    begins
With Columbus' victims and continues
Even to our grandchildren who will be
    named in their honor.

Because isn't it true that even the summer
Grass here in this land whispers those
    names,
And every creek has accepted the responsi-
    bility
Of singing those names? And nothing can
    stop
The wind from howling those names
    around
The corners of the school.

Why else would the birds sing
So much sweeter here than in other lands?

Jimmie Durhan, "Columbus Day"
In *Sojourners*, October 1991, 12

question anyone from the ghetto for crossing over. Sometimes the border is in the mind. This is what Franz Fanon calls taking on the mind of the colonizer, believing the official America's version of history.

The first step to creating history, according to Fanon, is to decolonize the mind. Brazilian Bishop Pedro Casaldaliga, who is considered the new de Las Casas of the Americas, has this to say about decolonization: "Decolonizing, reaching back for Latin America's identity, means allowing the overall Latin American culture—which is the sum total of many cultures, first of many indigenous peoples, and of the black people, enslaved and brought to Latin America, and then of the resulting mixture in many places— allowing this culture to be expressed . . . " (Casaldaliga, 2). How is culture to be recovered when it is no longer simply the culture it once was but the "sum total of many cultures . . indigenous . . . black . . . the resulting mix"? Dangerous memory must take back its own bruised and bold history. But even more than that, it must reckon with the fences that held captive the native, the black, red, brown peoples of the Americas, the fences staking land and the terrain of the heart and mind.

Historically the mixed blood person represented an affront to both the colonizer and the colonized. Mulattoes in the Caribbean were despised by the Europeans because they had black blood; they were rejected by the maroons and slaves because they were upwardly mobile and sought status in the white colonial society.

Even some colonized hold to the myth of pure blood and reject those who sympathize with or marry the colonizer. For the colonized, adherence to one's race is a necessary part of the decolonization process in which the colonized throw off the dominant culture and recover their own. Yet after five hundred years we have a racial mix that makes the notion of pure blood a myth. Historian Lerone Bennett, Jr., says that seventy to eighty percent of blacks have white and Indian ancestors. Moreover, he cites a study by Professor Robert Stuckert which indicates that one out of five American whites have African ancestors.

The most authoritative and scientific study in this area was made by Melville J. Herskovits . . . [whose study of 1551 blacks found] 71.7 percent of the same had white ancestors and 27.2 had some Indian ancestry. Since that time the number of mixed blacks has increased, not only because of additional black-white marriages but also because of the marriage of blacks (mixed) and blacks (unmixed). In the Herskovits sample, only 22 percent of black Americans were of unmixed ancestry. Nantu, Mandingo, Yoruba, Akan, Semite, British, Irish, German, French, Spanish, Dutch, Creek, Choctaw, Seminole, Pequot, Marshpee—the American black is an extraordinary amalgam of different amalgamations. The end product of 260 years of amalgamation, he is a genetic meta-

phor of the impossible possibilities of the peoples of the world, who are not so much equal as complementary, which is, as Teillard Chardin and Leopold Senghor said, a higher form, perhaps the highest form of superiority.

Lerone Bennett, Jr., Before the Mayflower, 325

The mix of races reveals "the impossible possibilities of the peoples of the world." But the colonizers have not welcomed the crossing of genetic borders. Ironically, the early colonists of North America lacked the taboos that would circumscribe such intermingling. Contrary to most accounts, there were many marriages between blacks and whites in the early U.S. colonial period before slavery was introduced. Bennett argues that a system of racism had not yet developed which could focus white fears and that marriage between blacks and whites was a commingling of the poor black and white indentured servants who made up the majority of the early colonial population. The state of Virginia was composed largely of mulattoes resulting primarily from the union of black men and white women who, without social prohibition, chose each other across race lines.

When the colonial planters sought more mass agricultural labor in the latter part of the seventeenth century, slavery was introduced and with it systematic separation of the races. This took some orchestrating because, according to Bennett, whites didn't as yet understand the concept of whiteness implying racial superiority.

> *To teach them their roles, the colonial ruling class organized a systematic campaign against mixing, which was perceived as a threat not only to Puritan morality but also to Puritan economics. "The increasing number of mulattoes, through intermarriage and illicit relationships," Dr. Lorenzo J. Greene wrote, "soon caused alarm among Puritan advocates of racial purity and white dominance. Sensing a deterioration of slavery, if the barriers between masters and slaves were dissolved . . . they sought to stop racial crossing by statue."*

Lerone Bennett, Jr., Before the Mayflower, 309

If the colonists of North America tried to hold color lines fast, the Spanish colonialists did not. Sexual relations between the Spaniards and the Indians produced a mixed race, the *mestizos*. *Mestizas* were represented by la Malinche *(la Chingada)*, the Indian woman who "betrayed" her people and slept with Hernan Cortes. The mix of bloods which resulted from mating between the Spanish and the Indian is the *Ladino*. Even today the most vulgar put-down one can say to a Mexican woman is to refer to her as *la chingada* (whore). Writer Gloria Anzaldua insists that such an interpretation of history fails to analyze Aztec class and gender relations. The Aztecs' weakness was their apparent strength. The Aztecs were themselves conquerors of other tribes who hated them because of the rape by the Aztec nobility. The conquered Tlaxcalans helped the Spanish defeat the Aztecs. "Thus the Aztec nation fell not because [Malinche] interpreted for and slept with Cortes, but

1992 could be the beginning of a reflection on the 500 years, the beginning of a discovery of what we have—the bad things which exist on this continent and the good things which we must plant, or cultivate, or irrigate, so that they can grow in the future. But it is not a question of 1992 being a great happening after which it can be said that the oppression, the discrimination, the racism, the poverty, and all the other evils have ended. It is the moment to begin creating the conditions for an encounter between two worlds, two cultures.

Rigoberta Menchu
In Sojourners, October 1991, 29

213

Sisters and brothers, the time is at hand. We cannot continue with business as usual. The threats to life in this nation and around the globe demand from all of us a new way of thinking, acting, and being. It is time for new affirmation and new covenants. A radically new orientation is required; a movement of unity, solidarity, and resistance is required in all parts of the world if we are to pursue a vision of a just peace for all of creation.

I believe that 1992 presents us with a pivotal moment in history. This is a truth-telling time, a world-changing time, that can provide us with new identities, new behavior, and a renewed mission for life, liberty, and the pursuit of happiness for all of God's people. This is a time for unity, solidarity, and resistance—not fragmentation and division.

The question has come up over and over again with regard to whether 1992 is a time for Native Americans to take the lead, to offer out of their pilgrimages insights and wisdom for the facing of these days. To teach us out of their rootedness to Mother Earth their understanding of peace, harmony, justice, wisdom. And the answer is obviously yes. We all—African Americans as well as Hispanic Americans, Asian, and white Americans—have much to learn from our Native American sisters and brothers. The shameful reality of our histories is how little we know of one another and how the history of divide and conquer has defined and continues to define the relationships among us.

Yvonne V. Delk, "A Moment of Turning," *Sojouners*, October 1991, 20

because the ruling elite had subverted the solidarity between men and women and between noble and commoner" (Anzaldua, 34).

The culture of the *mestizo* and the mulatto is the culture of the wretched of the earth. This is the juncture in history where worlds collide. It is the borderland, the land of nobodies, those cast-offs who "belong" to no one—but themselves. The *mestiza* is the mixture of races, the flesh in which the blood of oppressor and oppressed flows. The *mestiza*, sign of contradiction, rejected, shoved to the margins of history, stands at our border, those racial, and often class lines that separate us from each other. The border is the place of reckoning and hope. There, in the places of "fences," is another culture which transforms the old but remembers everything.

This is not an "integrated" or assimilated culture which imitates or seeks acceptance from the dominator. It is its own culture, struggling to know its identity, to make sense of the senseless, to make meaning of suffering, of absurdity, of duality. "We question the 'integration' of these cultures and peoples into what is supposedly a greater nation or a better culture. We do say we would be willing to accept an interintegration, one continent meeting another. . . . . Latin America can and must provide Europe with a great deal in the way of ecology, nature, sense of gratuity, joy, color, hospitality, solidarity, hope, utopia. . . ." (Casaldaliga, 2).

Who can see a world without fences, imagine the world beyond walls of captivity? Certainly not the fence-makers whose legacy to their children is a legal system which upholds their right to land, to boundaries that scar the earth with possession, and armies to enforce the "rights" of fences and walls. Those whose children and dreams were broken on the walls know the perniciousness of "ownership." Theirs is the vision showing that "boundaries are all lies" (Hogan, 68).

Poet Gloria Anzaldua expands the idea of Mexican philosopher Jose Vascocelos who spoke of the synthesis of races, a *mezcla* (mixture) resulting in a cosmic race. It is the *mestiza* who bridges borders, having been torn apart by them. Anzaldua is not speaking of a kind of universal *mestiza*, that is, an idealized human person without a concrete history mired in the pain of colonialism. The new frontier, peopled with those whose minds are free of fences, is not a "melting pot," nor a place for "individuals without an anchor, without a horizon, colorless, stateless, rootless, a race of angels" (Fanon, 218). On the contrary, those who stand at the borders refuse to forget their people's history of slavery, of colonization. They embrace the border as a meeting place rather than a place of separation. Whether the border is a state of mind or a fence in the earth, crossing over is an act of defiance, an act of decolonization. The *mestiza* understands that colonialism's intention is to obliterate her people's culture.

Photo by Jim Harney

Colonialism is not satisfied merely with holding people in its grip and emptying the natives' brain of all forms and content . . . it turns to the past of oppressed people and distorts, disfigures, and destroys it. . . . We have taken everything from the other side; and the other side gives us nothing . . . unless by a thousand wiles and a hundred tricks they manage to draw us toward them, to seduce us, and to imprison.

Franz Fanon, *The Wretched of the Earth*, 210

Decolonization is the process in which the colonized person refuses seduction. The task of the oppressed person is to discover his or her identity free of the definitions of the dominant culture. To be free is to affirm one's own stolen history. But what of the mix, the new breeds created in the clash of cultures? Are they the cast-offs of the world or the harbingers of culture, and signs of a new humanity? People who identify with the dominator die internally, strangled by their own betrayal. The racially mixed person who embraces her subjugated selves recognizes the gifts of mixed blood, having suffered the pain of difference. The *mestiza* incorporates in her flesh our common blood.

For Franz Fanon, "It is not enough to try to get back to the people in the past out of which they have already emerged; rather we must join them in the fluctuating movement which they are just giving shape to, and which, as soon as it has started, will be the signal for everything to be called into question. . . . It is [in] this zone . . . where . . . our souls are crystallized and our lives are transfused with light" (Fanon, 227).

Part of the blood that is mine has laboured endlessly four hundred years under the heel of lustful Europeans.
I am still here!

Rodolfo Gonzales, *I Am Joaquin*, 82

215

The point is hardly to blame Columbus for every atrocity of the West since his first voyage. . . . The real issue is the social paradigm and economic order that the Columbus event set into motion and the fact that it has dominated all of our lives and, in particular, the lives of marginalized peoples for the past 500 years. There is, in fact, no new world order; we are still being governed by an old one whose economic, political, philosophical, environmental, and especially spiritual roots can be traced back to the conquest and colonization of the Americas.

What are the values of that social order? What is their relationship to people of color, to the Earth, to technology, to the economy, to security, and to so many other vital questions that now face us? Most important, can the values and structures of the old social paradigm carry us into the future? If not, what must we do? . . .

The future of the American experiment depends on our remembering the past, transforming the present, and altering the future.

Jim Wallis, "Rediscovering America," *Sojourners,* October, 1991, 5

It is there at the border, in the shadows of fences, that light pours in, dispelling the clouds of forgetting. The struggle of the borderland is a struggle for culture. But this liberation struggle is not without anguish. "The area of culture," says Fanon, "is then marked off by fences and signposts. . . . Every effort is made to bring the colonized person to admit the inferiority of his culture" (Fanon, 236).

Gloria Anzaldua expresses the internalized shame and self-hatred produced by colonial domination:

In the Gringo world, the Chicano suffers from excessive humility and self-effacement, shame of self and self-deprivation. Around Latinos he suffers from a sense of language inadequacy and its accompanying discomfort; with Native Americans he suffers from a racial amnesia which ignores our common blood, and from guilt because the Spanish part of him took their land and oppressed them. He has an excessive compensatory hubris when around Mexicans from the other side. It overlays a deep sense of racial shame. . . .

Chicanos and other people of color suffer economically for not acculturating. This voluntary (yet forced) alienation makes for psychological conflict, a kind of dual identity—we don't identify with the Anglo-American cultural values and we don't totally identify with the Mexican cultural values. We are a synergy of two cultures with varying degrees of Mexicanness or Angloness. I have so internalized the borderland conflict that sometimes I feel that one cancels out the other and we are zero, nothing, no one.

Gloria Anzaldua, *The Borderland/La Frontera,* 63, 83

Amoja Three Rivers describes the burden of not knowing the racial mix that constitutes one's peoples as a fate as damaging as trying to straddle the known mix of one's race.

One of the most effective and insidious aspects of racism is cultural genocide. Not only have African Americans been cut off from our African tribal roots, but because of generations of whites pitting African against Indian, and Indian against African, we have been cut off from our Native American roots as well. Consequently most African Native Americans no longer have tribal affiliations, or know for certain what people they are from.

Amoja Three Rivers, "Cultural Etiquette: A Guide," *Ms.,* 42

Guillermo Gomez Pena sees whole generations "as the world's biggest floating population"—the refugees, the war and border displaced, the impoverished seeking work only the desperate want. The colonial project set in motion, and continues to drive, vast displacement of peoples. Gomez Pena calls this the borderization of the world.

The borders either expand or are shot full of holes. Cultures and languages mutually invade each other. The South rises and melts, while the North descends dangerously with its economic and military pincers. . . . Europe and North America daily receive uncontainable migrations of human beings, a majority of whom are being displaced involuntarily. . . .

The demographic facts are staggering: The Middle East and Black Africa are already in Europe, and Latin America's heart now beats in the United States. New York and Paris increasingly resemble Mexico City and Sao Paulo. Cities like Tijuana and Los Angeles, once socio-urban aberrations, are becoming models of a new hybrid culture, full of uncertainty and vitality. And border youth—the fearsome "cholo-punks," children of the chasm that is opening before the "first" and the "third" worlds, become the indisputable heirs to a new mestizaje *[the fusion of the Amerindian and the European races].*

Guillermo Gomez Pena, in Rick Simonson and Scott Walker, eds., *Multicultural Literacy,* 131

What emerges from the *mezcla* of cultures, from five hundred years of fences, is not only cultural damage and pyschic scars but a new wisdom, a new path. Creoles, mulattoes, and *mestizas,* the issue of crossed blood, of people who have crossed over the forbidden frontiers, are people who represent a new human enterprise. The new path is made by the despised. It is not an easy road, it is a way that reveals our common journey and common frailty.

The mixed blood person, like all subjugated people, bears the memory of lash, shackles, humiliation, and rape. Here is the testimony of Mary Crow Dog, a Lakota woman who gave birth during the siege of Wounded Knee.

> *. . . After I had a baby during the siege of Wounded Knee they gave me a special name, Okita Win, Brave Woman, and fastened an eagle plume in my hair, singing brave heart songs for me. I am a woman of the Red Nation, a Sioux woman. That is not easy.*

> *I had my first baby during a firefight, with bullets cracking through one wall and coming out the other. When my newborn son was only a day old and the marshals really opened up on us, I wrapped him in a blanket and ran for it. We had to hit the dirt a couple of times. I shielded the baby with my body, praying, "It's all right if I die, please let him live."*

> *When I came out of Wounded Knee I was not even healed up, but they put me in a jail at Pine Ridge and took my baby away. I could not nurse. My breasts swelled up and grew hard as rocks, hurting badly. In 1975 the feds put the muzzle of their M16's against my head, threatening to blow me away. It's hard being an Indian woman.*

The prophecy reports that many years ago the indigenous people of the Americas were divided into two groups, the people of the Eagle (those from the North) and the people of the Condor (those from the South). According to the prophecy, when the tears of the Eagle and the Condor are joined, a new era of life and spirit will begin for Native people.

Winona LaDuke, "We Are Still Here," *Sojouners,* October, 1991, 14

Photo by Jim Harney

You have sanitized death, put it under a rug, robbed it of its honor. But we Indians think a lot about death. I do. Today would be a perfect day to die— not too hot, not too cool. A day to leave something of yourself behind, to let it linger.

John Lame Deer, in Alan R. Velie, ed.,
American Indian Literature, 232

My best friend was Anna Mae Aquash, a young, stronghearted woman from the Mic Mac Tribe with beautiful children. It is not always wise for an Indian woman to come on too strong. Anna Mae was found dead in the snow at the bottom of a ravine on Pine Ridge Reservation. The police said she died of exposure, but there was a 38 caliber slug in her head. The FBI cut off her hands and sent them to Washington for fingerprint identification, hands that helped my baby come into the world.

My sister-in-law Delphine, a good woman who had lived a hard life, was also found dead in the snow, the tears frozen on her face. A drunken man had beaten her, breaking one of her arms and legs, leaving her helpless in a blizzard to die.

My sister Barbara went to the government hospital in Rosebud to have her baby and when she came out of anesthesia found that she had been sterilized against her will. The baby lived only two hours and she had wanted so much to have children. No, it isn't easy.

When I was a small girl at St. Francis Boarding School, the Catholic Sisters would take a buggy whip to us for what they called "disobedience." At the age of 10 I could drink and hold a pint of whiskey. At age 12 the nuns beat me for "being too free with my body." All I had been doing was holding hands with a boy. At age 15 I was raped. If you plan to be born, make sure you are white and male.

Mary Crow Dog and Richard Erdoes, *Lakota Woman*, 1-3

Born in this suffering is a defiance that offers hope. Indian poet Joy Harjo uses the metaphor of horses to describe Indian shame and defiant hope in response to the white way.

She had some horses who whispered in the dark,
who were afraid to speak.
She had some horses who screamed out of the fear of silence,
who carried knives to protect themselves from ghosts.
She had some horses who waited for destruction.
She had some horses who waited for resurrection. . . .

These were the same horses.

Joy Harjo, in Rayna Green, ed., *That's What She Said*, 45

The borderland is woman's "place" because it is no man's land. It is woman who locates in her bodiliness the wounds of centuries. It is woman who envisions a new humanity without borders, without a "place" for women, for the elderly, for those who are outcasts, who are "different" racially, sexually, culturally.

Women at the Crossroads

The dark-skinned woman has been silenced, caged, gagged, bound into servitude with marriage, bludgeoned for 300 years, sterilized and castrated in the twentieth century . . . she has been a slave, a source of cheap labor, colonized by the Spaniard, the Anglo, and by her own people (in Mesoamerica her lot under Indian patriarchs was not free of wounding). For 300 years she was invisible, she was not heard. . . . Every increment of consciousness, every step forward, is a travesia, a crossing. . . . Every time she makes "sense" of something she has to "cross over," kicking a hole in the old boundaries.

I saw Strikes-Two, a woman sixty years old, riding around the camp on a grey horse. She carried only her root-digger, and she was singing her medicine-song, as though Lakota bullets and arrows were not flying around her. . . .

When the men and even the women began to sing as Strikes-Two told them, she rode out straight at the Lakota, waving her root-digger and singing that song. I <u>saw</u> her, I <u>heard</u> her, and my heart swelled because she was a woman.

Pretty Shield
In Paula Gunn Allen, ed., *Spider Woman's Granddaughters*, 33

This weight on her back—which is the baggage from the Indian mother, which is the baggage from the Spanish father, which is the baggage from the Anglo?

Gloria Anzaldua, *The Borderland/La Frontera*, 82

In a few centuries, the future will belong to the mestiza. *Because the future depends on the breaking down of paradigms, it depends on the straddling of two or more cultures. By creating a new mythos—that is a change in the way we perceive reality, the way we see ourselves and the ways we behave—*la mestiza *creates a new consciousness. The answer to the problem between the white race and the colored, between males and females, lies in healing the split that originates in the very foundation of our lives, our culture, our language, our thoughts. A massive uprooting of dualistic thinking in the individual and collective consciousness is the beginning of a long struggle, but one that could, in our best hopes, bring us to the end of rape, of violence, of war. . . .*

As a mestiza *I have no country . . . yet I am cultured because I am participating in the creating of yet another culture, a new story to explain the world and our participation in it, a new value system with images and symbols that connect us to each other and to the planet.* Soy un amasamiento, *I am an act of kneading, of uniting and joining that which not only has produced both a creature of darkness and a creature of light, but also a creature that questions the definitions of light and dark and gives them new meaning.*

We are the people who leap in the dark, we are the people on the knees of gods. In our very flesh (r)evolution works out the clash of cultures. . . . Indigenous like corn, the mestiza *is a product of crossbreeding, designed for preservation under a variety of conditions. Like an ear of corn a female seedbearing organ, the* mestiza *is tenacious, tightly wrapped in the husks of her culture. Like kernels she clings to the cob; with thick stalks and strong brace roots, she holds tight to the earth—she will survive the crossroads.*

Anzaldua, *The Borderland/La Frontera*, 22-23, 48-49, 80-81

Liberated Zones Within the Borders of Empire

In 1663 in the mountains of northeastern Brazil, black slaves fled to Palmares. The governor general of Brazil sent expeditions to route the dissenters, to no avail. The Portuguese sent twenty-three expeditions against Palmares and failed to crush them. It is in Palmares that the many "petals" of language and custom become "a single rose."

*Let us summon the petals
of all the accents sometimes fratricide
to a single rose called
Amerindian America, Afroamerica,
Creole America. . . .*

Pedro Casaldaliga

Palmares remained dangerous memory, the place of resistance and new culture, black culture, the culture of the Quilombos, those escaped blacks who formed settlements in the mountains and jungles of Brazil. The culture which they made was a mix of many different languages, cultures, and national identities.

As a precursor to the slave revolts of the eighteenth and nineteenth centuries, Palmares symbolizes the formation of an autonomous "state" within empire. Only one slave revolt, however, became a soverign national power. The Haitian revolution, led by Touissant l'Overture and Dessalines, embodied the struggle for freedom and rights epitomized in the French revolution. But the Haitian revolution added a historical depth lacking in the French revolution. It was led by slaves. Such a fire threatened to spread.

The tragic counterrevoltion which followed reduced the island to isolation, savage poverty, and rule by brutal dictators. Yet the spirit of resistance rises from the ashes of history. A new leader, devoted to the impoverished majority, has given the people hope. On his presidential inauguration day Jean Bertrand Aristide invited the masses into the palace for a banquet. President Aristide, a Catholic priest whom the people call "our Liberator," moved throughout the courtyard offering the Haitian poor an inaugural meal as a sign of his desire to serve the people.

Aristide's uncompromising defense of the poor masses so angered the elites and military that he was captured and exiled in October 1991. The generals soon learned that the country might be ungovernable. Resistance remains clandestine, wily, and massive. The people do not forget the revolutionary priest who believed in them, who believed that the poor of Haiti are its future. So they wait as their ancestors waited for the right moment. They will fill the years with sabotage, defiance, underground organizations, secret codes, and memory. They will remember Aristide as they remember l'Overture. Poet Ntosake Shange calls on leaders l'Overture, Petion, and Dessalines to observe the suffering of the people:

> can you stand it dessalines?
> can you stand it Petion\l'Overture?
> can you stand these children
> with the red eyes and dacron brassieres for sale? . . .
>
> will you come again\some of you
> sweep through the alleys and the stink\come here
> with yr visions
> l' liberte l'egalite l'fraternite.
> come visit among us that we might know
> again/some hope.

Ntosake Shange, "A Black Night in Haiti, Palais National, Port au Prince," *A Daughter's Geography*, 33-34

Mass of the Quilombos

We are coming from the depths of the earth,
we are coming from the bosom of night;
of the flesh under the lash we are made
we have come to remember.

We are coming from death out at sea,
we are coming from the packed holds of ships;
we are heirs of melancholy
we have come to weep. . . .

We are coming from the old slave quarters,
we are coming from the new favelas;
we are the outcasts of the world
we have come to dance.

We are coming from the land of the quilombos,
we are coming to the beating of drums;
we are the new Palmares
we have come to struggle.

Pedro Casaldaliga, *In Pursuit of the Kingdom*, 67-68

So That You May Not Forget

Dedicated to Miguel, a Baptist minister killed with three others in El Salvador on Nov. 15, 1989.

You tried to rip out the roots of my life.
One time, ten times, a thousand times, a
million times.
To erase me from the earth
so as not to leave traces of my existence.
But today I am more alive than when you
killed me.
I give you back your death
so that you will always carry it like a
shadow
that does not allow you to forget—
that the bread you raise to your mouth
is the bread that was paid for with the
sweat of our workers;
the coffee that delights you
you took from campesinos blood;
the latest fashion that you wear
you robbed from women who worked long
hours.
Because of your luxury, billions of my
brothers and sisters
were left without food, without sleep,
without rest, without schools.
When you sleep, may you draw in your
dreams
the faces of the disappeared
the pain of their children
the bodies you mutilated
and the tortures you designed.
I give you back your death.
Because today I am more alive than when
you killed me.

Secundino Ramirez

L'Overture, Petion, Dessalines can never, of course, return. But the spirit of their resistance can. It is the memory of that spirit that Shange calls upon. This book has sought to remember the "l'Overtures" of history. But the book's dedication is to those anonymous masses who make such liberators possible. Those nameless peasants, slaves and workers are the spiritual and material forces that drive history. Shange calls upon the spirit of Haitian revolutionareies to return. But it is, and it was, the peoples' spirit of resistance which will determine the struggle for justice, not an individual leader. L'Overture cannot return. Aristide can. The people say he'll come again. They'll see to it.

They plucked our fruit, they cut our branches, they burned our trunk, but they could not kill our roots.

Committee of United Campesinos, Guatemala

Culture Bibliography: Works Cited in Chapter Three

Allen, Paula Gunn, *The Sacred Hoop*. Boston: Beacon Press, 1986.

___, ed. *Spider Woman's Granddaughters: Traditional Tales and Contemporary Writing by Native American Women.* Boston: Beacon Press, 1989.

Anglesey, Zoe, ed. *Ixok Amar•go.* Penobscott, Maine: Granite Press, 1987.

Anzaldua, Gloria. *Borderlands/La Frontera.* San Francisco: Spinsters/Aunt Lute, 1987.

Barreiro, Jose. "A Note on Tainos: Whither Progress? *View from the Shore: American Indian Perspectives on the Quincentenary. Northeast Indian Quarterly.* 7:3 (Fall 1990) 66-77.

Bennett, Lerone, Jr. *Before the Mayflower.* New York: Penguin Books, 1982.

Black, Irwin and Henry Rosen. *The Conquest.* New York: Grosset and Dunlap, 1961.

Campos, Pedro Albizu. *Claridad.* San Juan, Puerto Rico, Sept. 12, 1991.

Carew, Jan. *Fulcrums of Change.* Trenton, New Jersey: Africa World Press, 1988.

Casaldaliga, Pedro. *In Pursuit of the Kingdom.* New York: Orbis Books, 1990.

Césaire, Aimé. *Aimé Césaire: Collected Poetry.* Berkeley: University of California Press, 1983.

Chu, Daniel and Bill Shaw, "About Faces," *People Magazine.* July 22, 1991.

Collins, Sheila. "Are the Multiculturists Politically Correct?" Paper delivered at Walden University, July 10, 1991.

The Council on Interracial Books for Children. *Stereotypes, Distortions and Omissions.* New York, 1977.

Crow Dog, Mary and Richard Erdoes. *Lakota Woman.* New York: Harper Perennial, 1991.

Delk, Yvonne V. "A Moment of Turning," *Sojourners*, October 1991, 20.

Drake, Samuel. *Biography and History of the Indian of North America.* Boston, 1851.

Esquivel, Julia. *You Can't Drown the Fire.* Edited by Alicia Partnoy. Pittsburg: Cleis Press, 1988.

Fanon, Franz. *The Wretched of the Earth.* New York: Grove Press, 1963.

Galeano, Eduardo. *Memory of Fire.* Vol. 1, *Genesis.* New York: Pantheon Books, 1985.

Genovese, Eugene. *From Rebellion to Revolution.* New York: Vintage Books, 1979.

Gonzales, Rodolfo. *I Am Joaquin.* New York: Bantam Pathfinder, 1972.

Green, Rayna, ed. *That's What She Said: Contemporary Poetry and Fiction by Native American Women.* Bloomington: University of Indiana Press, 1984.

"Have You Seen *'La Nueva Mujer Revolucionaria Puertorriqueña?'" Que Ondee Sola.* Northeastern University student newspaper, March 1981.

Hogan, Linda, ed. *Seeing Through the Sun.* Amherst: University of Massachusetts, 1985.

Jojola, Ted. "American Indian Stereotypes," *View from the Shore: American Indian Perspectives on the Quincentenary. Northeast Indian Quarterly* 7:3 (Fall 1990) 26-28.

LaDuke, Winona. "We Are Still Here," *Sojourners*, October 1991, 14.

Lame Deer, John and Richard Erdoes. "Lame Deer, Seeker of Visions," *American Indian Literature: An Anthology.* Edited by Alan R. Velie. Norman: University of Oklahoma Press, 1988.

Matthiessen, Peter. *In the Spirit of Crazy Horse.* New York: Viking, 193.

McLuhan, T.C., comp. *Touch the Earth.* New York: Touchstone Books, 1971,

Memi, Albert. *The Colonizer and the Colonized.* Boston: Beacon Press, 1965.

Mohawk, John. "Discovering Columbus: The Way Here," *View from the Shore: American Indian Perspectives on the Quincentenary. Northeast Indian Quarterly* 7:3 (Fall 1990): 37-46.

____. "Toward a Reverence for Nature." Unpublished paper, 1991.

Murguia, Alejandro and Barbara Paschke. *Volcán.* San Francisco: City Lights, 1983.

Prucha, Francis Paul, ed. *Documents of United States Indian Policy.* Lincoln: University of Nebraska Press, 1990.

Shange, Ntozake. *A Daughter's Geography.* New York: St. Martin's Press, 1983.

Simonson, Rick and Scott Walker, eds. *Multicultural Literacy.* St. Paul, Minnesota: Graywolf Press, 1988.

Three Rivers, Amoja. "Cultural Etiquette: A Guide," *Ms.*, October 1991, 42.

Vanderwerth, W.C., ed. *Indian Oratory.* Norman: University of Oklahoma Press, 1971.

Venables, Robert W. "Commentary: The Cost of Columbus," *View from the Shore: American Indian Perspectives on the Quincentenary. Northeast Indian Quarterly* 7:3 (Fall 1990) 29-36.

Wallis, Jim. "Rediscovering America," *Sojourners*, October 1991, 5.

Weatherford, Jack. *Indian Givers: How the Indians of the Americas Transformed the World.* New York: Fawcett

T·E·A·C·H·I·N·G S·T·R·A·T·E·G·I·E·S

To make a quake of victory
to make a cluster of liberated world
to make a song in flood

It is the earth
It is the earth
that triumphs.

Para hacer un temblor de victoria
para hacer un racimo de mundo libre
para hacer una canción inunda

Es la tierra
Es la tierra
La que triunfa.

Juan Felipe Herrera
Akrilica

The Invasion
Europe Before the Conquest

Pre-Reading Strategies

Recollections of European History

What images and memories come to mind from your previous study of Europe and Spain around the end of the Middle Ages? From recollections of art, literature, and history, write down your impressions of everyday life, work, and social conditions at that time.

- Who had power?
- What were the main kinds of political structures?
- How did governments work?
- Who dominated in Spain and what had transpired there for the last millennium?

Recalling Images of Columbus

Write a portrait of Columbus from your study of history, from pictures and movies you have seen. Describe him and his compatriots as you recall them. Write what you think were his intentions in sailing west from Europe.

Identifying the Source

After doing either or both of the above tasks, identify and discuss the source of your memories and viewpoints. Where did you get these ideas? How accurate do you think your images are?

Post-Reading Strategies

The End of the World: Questions for Discussion

- How would you describe everyday life in Europe and/or Spain after reading the chapter? How does this image agree or contrast with the image you had of Columbus's time before your reading?
- Fifteenth-century Spain had a heavy emphasis on military advancements. How does that emphasis compare with current priorities in the United States?

Getting Inside the Minds of the Colonizers: Cartooning

Draw a cartoon which presents in "imagination bubbles" the mindsets of the merchant and ruling classes of Europe which prepared them for a "conquest" over the people they were about to encounter across the Atlantic. Draw a contrasting cartoon which shows the mindsets of other groups of people who also sailed the Atlantic and Pacific, landed on the coasts of the Americas, and did not proceed to conquer its inhabitants.

Refer to the requerimiento *information in the chapter and the section on European views of the natural world.*

The First To Land or the First To Conquer? A Role-Play

Divide into three groups. The first group represents a part of the world with the following characteristics:

- government with a high degree of participation of the people
- equitable distribution of land, goods, and benefits
- development of sophisticated navigation techniques
- widespread curiosity and interest in exploration
- no expansionist warfare over neighboring populations

The second group represents another part of the world, which has

- an autocratic pattern of government, with power and goods in the hands of a few
- sophisticated navigation techniques and also highly advanced weapons
- a long history of engagement in military battles for power and territory

The third group represents the indigenous peoples of the Caribbean.

The first two groups take turns "landing" in the Americas, pretending to be sailors from the vessels which have sailed long distances and are now meeting natives for the first time.

How do the sailors talk with the natives? What are their goals? What arrangements do they make, out of what worldviews and assumptions? How are the two experiences different?

Charting Key Connections

Several "isms" are mentioned in this chapter as influential ideas and movements at the time of Columbus. On a large piece of newsprint write these terms, spacing them all over the page. In a discussion group draw lines which connect terms and discuss any connections you can make between those "isms." Write notes on each "connecting" line which summarize your thoughts on how these terms are connected.

Inquisition   Nationalism   Rationalism   Catholicism   Humanism
Capitalism   Feudalism   Materialism   Judaism   Islam
Militarism

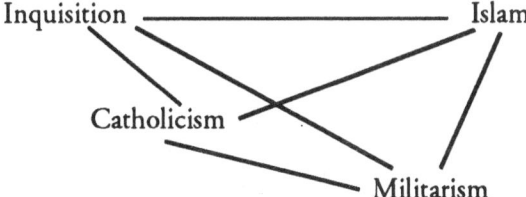

Impact of the "isms"

Sketch a map of Europe and one of the Western Hemisphere. Fill in the "isms" listed above on the European map and draw lines to the Western Hemisphere showing transference of these notions beginning with the arrival of Columbus and the subsequent Spanish conquest. Again write notes on each "connecting" line which summarize your thoughts on how these ideas were key factors in the conquest of the indigenous people on the other side of the Atlantic Ocean.

Expansionism and Militarism

Study the maps shown on the following pages and discuss the questions presented here:

- What group controlled the major portion of the Iberian Peninsula in the tenth century? How do you know?
- By the end of the eleventh century what had happened to the political control of the Iberian Peninsula? From your reading of this section, explain what had transpired in the politics of Spain.

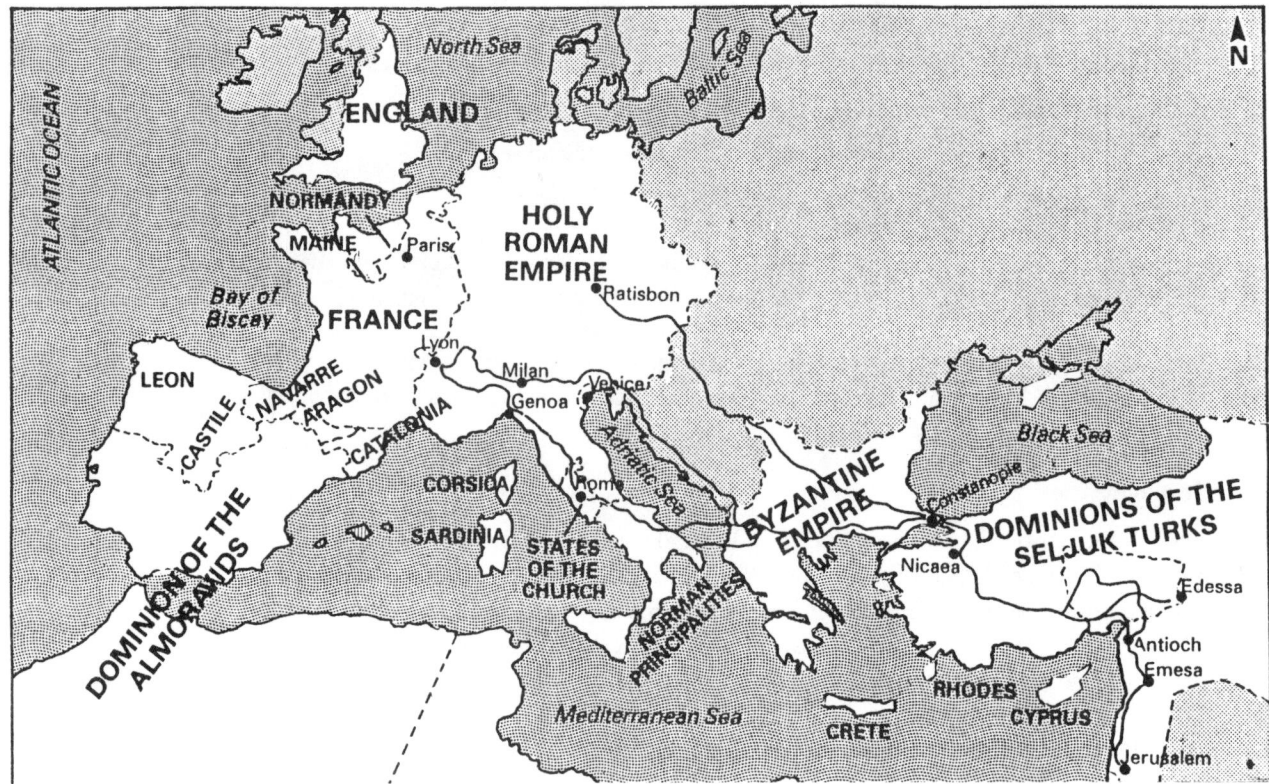

Map above:
The First
Crusade,
1096-1099

• Identify the political powers which controlled the peninsula at the time of Columbus's first voyage. Describe the importance of the reconquest of Granada for Spain.

Explain why Portugal's position was better suited for Atlantic conquest and why Columbus's journey would be perceived by the world as one of conquest and colonization rather than exploration.

The Western Hemisphere Before the Conquest

Pre-Reading

Strategies

Civilizations for Centuries

Draw up a timeline from your memory which indicates how far back indigenous people lived on the continent now known as America. Show as much as you can remember of the different civilizations which existed throughout the centuries before Columbus. As you read the chapter, correct any misconceptions you may have had and add any new information you gain to your timeline.

The Power of the Word

The terms on page 230 have all been used in reference to the people who were on this continent when Columbus arrived and the space they inhabited. Discuss in writing or in a group what you know about the meaning of these terms, how they originated, and what they conveyed about the people who used them. Discuss in a group how such language was (and is) used to oppress people.

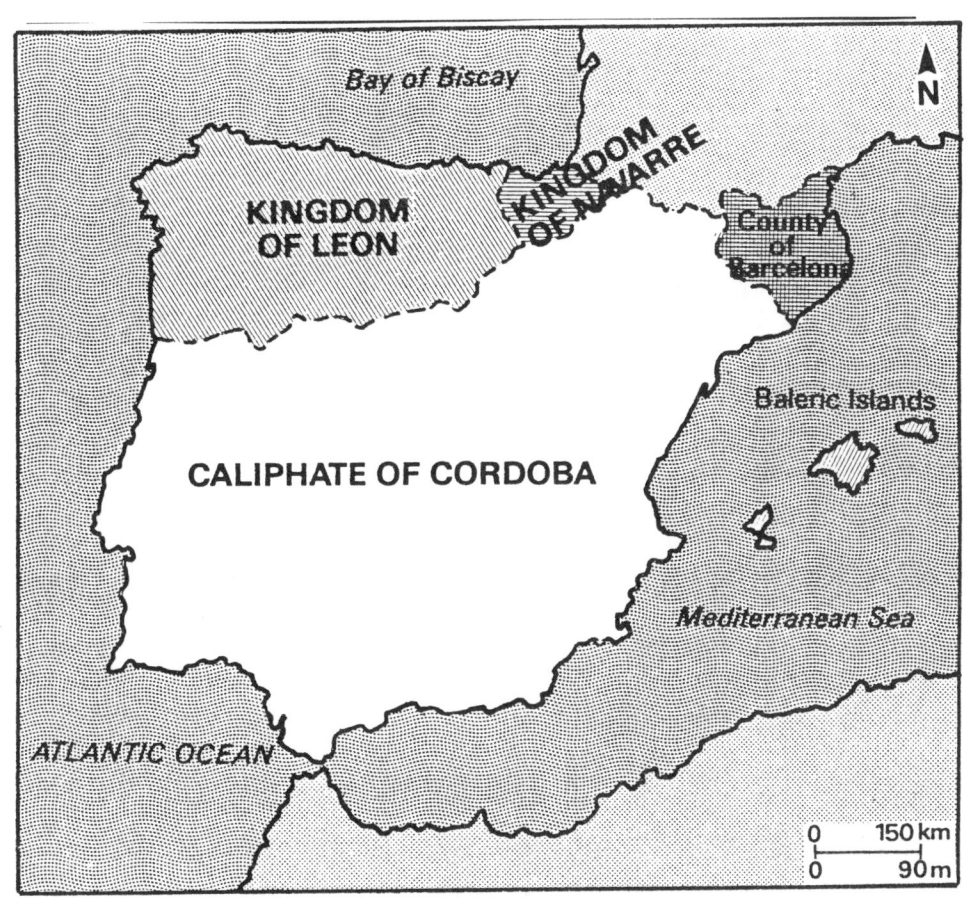

*Iberian
Peninsula, 910*

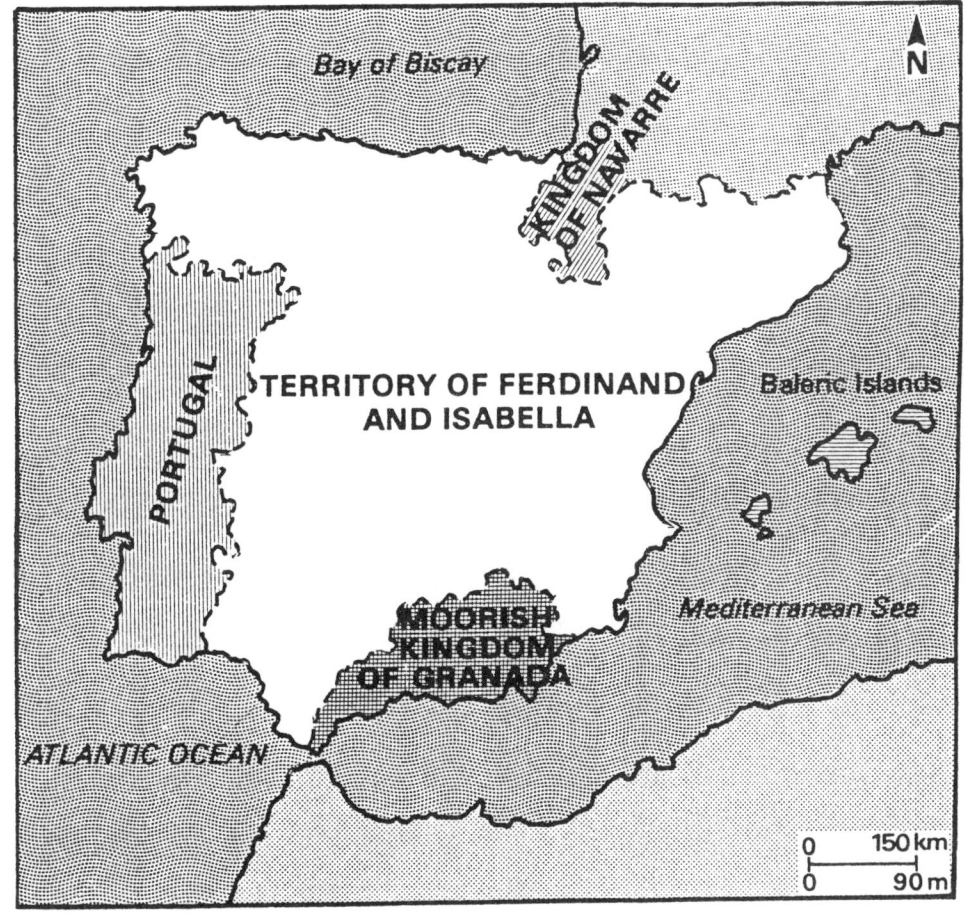

*Iberian Peninsula at
the time of King
Ferdinand and Queen
Isabella, 1492*

Native Americans	First Americans	indigenous	Indians
primitive	civilized	uncivilized	savage
wilderness	the "wild"		

Myriads of People

Brainstorm a list of as many groups of Native American peoples (nations) that you can. Don't consult any books to do this. Rely on your memory. Compare your list with a comprehensive list in an encyclopedia. Discuss how well you did and how limited our knowledge is of the people who inhabited this continent first. Why do we not know more about the people who lived here in the millions when Columbus landed?

Geographic Regions and Peoples

On a blank map of the Americas, label the regions identified in this section of *Dangerous Memories* and show what groups resided where at about the time Columbus arrived. You will need to obtain a list of names of the hundreds of groups and nations that existed and develop a wall-sized map in order to make the names readable. This is best done as a group task. If you do this as an individual, it would be best to choose one region to research and map only the groups in that region (e.g., Meso-America or your own region of the United States).

Languages and Cultures That Far Outdistance the Conquerors

Linguists and anthropologists have shown that more than three thousand languages were once spoken in the Americas and about two thousand were in existence at the time the Europeans invaded the continent. On the map shown on the following page, Native American languages of North and Central America have been divided into families. Locate the "family" of languages which once was spoken in the area of the United States where you live. Research in an encyclopedia what specific languages belong to this family. Chart these languages on the language map shown here or a map of your own region.

Indigenous Identity and the Land

Read the following thoughts of indigenous people about their relationship to the land. As you read:

- Take note of the ways in which native people feel linked or connected to the land.
- Consider reasons why they may not feel that any one can own the land.
- Think about how their ideas of sharing the goods of the earth might stem from their ideas about their relationship to the land.
- Consider how they felt seeing the land exploited by the Europeans.
- Try to imagine whether Columbus and the Europeans **could** have understood the natives' perspectives about the land. **Could** they have understood this radically different perspective if they had been more observant and less driven by the search for material wealth?

How can you buy or sell the land—the warmth of the land? The idea is strange to us. We do not own the freshness of the air or the sparkle of the water. How can you buy them from us?

Duwamish Chief

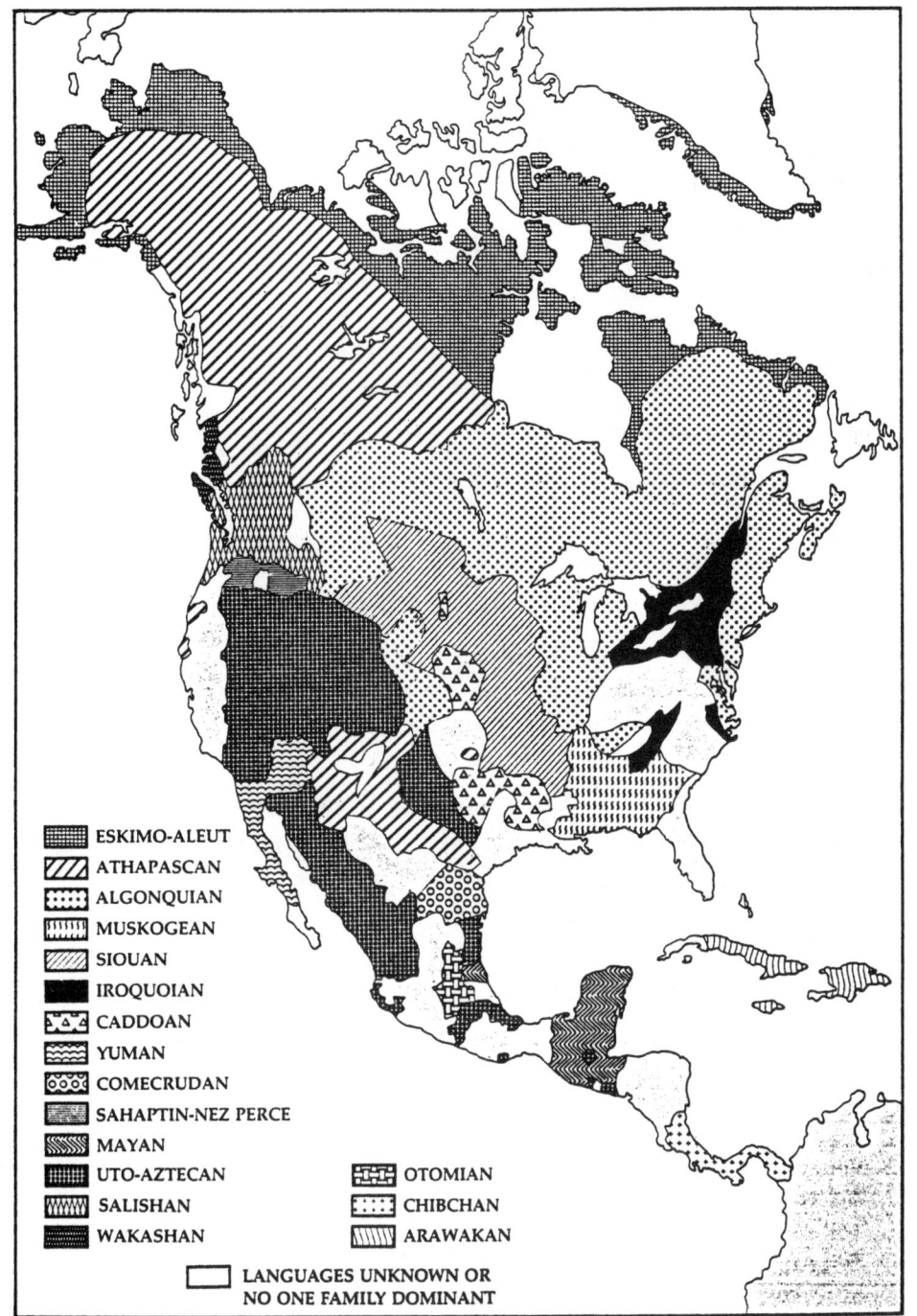

*Dominant
Language
Families
(Waldman, 67)*

LEGEND:

ESKIMO-ALEUT
ATHAPASCAN
ALGONQUIAN
MUSKOGEAN
SIOUAN
IROQUOIAN
CADDOAN
YUMAN
COMECRUDAN
SAHAPTIN-NEZ PERCE
MAYAN
UTO-AZTECAN
SALISHAN
WAKASHAN

OTOMIAN
CHIBCHAN
ARAWAKAN

LANGUAGES UNKNOWN OR
NO ONE FAMILY DOMINANT

One has only to develop a relationship with a certain place, where the land knows you, and experience that the trees, the Earth and Nature are extending their love and light to you to know there is so much we can receive from the Earth to fill our hearts and souls.

Inca Shaman

The earth is our historian, the keeper of events and the bones of our forefathers. Earth provides us with food, medicine, shelter, and clothing. It is the source of our independence, it is our Mother. We do not dominate her; we must harmonize with her.

Native Hawaiian

We think the land is there for everyone to use, the way our hand is there, a part of our own body.

Miccosukee Indian

Traditional people, still in harmony with the world around them, do not isolate themselves from other living things, nor consider one creature superior to another.

California Indian

Julian Burger, *GAIA, First Peoples*, 20, 23

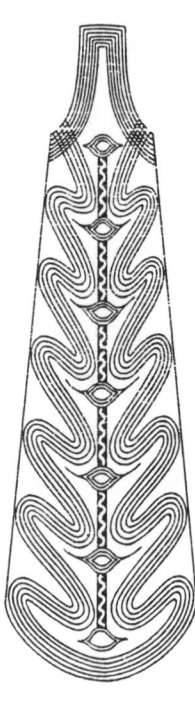

The Word Speaks

Reread the words of the Native Americans quoted in this section of the book about the connectedness of humans to the earth. Choose one piece or passage from a piece and respond as you would if it were written directly to you. Write in whatever style you wish (poetry, a letter, a stream-of-consciousness response). Try mainly to listen carefully to the words and hear the spirit in which they were spoken.

Potlatch—All Wealth Must Circulate

"Potlatch" was a widespread practice among the indigenous peoples of the Pacific Coast.

> *Potlatch takes place whenever anyone undergoes a significant personal change, such as puberty, marriage, accession to chiefdom, or death. It is based on the idea that all wealth, material or symbolic, must circulate; it honours non-acquisitiveness, generosity, and redistribution of wealth through exchange.*
>
> *When ritual privileges are publicly transmitted to the next generation, prestigious objects are given away, accompanied by feasts, speeches, songs, and dancing. Traditionally the potlatches were a means of affirming social and political prerogatives as well as placing obligations on friends, strengthening kinship ties and village solidarity. They could also end hostilities and re-establish good relations.*

Julian Burger, *GAIA, First Peoples*, 43

This perspective of wealth is obviously quite different from the perspective of the gold- and silver-seekers from Europe.

- Why was such sharing outlawed during the colonial period and seen as subversive?
- How and why might you initiate this practice in your own community?

Who Then Was Civilized?

The text of this chapter describes how among most of the groups of people living in the Americas "freedom and equality prevailed, with no division between rich and poor, no form of servitude, no money, no meddling governmental constructs, no private property." Note that, though individual nations and groups may have had different customs and life-patterns—both in the Western Hemisphere and in Europe—in general the viewpoints can be characterized in such a way that they apply to most of the people in the group. You could also complete the following chart making reference only to the Taino and the Spanish.

Imagine what might have happened if the values of the indigenous had prevailed in the continent rather than those of the Europeans. How might our lives and the world be different—ecologically, economically, socially, governmentally, spiritually?

Values/Beliefs	Indigenous American (or Taino in particular)	European (or Spanish in particular)
Economic		
Governmental		
Social		
Ecological		
Religious/Spiritual		

From your reading in this chapter and in Chapter Three draw up a comparison chart to show how societal values in the Western Hemisphere differed radically from those in Europe at the time of the invasion.

The Tainos, Our Teachers

The Tainos of Columbus's time might have some advice to offer a twentieth-century audience about how to save the planet. Imagining you are a Taino, write a message about ecosurvival, including your reaction to the "progress" and "civilization" brought by the Europeans and your feelings about the destruction of your own people.

The Conquest and Its Consequences

When Is a Discovery Not a Discovery?

The expressions listed below are terms which you have probably encountered often in reading about the history of Columbus. Reading history with a critical eye and ear entails questioning terms very carefully. Review the following terms. Discuss how they have been used in textbooks in talking about this period. For each term write or discuss ways in which the term might not be altogether true.

Pre-Reading Strategies

Terms in Text   Contradictions in Terms

"discovery"	When is a discovery not a discovery?
"new world"	In what way was this "new world" really an "old world"?
"explorer"	How could Columbus, Cortes, Lewis and Clark, et al, be called explorers of lands, rivers, mountains, valleys, and territories occupied for centuries by nations of people?
"wilderness"	What concepts were conveyed to the Europeans when the "virgin land" voyagers perceived this land as a wild, uninhabited place?
"the West"	To whom was the West not west? To whom was this land north? south? east?
"pagans"	In what way were these terms absolutely false about indigenous people?
"infidels"	Which terms were used by the Europeans and why? Which terms have
"cannibals"	you seen in textbooks describing the people Columbus encountered?
"hostile"	
"primitive" vs.	
"civilized"	

- How does terminology become important in conveying an historical, geographic, and political perspective in a text book?
- What perspectives were/are fostered by those who use these terms to define Columbus's and the colonialists' activity in the Americas? Whose perspectives are left out?
- What other terms would be more accurate in describing what Columbus and the colonialists did?

To Name = To Own = To Subjugate

Language can be powerful. To give a new name to people or places is symbolically to exercise power and authority over them.

- Brainstorm a list of the names Columbus and the Europeans "gave" to the people they met. If you can, try to write the names the indigenous used for those same people and places.

- Discuss the way in which Columbus's act of naming the indigenous people (Indians) and the land he encountered (West Indies, capes, mountains, ports, islands) was a powerful act on the part of the Europeans. How did it influence beliefs of ownership over these groups of people and this land for centuries?

- Research how indigenous people of the Americas today feel about being called "Indians." What did they call themselves before Columbus arrived? How do they refer to themselves today? How might it alter our thinking if people could be called by names which they have chosen for themselves rather than names which are superimposed on them (e.g., the slaves being given names of their masters)?

- Talk about how this phenomenon works in your own life or experience. How are powerful images of you created by others, by history, or by society?

Invasion Timekeepers

As you read this chapter create a timeline which charts events related to the invasion of the continent which came to be known as America. Though you may want to concentrate on the beginning years of the invasion, be sure to show in some way the history of the millions of people who were here prior to Columbus's landing (as a reminder that American history did not begin in 1492).

One kind of specific timeline to construct as you read this chapter is a detailed summary of the events which occurred surrounding the four voyages of Columbus. As you develop this timeline, create a map of the Caribbean to track Columbus's travels and the territories invaded by the Europeans.

There are many ways of doing timelines. You can construct one in a linear fashion, write a timeline as a kind of diary (with a page per day or week or month), or make a kind of storyboard which can later be illustrated. A group could divide this project into smaller tasks.

Charting the Consequences

Chart or graph the immediate consequences of the invasion of the Europeans into the Americas. Among the changes you may graph beginning with the information in this chapter, consider doing any or all of the following in a graph form:

- Population changes among the indigenous peoples
- Environmental changes in specific areas (e.g., Hispaniola)
- Language changes

Genocide Trials: Five Hundred Years Overdue

In a mock court room each of the defendants indicted below is put on trial for the atrocities begun five hundred years ago. Groups can limit or extend the number of roles depending on time and the number of persons available, but there should be an opportunity for all the indictments to be heard and responded to by the accused. To prepare for your role, read the indictments and prepare your own argument or points to bring before the court, using the material in this chapter as a starting point.

Participants in Each Trial
Defendants (to respond to the indictments—list below)
Judge (to read the indictments and run the trial)
Prosecutor (to question and dialogue with the defendants)
Jury (to determine guilt)
Witnesses (whoever the defendant or prosecutor may choose to have testify)

Christopher Columbus

- Your first act in the lands you "discovered" was to take possession of another people's territory in the name of an empire thousands of miles away.
- From the very beginning of your time in the Indies you kidnapped Indians. Even when they attempted to escape, making it clear that they wished to leave, you refused to release them.
- Your journal shows that your only wish in the Indies was to find gold. The only reason that you showed any kindness to the Tainos on your first trip was so they would agree to show you the source of their gold.
- On your second voyage to the Indies, you ordered your men to round up Indians and had over five hundred shipped to Spain as slaves. You told your men to help themselves to the remaining Indian captives, which they did.
- In 1495 you started the policy of forcing Indians, age fourteen and older, to collect gold for you. Those who didn't return every three months with the amount of gold you wanted were punished by having their hands chopped off.
- You ordered your men to spread "terror" among the Indians when there was rumor of resistance.
- The list goes on. When you arrived on Hispaniola there may have been as many as a million or even three million Tainos on the island. According to Bartolomé de Las Casas, by 1542 there were two hundred Tainos left. There is no one to blame but you. You were Admiral, you were viceroy, you were governor of the island.

Indictment of Columbus: Charged with committing genocide against the Taino Indians of Hispaniola

Columbus's Crew

- Without you, Columbus's orders to enslave and kill Tainos would have been empty words.
- There is no evidence that Columbus <u>personally</u> captured slaves or killed anyone with his own hands. <u>You</u> are the ones responsible for the enslavement of first hundreds, then thousands, of Taino Indians. You did the dirty work. You raped women. You set dogs on infants. You cut the hands off Indians who didn't deliver

Indictment of Columbu's Crew: Charged with the murder of Taino Indians on Hispaniola, leading to complete genocide

235

enough gold. You whipped Indians if they didn't work hard enough in the mines. Without you there were no crimes.

- You may try to blame your superiors—Columbus or even King Ferdinand and Queen Isabella. But because someone orders you to commit a crime does not free you of the blame for committing it. You could have said no. Some Spaniards, like the priests Antonio de Montesinos and Bartolomé de las Casas, refused to mistreat Indians and spoke out on their behalf. Why didn't you?
- Without the soldier there is no war. Without you there would have been no genocide.

King Ferdinand and Queen Isabella

Indictment of Ferdinand and Isabella: Charged with being responsible for genocide of the Taino Indians on the island of Hispaniola

- Without your money, Columbus couldn't have launched his plan to find the East Indies by sailing west. Without you, he was an unemployed sailor with incorrect ideas about the distance from Spain to Japan.
- You hired him to "discover" and claim new lands. Thus you are guilty of conspiracy to steal the territory of people you didn't even know, who had never bothered or harmed you.
- When Columbus returned after his first voyage with several Indian captives, and you approved, you became guilty of kidnapping. You could have ordered Columbus to stop kidnapping Indians. You could have punished him for this illegal act. By not doing anything to stop Columbus and his men, you legalized every crime they committed.
- In his first letter to you, Columbus wrote that the Indians would make excellent slaves. Right away, you could have ordered him to take no slaves. You did no such thing and thus became accomplices in all future slave taking. True, after a while you discouraged Columbus from taking slaves—they mostly died, anyway—but you never punished him for these crimes which killed hundreds of human beings.
- Really, you didn't care what Columbus did, so long as you became rich. At times, you would order that the Indians should be treated humanely. But you took no action to stop the Indians from being forced to work in the mines. They were slaves in everything but name. Had you wanted the cruelty to stop, you could have ordered all your subjects home. But then you wouldn't have obtained any more gold. And that was what you wanted, right?
- Because Columbus was unpopular with other Spaniards, you replaced him as governor. But you never punished him for the crimes committed against Tainos when he was governor. And these crimes continued under the next governor.
- Because you were the bosses and because you paid the bills, you have more guilt than had you been the ones wielding the swords and hangmen's nooses.

Taino Indians

Indictment of the Taino Indians: Charged with responsibility for the deaths of Taino Indians on Hispaniola leading to complete genocide

- While you are the victim of this crime, you are also guilty of committing it. You failed to fight back against the Spaniards. This meant that you brought the fate of slavery and death upon yourselves.
- From the very beginning you must have known what Columbus meant to do. He took Indian captives from other islands and held them against their will. He claimed your land as his own. He was only interested in finding gold. When your people were cut by Spaniards' swords, he and his men didn't care at all. All this you must have known.

236

- Tragically, you let this greedy, violent man get away, so he could return. This time, however, he brought seventeen ships and between twelve and fifteen hundred men, all heavily armed. You allowed, even invited, this invasion.
- Stupidly, your *cacique* (leader), Caonabo, killed the thirty-nine men Columbus left behind. Why didn't Caonabo and the Tainos kill all the Spaniards—including Columbus—before they had a chance to return? Imagine the different outcome had the Tainos been smart enough to stop Columbus before he could launch the invasion.
- Who knows why the Tainos of Hispaniola did not unite to throw out all the Spaniards? Had Tainos worked together they might have beaten the Spaniards, even after Columbus returned. After all, the Spaniards numbered less than two thousand, and Tainos numbered in the hundreds of thousands, possibly as many as three million. However, as a result of this Taino failure, all the native peoples of the Americas suffered.

The System of the Empire

- This gets complicated. You are not a person, but a system. We like to blame crimes on people. But in this case, the real criminal is not human.
- True, Columbus's men did the killing, Columbus gave the orders and King Ferdinand and Queen Isabella paid the bills—and took the profits. But what made them behave the way they did? Were they born evil and greedy? The real blame lies with a system that values property over people.
- European society was organized so that for an individual to feel secure, he or she must own property. The more property one owned, the more security, the more control over one's destiny. There was no security without private ownership of property. If you were poor you could starve. The Tainos were not perfect, but they had no "poor" and no one starved. Indians commented that Europeans' love of gold was like a disease. In fact, this attitude was a product of a diseased system.
- In order to get more wealth, Columbus and his men took Indians as slaves, terrorized them into searching out gold, and forced them to work on their farms and in their mines. They justified all this by telling themselves that the Indians weren't Christian, so "we" can control "their" land and labor. The European system saw only white Christians as full human beings.
- It was life in a system that valued private property (especially gold), and approved of violence against foreigners and non-Christians to get it, that made Columbus and his men enslave and kill. Sane people do not kill hundreds of thousands of other human beings. It was a rotten, <u>insane</u> system that led Columbus and the others to behave the way they did. You, as the representatives of this system, are guilty for the genocide committed against Tainos.
- As a final test to see who is guilty for the mass murder of the Tainos, ask yourself these questions:
  - If it had been some other "European explorer" besides Columbus to "discover America," would he have let the Tainos keep their land?
  - Would he not have taken slaves?
  - Would he not have made them search for gold and work in the mines?

You know the answer: <u>Any</u> European conqueror would have been every bit as bad as Columbus. Why? Because the system of empire was to blame, not any particular individual.

Indictments quoted from *Rethinking Columbus*, Bill Bigelow. Washington, D.C.: NECA, 1991

Indictment of the System: Charged with being guilty for the genocide committed against the Taino Indians of Hispaniola

Roots of Racism

Discrimination began when the Spanish arrived, invading our land, destroying our culture and our lives. They tied up our kings and burned them alive because our kings would not betray the population to the foreign invaders who only brought deceit, pain, destruction, and death as they attempted to seize a rich history and culture. . . . The indigenous population, the true owners of the lands, were relegated to the bottom of the new society.

Isabel Gutierrez, "Constructors of Our Own History: The Indigenous of Guatemala," *¡Basta!*
December, 1990

Though the word itself did not exist at the time, the incidents which transpired between Columbus, the European nation-states, and the indigenous people of the Americas could today be labelled "racist." Many historians and social critics have suggested that these incidents triggered and extended into the Western Hemisphere a system of economic, political, and social assumptions and of aggressive institutional and individual behavior against people of color which prevails to this day and is known as racism.

Select an approach from among the following activities to examine your own concepts of racism, its existence today,and its connections with the history presented in this chapter and in this entire book of *Dangerous Memories.*

1. Debating the Roots of Racism

Choose a debate topic from the following or create a statement of your own for debate.

Resolved: That the roots of racism which took hold in the Americas when Columbus reached the shores of this continent were inevitable, given the religious, economic, political, and social conditions of the European nation-states of the fifteenth and sixteenth centuries.

Resolved: That racism is a vital part of the global economic system sparked in 1492.

Resolved: That the Europeans brought civilization to the Western Hemisphere.

2. Coding Racism

Understanding the ways in which we are connected to this history of five hundred years ago requires that we look at our own experience today and recognize the ways in which the economic, political and social systems begun by colonization extend into our lives. For this activity you will be asked to develop a "code." A "code" is

Step 1. Developing a Code

- a concrete example of a common experience or problem situation;
- a familiar situation/dilemma with no particular solution presented;
- a problem that can be broken down into parts; and,
- a motivator for thinking about situations and dialoguing about them

After the presentation of the code, members of the group or class dialogue about the incident portrayed, analyze the situation, try to "connect" it to their own experience, and generate alternatives and resolutions. The codes you develop here should reflect present day experiences of discrimination and/or racism.

Within a small group develop the "code" (a story, a role-played scene, a drawing, a cartoon, a photograph, or a collage) which can be presented to a class or larger group. This story or representation should reflect an incident, a concrete common experience, or a physical image which demonstrates some aspect of discrimination and/or racism.

Examples of Codes:

A dialogue heard at a school board meeting:

President: We'll open the meeting now to comments from the public.

Parent: I want to bring up a concern of mine—and of several other parents who've been meeting informally. We think the school should spend less money on teachers who have only small groups of children.

President: What kind of classes are you referring to?

Parent: Those classes with only ten or fifteen children in them where they are always speaking in Spanish. That takes too many teachers. Furthermore, they should be speaking English.

Person #1: I want my pen.
Person #2: You gave it to me to use.
Person #1: Well, now I need it back.
Person #2: You're an Indian giver.

Use the following descriptions to help you develop codes which show critical aspects of racism.

Step 2: Defining Racism

Racism— ". . . any attitude, action or institutional structure which subordinates a person or group because of their color. . . . Racism is not just a matter of attitudes: actions and institutional structures can also be a form of racism." (From *Racism in America and How to Combat It*, U.S. Commission on Civil Rights, 1970)

Cultural racism—". . . when whites use power to perpetuate their cultural heritage and impose it upon others, while at the same time destroying the culture of ethnic minorities." (From *Teaching Ethnic Studies*, National Council for the Social Studies, 1973)

Racism—". . . imposition of a system of exploitation and elimination of a culture and people." (From "Listen, People of the World: Racism in Guatemala," Daniel Eduardo Matul Morales in *¡Basta!* December, 1990)

Racism—". . . a tool used by the dominant society to keep people divided and distracted from the real issues of life." (From "A Voice from Home," James Yellowbank in *¡Basta!*, December, 1990.)

Racism—". . . is not a desire to wake up every morning and lynch a black man from a tall tree. It is not engaging in vulgar epithets. These kinds of people are just fools. It is the day to day indignities, the subtle humiliations, that are so devastating. Racism is the assumption of superiority of one group over another, with all the gross arrogance that goes along with it. Racism is a part of us. . . ." (Whitney Young, Congress for Racial Equality)

Racism—". . .is enforced and maintained by legal, cultural, religious, educational, economic, political, and military institutions in societies." (From "Policy Statement on Racial Justice," National Council of Churches of Christ in the U.S.A., in *¡Basta!*, December, 1990)

On racism—"If white people have suffered less obviously from racism than black people, they have nevertheless suffered greatly; the cost has been greater perhaps than we yet know. If the white man has inflicted the wound of racism upon black men, the cost has been that he would receive the mirror image of that wound into himself." (From Wendell Berry, *The Hidden Wound*)

On child development and racism—"Children who develop in this way (white-centered and reacting to skin color) are robbed of opportunities for emotional and intellectual growth, stunted in basic development of the self so that they cannot experience or accept humanity. It is quite possible to build into children a great feeling and compassion for animals and an unconscious fear and rejection of differing human beings. Such persons are by no means prepared to live and move with either appreciation or effectiveness in today's world." (From A. Citron, *The Rightness of Whiteness,* in Judith Katz, *White Awareness*)

Step 3: Decoding

After demonstrating or enacting a code, "decode" the incident or representation of this common experience by using the following framework:

- Name the key problem(s) presented in the incident.
- Analyze it. (Why did people say what they said? Why does the problem exist?)
- Reflect. (What do our responses reveal about our own experiences? Where do we see ourselves in relation to this issue?)
- Generate actions. (If we could re-do the scene by walking into it, where would we place ourselves? What kind of action can we take when we identify situations like this in our everyday lives?)
- Move beyond. (Are there more serious issues related to racism in our community which need to be addressed? What are they? Develop a new code to show how racism impacts your community.)

Step 4: Moving back to the roots

After "decoding" the incident of racism/discrimination in today's world, discuss the ways this incident reflects the incidents and relationships between the Europeans, the Native Americans, the early colonialists, and the African American slaves.

Critical Reading of Columbus Texts

Obtain elementary, secondary, and/or college texts of American history. Read the sections on Columbus and the first years of the invasion from Europe. Examine the content and presentation of this material, considering areas such as the following to rate a text. Some groups may be able to construct their own list of questions and criteria for examining the perspectives and truthfulness of these texts.

- **Factual accuracy**
  Christopher Columbus's knowledge and motivations for travel
  The indigenous societies in the hemisphere, their diversity and complexity
  Enslavement of the indigenous
  Resistance of the indigenous
  Military dominance of the Europeans
  Virtual extinction of the Taino
  Role of the church
  Impact on the land
  Methods of obtaining gold

- **Concepts highlighted**
  Issues raised or omitted (issues of land rights, sovereignty)
  Connections of early invasion to European economic, religious, military situation
  Impact and change within the indigenous societies and lands

- **Perspectives/Viewpoints**

  Variety of viewpoints presented (e.g., how the indigenous viewed and reacted to the Europeans; how some Europeans objected to treatment of the indigenous)

  Sensitive and critical use of language (including critique of words like "discovery," "west," "exploration," "primitive," "wilderness")

  Events important to indigenous given equal weight to those of Europeans

  Values, beliefs, customs of the indigenous presented respectfully

- **Images/Illustrations**

  Descriptions and images of the indigenous

  Descriptions and images of the Europeans

  Messages conveyed by illustrations and descriptions

- **Overall viewpoint**

  Whose interest might it serve?

Re-Thinking What We Have Learned

After reading this chapter think through the ways the information given here contradicts perspectives and ideas you may have gained from your study of American history in the past. In particular, consider the following:

Pilgrims	Reasons for coming
	Relationship to the Native Americans/Who shared what with whom?
Colonialism	"Settlement" vs. "displacement"
	Empire building vs. empire destruction
Militarism	Use of force in the "settlement" of the Europeans
	Indigenous vs. European modes of warfare
Contributions	Who contributed what in the "exchanges" between the indigenous and the Europeans?
Slavery and Slave Trade	Why and how slavery arose in the Americas
	African presence in pre-Columbian America /First Africans in the Americas
	Commonality of experience among people of color in the hemisphere
Religion	Absence/presence of religious beliefs in the indigenous peoples
Resistance	Reality of resistance

Resistance
African American Resistance

American Revolutions and Resistance

Quickly brainstorm a list of events and people that come to mind when you think of revolution in the Americas. Discuss in a group or individually write about your present knowledge of resistance and revolution in the Americas. Review what you learned in school about revolutionaries in the U.S., in Latin America, and among "minorities" on this continent. Or you might sketch a timeline to indicate any revolutions you can remember and when they happened.

The Three R's: Resistance, Revolt, Revolution

Consider why it is that individuals or groups "resist." Brainstorm occasions when you or your group would resist. Consider the following questions:

- What would be your rationale for resisting?
- How would you go about planning your resistance?
- What form would your resistance take?
- What might be some differences, if any, between resistance and spontaneous revolts?
- What is the connection between revolt and revolution?

African American Resisters

The introduction to this section of the book states, "The invasion of this hemisphere was not a single event or a series of events of the late fifteenth and early sixteenth century. The invasion and destruction has been constant for five hundred years." So has been the history of resistance by indigenous people of the Americas and African Americans who were forcibly transported to these shores.

Although they have not been portrayed prominently in traditional history, African Americans have nonetheless played a significant role throughout the history of the Americas. Below are names mentioned in this part of the book. Review the names and list as many facts about each person or group that you have learned from conventional history. Some names may be new to you. After completing the reading of this section of the book, return to this exercise and review the names again, listing facts for each.

After doing this exercise, reflect on/discuss the following:

- How many of these individuals appear in traditional textbooks?
- How is your understanding of history altered when you read about people such as these who have been significant in resistance and yet have never been recognized for their involvement in history?
- Why may many of us not have heard of most of these significant persons in American history?

Joseph Cinque	Toussaint L'Ouverture	François Macandal
Jean-Jacques Dessalines	Mary Church Terrell	Maroons
Frederick Douglass	Tomba	Madison Washington
W.E.B. DuBois	Nathaniel Turner	Ida B. Wells
Henry Highland Garnet	Denmark Vesey	

Parallel Timelines

As you read through this entire chapter, develop parallel chronologies of resistance in different parts of the Americas (African American and Caribbean resistance, indigenous resistance throughout the Americas, and the more recent Central American/Mexican resistance). Against these three parallel timelines develop a fourth timeline of the events and periods of American history typically covered in American history classes. Use these timelines to organize your awareness of movements and issues in American history and world history.

Contrasting Chronologies: Critiquing the Textbooks

Below is a synopsis of "important" historical events between the years 1642 and 1732 as they are presented in a popular U.S. history textbook. Reflect on the questions here as you consider the chronology:

- What's left out in this chronology?
- What are the (hidden) messages in such a chronology?
- How do history books convey belief systems?
- What is important, according to the authors of this text book?
- From your reading of this part of the book how would you alter this list?

Post-Reading Strategies

Important Events of the Period	
1642-46	English Civil War
1649	Charles I executed
1651	First Navigation Act passed
1660	Stuarts restored to throne; Charles II becomes king
1662	Halfway Covenant drafted
1663	Carolina chartered
1664	English conquer New Netherlands; New York founded; New Jersey established
1675-76	King Philip's War (New England)
1676	Bacon's Rebellion (Virginia)
1680-92	Pueblo revolt (New Mexico)
1681	Pennsylvania chartered; James II becomes king (1685)
1686-89	Dominion of New England
1688-89	James II deposed in Glorious Revolution; William and Mary ascend throne
1689-97	King William's War
1692	Witchcraft panic in Salem Village
1696	Board of Trade and Plantations established
1701	Iroquois adopt neutrality policy
1702-13	Queen Anne's War
1711-13	Tuscarora War (North Carolina)
1715	Yamasee War (South Carolina)
1732	Georgia chartered

Rereading History

Sometimes we are able to see errors in the past that go unnoticed in the present. The following is an excerpt from a sixth grade textbook of a major publisher that was used in the New York City schools in the 1930s. Many of the leaders of the United States over the past two decades grew up during that period and could have studied from this text or one like it. What is wrong with this text taken from a section in the Reconstruction Era?

> *When they (Negroes) realized that they were free, many thought they must get away from the plantations where they had lived as slaves, though they had little idea of where to go or what to do. They had no homes and no money. They began to wander about, stealing and plundering. In one week in a Georgia town, one hundred fifty Negroes were arrested for thieving.*
>
> *Many ignorant Negroes thought that the property owned by their former masters was theirs now and some even took possession of land and began building houses and planting their farms. Often they were insulting to the white people. In some localities conditions were so bad that the white women were afraid to go outside their homes even in the day-time. Many of the white people slept with a gun within reach so that they could protect themselves in case they might be attacked by a Negro.*
>
> *By 1871 Congress had pardoned most of the white leaders of the War, and they were again allowed to vote and hold office. But it was almost impossible for white men to be elected in four of the states, because there were many more Negroes than white men in these states. So the white men decided to take other means to get the power into their own hands. A secret society, known as the Ku Klux Klan, was organized, and its members set out to spread terror among the ignorant Negroes. Knowing that the Negroes were very much afraid of spirits, or ghosts, the members would dress in white robes with hoods over their heads and grinning masks hiding their faces. Disguised in this way, they would visit the home of a Negro in the dead of night. When they had roused the trembling Negro from sleep, they would make all sorts of threats about horrible things that would happen to him if he dared vote in the next election. The Negroes were quite terrified and nothing could make them go to the polls after such a visit.*

Herbert Aptheker, ed., *A Documentary History of the Negro People in the United States*, 694

Legacies

The thread of history is continuous with few outright breaks. Below are listed some facts of present reality. How do these realities relate to the past? What are some of the other legacies that we live with today?

- The United States has the highest incarceration rate in the world, 426 out of every 100,000 residents are incarcerated. For black men, the incarceration rate is 3,109 per 100,000.

Report of the Sentencing Project, *Chicago Tribune*, January 6, 1991: 5

- For black men age fifteen to twenty-four, homicide is the leading cause of death. One out of every three black men who dies is a homicide victim. This has pushed overall death rates for black men to alarming levels at a time when mortality rates for whites are decreasing.

Washington Post National Weekly Edition, February 12-18, 1990

- One out of every nine African American males are in jail or prison on any given day.

- Sixty percent of all women in prison are women of color.

- Of the more than three thousand people who have been executed since 1930, nearly half have been people of color.

- Eighty-five percent of those executed since 1977 were punished for crimes against white victims.

- In Mississippi, killers of whites receive the death penalty six times more frequently than killers of African Americans. In Illinois, killers of whites were four times more likely to be sentenced to death than killers of blacks.

- Only one white man in Ohio has been executed for killing a black person since 1884 (342 people have been executed during that period).

Fact Sheet, American Friends Service Committee, 1501 Cherry St., Philadelphia, PA

Meet the Press Programs

Identify panels of persons to interview from among the following heroes, heroines, and villains in this chapter. Schedule press interviews, giving every person a chance to be either a journalist or one of the panelists reporting on the conditions of life for African Americans and their action taken in resistance. Some are actual persons; others are characters who should represent the mentality of the time. Read the section on African American Resistance for background.

Program 1:   Toussaint L'Ouverture and Napoleon
Program 2:   A runaway slave living in a hidden maroon society (Francois Macandal); a woman rebel on board an African slave ship
Program 3:   A colonial "big" white (merchant or landowner); a colonial "small" white (clerk, artisan, grocer, vagabond, debtor, thief) in San Domingo
Program 4:   A colonial white child; a black slave child on a sugar plantation
Program 5:   Harriet Tubman; Sojourner Truth
Program 6:   Frederick Douglass; Ida B. Wells
Program 7:   African American veteran of World War I involved in the 1919 race riots; Rosa Parks
Program 8:   Martin Luther King Jr., Malcolm X, Henry Highland Garnet
Program 9:   J. Edgar Hoover, Fred Hampton, Mark Clark

Slave Commodities: White Gold
Research the story of sugar cane production in the Caribbean. Tell the story from the standpoint of a sugar cane slave at the time of the rebellion in San Domingo. In your story, tell why and how you resisted your chains and joined up with Toussaint L'Ouverture.

They Advance Singing
The more they fell, the greater seemed the courage of the rest. They advanced singing.
So noted a Frenchman recalling the blacks he was fighting in San Domingo in 1803. Write about this kind of courageous resistance from people who would give up their lives in order

to obtain freedom for their people. Note evidences of this kind of courage in the history of African American resistance described in this chapter. Have you ever witnessed such courage?

Indigenous Resistance: South and North America

Pre-Reading Strategies

Revolts to Revolution

Before beginning to analyze revolution and pinpointing its occurrence in the indigenous and Latin American communities, think carefully about the word "revolution." What does it mean? Complete the following activities as they relate to the term "revolution."

- On a blank sheet of paper write down everything that comes to mind when you hear the word "revolution."

- Interview people about what the word means. Get different age groups to respond and, if possible, talk to people who have come from different parts of the world. Reflect on all the responses you received and find commonalities and distinctions among these ideas.

- Write a dictionary definition of the word. Imagine that you have been asked by Webster or Random House to write a new definition for the word revolution. Without going to the dictionary compose the definition.

- Compare your dictionary definition of revolution to the meaning given in the dictionary. How do they compare? Do you have anything in your definition that is not given in the dictionary? Does the dictionary have something you have not considered in your meaning?

- What do you anticipate you will read in this section about revolution among the indigenous peoples of the Americas? Among the countries of Latin America and the Caribbean in modern history?

Connecting Ideas and Thoughts on Revolution

Presented here are a number of quotes on revolution that come from people of the Americas as well as from other areas of the globe. Select a quote that appeals to you. Write your response to this quote. Begin your writing in a random style, responding freely with whatever comes to mind regarding this quote. Follow up your random writing with a more formal composition which organizes and expands on your initial ideas.

The highest virtue is always against the law. (Ralph Waldo Emerson)

I do not carry innocence to the point of believing that appeals to reason or respect for human dignity can alter reality. For the Negro who works on a sugar plantation in Le Robert, there is only one solution: to fight. He will embark on this struggle and he will pursue it, not as the result of a Marxist or idealistic analysis but quite simply because he cannot conceive of life otherwise than in the form of a battle against exploitation, misery and hunger. (Franz Fanon)

It is organized violence on the top which creates individual violence at the bottom. (Emma Goldman)

Let us say at the risk of seeming ridiculous, that the true revolutionary is guided by great feelings of love. (Che Guevara)

I know, and all the world knows, that revolutions never go backward. (William Seward)

Beginning reform is beginning revolution. (Duke of Wellington)

Make the revolution a parent of settlement, and not a nursery of future revolutions. (Edmund Burke)

Spirits of Resistance

> *The Spaniards find it easier to kill Indians than to kill the spirit of rebellion.*
> Eric Williams, *Documents of West Indian History*

The courage to maintain the struggle against their oppressors is in many cases in Latin America and among the indigenous people strengthened and fed by the memory of ancestors who struggled years before. As you read this section, take note of some of these leaders whose spirits are remembered by their compatriots today. Using the material in this book, develop a dramatic reading which retells the stories of these leaders and notes how they inspired others to struggle against their oppressors.

Cacique Hatuey, 1511	Cuban national hero
Tupac Amaru	Andean hero of the "Tupamaros" (Uruguayan guerrillas)
Micaela Bastidas	Andean heroine
Miceala Bastidas Committee	Peruvian women's group
Sandino	Nicaraguan Sandinistas

Forms of Repression

Review the forms of repression that you have learned were used by the Spaniards, the early colonialists, and later the U.S. government against the indigenous. If you are working in a group, divide the research and teach one another the meaning of each one by performing a role-play or presenting a small "code" which enacts some aspects of the system. (See strategies under Invasion Chapter). In your discussion after each example, generate ways in which the Indigenous tried to fight against these systems and patterns of repression.

> *Encomienda*
> *Requerimiento*
> *Corregidores*
> *Repartimiento*
> Tribute system
> Forced labor
> *Mita* system
> Charges for church services (Catholic Church in South America)
> Religious righteousness and political imperialism of the Puritans
> Unfair trading practices by the early English settlers
> War against the Indians by the British trading companies
> Loss of sovereignty over the land by treaties
> Broken treaties and manipulation of treaties
> Bureau of Indian Affairs governance
> Mission schools

Women in the Resistance

Stories abound about the women who not only participated in the resistance but directed the forces, fought in battles, and gave their lives to fight the colonialist injustices. Reread the section on Micaela Bastidas, the wife of Tupac Amaru in Peru, including her letter to her husband and the account of her torture and execution.

Write a response letter or poem to her in which you comment on her clarity of purpose and willingness to take the necessary action for her cause. You may want to write a tribute which names and gives testament to all the brave women who led and participated in resistance struggles in the Americas.

The Ultimate Irony

To tame a savage you must tie him down to the soil. You must make him understand the value of property, and the benefits of its separate ownership.

U.S. Secretary of the Interior, 1851

Contrast this "policy" of the nineteenth century with the events of the three hundred years which led up to this time which forced the removal of the Indians from the land.

Native American Resistance to This Day: The Struggle for the Earth

Someday I will embrace our brothers' tribes and draw them into a bundle and together we will win our country back from the whites.

Tecumseh, 1795

There are tens of millions of Indian people in the Western Hemisphere today. They are united in their struggles to return to and win back the earth and to have their voices heard. Research one of the following areas where the struggle to resist continues. Report in what ways this struggle resembles those of the past and renews the hope of the indigenous:

Black Hills of South Dakota: Lakota struggling to save the Lakota sacred ground from mining and toxic waste dump.

Hopi and Navajo Reservations: Hopi and Navajo struggling to prevent relocations off the land.

White Earth Reservation, Minnesota: Struggling to win back thousands of acres of land taken and sold to whites.

Oka, Canada: Mohawk struggling to save ancestral burial grounds from being used as a golf course.

Quebec, Canada: Cree and Inuit struggling to save traditional lands from environmental ruin due to hydroelectric development.

Amazon: Struggling to receive international aid to the Amazon to save it from mining and logging.

Cheyenne, Montana: Struggling to stop the U.S. government's largest coal sale in the history of the country.

Yukon Territory: Struggling to stop oil development in the Arctic National Wildlife Refuge.

Northern California: Hoopa and Yurok struggling to stop the U.S. Forest Service from constructing a logging road in the area.

Ixil Triangle, Guatemala: Communities of the Populations in Resistance struggling to survive and to protect their right and access to the land from government-supported military incursions and destruction.

British Columbia: Lillioett people working to protect an undeveloped mountain from development and logging.

Wisconsin: Ojibway and the LaCourte Oreilles opposing the construction of a copper and zinc mining facility.

Bolivia: Sirionos fighting to save lands from destruction by cattle ranchers.

Brazilian rainforest: Wauja people organizing to defend their land from ranchers and poachers.

"Struggles Unite Native People: Interview with Chief Tayac," in *Rethinking Schools* Special Edition, 56-58
"Our Land, Our Life: Native Peoples Organize for Justice in the Americas" in *Rethinking Schools* Special Edition, 63

Rebellion and Revolution: Mexico and Central America

Resistance and Revolution

Below is a selected listing of revolutions that have occurred in Latin America since the time of the revolutionary war within the United States. Since revolutions which evolve within countries involve a great deal of bloodshed, human suffering, and loss of life, it seems fairly safe to say *revolutions aren't fashionable.* Therefore, there must be serious reasons that individuals are willing to risk everything they own—including their lives—when they make a decision to participate in a revolution. Certainly there are some people, and at times many people on the fringe of a revolution, who just wish it weren't happening. However, once a revolution begins in your region of the world, there is very little you can do to escape it.

Revolutions in the Americas			
Geographic Area	Date(s) of Revolution	Identifying Statement	Reason(s) for the Rebellion
North America	1765-75	American Revolution	
Peru	1780	Tupac Amaru II	
Guatemala	1838 1944	The peasant revolt Cadet and student revolution	
Nicaragua	1961-79	Sandinistas' revolt	
El Salvador	1932	Farabundo Martí	
Cuba	1956-60	Revolution	

Researching and Illustrating Resistance

Select an act of resistance, revolt, or revolution from the chronology above or take an individual country's act of resistance. Begin to do research on the topic you selected. As you undertake your research look at your topic in stages. Make certain you document your research. Think about preparing a pictorial presentation of your topic. Include enough writing with each of your pictures so that a person unfamiliar with the topic would have enough understanding about the revolution to ask significant questions.

Revolution and Art

Art is frequently used as a vehicle for people to express their values, concerns, and hopes for the future. Some very poignant graphic and poster art has had its origins in the context of political revolutions. The art of the Cuban and Mexican Revolutions is especially significant.

Viewing the art of a particular country during a critical period in its history can help us understand more completely the reality of that time.

One of the prime examples of art connected with revolutions can be found in Mexico. José Clemente Orozco, José David Alfaro Siquerios, and Diego Rivera are three prominent artists whose numerous and important works provide insight into the revolutionary history of Mexico in the nineteenth and twentieth centuries.

Many other artists in Latin America, though less well known, have chronicled visual impressions of their countries' histories. Below is a listing of many such artists.

Argentina: Roberto Alzenberg, Marcelo Bonevardi, Victor Chab, Kenneth Kemble, Rodolfo Krasno, Miguel Ocamp, Marta Peluffo, Pucciarelli, Francisco Sobrino, Clorino Testa, Luis Tomasello, and Alicia Partnoy.

Brazil: Antonio Henrique Amaral, Milton Dacosta, Djanir, Gontran Netto, Arthur Luiz Piza, Heitor dos Prazeres, Flavio de Resende Carvalho, Alberto da Veiga Guinard, and Alfredo Volpi.

Chile: José Balmes, Eduardo Bonati, Roser Bru, Gonzalo Cienfuegos, Juan Dávila, Eugenio Dittborn, Pedro Irarrázavl, Benjamin Lira, Guillermo Nuñez, Rodolfo Opazo, Eugenio Tellez, Mario Toral, and Isabel Allende.

Cuba: Cundo Bermudez, Jorge Camacho, Mario Carreño, Julio Herrera Zapata, Raul Martinez, and Mariano Rodriquez.

El Salvador: Armando Solis and Claribel Alegria.

Guatemala: Diaz Aldana, Roberto Cabrera, Julia Esquivel, Recino, and Elmer Rojas.

Mexico: In addition to those individuals already mentioned: José Luis Cuevas and Oswaldo Guayasamin.

Peru: Herman Braun and Tilsa Tsuchiya.

Divide the task of researching some of this art and bring it to the class or study group. A similar research project can be done with musicians and poets. Some key artistis to investigate: Pablo Neruda, Claribel Alegria, Victor Jara, and Roque Dalton.

Culture

Reflecting on *Dangerous Memories*

The title of this book is *Dangerous Memories*. What are some of the memories included in this book thus far that you consider dangerous?

- To whom are they dangerous?
- How did those in power seek to erase or distort those memories?
- What are some "dangerous memories" or "dangerous ideas" that exist today?
- Do you see any similar erasures or distortions happening today?

Reflecting on Culture: A Preliminary Discussion

Culture provides a background to the world in which we live. This chapter of *Dangerous Memories* presents the evidence, the story of the manipulation and annihilation of that background for millions of people in this hemisphere in the five hundred years since Columbus. The cultural context of some people's lives have been painted over, and integrated with or subsumed by the more dominant culture. The cultural backgrounds of some people's lives are visible now only to them.

This chapter looks at the impact of this sometimes subtle and sometimes blatant war against culture. To prepare for reading, reflect on the meaning of the following terms: culture, dominant culture, "minority" culture, subculture, popular culture, and multiculture. These words may often be heard, but seldom do we consider the extent to which our lives are framed by the substance of those words.

Use the following quotes to discuss what culture is (beyond the dress, the food, the customs, the traditions) and the way that culture deeply affects all of us. Begin to consider the issue of imposition of culture and the whole question of the ethics of a "dominant" culture in a hemisphere such as this one.

Then, as you read this chapter, begin to analyze the way in which people's cultures and lives can be radically different and whether they can ultimately integrate without doing injustice to some.

- Should cultures be assimilated? Can they be?
- What is it to which they are being assimilated?
- What would Native Americans have to do to "fit" into the dominant society? Should they?

If we are to achieve a richer culture, rich in contrasting values, we must recognize the whole gamut of human potentialities, and so weave a less arbitrary social fabric, one in which each diverse human gift will find a fitting place. (Margaret Mead)

Until he [sic] has become fully human, until he learns to conduct himself as a member of the earth, he will continue to create gods who will destroy him. (Henry Miller)

North American civilization is one of the ugliest to have emerged in human history, and it has engulfed the world. Asphalt and exhaust fumes clog the villages. . . . This great, though disastrous, culture can only change as we begin to stand off and see . . . the inveterate materialism which has become the model for cultures around the globe. (Arthur Charles Erickson)

Worldview: What Is It? What Is My Worldview?

Most people recognize different cultural practices, habits, customs, languages, art forms, food preparations, celebrations, dress styles, and physical appearance. What is more difficult to observe is cultural worldview which contains cultural values, the deeper expressions of culture. Worldview cannot be seen because it is held in mind and heart. Worldview is a framework through which we see the world and the perspective with which we interpret the world.

Our own cultural worldview is often partially hidden from our conscious awareness because our world perspective appears to us as "natural," as a universal point of view. Thus different worldviews are seen as wrong, aberrant, exotic, cute, unscientific or the like. To be challenged by another worldview requires an ability to see our own worldview and to recognize different cultural perspectives. The key to examining cultural perspectives is history.

As an exercise before you read this chapter, consider your own beliefs and viewpoints regarding some of the concepts listed on the following page. To do this think about how you would define each area and how something you do is connected to that definition. For example, I might think of time as linear and an evidence of that is the calendars, date and appointment books that I keep as well as expressions I use (e.g., "That event is on down the line," i.e., "in the future"). I might also think of process and progress as moving forward in one direction and from one point to the next. I might also think that as we go forward in time progress is inevitable and that we are more advanced now than we were fifty, five hundred, or five thousand years ago.

After you consider your own beliefs and frameworks and begin to read the chapter, be alert to the voices, stories, poetry of the indigenous and African Americans. Fill in the chart on the following page.

Historical Research

Research an historical event, movement, or law that is of interest to you. Events that are referred to and/or highlighted in this chapter of the book include the following:

American Indian Movement	Palmares
Bureau of Indian Affairs	*Quilombos*
Commonwealth of Puerto Rico	The *Requerimiento*
Encomienda System	Reform Law (Le Code Noir)
Ghost Dances	Sioux Nation
Iroquois League	Wounded Knee

Consult at least two different sources. Once you have some of the historical record, write the event as though you were writing fiction. Use present tense and describe the scene as though you and the reader are there. While sticking to the facts, be creative and imaginative. You can include dialogue, description of the scene, etc. Part of your research should include the dress, architecture, mannerisms of the period to give your story an authentic appeal.

Concept	Beliefs/Frameworks	Evidence/Behaviors that Indicate this Belief	Implications/ Extensions
Time	Linear and lateral	Time logs/calendars/date	Notions of progress and process
Space			
Human nature			
Animals and Nature			
Dreams			
Land and the Earth			
Identity as Individual vs. Community			
Community Family/Clan			
Property/ Ownership			
Body/Spirit Duality vs. Wholeness			
Power—what constitutes power?			

How Could It Have Been Different?: A Simulation Scene

Divide the group into two sections. One group made up of seventy-five percent of the people are the white Europeans. The other twenty-five percent are indigenous people of the Western Hemisphere.

The year is 1650.

Have each group think about their goals and aspirations and values. The following is a list to give to each group.

White European Values/Goals	Indigenous Values/Goals
Survival	Survival
Gaining more land for agriculture	Keeping lands for hunting
Christianizing the Indians	Accepting all religions
Freedom to exercise religion	Living in harmony with nature
Gaining wealth and prosperity	Sharing with community
Trading with natives for furs	Trading with whites for cloth, guns and other machine-made items
Making room for the Europeans still coming	Sharing with others the goods of the land

Both groups are deeply religious. The indigenous believe in the Great Spirit who has given them this land. They do not believe it can sold. The settlers are Puritans who believe that they were sent here by God to Christianize the heathen. They believe that they are to found a "city on a hill" that will be a "beacon to the world." If they fail in this mission God will eternally punish them.

A disagreement between the two groups has arisen. The indigenous people are complaining that the Europeans are settling on their land. Those settlements are destroying and scaring away the wildlife that the indigenous depend on for their food. The whites, on the other hand, say they have to find new land in order to feed the extra people who have been coming, fleeing the persecution in Europe and looking for a new way of life.

A negotiation session has been arranged. Each group must decide what they want from the negotiations, who will represent them and how the session will be organized.

The leader/teacher can interject new developments as the negotiations continue such as
  • A boat load of five hundred new settlers has just arrived from England.
  • Word has reached the negotiation session that a group of white settlers were killed by another tribe of natives (not included in this particular negotiation).

After the role play, debrief both groups:
  • Discuss both feelings and thoughts about what happened.
  • Was the solution reached a satisfactory one?
  • Would a satisfactory resolution have been possible in reality?
  • Did such meetings ever take place?

Myth and Memory

If we knew and understood fairytales—and by extension the myth—we would not need the scriptures.

G.K. Chesterton

Myths are complex. Many people view myths as fantasy stories and as forms of entertainment. Indeed there are some myths that fit this description. However, there are myths that fit a different definition. These are myths that teach about morals, give directions about living and aid individuals in communicating with the supernatural. Myths of this kind are viewed as "religious" in the lives of indigenous people. They are the source of spirituality and the guidepost for passing on values and morals from one generation to the next. Myths are a powerful way memories of a people are kept alive and not forgotten.

Read the myths that follow and discuss their significance and possible meanings. How might these myths be viewed as "religious"? What values are conveyed and what worldviews are transmitted in these stories?

Sliding Down a Rainbow

The ancestors of the Taos people have lived in their valley since the Stone Age. Before that, they lived in a less-favorable place in the north. So dissatisfied did they become with their home, they called upon the gods to move them.

The gods listened. They sent a rainbow to carry the poeple to a new home. After a long journey, the rainbow came down in beautiful Taos Valley. It settled down to the ground at such a sharp angle that the menfolk who came off last had a fast slide in getting off. They came down so fast, indeed, that the seats of their trousers were completely worn off. They had to cover themselves with blankets.

Even to this day, a Taos man never has a seat in his trousers. He never leaves his village without his blanket.

Maurine Grammer, The Bear That Turned White, 11-12

How Grandmother Spider Stole the Sun

When the Earth was first made, there was no light. It was very hard for the animals and the people in the darkness. Finally the animals decided to do something about it.

"I have heard there is something called the Sun," said the Bear. "It is kept on the other side of the world, but the people there will not share it. Perhaps we can steal a piece of it."

All the animals agreed that it was a good idea. But who would be the one to steal the Sun?

The Fox was the first to try. He sneaked to the place where the Sun was kept. He waited until no one was looking. Then he grabbed a piece of it in his mouth and ran. But the Sun was so hot it burned his mouth and he dropped it. To this day all foxes have black mouths because that first fox burned his carrying the Sun.

The Possum tried next. In those days Possum had a very bushy tail. She crept up to the place where the Sun was kept, broke off a piece and hid it in her tail. Then she began to run, bringing the Sun back to the animals and the people. But the Sun was so hot it burned off all the hair on her tail and she lost hold of it. To this day all possums have bare tails because the Sun burned away the hair on that first possum.

Then Grandmother Spider tried. Instead of trying to hold the Sun herself, she wove a bag out of her webbing. She put a piece of the Sun into her bag and carried it back with her. Now the question was where to put the Sun.

Grandmother Spider told them, "The Sun should be up high in the sky. Then everyone will be able to see it and benefit from its light."

All the animals agreed, but none of them could reach up high enough. Even if they carried it to the top of the tallest tree, that would not be high enough for everyone on the Earth to see the Sun. Then they decided to have one of the birds carry the Sun up to the top of the sky. Everyone knew the Buzzard could fly the highest, so he was chosen.

Buzzard placed the Sun on top of his head, where his feathers were the thickest, for the Sun was still very hot, even inside Grandmother Spider's bag. He began to fly, up and up toward the top of the sky. As he flew the Sun grew hotter. Up and up he went, higher and higher, and the Sun grew hotter and hotter still. Now the Sun was burning through Grandmother Spider's bag, but the Buzzard still kept flying up toward the top of the sky. Up and up he went and the Sun grew hotter. Now it was burning away the feathers on top of his head, but he continued on. Now all of his feathers were gone, but he flew higher. Now it was turning the bare skin of his head all red, but he continued to fly. He flew until he reached the top of the sky, and there he placed the Sun where it would give light to everyone.

Because he carried the sun up to the top of the sky, Buzzard was honored by all the birds and animals. Though his head is naked and ugly because he was burned carrying the Sun, he is still the highest flyer of all, and he can be seen circling the Sun to this day. And because Grandmother Spider brought the Sun in her bag of webbing, at times the Sun makes rays across the sky which are shaped like the rays in Grandmother Spider's web. It reminds everyone that we are all connected, like the strands of Grandmother Spider's web, and it reminds everyone of what Grandmother Spider did for all the animals and the people.

Michael J. Caduto and Joseph Bruchac. Keepers of the Earth, 49-50

Song of the World

In the beginning there was only darkness everywhere—darkness and water. And the darkness gathered thick in places . . .crowding and separating until at last out of one of the places where the darkness had crowded there came forth a man. This man wandered through the darkness until he began to think; then he knew himself and that he was a man; he knew that he was there for some purpose.

He put his hand over his heart and drew forth a large stick. He used the stick to help him through the darkness, and when he was weary he rested upon it. Then he made for himself little ants; he brought them from his body and put them on the stick. Everything that he made he drew from his own body even as he had drawn the stick from his heart. The stick was of greasewood, and of the gum of the wood the ants made a round ball upon the stick. Then the man took the ball from the stick and put it down in the darkness under his foot, and as he stood upon the ball he rolled it under his foot and sang:

> I make the world, and lo!
> The world is finished.
> Thus I make the world, and lo!
> The world is finished.

So he sang, calling himself the maker of the world. He sang slowly, and all the while the ball grew larger as he rolled, till at the end of the song, behold, it was the world. Then he sang more quickly:

> Let it go, let it go,
> Let it go, start it forth!

So the world was made. And now the man brought from himself a rock and divided it into little pieces. Of these he made stars, and put them in the sky to light the darkness. But the stars were not bright enough.

So he made Tau-muk, the Milky Way. Yet Tau-muk was not bright enough. Then he made the moon. All these he made of rocks drawn forth from himself. But even the moon was not bright enough. So he began to wonder what next he could do. He could bring nothing from himself that could lighten the darkness.

Then he thought. And from himself he made two large bowls, and he filled the one with water and covered it with the other. He sat and watched the bowls, and while he watched he wished that what he wanted to make in truth would come to be. And it was even as he wished. For the water in the bowl turned into the sun and shone out in rays through the cracks where the bowls joined.

When the sun was made, the man lifted off the top bowl and took out the sun and threw it to the east. But the sun did not touch the ground; it stayed in the sky where he threw it and never moved. Then in the same way he threw the sun to the north and to the west and to the south. But each time it only stayed in the sky, motionless, for it never touched the ground. Then he threw it once more to the east, and this time it touched the ground and bounced and started upward. Since then the sun has never ceased to move. It goes around the world in a day, but every morning it must bounce anew in the east.

Russell, Frank. "The Pima Indian," in *Annual Report of the Bureau of American Ethnology, 1904-1905,* 206-230, 277

Indigenous Prayers

What follows are prayers from various indigenous groups of the Americas. As you read them consider the following:

- What is being viewed as sacred in these prayers?
- How is the land viewed?
- How would you describe the nature of God in the lives of Native Americans?
- How does the Native American view his/her relationship to God?

Sometimes
I go about pitying myself
While I am carried by
The wind
Across the sky. (Chippewa Song)

Grandfather,
Sacred One,
Teach us love, compassion, and honor
that we may heal the earth
And heal each other. (Ojibway Prayer)

Beseeching the breath of the divine one,
His life-giving breath,
His breath of old age,

His breath of waters,
His breath of seeds,
His breath of riches,
His breath of fecundity,
His breath of power,
His breath of all good fortune,
Asking for his breath
And into my warm body drawing his breath,
I add to your breath
that happily you may always live. (Zuni Chant)

May the earth continue to live
May the heavens above continue to live
May the rains continue to dampen the land
May the wet forests continue to grow
Then the flowers shall bloom
And we people shall live again. (Hawaiian Prayer)

O God, my mother, my father, lord of the
        hills, lord of the valleys, lord of the
        forest, be patient with me. I am about to
        do what has always been done.
Now I make you an offering, that you may be
        warned: I am about to molest your
        heart. Perhaps you will have the
        strength to endure it.
I am going to work you in order that I may
        live.
Let no animal pursue me, no snake, no
        scorpion, no wasp annoy me, no falling
        timber hit me, no ax, no machete catch
        me.
With all my heart I am going to work you. (Kekchi Maya Prayer)

The Morelia Declaration

In October of 1991, for the first time in history, environmentalists, scientists and representatives from indigenous groups throughout the Americas met in Morelia, Mexico to discuss the state of the world. This group of people, coming from twenty different nations, created a declaration that expressed their concern for the planet. The reverence for land appeared throughout their statement. Before reviewing excerpts from the Morelia Declaration given below, create your own declaration considering what needs to be done regarding the following ecological problems:

- Global warming
- Rainforests
- Distribution of resources

- Nuclear Power
- Pollution
- Ozone Layer

Start your statement by providing a rationale, then address all or some of the issues listed above and outline an action statement that the peoples of the Americas should follow. Include as many facts in your statement as you can gather.

The Declaration

I. We the participants of the Morelia Symposium urge the leaders of the world at the Earth Summit to be held in June 1992 in Brazil to commit themselves to ending ecocide and ethnocide, and we propose the creation of an International Court of the Environment modelled on the International Court of Justice at The Hague.

II. Twenty percent of the world's population consumes eighty percent of its wealth and is responsible for seventy-five percent of its pollution. We believe there is sufficient knowledge and technology available to reduce the obscene disparity of wealth. We demand a genuine transfer of knowledge and resources from North to South, not the dumping of obsolescent and inefficient technologies and products. There must be an immediate end to the international traffic in toxic waste, urgent reduction of the pollution of rivers and oceans by industrial waste and human sewage, an end to the unprincipled export of banner pesticides and other chemicals to the economically desperate countries of the Third World, and the immediate availability of information and means to allow people to individually and voluntarily pursue the goal of population stabilization.

III. Traditional societies are generally the best managers of biodiversity. For the last five hundred years the knowledge and the rights of the native American peoples have been ignored. We believe that respecting the interests of indigenous peoples, both in the Americas and throughout the rest of the world, who have become exploited minorities in their own countries is crucial for the preservation of biological and cultural diversity. We deplore the cultural pollution and loss of tradition which have led to global rootlessness, leaving humans, through the intensity of mass-marketing, vulnerable to the pressures of economic and political totalitarianism and habits of mass-consumption and waste which imperil the earth.

IV. At the Earth Summit of June 1992 we demand that world leaders sign a Global Climate Change Convention. Industrialized countries must make a minimum commitment to a twenty percent reduction of their carbon dioxide emissions by the year 2000 A.D. We insist on rigorous implementation of the Montreal Protocol on Protection of the Ozone Layer. We also demand the signing of a convention to protect biological diversity, and the evidence of concrete progress in negotiations for a global forests treaty.

V. The proven economic folly of nuclear power coupled to the probability of environmental catastrophe necessitate the urgent substitution of nuclear energy by clean, safe and efficient energy systems. The military establishment must cease the proliferation of nuclear, biological and chemical weapons and convert a significant proportion of military expenditure to expenditure on environmental security. To ensure this, we demand an end to secrecy and a right to freedom of information in all matters concerning the world's environment.

The participants at this conference wish to stress that environmental destruction cannot be confined within the boundaries of any nation state. We urge our fellow writers, environmentalists, scientists, members of indigenous minorities, and all concerned people to join us in demanding the creation of an International Court of the Environment at which environmentally criminal activity can be brought to the attention of the entire world.

If the latter half of the twentieth century has been marked by human liberation movements, the final decade of the second millenium will be characterized by liberation movements among species, so that one day we can attain genuine equality among all living things.

Commemoration

One way people have kept dangerous memories alive is through the celebration of heroic events or significant moments in the life of heroes or heroines. Pick an event or person that you would like to commemorate and plan a celebration in honor of that occasion or person. Celebrate it on the actual date. As you plan think about what symbols, readings, ideas, and actions would be appropriate to commemorate the date. Small groups can each take a different date. Library research will be required to find exact dates when those are not given in this text.

Roots of Democracy—European or Native American?

Whereas the original framers of the Constitution, including, most notably, George Washington and Benjamin Franklin, are known to have greatly admired the concepts of the Six Nations of the Iroquois Confederacy;

Whereas the confederation of the original ThirteenColonies into one republic was influenced by the political system developed by the Iroquois confederacy as were many of the democratic principles which were incorporated into the Constitution itself;

Be it resolved by the Senate that . . . the Congress, on the occasion of the two hundredth anniversary of the signing of the United States Constitution, acknowledges the historical debt which this Republic of the United States of America owes to the Iroquois Confederacy and other Indian nations for their demonstration of enlightened, democratic principles of Government and their example of a free association of independent Indian nations.

Excerpts from a Congressional Resolution passed by the House and Senate, 1988

The United States takes great pride in its democratic tradition. It is not widely known that this tradition has a good portion of its historical roots in the Iroquois League's Great Law of Peace. The framers of the U.S. government looked to the Iroquois Confederacy as a model. Furthermore, even the early colonialists took back to Europe the notions of participatory decision-making that they observed in the Native American nations. To a Europe steeped in autocracy, the Native American governmental structures were a beacon of ideas which did not go unnoticed by philosophers and social theorists. Eventually these ideas made full circle and came back to the colonies when they began to frame the U.S. government.

Before reading the Iroquois Law of Peace, define "democracy." What does the word mean to you personally? Is this meaning different than what might be meant by the political definition of democracy? What do you perceive as the differences/similarities in these meanings?

What follows are some excerpts from the Iroquois League's Great Law of Peace. The Great Law was not written down until about 1800. It was an oral law which took two days to fully recite. As you read excerpts from the Great Law, note specific aspects of the Law which might correspond to aspects of the U.S. Constitution and governmental structures. What aspects were <u>not</u> borrowed into the U.S. government model? You may wish to research this issue in greater depth. Several books are noted in the bibliography which will provide you with resources.

The Great Law begins with the planting of the Tree of the Great peace, the white pine, which symbolizes the unity of the tribes that made up the league.

Roots have spread out . . . one to the north, one to the west, one to the east and one to the south. These are the Great White Roots and their nature is peace and strength.

If any man or nation outside the Five Nations shall obey the laws of the Great Peace and shall make this known to the statesman of the League, they may trace back the roots to the tree. If their minds are clean and they are obedient and promise to obey the wishes of the Council of the League, they shall be welcomed to ake shelter beneath the Tree of the Long Leaves.

The Great Law began to outline a complex system of checks and balances on the power of each nation against that of the others. The Great Law ensured that no measure (such as declaration of war) would be enacted by the Council of the League without the consent of all five represented nations, each of which would first debate the question internally:

The council of the Mohawk shall be divided into three parties . . . the first party shall listen only to the discussion of the second and third parties and if an error is made, or the proceedings irregular, they are to call attention to it, and when the case is right and properly decided by the two parties, they shall confirm the decision and refer the case to the Seneca statesman for their decision. When the Seneca statesman has decided in accord with the Mohawk statesman, the case or question shall be referred to the Cayuga and Oneida statesman on the opposite side of the house.

After a question had been debated by the Mohawks, Senecas and Oneidas and Cayugas on both sides of the "house," it was passed to the Onondagas, the "firekeepers," for their decision. The Great Law provided that every Onondaga statesman or his deputy be present in council and that all agree with the majority "without unwarrantable dissent". . . . While holding membership on the confederate council, the Great Law provided that a chief should be tolerant and attentive to constituent criticism.

The Chiefs of the League of Five Nations shall be mentors of the people for all time. The thickness of their skins shall be seven spans, which is to say that they shall be proof against anger, offensive action and criticism. Their hearts shall be full of peace and good will and their minds filled with the yearning for the welfare of the people of the League. With endless patience they shall carry out their duty. Their firmness shall be tempered with a tenderness for the people.

Bruce Johansen, *Forgotten Founders*, 23, 24, 27

The Native Americans Share with the World

Brainstorm your images of the native American people. What things in your life are "connected" with their lives and heritage? Go through a day in your life and identify what things you use or do that can trace their roots back to the native Americans' gifts to the world.

The contributions given to the world by various nations of the indigenous peoples of the Americas is an almost inexhaustible list. Learners can divide the task of finding out specific contributions within each of the following categories and then share these with the group. A few specifics are given in each case to get you started.

Contributions	Items
Agricultural Products	potatoes, maize, pumpkins, popcorn, pomegranates, papaya, pecans, paprika, rubber, cotton
Agricultural Processes	farming techniques (raised field agriculture of Peru)
Medicines and Practice	quinine, thousands of plants used for external and internal curatives, dental surgery
Language	thousands of vocabulary words "borrowed" into English (e.g., kayak, Chicago...)
Government	state/federal system; balance of powers; impeachment; caucus
Architecture	building techniques without contemporary tools of measurement
Clothing	dyes
Furniture/Furnishings	hammock; sisal
Mathematics	concept of zero
Astonomy	calendars
Spiritual Legacies	Great Spirit; the Sacred Circle

The U.S. Policy War Against Culture

Role play a short scene which enacts one of the following aspects of the centuries long war against culture waged by the U.S. government against the native Americans. Some details are in this chapter and some appear in Chapter 2 (Resistance). This list represents only a few of the acts and laws.

Policy of Separation (1625-1887)
Lands taken away from Indians and given to English colonists and settlers moving west
Cherokee Removal Act of 1838-39 (Trail of Tears)

Coercive Assimilation (1887-1934)
Allotment Act/Dawes Act of 1887 and Homestead Act of 1862
BIA Schools and missionary schools: language and culture assimilation
Curtis Act (Oklahoma tribes forced to terminate self-government)

Tribal Restoration (1934-1953)

Termination (1952-1968)

Zimmerman Act (Terminating the federal government's responsibility to specific tribes)

Ken Harvey, et al, "Conflict and Discrimination," in *Teaching About Native Americans*, 44-49

A Constitution, Economy and Environment for All

1. Divide into three groups: Native Americans, African-American Slaves, and White Colonialists. Each group should write their own <u>constitutional statement</u> as if they had the power to do so at the time the Constitution was written.

Allow approximately thirty minutes in groups to complete the above task. Then have each group share their "constitution" with the entire group. Allow another thirty minutes to discuss the differences in the way each group constructed their "law of the land."

2. Have groups reconvene. This time each group should write out a description of the type of <u>economy </u>the group would have created if you had the power to do so.

Allow approximately twenty to thirty minutes for the completion of this task and another twenty to thirty minutes to share the results of each group.

3. In the same groups decide what kind of <u>environmental protection laws</u> each group would adapt.

Allow fifteen to twenty minutes for each group to arrive at its policy and another equal amount of time for sharing among the groups.

Discussion: To what extent were the interests and voices of all groups of people addressed by the framers of the U.S. Constitution and the economic-political system? How might things have developed differently if the Iroquois Confederacy and the African Americans and the women been included in the framing of the system?

Colonialism Today
Answer the following questions:

- What is a colony?
- What does it mean to be colonized?
- What conditions enable one group of people to colonize another group of people?
- Are there any circumstances that would justify colonization?
- What is a reservation?
- Why are reservations needed? Are there any circumstances under which reservations should be created? What are the reasons?
- Does the United States government maintain colonies? Reservations? If so, what are the colonies? Where are the reservations?

Acting out Colonialism

Divide the participants into four groups. Two groups should be instructed to develop a skit, construct a picture or create a pantomine which defines or reveals what colonialism is. The two groups should then present their creation to the entire group. In effect, each of these groups will be presenting a code (see strategies under Invasion Chapter to review the meaning of codes). The groups presenting should not explain their presentation—the skit, picture, or pantomine should speak for itself. The audience should then be led to "decode" or tell the presenters what they saw in the code about some key aspects of colonialism. When the entire group exhausts their interpretations, the presenting group should share their ideas about their product and react to the insights the entire group brought to the topic. (Refer to Chapter 1 Strategies for framework for processing codes.)

The two remaining groups, who made up the audience for the former groups, can develop presentations that depict remnants and forms of U.S. colonialism as it exists today.

Quincentenary Commemoration: A National Debate

1. Divide a large group into small teams, each of which assumes one of the roles described below. Discuss the national resolution from your group's perspective. Decide whether you agree or disagree with the resolution.

2. If you basically agree with it but want to change it some, feel free to do so. If you decide to support or modify it, list as many reasons as you can think of for why this is a good resolution.

3. If you disagree with the resolution, list the reasons. Then, from your group's point of view, write a new resolution on how to deal with this anniversary. List reasons why your new resolution is better than the resolution below.

National Debate

Whereas: Christopher Columbus not only opened the door to a "new world," but also set an example for us all by showing what monumental feats can be accomplished through perseverance and faith, and

Whereas: Columbus's journey took just thirty-three days, but changed the outlook of the world forever, and

Whereas: His explorations in 1492 led mankind on a path of discovery that has never ceased to challenge and surprise us,

Therefore, be it resolved: That people in every country should plan to celebrate Columbus's great accomplishment and the "new world" it created, and

Be it finally resolved: That every American should support the quincentenary celebrations and discover the significance that this wonderful milestone in history has in his or her own life.

Tainos

You are a Taino Indian who lived on Bohio (Hispaniola) before Christopher Columbus arrived. In 1492, there were millions of Tainos in the Caribbean, possibly as many as three million on the island of Bohio, alone. Within fifty years the Spanish had wiped out all but two hundred Tainos on Bohio. The Spaniards under Columbus's leadership stole land, took slaves, tortured poeple, raped women, and murdered untold numbers. Others were worked to death in the mines or on Spaniards' plantations. In your view, absolutely nothing good came of Columbus's arrival.

The Tainos were the first to suffer from the arrival of the Europeans, but not the last. The Spaniards invaded the land of the Aztecs, the Mayans, the Incas, and countless others. The story was always the same: rape, theft, murder. Later the English, Portuguese, French and Dutch also exploited and killed Native peoples. With the Europeans came their diseases —measles, smallpox, diphtheria, etc.—which wiped out millions, weakened by forced labor, poor nutrition and demoralization. In 1992, native peoples of the Americas still suffer. In the United States, Indians have the shortest life expectancy, the highest unemployment and have been left on the least desirable patches of land.

Europeans raped native women, but they also raped the earth. Native peoples had lived in the Americas for thirty thousand years or more without harming the environment. The Winnebagos had a saying: "Holy Mother Earth, the trees and all nature, are witnesses of your thoughts and deeds." Mother Earth provided the Tainos with great abundance, and with little labor you were able to live in harmony with other living creatures. But the Europeans wanted to control nature, and called it wilderness, "wild land." They brought new animals and plants that destroyed much that had existed. In the North, they killed millions of buffalo and beaver. Today, in the Amazon region and Central America the Europeans continue to make war on the Earth, cutting down ancient forests; in James Bay, Canada they destroy huge areas of land and rivers with massive dams; everywhere, they pollute the air and spill their chemical and nuclear poisons. Europeans refused to learn from the Indians that the Earth is not to be conquered and abused, but to be loved and nurtured.

When Columbus first arrived, you were willing to share what you had. He had a love of gold, so you gave him some and told him where you thought he could find more. You fed him and his men. When his ship the Santa Maria crashed in December, 1492, one of your leaders, Guacanagari, wept. He organized a group of Tainos to help Columbus unload his cargo. Not a shoelace was stolen. When Columbus began to treat your people cruelly, one of your leaders, Guarionex, even volunteered to plant fields of crops to feed all the Spaniards. But Columbus didn't want food, he wanted gold. Had the Europeans wanted to live with you in peace, you would have accepted. You had much to teach them about life and about the earth. Perhaps the Europeans could have taught you something. We'll never know.

And now they want to celebrate. Celebrate? Exactly what is to be celebrated? You believe there should be a commemoration marking the last five hundred years, but what kind?

U.S. Businessperson

In the beginning there was Columbus. If not for his vision, bravery and skill, the discovery of America would have been postponed. Who knows for how long?

But a celebration of the five hundredth anniversary of Columbus's voyage is not just a tribute to Columbus the man. It is more a tribute to the modern world, and what Columbus's voyage made possible. The first and most tangible result of his journey in 1492 was a vastly broadened picture of the world. Europeans now knew that by sailing West they could make contact with new peoples, establish new trade routes and locate new resources. It pointed all Europe towards the west as well as the east and launched an exciting and productive era of exploration, the scale of which the world had never before seen.

Ultimately, Columbus deserves credit for founding the American colonies and settling the American frontier. Columbus's descriptions of the Indies were almost immediately translated into over a dozen languages. English colonists had Columbus to thank for the knowledge that there was a "new world" awaiting settlement. Thus, it's not an over-statement to say that America owes its very existence to Christopher Columbus. The Declaration of Independence, the Constitution, ideas of individual rights, and other freedoms all originated in the Americas that Columbus discovered. Likewise, the American ingenuity that developed the radio, the telephone, the automobile, the airplane, the television, and thousands of other devices that make our lives richer can be traced back to Columbus's discovery in 1492.

None of this is to overlook the contributions of the Native Americans. They contributed a great deal to the world. They grew many important food crops: potatoes, corn, squash, tomatoes, avocados, chillies. All these foods were native to the Western Hemisphere. Indians gave inventions like the canoe and hammock to the world. Tremendous amounts of gold and silver found their way to Europe and boosted industry and commerce. The Quincentennial also celebrates these important contributions.

The values Columbus brought to the "new world" are cherished by today's Americans. **Independence**: Columbus wouldn't take no for an answer; he refused to be discouraged by the smaller minds of his time. **Faith**: Columbus drew strength and hope from his deep religious beliefs; his trust in God never wavered. **Perseverance**: He never gave up his dream of sailing west, even when turned down by kings and queens time and again. **Courage**: Columbus sailed into the unknown, leaving safety and the comforts of home behind; he was willing to risk everything for his dream. **Leadership**: Columbus inspired, cajoled and, at times, bullied his men; he pushed them to overcome their fears and to believe in his dream. **Skill**: Quite simply, Columbus may be the greatest sailor of all time. In a certain respect Columbus is America. (It's no wonder the country was almost named The United States of Columbia.)

Now is the time to remind ourselves and teach our young about the significance of Columbus's great accomplishment. You are delighted that you were selected as a member of the Quincentenary Jubilee Commission. It's a chance that comes only once every five hundred years.

African in Hispaniola

You were born in northwestern Africa. When you were young, you were seized, marched in chains to the coast, branded with a hot iron and loaded onto a stinking, filthy, crowded ship with hundreds of others. The journey to Spanish Hispaniola took several weeks. Many Africans died. On arrival you were put to work as a slave on a sugar plantation.

You have Christopher Columbus and the profit system he represented to thank for destroying your life and the lives of millions of other Africans. The very first day Columbus arrived in the Americas he took Indian captives and began talking about what great slaves they'd make. On his second voyage, he captured hundreds of Tainos and sent them to Spain as slaves. As Indian slaves began dying off, the Spaniards got the idea of bringing in slaves from Africa. In 1501, Spain issued the first laws regulating the African slave trade —the first slaves arrived shortly thereafter.

From the beginning, Africans resisted slavery. In 1503 the Spanish governor of Hispaniola complained that runaway African slaves were getting together with the Indians and encouraging them to disobey. He said that they were impossible to recapture. The first reported African slave revolt on Hispaniola was in 1522 and within ten years Spain had to establish a special police force to chase after escaped slaves. You Africans were used to freedom and weren't about to quietly accept the Spanish ships. (Three centuries later, in Florida, Africans and Seminole Indians fought side by side against the U.S. Army, which was on a mission to reenslave Africans and take Indian land.)

In the meantime, Europeans got rich off African labor. Slave-harvested sugar was first shipped back to Spain in 1515 and after that, every year, thousands of Africans were captured and sent to work in the Americas. Soon other European countries realized that huge profits could be made and began to ship slaves to the "new world." Many millions of Africans were enslaved or killed in raids.

As Europe got richer and richer, Africa got poorer and poorer. In the late 1800s, weakened by over four hundred years of the slave trade, Africa was carved up into colonies by Europeans. The invaders began to steal even more massive amounts of gold, diamonds, ivory and other resources. Forced to go to work to pay taxes to European colonial authorities, Africans again became a cheap source of labor and created enormous wealth for their white masters.

In 1492, when Columbus first arrived on Bohio (Hispaniola—now the countries of Haiti and the Dominican Republic), he reported seeing only well-fed, contented people. Today, the island's mostly African inhabitants are among the poorest in the world. In Haiti, one child dies every five minutes from malnutrition, dehydration and diarrhea. Out of every 1,000 babies born there, 135 die before their first birthday—the worst infant mortality rate in the Western Hemisphere. In the countryside, wages average less than $1.50 a day. Thank you Christopher Columbus, father of slavery and poverty in the Americas.

Still, African people in the Americas can be proud of a long tradition of resistance: from Tousaaint L'Ouverture's slave revolution in St. Domingue (Haiti) against French rule, to the runaway slave maroons of Jamaica, to the 1930's tenant farmer organizing in Arkansas to the 1991 struggle for educational equity in Selma, Alabama. Several years ago the Haitian people toppled a brutal dictatorship and today are still working for democracy and justice. You Africans never suffered your oppression without offering some kind of fight.

Christopher Columbus

You may be biased, but you believe that your voyage five hundred years ago is, after the birth of Christ, the greatest event in world history. Its anniversary should be celebrated in grand style.

You opened up vast new areas of the world to the influence of Christianity. You first landed on islands in what you believed at the time were the East Indies, but later became known as the West Indies. True, the people were kind, gave you gifts, and tried to give you helpful directions. But they were pagans, heathens, unbelievers. They went naked and had no knowledge of the Bible. Thanks to your voyage, millions of people were discovered and could be converted to Christianity, the one true faith.

Five hundred years after your discovery, it looks even more significant. Countries all over the Americas are now predominantly Christian. This Christian and civilizing presence in the Western Hemisphere has replaced the cannibalism, idol worshipping and laziness of the Indians. If not for you, where would these savages be today?

Your voyage gave the Christian world a tremendous source of wealth. From the mines of Hispaniola came gold. Later, still more gold came to Spain from the Aztecs and Incas. The silver which flowed to Spain greatly expanded the money supply and thus made possible much more business and trade. Other valuable minerals, spices and foods were also imported to Spain and other Christian countries from the colonies in the New World. At the time, you may not have fully understood the importance of the land you discovered. What you had thought to be Asia turned out to be fabulous new continents. But every ounce of gold, every bar of silver, every cup of sugar returned to Spain was a direct result of your courage, skill and determination.

There were some who complained that you were not a good governor of the islands, that you played favorites, and treated some cruelly. During your third stay in the Indies you were even arrested and sent back to Spain in chains. History teaches us that many great men are misunderstood and mistreated by their inferiors. You had to deal with frightened, lazy and greedy men—men who did not share your deep belief in God and your commitment to the king and queen. Yes, at times you dealt with them harshly and even had some of them executed. But yours was a difficult, even impossible job. Whatever mistakes you may have made are greatly outweighed by the glories of your enormous accomplishments.

Cherokee Historian
You are an historian and a Cherokee Indian. You've read a great deal about the five hundredth anniversary of the arrival of Christopher Columbus and about the people who are planning big celebrations around the event.

Your first reaction is: How can they celebrate the killing of millions of Indian and African people? By now everyone should know that Columbus stole Indians' land, took hundreds of Indian slaves, cut the hands off Tainos who did not bring in enough gold, forced thousands upon thousands to work in Spanish mines, and, in killing off the Indians, created the conditions which led to the bringing to America of millions of African slaves. His so-called "discovery" led to tremendous human misery. This is something to celebrate?

But as an Indian yourself, you don't just want the world to think of Indian people as victims. For the last five hundred years Indians have fought back against the European invaders. From the very beginning, when the Taino leader, Caonabo attacked and killed the thirty-nine rapists and murderers Columbus left behind on Bohio (Hispaniola), Indian people have fought for their rights. In the 1830s, Seminole Indians in Florida fought side by side with escaped black slaves against the U.S. Cavalry, sent to throw the Seminoles off their lands and to reenslave the blacks. In 1876, a combined force of Sioux and Cheyenne wiped out the 225 men led by Colonel George Armstrong Custer. It wasn't the worst defeat Indians had handed the U.S. government, but it came close. In more recent times Indians have fought against toxic waste dumps on their land, against loggers destroying forests and to restore land and fishing rights. No, Native Americans are not just victims.

On the five hundredth anniversary of the arrival of Columbus there is much America should learn and remember about the people who were here first. When Spain, Great Britain and France were ruled by rich kings and queens, the Hurons built a society without social classes or bosses. As one Huron explained to a visiting Frenchman, "We are born free . . . while you are all the slaves of one sole man." In 1739, over thirty years before the American revolution, Yaqui Indians in what is now northwestern Mexico demanded free elections with one person, one vote. Thomas Jefferson and George Washington owned slaves, but the Iroquois permitted no slavery.

Some quincentennial celebrators admit that foods like corn and squash came from the Indians. But Indians didn't just **find** these foods, they **developed** them. They were scientists. By the time Spaniards arrived, the Incans had cultivated three thousand different varieties of potato. They even had learned how to freeze-dry potatoes so they could be transported more easily. Indians taught the whites how to dry meat. Our word "jerky" comes from the Quechua word, *charqui*. From lima beans, to corn, to tapioca, Native Americans taught Europeans how to grow and process new foods. **Sixty percent** of all the food grown in the world today originated with the hard work and creativity of the American Indian.

The Incans discovered the healing powers of the bitter-tasting Peruvian bark. They called it *quinaquina* (bark of barks, what the Europeans called quinine when they extracted the active ingredient.) Prior to the availabilty of quinine it's estimated that malaria killed about two million people a year throughout the world. Novocaine, *ipecac* (an Amazon Indian word), petroleum jelly—all originate with medical discoveries of Native Americans.

Of course, much native agricultural and medical wisdom has been ignored by the European invaders. In their rush to control land and people much has passed them by, and much has been destroyed. Sadly, what seems to have been almost totally ignored is the Indian knowledge that the Earth is our mother. Because our mother continues to give us life we must care for and respect her. There is a saying your people have: The frog does not drink up the pond it lives in. In a country of toxic chemical dumps, nuclear power plants, and polluted air, isn't it about time we learned this piece of native wisdom? Isn't it about time people tried to **really** discover the Indians' America?

Bill Bigelow, *Rethinking Columbus*, Washington, D.C.: NECA, 1991.

Rediscovering America

One-half a millennium ago, two vastly different cultures met on the shores of this continent. The "discovery" of America with which Columbus has been credited was not only <u>not</u> a discovery of something new. In many ways, on the contrary, it was exactly the opposite, an inability to see.

Dangerous memories are ones which enable us to see some very painful aspects of our history. But they are also enabling memories. They enable us to take hold of a real discovery of the cultures and perspectives and richness that has been suppressed and devalued. Read the poem on the right by Maya Angelou. Listen to the voice of this African American woman who challenges us to begin now the real discovery. What part will you play?

The gold of her promise
has never been mined

Her borders of justice
not clearly defined

Her crops of abundance
the fruit and the grain

Have not fed the hungry
nor eased that deep pain

Her southern exposure
black death did befriend

Discover this country
dead centuries cry

Erect noble tablets
where none can decry

"She kills her bright future
and rapes for a sou

Then entraps her children
with legends untrue."

I beg you

Discover this country.

Maya Angelou
In Daniel Gioseffi, ed., *Women on War*

269

Teaching Strategies Bibliography: Works Cited in Chapter Four

Amidon, Elias and Elizabeth Roberts, eds. *Earth Prayers: From around the World.* San Francisco: Harper, 1991.

Appleton, LeRoy H. *American Indian Design and Decoration.* New York: Dover Publications, Inc., 1971

Aptheker, Herbert, ed. *A Documentary History of the Negro People in the United States.* New York: Citadel Press, 1990.

Barreiro, Jose. "A Note on Tainos: Whither Progress?" *View from the Shore: American Indian Perspectives on the Quincentenary. Northeast Indian Quarterly 7:3* (Fall 1990) 66-77.

Bierhorst, John. *The Mythology of Mexico and Central America.* New York: William Morrow and Company, Inc., 1990.

Bigelow, Bill, Barbara Miner, and Bob Peterson. *Rethinking Columbus.* Somerville, MA: Rethinking Schools, 1991.

Braudel, Fernand. *Civilization and Capitalism 15th-18th Century.* Vol. 1. *The Structures of Everyday Life.* Vol. II. *The Wheels of Commerce.* New York: Harper and Row, 1979.

Burger, Julian. *GAIA, Atlas of First People: Future for the Indigenous World.* New York: 1990.

Caduto, Michael J. and Joseph Bruchac. *Keepers of the Earth.* Golden, Colorado: Fulcrum, Inc., 1989.

Gioseffi, Daniela. *Women on War.* New York: Touchstone Book, Simon and Schuster, Inc., 1988.

Grammer, Maurine. *The Bear That Turned White.* Flagstaff, Arizona: Northland Publishing Company, 1991.

Greenwald, Martin Associates. *Historical Maps on File.* New York: Facts on File, Inc., 1984.

Harriot, Thomas. *A Briefe and True Report of the New Found Land of Virginia.* New York: Dover Publications, Inc., 1972.

Honour, Hugh. *The Image of the Black in Western Art.* Cambridge: Harvard University Press, 1990.

Horne, Gerald, ed. *Thinking and Rethinking U.S. History.* New York: Council on Interracial Books for Children, Inc., 1988.

Jane, Cecil, ed. *The Four Voyages of Columbus.* New York: Dover Publications, Inc., 1988.

Johansen, Bruce. *Forgotten Founders.* Cambridge: Harvard Commons Press, 1982.

Lopez, Barry. *The Rediscovery of North America.* Lexington, Kentucky: The University of Kentucky Press, 1990.

Lunenfeld, Marvin, editor. *1492: Discovery/Invasion/Encounter.* Chicago: The Newberry Library, 1989.

Milanich, Jerald T. and Susan Milbrath. *First Encounters: Spanish Explorations in the Caribbean and the United States, 1492-1570.* Gainesville, Florida: University of Florida Press, 1989.

Norton, Mary Beth, David M. Katzman, et al. *A People and a Nation: A History of the United States, Volume A: to 1877.* Boston: Houghton Mifflin Company, 1991.

The Oxford Dictionary of Quotations. 3rd Ed. Oxford: Oxford University Press, 1980.

Peterson, Scott. *Native American Prophecies: Examining the History, Wisdom and Startling Predictions of Visionary Native Americans.* New York: Paragon House, 1990.

Priego, Joaquin. *Prehistoria de Quisqueya Cultura Taina.* Santo Domingo, Dominicana: Publicaciones America, 1977.

Rothenberg, Jerome, ed. *Shaking the Pumpkin: Traditional Poetry of the Indian North Americas.* Garden City, New York: Doubleday and Company, Inc., 1972.

Russell, Frank. "The Pima Indian," *Annual Report of the Bureau of American Ethnology, 1904-1905.* Washington, D.C.: Government Printing Office, 1908.

Rydberg, Pal, Gittan Jonsson, et al. *The History Book.* Culver City, California: Peace Press, Inc., 1974

Sale, Kirkpatrick. *The Conquest of Paradise: Christopher Columbus and the Columbian Legacy.* New York: Alfred A. Knopf, 1990.

Semer, Robin, Mary McCann and Paul Kapczuk. "Decoding Racism: A Collective Task." *¡Basta!* December 1990.

Simonson, Rick and Scott Walker, eds. *Multicultural Literacy.* Saint Paul, Minn.: Graywolf Press, 1988.

Viola, Herman J. and Carolyn Margolis. *Seeds of Change.* Washington, D.C.: Smithsonian Institution Press, 1991.

Waldman, Carl. *Atlas of the North American Indian.* New York: Facts on File Publications, 1985.

Organizations and Publications with a Focus on the European Invasion

Africa World Press, 15 Industry Ct., Trenton, NJ 08638, 609-771-1666; publishes and distributes excellent books on Africa and the Americas.

Akwesasne Notes, Mohawk Nation, PO Box 196, Rooseveltown, NY 13683-0196. A long-established quarterly on Native American affairs.

Alliance for Cultural Democracy, P.O. Box 7591, Minneapolis, MN 55407, publishes excellent networking journals, *Cultural Democracy* and *huracán* ($15/year).

American Friends Service Committee, 1501 Cherry Street, Philadelphia, PA 19102, 215-241-7169; special project is called "500 Years Is Enough."

American Indian Law Alliance, 488 Seventh Avenue, Suite 5K, New York, NY 10018, 212-268-1347; resource center and advocacy group.

American Indian Library Association, c/o Lisa Mitten, Secretary, 207 Hillman Library, University of Pittsburgh, Pittsburgh, PA 15260; 412-648-7723.

Continental Campaign: 500 Years of Indigenous and Popular Resistance—the leading organizer of North, Central, and South American indigenous struggles, sponsoring conferences and putting out good materials. Write to Campaña Continental, Secretaria Operativa, Apt. Postal 7-B, Sucursal El Trebol, 01903, Guatemala Ciudad, Guatemala, C.A.

Canadian Alliance in Solidarity with Native Peoples, P.O. Box 574 Station P, Toronto, Ontario M5S 2T1, Canada.

Central American Resource Center/Quincentennial Education Project, 1407 Cleveland Avenue N, St. Paul, MN 55104, 612-644-8030; excellent materials for teachers with good ideas about how to use them.

Clergy and Laity Concerned, P.O. Box 1987, Decatur, GA 30031, 404-377-1983; publishes an organizers' packet and information about activists around the country as well as a regular journal with good information and analysis.

Cultural Survival, 53 Church Street, Cambridge, MA 02138, 617-495-2562; events, newsletter, information packets.

In the Heart of the Beast Puppet Theater, 1500 E. Lake Street, Minneapolis, MN 55407, 612-721-2523.

Indigenous Thought, c/o Jan Elliott, 6802 SW 13th St., Gainesville, FL 32608, 904-378-3246. A networking newsletter from the Committee for American Indian History with exciting articles addressing concerns crucial to both natives and nonnatives in their struggles to end oppression.

Indigenous Women's Network, P.O. Box 174, Lake Elmo, MN 55402; publication, *Indigenous Woman*, and community involvement on peace and justice issues.

Latin America Council of Churches, Av. Patria 640 y Amazones, Piso 11, Quito, Ecuador, coordinating 500 years' activities in Latin America, producing materials in Spanish.

NAES Bookstore, 2838 West Peterson, Chicago, IL 60659; a good source of books by and about Indian communities.

National Council of Churches of Christ, 475 Riverside Drive, New York, NY 10115; issued a public statement calling for 1992 to be a year of reflection and repentance.

Network of Educators on Central America (NECA), 1118 22nd St. NW, Washington, DC 20937; excellent classroom resources and programs.

North American Congress on Latin America (NACLA), 151 W. 19th St., 9th Floor, New York, NY 10011, publishes *NACLA Report on the Americas;* several issues will focus on themes reflecting on the past 500 years in the Americas.

Northeast Indian Quarterly, published by American Indian Program, Cornell University, 300 Caldwell Hall, Ithaca, NY 14853, 607-255-6587, which also publishes program guides and curriculum packages for teachers. Well-produced, attractive, timely publications.

Our Developing World, 13004 Paseo Presada, Saratoga, CA 95070, 408-379-4431; working on multicultural curriculum.

Peace and Dignity Journeys, 1301 W. 16th Street, Chicago, IL 60608, 312-733-6363; sponsoring dual relays north from Argentina and south from Alaska, beginning in April and culminating in Mexico in October 1992.

Pueblo to Pueblo, 1616 Montrose #4500, Houston, TX 77006, 800-843-5257; non-profit group which sells products from coops in Latin America.

Rethinking Columbus: Teaching about the 500th Anniversary of Columbus's Arrival in America. A Special Issue of *Rethinking Schools*, 1991. Articles, teaching aids, poems, stories by a wide variety of authors, and a much more comprehensive list of organizations and publications than this one. For information write 1001 E. Keefe Ave., Milwaukee, WI 53212 or phone 414-964-9646.

South and Meso-American Indian Information Center (SAIIC), PO Box 28703, Oakland, CA 94604; publishes a newsletter and was one of the convening groups for the First Continental Meeting of Indigenous Peoples—500 Years of Indian Resistance in Ecuador, July 1990.

Underground Railway Theater, 41 Foster Street, Arlington, MA 02174, 617-643-6916; producing "The Discovery of Columbus," a lively and involving performance available for bookings nationwide.

WBAI-99.5 FM, "Columbus in Context," 505 Eighth Avenue, 19th floor, New York, NY 10018, 212-279-0707; special radio programs to be produced by this Pacifica Radio Network station.

Witness for Non-violence, 1759A N. Marshall, Milwaukee, WI 53202, 414-271-3309; active in training for witnessing at Chippewa boat landings.

Witness for Peace, P.O. Box 33273, Farragut Station, Washington, DC 20033, 202-797-1160; year-long study guide materials.